Enigma Books

Also published by Enigma Books

Roman Brackman

Israel at High Noon

From Stalin's Failed Satellite to the Challenge of Iran

Enigma Books

Enigma Books
580 Eighth Avenue, New York, NY 10018
www.enigmabooks.com

ISBN 1-929631-64-2

Printed in the United States of America

Library of Congress Cataloging-in-Publication Data

Brackman, Roman 1931-
  Israel at high noon : from Stalin's failed satellite to the challenge of iran / Roman
Brackman.

    p. ; cm.
    Includes bibliographical references and index.
    ISBN: 1-929631-64-2

1. Israel--History--20th century. 2. Antisemitism--Soviet Union--History. 3. Soviet Union--
Foreign relations--Middle East. 4. Soviet Union--Ethnic Relations. 5. Russia--Foreign
relations--Middle East--21st century. 6. Russia--Ethnic relations--21st century. 7. Middle
East--Politics and government. 8. Middle East--Foreign relations. I. Title.

DS125 .B73 2005
956.940/5

Israel at High Noon

Dedication

This book is dedicated with love and gratitude to my wife Nadine, my sons Alex and Peter, my daughters Yvette and Natasha, for their support, patience, and help in the effort required to complete this work.

This book is also dedicated to Vitaly Svechinsky and Mikhail Margulis, my childhood friends, classmates, and fellow inmates in the Siberian Gulag, and to my closest and oldest American friend Michael Steinhardt in deep appreciation for his trust in me, his loyalty, and his love and support for Israel.

Finally, I wish to thank the Provident Foundation for its generous help.

Roman Brackman
August 2006

Table of Contents

Foreword
by
Vitaly Svechinsky*

Roman Brackman's new book *Israel at High Noon* is about Israel's lonely struggle for survival. Israel, like the marshal in the movie *High Noon*, as played by Gary Cooper, faces the same predicament. The Hamas dominated "Palestinian Authority" becomes a launching pad for Iranian and Arab suicide bombers. On February 19, 2006, students at the University of Tehran were asked to name the enemies against whom they would like to carry out suicide bombings. They named Israel. On the stage was the slogan "Israel must be wiped off the map." One of the speakers declared that "1,000 loyal and trained suicide bombers were ready and another 5,000 were placed on a waiting list."[1] These blood-thirsty murderers on the *High Noon* train are now ready to cross into Israel. Hamas leader Khaled Mashaal declared:

> Our delegation was in Tehran today and will be in Moscow tomorrow. We will try to look for political and financial support.[2]

The reader will find in Roman Brackman's *Israel at High Noon* many revealing insights.

I want to share with the readers of this book what I know about the author. I met Roman for the first time in 1935 when we both were four-year-old kids in a kindergarten on Trubnikovsky Lane in the center of Moscow. When we met again years later all we could remember of this kindergarten was the playground on the roof of a tall building and the large wine barrels stored in its courtyard. When Roman was a four-year-old boy, his father, an engineer,

---

* Vitaly Svechinsky, the original leader of the Soviet Jewish movement, is now a prominent architect living in Israel.

was imprisoned in the Gulag camp in Dmitrov, some 100 kilometers from Moscow. Roman's mother used to take him to visit his father, leaving him for weeks in the inmates' barracks. Roman remembered vividly the barb wire, the watch towers, the columns of inmates and the armed guards with their German Shepherds at the prison camp.

In 1946 we met again as classmates at school #103, one of the best schools in the center of Moscow. We loved our teachers, who had taught years earlier in the pre-revolutionary gymnasiums. A large percentage of pupils in this school were boys from Jewish families. We all loved life and cheerfully greeted the future. But our graduation in 1948 coincided with the beginning of the vicious anti-Semitic campaign launched by Stalin. It was difficult time for us— after all, spiritually we were a sad product of Soviet ideological indoctrination. Among all the 1948 graduates, only Roman Brackman had a sober and daring view of what was happening around us. Roman was the first among us students to understand the criminal nature of the totalitarian Stalinist regime which he compared to German fascism. Mikhail Margulis and I were Roman's close friends. We could not live in peace with anti-Semitism that assailed our ethnic pride. Roman could not live in peace with the totalitarian regime which assailed his human pride.

Roman enrolled in the Moscow Oriental Institute's Arabic division; I chose the Moscow Architectural Institute and Mikhail Margulis went to Moscow University. We discussed plans for an escape to Israel by crossing the Soviet-Turkish border. At that time, the mere intention of escaping from the Soviet Union was considered the most horrendous crime (treason of the motherland which was punishable by death). We were arrested in the summer of 1950 and wound up in the cells of the MGB (Ministry of State Security) prison. The Secret Police interrogated us for a year in the Lubyanka and Butyrki prisons. In May 1951 each of us was sentenced to 10 year in special regime Gulag camps. Roman and I were transported together to the Novosibirsk transit prison. From there Roman was shipped north in the cargo hold of a barge down Yenisey River to Norilsk Gulag and I was transported to Kalyma in Eastern Siberia. Mikhail Margulis was sent to Potma.

Imprisonment did not break Roman's rebellious spirit. He was certain that uprisings of enslaved fellow camp inmates awaited us in the future. And this actually happened to him: in the summer of 1953 the Norilsk Special Regime Political camp exploded in an uprising. Roman became one of the active participants as a member of the uprising committee. He, together with Chabuk Amiragibi and Max Mintz, wrote the declaration of the inmates' demands. The uprising was put down with the usual Soviet brutality. The inmates stood holding hands in front of the soldiers who opened fire. The bullets did not touch Roman—fate had decided on a different course for his life. In the autumn of 1954 Roman, Mikhail Margulis, and I were brought back to Moscow for a review of our case. On January 29, 1955, the Moscow Military Tribunal reduced each of our sentences from ten to five years and released us in accordance with the first post-Stalin amnesty. We went home to our parents. Roman went to work as a draftsman and in the evening studied at the Engineering Institute. He got married in 1957. He and his wife, who had Polish citizenship, applied for exit visas to Poland. A year later, their son Alex was born. Finally, in May 1959, after several refusals, Roman's family was allowed to leave for Poland. At that time this was a miracle. I saw them off as they boarded the Moscow-Warsaw train. A year later, Roman's parents were also allowed to leave for Poland. It was the second miracle. Shortly afterwards Roman's entire family left for Israel.

Roman's life was propelled towards freedom, as if by compass. Roman was one of the first to escape from the Soviet Union in 1959. His escape left a deep impression on the people who knew him. In Soviet Russia, where lawlessness reined supreme, his struggle for an individual's right to live in freedom, inspired hope for everyone. At the time, Roman's example meant that resistance was not hopeless. He showed the way to all of us. I learned from his Moscow aunt that he went to America. Roman became an American citizen. For thinking people in Soviet Russia, America represented a country where the ideals of spiritual and human freedom had been realized. And there were no better candidates than Roman for the right to be an American citizen. He earned that right by the struggle of his whole life.

In the Soviet Union the late 1960s were also the beginning of an unprecedented fight for human rights. Roman was very actively involved in the fight of Russian dissidents for human rights and for the right of the Jewish people to return to their ancient homeland—Israel. Twentieth-century totalitarianism was the subject of Roman's intense historical research and his NYU dissertation—"The Anti-Semitism of Joseph Stalin."

For several years I had no contact with Roman. In 1968 I asked a friend, who had received an exit visa to Israel, to find Roman's mother in Israel and ask her to send me an official invitation to travel there as her nephew. This friend accidentally ran into Roman in Jerusalem and gave him my letter. Soon I received an invitation from Roman's mother and applied for an exit visa. I received a negative reply. A group of ten Moscow Jews, including myself, signed the first open letter with an appeal to free people to help us immigrate to Israel. Another thirty-nine Jews later signed a similar letter. Roman helped publish these letters and joined the 1970 election campaign of James Buckley, who was then running for the Senate from New York. Buckley was the first US politician to introduce the issue of Soviet Jews to the American public. He won election to the Senate.

In late January 1971, as Roman was driving to his summer place in Sag Harbor, Long Island, he heard on the radio that Vitaly Svechinsky and his family had received exit visas and on February 1 were leaving Moscow for Israel via Vienna. Roman turned his car around, stopped to make a telephone call to reserve a plane ticket and we met in the Vienna airport for the first time in twelve years. We flew to Israel together and then met again in Brussels, where I had to address the First Congress for Soviet Jews. Then my family and I spent the most wonderful month at his summer place on Long Island. Since then we often see each other in America and in Israel.

Who can say that miracles don't happen? A small British publisher published Roman's book, *The Secret File of Joseph Stalin—A Hidden Life* in 2001 in English. It was later published in French and Russian. It is the most revealing account of the history of Stalin's rule, and of the life and crimes of that brutal dictator. The book exposes the roots of anti-Semitism of both Stalin and Hitler. Their hatred of the Jews was the irrational motive behind Stalin's alliance with Hitler that led to the partition of Poland in 1939 that started WWII. His book exposes the twentieth century epidemic of totalitarianism that engulfed not only Russia, Germany, and Italy, but also countries in Asia and Africa. The phenomenon of Stalin is an example of mass psychology which helps to answer the question: How can civilized people succumb to mindless barbarity and allow depraved pathological personalities like Stalin and Hitler reach the pinnacle of power in their countries and for years dominate the lives of millions of people? Roman's personal experience helped him in the search for the answer to this question.

Who could say that miracles do not happen? Recently Irina Resnikov, a sister of our classmate, Boris Resnikov, called from Moscow and said that she had watched a TV interview with V. A. Kriuchkov (the last head of KGB). She noticed a Russian copy of Roman's book, *The Secret File of Joseph Stalin,* on his desk. When Roman was being shipped in the cargo hold of a barge down the Yenisey River to Norylsk Gulag, he could not have imagined that some day a KGB chief would read his book. Miracles happen! Roman has written numerous articles, among them in 1968 the article "Israel—The Middle Eastern Vietnam," and a 1980 book, *Jimmy Carter, Provocateur-in-Chief.*

Roman Brackman's *Israel at High Noon* places the Arab-Israeli conflict in focus, along with the insane ravings of Iran's President Mahmoud Ahmadinejad, the present-day reincarnation of such pathological Jew-haters as Hitler and Stalin. As if history threatens to repeat itself, Ahmadinejad, like a mix of a miniature Mickey Mouse and Lucifer, inflames large frenzied crowds enthralled in adoration.[3] *Israel at High Noon* is about the struggle for survival of a country which is threatened by a raving lunatic. The Jews have faced "High Noon" many times throughout their long history. Roman Brackman has researched this history. He believes they will survive this time too.

Vitaly Svechinsky

June 6, 2006

Introduction

The Middle East has been at the center of world conflict for the last two centuries, as Germany, Austria, and Russia have competed for their share of the spoils of the decaying Ottoman Empire. As a way of compensating each other for mutual concessions, the Great Powers used to settle their disputes by partitioning Poland among themselves. Adolf Hitler and Joseph Stalin did so in 1939, but within a year their interests clashed. Stalin demanded that the Soviet Union be allotted the sphere of interests in the "area south of Batum-Baku line in the general direction of the Persian Gulf," which included Iran, Iraq, and what was then known as British Palestine. Stalin and Hitler intended to destroy the Jews of Palestine. Stalin was also planning to join the axis of Germany, Italy, and Japan. But Hitler also decided that this area of the Middle East should be allotted to Germany, and offered India to Stalin as the Soviet share of the spoils of the British Empire. Since Hitler and Stalin had already partitioned Poland in September 1939 they could no longer settle their dispute at Poland's expense.

A great deal has been written about Hitler's hatred for the Jews, but so far very little has been revealed about Stalin's anti-Semitism and his plan to destroy Soviet Jewry on the eve of his death. This book intends to fill that void. After the Second World War, Stalin continued to pursue the policy of expansion in the "direction of the Persian Gulf," and hoped to turn Palestine into a Soviet satellite. After Stalin's death, Soviet leaders supported Arab plans to annihilate Israel, and pressured Israel to make concessions to the Arabs in the Palestinian-Israeli conflict. As the conflict intensified, it became fashionable to suggest that world peace was dependent upon the successful resolution of the Israeli-Palestinian clash. Senator Dianne Feinstein stated that the Israeli-Palestinian conflict was the "Number One issue precipitating a real clash of civilizations between the Western world and the Muslim world." She wished to hear something from President Bush "about the United States pushing the peace process."[4] Tony Blair called the Israeli-Palestinian issue "the most pressing political challenge in the world today." On the occasion of Yasir Arafat's death on November 11, 2004, former vice-presidential candidate Geraldine Ferraro suggested to Fox News that the war on terror could not be won without a peaceful resolution of the Israeli-Palestinian conflict. Mark Ginsburg, the former American ambassador to Morocco, advanced the same argument on the same program which boils down to pressuring Israel to make concessions to the Palestinian Arabs.

The first time this idea was promoted so explicitly came after Saddam Hussein invaded Kuwait in August 1990. At that time, Evgeny Primakov, the special envoy of the Soviet leader Mikhail Gorbachev, shuttled between Washington and Baghdad trying to derail President George H. W. Bush's plan to liberate Kuwait. Primakov advanced the idea, novel at the time, of linking the Iraqi aggression in Kuwait to the Arab-Israeli conflict. Photos of Primakov, hugging and kissing Saddam Hussein, were displayed on the front pages of major newspapers. Photos of Yasir Arafat embracing Saddam Hussein received similar coverage. On July 31, 1991, President George H. W. Bush at a joint press conference with Gorbachev in Moscow said that the United States and the Soviet Union would promote peace by acting as "co-sponsors" in the forthcoming Arab-Israeli talks. On January 29, 1991, U.S. Secretary of State James Baker and Soviet Foreign Minister Alexander A. Bessmertnykh had issued a Soviet-American communiqué, in which they linked the Iraqi invasion of Kuwait to "the sources of conflict, the Arab-Israel conflict. They agreed to pursue "a meaningful peace process" to promote Arab-Israeli "peace and regional stability."

The Baker-Bessmertnykh communiqué produced an outcry in America and Israel against the "linkage" of the Gulf War to the Arab-Israeli conflict. This statement was similar to the Soviet-American Joint Declaration of October 1, 1977, demanding Israeli concessions. State Department spokesperson Margaret D. Tutwiler tried to downplay the importance of the Baker-Bessmertnykh communiqué, saying, "We did not, in all candor, view this [communiqué] as any big deal." The linkage idea survives to the present day, playing an important role in the public debates about President George W. Bush's policy in the second Iraqi war, the war on terror, and the "road map to comprehensive peace" in the Arab-Israeli conflict. Evgeny Primakov deserves a prominent place this story not only because he was the first to promote the idea of "linkage," but also because he was one of the most sinister promoters of anti-Semitism in the Soviet Union. Yakov Etinger, the stepson of Dr. Y. G. Etinger, the murdered Kremlin doctor, wrote:

> By his articles directed against "world Zionism" and against the State of Israel, Primakov was enflaming anti-Semitism among wide circles of the population in the USSR. It was because of his writing that tens of thousands of Jews . . . had to leave in fear of anti-Semitic excesses, as the result of which Russia has lost a large number of first-class specialists.[5]

Ernest Henry, a prominent Soviet journalist and diplomat, wrote:

> Primakov drained Russia's blood by compelling [Jewish] intellectual cadres to leave the country.[6]

KGB Lieutenant-General V. Kirpichenko wrote that Primakov "maintained permanent working contacts with the KGB."[7]

I met Evgeny Primakov for the first time at the beginning of the 1948–49 academic year at the Moscow Oriental Institute, in the Arabic Department. For the next two years, until I was arrested in May 1950, we sat next to each other during the lectures. He told me that because he had some health problems, he had been transferred from Nakhimov Naval Cadet School in Baku, the capital of Azerbaijan. In that naval cadet school, Primakov had been a classmate of my cousin, Ilya Gold whom our uncle, Admiral G. I. Brakhtman (Chief of Staff of the Caspian Fleet) had helped to enroll there.

Evgeny was born in 1929 in Kiev, where his father, General Vitaly Primakov, was then commander of the Ukrainian Military District. Evgeny was about five years old when his parents divorced in 1934. His Jewish mother, Anna Yakovlevna Kirshenblat, a gynecologist, moved with Evgeny to Tbilisi, the capital of Georgia, where her cousin Dr. David Abramovich Kirshenblat was a prominent physician. Evgeny referred to him as "my uncle." Evgeny grew up in Tbilisi in a Jewish family. I remember Evgeny's mother, who used to come to Moscow to visit her son. Evgeny used to imitate a Georgian accent, but I never heard him speaking Georgian with any of our classmates who were Tbilisi natives and spoke their native tongue among themselves. I knew Evgeny's Georgian accent was a fake, which he thought would be helpful in advancing his career, because Stalin and Lavrenty P. Beria, the chief of the Soviet secret police, spoke Russian with authentic Georgian accents.

I was aware that Evgeny's father, General Vitaly Primakov, had been executed with Marshal Tukhachevsky and a group of top Red Army generals in June, 1937. The members of this group were accused of being "enemies of the people, traitors to the motherland, and Trotskyites." I felt a great sympathy toward Evgeny, who had lost his father so early in life. I knew about the executed generals because one of them, Yona Yakir was related to my mother. I had heard Yona Yakir's name whispered in fear by my parents during my childhood. I knew that children, wives, and even distant relatives of the executed "enemies of the people," were often either murdered or imprisoned themselves. My cousin, Peter Yakir (General Yakir's teenage son) was incarcerated.

I never discussed my political views with Evgeny, although at that time I did not suspect him of being an informer of the MGB (Ministry of State Security, the predecessor of the KGB). I knew that it was dangerous to discuss political subjects with anybody. My high school classmates, Vitaly Svechinsky, Mikhail Margulis, and I felt that we had no future in the Soviet Union. We were arrested in the summer of 1950 for "anti-Soviet propaganda," and for our attempt to escape across the Soviet-Turkish border near Batumi. While in the MGB's Lubyanka prison, I tried to figure out who might have been an informer in our "Batumi case." and I recalled one episode, which I still remember vividly.

It took place shortly before my arrest: my classmates Evgeny Primakov, Suren Shiroyan, and Eduard Markarov and I stood near our classroom in the hall of the Moscow Oriental Institute. I do not remember what we were talking about. Evgeny suddenly turned to me and said: "Romka, you are a Trotskyite!" I managed to turn this very dangerous accusation into a joke. When, after my arrest, I was in the Lubyanka prison, I recalled Evgeny's provocative remark and began to suspect that the "organs" had recruited him and that his MGB handlers had asked him about me without telling him of what crime I was suspected. I could not recall any politically dangerous conversation with Evgeny and thought that the "Trotskyite" accusation was his surmise, because it was the most common accusation during Stalin's rule. Later I learned that the "organs" were routinely recruiting informers among children and relatives of the "repressed enemies of the people." The interrogators did not mention Evgeny Primakov's name to me. They were not supposed to reveal their secret sources, which were kept in "operational files." These files, no matter how old, are kept secret even today.

My friends and I were sentenced to ten years in the Siberian Gulag prison camps by the MGB "Special Council." In 1955, two-and-one-half years after

Stalin's death, my friends and I were brought back to Moscow for the reinvestigation of our "Batumi case." KGB Captain Ushakov, who interrogated me, said that "someone here" remembered me. He did not say who that person was, but I suspected Primakov. On January 29, 1955, the Moscow Military Tribunal reduced our sentence from ten to five years, and my friends and I were released in accordance with the first post-Stalin amnesty of March 27, 1953, which was applied retroactively to us. We went home to our parents.

Shortly thereafter, Primakov phoned me and suggested we get together in Moscow's Maxim Gorky Park. We sat on a bench and talked for a couple of hours. He said he was glad to see me back and was interested in my prison camp experiences. I was not sure whether he had decided to see me out of curiosity as a former classmate, or had been told by his KGB handlers to question me. Perhaps, he wanted to find out whether I knew anything about his role in my case. I was in the dark about it. Even if he played some role, it would not have made any difference. I did not remember ever telling him anything "anti-Soviet," so he had nothing to report on me; but I did not mention that. We parted on friendly terms.

My family and I left the Soviet Union for Poland four years later, at the end of May 1959, and a year later we went to Israel. We immigrated to the United States in April 1962. I did not see Primakov for the next ten years, but I read his articles in which he castigated "Zionist aggressors" and praised "progressive" Arab leaders, such as Gamal Abdel Nasser, Saddam Hussein, Hafez al-Assad, and Yasir Arafat. I knew that his reports were covers for his KGB missions in various Arab countries. In 1970, I spotted Primakov's name in a brief article in the *New York Times*, stating that he and several members of the Soviet delegation were at the New York Hilton Hotel for a roundtable discussion with American scholars.

I decided to go and see Primakov. At that time I had just returned from Israel, where in 1968–69 I had interviewed many people for my Ph.D. dissertation. While I was doing my research, the first small group of Soviet Jews was allowed to leave Russia for Israel. One of the arrivals brought a letter to my mother from my classmate and codefendant Vitaly Svechinsky, who asked that my mother send him an invitation as if she was his aunt to help him emigrate to Israel. His application for an exit visa was refused and his name appeared on published open letters of appeals to allow Jewish emigration to Israel. When I came back to the United States, I became involved in the 1970 New York senatorial election campaign of James Buckley who brought up the issue of Jewish emigration from Russia. I thought that Primakov, being an important Soviet Middle East expert, should know a great deal about the Soviet policy toward Jewish emigration to Israel. I naïvely thought that because of Primakov's Jewish mother and uncle, who had raised him, he might have some sympathy for the Soviet Jews. During the roundtable discussion, several young American Jews from Meir Kahane's "Jewish Defense League" entered the stage, shouting "Let My People Go!" Police removed them from the hall.

During the intermission I went downstairs and found Primakov sitting in the recreation area at a table with a group of his colleagues. As I came near him, he got up, and we embraced as old friends. He introduced me to his colleagues at the table, but I noticed his fleeting wink, hinting to them that I was not their "kind." Indeed, I was not.

Primakov and I walked up and down the hotel corridors for about an hour. I asked about his mother, his uncle, his family, and our former classmates. At that time, his mother and uncle were still alive, and he said that they were fine. He mentioned his disapproval of my "anti-Soviet" articles and said, "Stalin murdered my father, but that did not make me anti-Soviet." A few years earlier, in the mid-1960s, his father and other generals in Tukhachevsky's group were "posthumously rehabilitated" (declared to be not guilty of any crimes). When I mentioned the problem of Jewish emigration, Primakov said:

> Why should we allow Soviet Jews to go to Israel, where they will be drafted into the army to fight our Arab friends? Do you realize what awaits them in Israel, which is a tiny speck of sand in the ocean of one hundred million Arabs? Israel will not survive for long.

There was no point arguing. We parted amicably and I never saw him again.

Even after the collapse of the Soviet Union I kept spotting his articles in the press, in which he castigated "Israeli aggression." It was also reported that Primakov's KGB code name was "Maxim" and his patronymic was "Maximovich." I knew his patronymic should have been "Vitalievich," because his father's first name was Vitaly. I assumed that his patronymic was changed in 1947 when he had turned eighteen and was recruited as a MGB informer. I knew that the children of the "repressed enemies of the people" were usually summoned to the MGB office at that age, and told that the MGB would imprison them unless they agreed to sign a pledge to inform the MGB about anything they might know about "anti-Soviet activities." Lev Golovchiner, who was an informer not only in my case but also in many others cases, including that of my friend, a prominent movie director Mikhail Kalik, told me about his experience when we met following my release from prison. However, Evgeny Primakov's story was more complicated then that of Golovchiner, because Evgeny's father was not the usual "enemy of the people" but an executed member of the "Tukhachevsky military conspiracy." No MGB officer would have dared to recruit the son of such a prominent "enemy" of Stalin without first eliciting Stalin's permission. Stalin must have given his consent and he probably also chose Evgeny's code-name "Maxim" and his patronymic "Maximovich," because Stalin knew that Evgeny's father had nothing to do with the Tukhachevsky conspiracy but was involved in the case of Soviet writer Maxim Gorky.[8] The generals in Tukhachevsky's group were arrested in May 1937, and executed on June 11, 1937. General Vitaly Primakov had been arrested in June 1936. Stalin "inserted" General Primakov into the Tukhachevsky group and he was executed the same day as the other generals in that case.[9]

In 1991, when Evgeny Primakov was appointed chief of Russia's Foreign Intelligence Service (SVR) he used his first press conference to deny any affiliation with the KGB. Privately, however, he told Evgenia Albats (who at that time was writing a book on the history of KGB) that it was "naïve not to know that no one who wanted to work abroad could leave without some contact with the organs." By "organs," he meant the MGB and KGB. In January 1992, the Russian Parliament and the Russian Prosecutor-General accused the KGB of transferring "six billion Russian rubles from the Communist Party accounts to foreign banks." It also accused KGB agents of setting up six hundred joint venture firms abroad in case the Party would have to work in exile." The report further stated:

> Despite all the facts, the numerous requests by investigators from Russia's Office of the Prosecutor-General to Evgeny Primakov, the current foreign intelligence head and former Gorbachev adviser, have fallen on deaf ears. Invariably, the reply has been: 'We have no right to expose our agents' network.'[10]

Primakov's story is an example of how Stalin morally crippled generations of people by coercing them into rejecting their parents and forcing them to become secret police tools. By agreeing to change his patronymic to "Maximovich," Primakov symbolically rejected his father and switched his identification and his loyalty to the "organs" that provided him with a sense of security. The "organs" became the linchpin of Evgeny's personality. The transfer of his allegiance to the "organs" was made easier by the fact that very early in his life he had been abandoned by his father, who had left the family and remarried.

In October 2004 I learned that Evgeny's mother had died in the early 1980s and was buried in a Jewish cemetery in Tbilisi while he was abroad. When he returned to Russia he ordered that her remains be moved to the Georgian Christian Orthodox cemetery in Saburtalo, near Tbilisi.[11] On his seventy-fifth birthday, Evgeny gave an interview and provided a photograph of himself (in the uniform of the Nakhimov Naval Cadet School with his mother, giving her name only as "Anna Yakovlevna" and omitting her Jewish surname, Kirshenblat.[12] Primakov did not change his patronymic back to "Vitalievich" after his father's rehabilitation. For him, "Maximovich" and his code name "Maxim" remained the symbol of his identification with the "organs." He rose to the post of Chief of the Russian intelligence service, and was later appointed Prime Minister of Russia by Boris Yeltsin.

Primakov's name appeared in the Moscow newspaper *Novaya Gazeta* in an article by Anna Politkovskaya, in which she stated:

> Perhaps Evgeny Primakov, the former Prime Minister, might be able to open new talks. He is not hated by the Chechens and he has direct access to Mr. Putin. Moreover, the Kremlin hawks respect him—he is a former intelligence chief, he has demonstrated remarkable political survival skills.[13]

On April 11, 2003, Primakov revealed that he had been instructed by President Putin to convince Saddam Hussein to leave power and move to another country.[14] Primakov guided Hussein in manipulating the Iraqi charade of "disarmament" in order to forestall the American invasion of Iraq and the destruction of Hussein's regime. According to a *Times* (London) report, recently discovered documents in the Iraqi archives reveal that, up to the last minute prior to the fall of Baghdad, Saddam Hussein was living under the delusion that he was winning the war and could "clinch a negotiated settlement through French and Russian mediation." Iraqi diplomats told him, "President Putin has instructed us that Russia is very clear in its opposition to any attack on Iraq." The documents also reveal that "Evgeny Primakov, Russia's former intelligence chief and top "Arabist" had warned Saddam Hussein:

Bush is determined to start a large-scale military operation against Iraq.[15]

This time Primakov realized that there was no need to connect Iraq to the Arab-Israeli conflict, because by then the multitude of leftist and Arab promoters of such a linkage had multiplied and he didn't have to advocate linking the Israeli-Palestinian conflict to the Iraqi war. Primakov failed to prevent American action, the same way he had failed to thwart the liberation of Kuwait in the 1991 Gulf War. Primakov left Baghdad in the convoy of Russian diplomats, who were later attacked on the road to Syria, but Primakov survived.

Primakov remains part of Stalin's legacy, which has influenced Soviet and Russian policy toward Israel and Russian Jews for many years after Stalin's death. Dr. Jerrold M. Post, a psychiatrist at George Washington University, and Dr. Amatzia Baram, an expert on Iraq at the University of Haifa, described the psychological profile of Saddam Hussein to the Central Intelligence Agency. They described Hussein as a "malignant narcissist," a diagnosis that they also applied to Stalin and Hitler. Dr. Otto Kernberg, a professor of psychiatry at Cornell University and an expert on personality disorders, observed that "malignant narcissists" suffer from "paranoia and aggression" and an "absence of moral or ethical judgment." Psychoanalyst Dr. Kerry J. Silkowicz stated that "occasionally in history there is a confluence of events in which the severe psychopathology of a leader is allowed to flourish."[16] Such a confluence of events had occurred in Russia (the country that introduced the word *pogrom* into the international vocabulary), and had proven to be the fertile ground for a pathological anti-Semite like Stalin to flourish. Anti-Jewish discrimination was rampant in Russia during centuries of bloody *pogroms* where the Jewish population was put in ghetto-type "pales of settlement."[17] Toward the end of his life, Stalin's anti-Semitism drove him to plan the total annihilation of the Soviet Jews and the destruction of Israel as a Jewish state. Stalin's legacy is perhaps the biggest single influence on post-Stalin Soviet and Russian policy toward the Jews and Israel.

Linking the Arab-Israeli conflict to all the problems in the Arab states and the Muslim world is part of Stalin's legacy which points to remarkable continuity in Soviet policy. It revealed itself when the Soviets provoked the 1967 Six-Day War; in their support for the 1970 PLO attempt to overthrow King Hussein of Jordan; and in their inciting the 1973 Yom Kippur War—not to mention their consistently hostile attitude toward Israel and the Jews before and after the collapse of the "Evil Empire," the glib denials by Russian officials notwithstanding.

Roman Brackman

Chapter 1

The Unidentified Vasily

Stalin's childhood began in the small Georgian town of Gori, which then had a population of approximately eight thousand people, mostly Georgians. But many Armenians, Ossetians, Tartars, and several families of Georgian Jews also lived there. The Jews have lived in the Caucasus for twenty-five hundred years. According to tradition, the Assyrians brought many Jewish captives to the Caucasus after the destruction of the Samarian kingdom in 696 BC. The Babylonian King Nebuchadnezzar had destroyed the First Jerusalem Temple in 586 BC. His ally, the Armenian King Gaik II, settled a large number of Jewish captives around the city of Mzkheta, the ancient capital of Georgia, which was at that time a part of Armenia. Among the Jewish captives was High Priest named Shambat. His descendant, Shambu Bagarat, was appointed hereditary *tagadir* (commander of the Armenian cavalry). The Armenian noble family Bagratuni traces its origins to Shambu Bagarat. His descendants remained true to the Jewish religion until the reign of the Armenian King Tigran the Great, who in 95 BC tried to force them to worship idols (the official religion of Armenia at the time). Many of them refused and were executed. During the following centuries, the Bagratuni family abandoned Judaism.

A large number of Jews came to the Caucasus after the destruction of the

Second Jerusalem Temple by the Romans in 70 AD and settled around Mzkheta, joining the Jews who had lived there since earlier times. In 314 AD, Saint Nina, a Byzantine nun, and a niece of the Jerusalem Bishop, visited Mzkheta and found many Jews with whom she could converse in Hebrew. She baptized a local rabbi, Aviatar, who proselytized in Georgia and Armenia. In 886 AD, Turkish caliph Mutamid Billahi placed the crown of Armenia and Georgia on Bagrat Ashkhot, who started the royal families of Bagration in Georgia and of Bagratuni in Armenia.[18] Although people in some Armenian villages have retained vague memories of their Jewish ancestors, most of the Jews in Armenia were assimilated a long time ago. The descendants of the Jews who in ancient times had settled in the area of Mzkheta were converted to Islam by the Arab, Turkish, and Persian conquerors. They became known as *Meskhi,* all of whom Stalin would exile to Siberia in the early 1950s when he learned of their Jewish roots. The Georgian Jews have lived in most of the Georgian provinces, but since the early 1970s, a large number emigrated to Israel and the United States. During World War II, the Nazis spread rumors that Stalin was a Georgian Jew.

Few fragmentary recollections about Stalin's ancestors have survived. His great-grandfather, Zaza Dzhugashvili, was born a serf in about 1800 in a village named Ger, near the small town of Gori in the province of Kartvelia. Zaza took part in several uprisings, which were suppressed by Russian troops. He was captured twice, but managed to escape and settled in the village of Didi-Lilo.[19] One of Zaza's grandsons was Vissarion Dzhugashvili, Stalin's father. He left Didi-Lilo in 1864 at the age of fourteen, shortly after the abolition of serfdom, and went to work at the Adelkhanov shoe factory in Tiflis, the capital of Georgia. Ten years later, Vissarion moved to another shoe factory in Gori where his peasant ancestors had lived in a nearby village for centuries.[20] The name Dzhugashvili consists of two words: *dzhuga* and *shvili*. In the Old Georgian language, *dzhuga* meant "yoke for oxen." Words of the same root and similar meaning, such as the Russian word *igo* (yoke), are common to many Indo-European languages. The word *dzhuga* was absorbed into Old Georgian from a language spoken by an Indo-European tribe who had dwelt in the area in ancient times.[21] *Shvili* means "son of." The Dzhugashvili family name dates back to ancient times, when a remote family ancestor was a craftsman who made yokes for oxen, then a device in great demand. In an 1895 scholarly article (and later a 1907 pamphlet), Niko Marr, a young Georgian linguist, would argue that the Georgian language belonged to the Semitic group of languages.[22]

Vissarion opened his own shoemaking business and bought a small house in Gori. On May 17, 1874, he married seventeen-year-old Katerina Geladze, or Keke, as everyone called her.[23] The couple had a Georgian Orthodox ceremony conducted by Koba Egnatashvili, a local priest, who walked at the head of the wedding procession.[24] Keke gave birth to three babies who died in infancy or were stillborn. She once mentioned that she had two sons, and another time she spoke of three babies, which suggests that one of the babies was a girl.[25] The causes of the babies' deaths have remained unknown. The fourth child, a boy, was born a month before the Eastern Orthodox Christmas. An entry in the records of the *Uspensky Sobor* (the Cathedral of the Assumption) in Gori states:

> Iosif Dzhugashvili was born December 6, 1878. Christened December 17, 1878; parents Vissarion Ivanovich Dzhugashvili, peasant, and his lawful wedded wife, Katerina Geladze, residents of the town of Gori.[26]

The boy survived. Everyone called him Soso, the diminutive of Iosif, or Joseph. He was to become known to the world as Iosif Vissarionovich Stalin.

Soso appeared to be a normal child except for an abnormality of his left foot: the second and third toes were webbed.[27] This defect attracted attention and started gossip, which with the passage of time was distorted and turned into a rumor, still alive in Georgia today, that Stalin had six fingers.[28] As late as the Middle Ages, it was common to kill babies with various physical abnormalities, which to superstitious minds signified the mystical intervention of diabolical forces. Some of these superstitions have survived into current mythology. Grigory, one of the characters in Dostoyevsky's *The Brothers Karamazov*, believes that his six-fingered son is a "dragon." He is relieved when his son dies.

The one-room mud hut where Soso grew up had an "ancestral bed that took up half the room. It was the resting place for the entire family."[29] A great scare gripped Georgia at the time Stalin was born. Russian police were investigating the death of a Georgian girl, Sara Madubadze, whose body was found near the village where she had lived. There were numerous small wounds on the girl's body. The Russian police stated that several Georgian Jews, who were traveling on horseback through the village at that time, had murdered the girl and placed her body into a wooden barrel studded with nails in order to drain her blood for baking matzoth.[30] Such a blood libel had been common throughout Russian history, but this was its first appearance in

Georgia, and the accusations instilled fear in many Georgian families. The mass hysteria continued for some time, even after several prominent Russian lawyers repudiated the police version and proved in court that the girl had drowned during a heavy rain, and that her wounds had been caused by bites from small animals. The accused Georgian Jews were acquitted.[31]

No recollection has come to light to suggest that Stalin's parents were affected by this hysteria. Yet shortly before Stalin's death, when he was preparing to unleash a Jewish pogrom and to exile the Jewish population to Siberia, he ordered Georgian secret police to instigate one of their collaborators, Natalia Kavtaradze, to yell through the streets of Tbilisi, "The Jews murder Christian children and roll them in wooden barrels studded with nails to drain their blood for use in matzos."[32] The roots of Stalin's hatred of the Jews might, or might not, be traced to this particular childhood memory.

The neighbors remembered Vissarion brutally beating Soso.[33] The rumor in Gori was that Vissarion hated Soso because he suspected Keke of infidelity and thought that Soso was not his son. He cursed Soso and called him a *nabichuari* ("bastard" in Georgian).[34] Suggestions of Soso's illegitimacy appeared early in Stalin biographies. Trotsky cited "ticklish facts."[35] Boris Souvarine refers to Georgian Bolsheviks who "adduce rather unpleasant facts by way of proof."[36] Roy Medvedev states, "In Georgia, even today, there are rumors which attempt to give Stalin higher status as the illegitimate son of an aristocrat or high-placed clergyman."[37] Illegitimacy is considered a disgrace and the ultimate insult for Georgians, who cherish their traditions of family ties, kinship, and honor. The name that invariably comes up in rumors about Stalin's "true" father has been Koba (Yakobi) Egnatashvili, a Gori priest who officiated at Vissarion's and Keke's wedding.[38]

The Egnatashvili family belonged to the ranks of the *aznauri*, a well-established and proud Georgian gentry, whose members traditionally went into military or civil service or took the cloth. The priest was married, but of all his children, only two sons had survived the smallpox epidemic of the winter of 1887 that had almost claimed Soso's life as well (leaving his face heavily pockmarked).[39] For many years during his rule, Egnatashvili's two sons were in Stalin's good graces. One of them, Alexander Yakovlevich Egnatashvili, later became a general and Stalin's personal bodyguard. He was known among them as Stalin's "brother."[40] He was also known as a "rabbit," because his main responsibility was to taste all of the food that was served at the table of his "brother" to make sure that it was not poisoned.[41] (General Egnatashvili mysteriously disappeared at the time of Stalin's death.)[42]

Priest Egnatashvili's other son, Vasily Yakovlevich Egnatashvili, was a high Georgian Communist Party official. He could not resist the temptation to brag that he was Stalin's "brother." Stalin was annoyed and ordered his arrest, but he was released after Stalin's death.

Keke and the priest were the only people who could have answered the question of Soso's paternity, but they are both long dead. Their confession would have surely started a bloody feud between the Dzhugashvili, and Egnatashvili, and Geladze families. The ancient tradition of *siskhus akheba*, or bloody revenge for a man's injured pride, still exists in Georgia. This suspected adultery destroyed the Dzhugashvili family. Vissarion turned from an outgoing, cheerful man, an engaging storyteller and a fine singer, into a bully and a drunkard who spent all his earnings on alcohol, and who was feared and avoided by Soso.[43] Soso was five years old when Vissarion left Gori for Tiflis, where he again worked at the Adelkhanov shoe factory.[44] Soso was enrolled in the first grade of Gori's Preparatory Ecclesiastic School in September 1888. Priest E. Egnatashvili had arranged the stipend and had given Keke a job in the school.[45]

Vissarion came back to Gori sometime in the early spring of 1890, and, despite Keke's and Egnatashvili's objections, took Soso out of school to work with him in Tiflis. "Do you want my son to become a priest?" shouted Vissarion. "You will not live to see that happen! I'm a shoemaker. My son must also be a shoemaker."[46] Soso did not want to leave Gori. This further enraged Vissarion. "Look at this *nabichuari!* [bastard]" he shouted. "He doesn't want to be a shoemaker like me!"[47] Soso threw a knife at Vissarion, who ran after him screaming.[48] A neighbor recalled a fight in which Vissarion had called Keke a "whore," knocked her down, and tried to strangle her. The neighbors restrained Vissarion.[49] Vissarion forced Soso to labor as an errand boy for the workers of the Adelkhanov shoe factory.[50] Keke and Egnatashvili asked the Exarch of Georgia, the head of the Georgian Orthodox Church, to remove Soso from Vissarion. The Exarch offered a compromise: to leave Soso in Vissarion's custody so that he would attend a church school in Tiflis and sing in the Exarch's choir. Vissarion rejected this proposal. Vissarion injured Soso's left arm during his son's stay in Tiflis. Years later Stalin explained that his left arm was shorter than his right one by a couple of inches because Vissarion had injured it during his childhood.[51]

The police arrested Vissarion and he was tried in court for gravely injuring his son. Soso testified about the beatings he had suffered. The court sentenced Vissarion to a prison term and voided his custody rights.[52] (Decades later,

Stalin staged show trials in which the scene of boys testifying against their fathers was reenacted over and over again. Stalin also glorified Pavlik Morozov, a young peasant boy who had testified against his peasant father in a Soviet court. In doing so, Stalin was also glorifying himself.)

After serving his term, Vissarion did not return to his family, and became a vagrant and a drunk. Soso returned to Gori at the end of September 1890. He and Keke kept silent about what had happened in Tiflis.[53] Soso's injured left arm healed, but the damaged bone developed osteomyelitis, a bone disease, which at that time was generally a fatal malady. Soso's left arm grew short by a couple of inches. Soon after returning to Gori, Soso adopted the nickname Koba. His classmates assumed that he chose this name after Koba, the hero of the popular novel *Father Killers* by Georgian writer Prince Kazbegy.[54] But there was a more important hero in Soso's life; his benefactor, Koba Egnatashvili. Children traumatized by brutal fathers often reject them and postulate a new origin for themselves, choosing a different father figure and adopting his name.[55] It was natural for Soso to reject Vissarion as his father and to appoint Koba Egnatashvili in his place. He may even have known of the rumor circulating in Gori that Koba was his true father.[56] Koba Egnatashvili was Soso's obvious choice for a worthy father. He never explained his choice of the nickname Koba, but he insisted on being called by it.

In the spring of 1894, Koba graduated from the Gori School and enrolled in the Tiflis Orthodox Seminary, where he got free tuition, room, and board.[57] Egnatashvili had arranged for all of these benefits.[58] Until the beginning of his third year at the seminary, Koba was a good student.[59] Then the trouble began. The record book reports state that he was "disrespectful and rude."[60] In 1897, Koba and several of his classmates joined a Young Socialists Circle, which split into supporters and opponents of Koba. "Only the intellectually shallow types, who were willing to toady up to Koba, remained with him."[61] Toward the end of 1898, Koba smuggled inflammatory leaflets into the seminary dormitory, and placed them under students' pillows and mattresses. Then he denounced those students to the Rector, who ordered the dormitory searched.[62] Soon thereafter, some forty-five students who had been implicated by Koba in the illegal leaflet scandal were expelled from the seminary. They found out that it was Koba who had planted the leaflets, and that it was also he who had informed on them. Their parents besieged the rector with petitions to reinstate their sons and complained that they were innocent victims of Koba's provocation. Koba did not deny the charge. He remarked blithely that he did it to create the opportunity for them to be "good revolutionaries."[63] This was

Koba's first such recorded provocation.

Koba failed to take the necessary exams to be transferred to the fifth and final grade, and he did not respond to Rector Germogen's offer to take the exams at a later date. Rector Germogen was one of the leading anti-Semites in the Russian Empire, and he shared his hostile views about the Jews with his students. (Whether he had any personal contact with Koba is not indicated in the corresponding records.) But he had no other choice but to expel Koba. On May 29, 1899, a laconic entry was made in the Seminary's record book: "Iosif Dzhugashvili was expelled for not taking the examinations; reason unknown."[64] Stalin's childhood biography contained the poem *"Musha"* (vagrant) by the Georgian poet Prince Ilia Chavchavadze.[65] This poem tells a story of a vagrant (which is Vissarion's story), and hints at Koba's accidental encounter with this vagrant on a Tiflis street at the end of 1897. Vissarion had been released from prison. Koba's childhood friend Iosif Iremashvili wrote:

> When Koba left the Seminary, he took with him a grim, sullen hatred. It was a hatred for every form of authority. . . . Everywhere and in everything he saw only the negative, the base, and he did not credit mankind with any lofty ideals or noble qualities.[66]

Koba's childhood traumas might provide some explanation for the carnage and bloodshed of his subsequent years.[67]

Planting illegal leaflets was a typical provocation by the *Okhrana*, the Russian secret police, officially known as the *Okhrannoe Otdelenie* (Security Section of the Department of Police). At the turn of the century, the Okhrana extensively employed *provokatsiya* (provocations).[68] The leading proponent of provocations was the chief of the Moscow Okhrana section, Sergey Vasilievich Zubatov, who advocated the theory of "Police Socialism," by which he meant the infiltration of revolutionary parties (who were printing inflammatory leaflets on illegal printing presses) by Okhrana agents and informers. The purpose was to arrest revolutionaries, thus creating vacancies for Okhrana agents to be promoted to leadership roles in the revolutionary organizations. Zubatov's tactics were mimicked by other Okhrana agents, who often caused scandals that embarrassed the secret police. Zubatov's methods became known as *zubatovshchina*.

Such a scandal rocked the Tiflis Okhrana in 1901. Okhrana informers Iosif Dzhugashvili and Lado Ketskhoveli had printed illegal leaflets on a primitive printing press. They were assisted by a deranged Armenian criminal, Simon

Ter-Petrosian (nicknamed "Kamo"), who operated this press. Kamo printed a leaflet, which alarmed the chief of the Tiflis Okhrana, Captain Lavrov, who started an investigation. Koba and Ketskhoveli told their Okhrana handler, Samedov, that this leaflet had been printed on a private printer owned by Kheladze for the Marxist "secret circle" headed by Victor Kurnatovsky in Tiflis. Kheladze was arrested, along with every member of Kurnatovsky's secret circle.[69] The provocation was discovered and Kheladze was released. The members of Kurnatovsky's circle remained behind bars to face charges of revolutionary activity, although the charge related to the criminal leaflet was dropped.[70] To avoid the exposure of an embarrassing Okhrana scandal, the case of the Okhrana officer Samedov and his informers Koba and Ketskhoveli was sent to St. Petersburg for a "secret investigation." Captain Lavrov was dismissed from his post.

Koba's nickname in the criminal underworld was "*Chopur*" ("pockmarked," in Georgian), because he had a heavily pockmarked face. Similarly, at the Tiflis Okhrana, Koba's nickname was recorded as "*Riaboy*" ("pockmarked," in Russian).[71] Criminal nicknames often reflect physical defects, habits of speech, or ethnic background. Koba, Ketskhoveli, and Kamo came to Tiflis from Gori, which may well have initially contributed to their friendship. More importantly, they shared similar childhood experiences of abuse at the hands of their fathers. They shared habits of thought and attitudes. They hated authority and all of its symbols. Koba watched the bloody confrontation between workers and the Cossack troops during the demonstration from a safe distance. It had been provoked by the leaflet that he, Ketskhoveli, and Kamo had printed. Afterwards, he gleefully told his childhood friend Iosif Iremashvili how Cossack sabers and whips had spilled the blood of "proletarian workers." Iremashvili thought that Koba was "intoxicated by workers' blood."[72] In one of his articles Koba, drew a portrait of a "typical proletarian worker." He stated:

> Imagine a shoemaker who had a tiny workshop but could not stand the competition of big business. That man closed his shop and hired himself out to, say, Adelkhanov at the Tiflis shoe factory.[73]

This was Vissarion's story, including such detail as the Adelkhanov shoe factory, where Vissarion had worked—and where, as a ten-year-old boy, Koba had been an errand boy for the "proletarian workers" and had been abused by his father. The passage barely veils Koba's contempt for the workers whose champion he proclaims himself to be.

In late November 1901, Koba left Tiflis for Batum, a growing Black Sea port near the Turkish border, where he accused the leaders of the Batum workers of "cowardice, lack of ability, and treason against the working class."[74] They in turn called Koba a "madman" and "troublemaker."[75] Koba was arrested by the Batum criminal police, which was conducting an investigation of a local criminal gang that was running a counterfeiting operation and was also involved in armed robbery. In his report, the arresting officer stated:

Iosif Dzhugashvili: Expelled from the Theological Seminary; has been living in Batum without a definite address or passport.[76]

Koba offered to provide information about the revolutionary underground. Colonel Shabelsky, the chief of the Batum Okhrana, decided to recruit Koba and ordered:

Free him if he agrees to give information about the activities of the Social Democratic Party to the Gendarmerie Department.[77]

Back in his cell, Koba accused one of the prisoners of being a police informer, and incited his fellow prisoners to attack this man. The guards later removed the man's blood-spattered body.[78]

This was Koba's first recorded instance of his offering to provide information to the Okhrana in exchange for release from prison and it was also the first recorded instance of him accusing innocent people of being Okhrana informers. This pattern of behavior would continue to punctuate Koba's Okhrana career for years to come. On June 17, 1903, Colonel Shabelsky received an Okhrana communication stating that Koba should be arrested "in connection with the case of the secret circle in Tiflis."[79] That day Colonel Shabelsky made an entry in Koba's file:

Iosif Vissarionov Dzhugashvili; Height: 2 arshina, 4.5 vershkov [5 foot, 4 inches]; Body type: medium; Age: 23. Second and third toes on left foot fused together. Appearance: ordinary. Hair: dark brown. Beard and mustache: brown. Nose: straight and long. Forehead: straight and low. Face: long, swarthy, and pockmarked.[80]

Shabelsky recorded Koba's criminal nickname *Riaboy* (pockmarked, in

Russian) and provided the Okhrana with Ketskhoveli's address in Baku, where Ketskhoveli was arrested shortly thereafter, then taken to the Metekh prison in Tiflis. The Okhrana was still unable to arrest Kamo, who kept moving from place to place, leaving a trail littered with leaflets. The "secret case" of Okhrana officer Samedov and his informers Koba and Ketskhoveli was decided in midsummer 1903. Koba was sentenced by the "Highest Authority" decree of June 9, 1903, to be exiled "administratively to the Balagan region of the Irkutsk province in eastern Siberia, to remain there under open police surveillance."[81] Samedov was fired and exiled to Siberia. The members of Kurnatovsky's secret circle were sentenced to various terms of exile. The members of the Tiflis Okhrana sarcastically labeled the provocations involving these officers (and their informers) as "Samedov's Disease."[82]

Ketskhoveli was brought to the Metekh prison. On August 4, 1904, Ketskhoveli was shot and killed as he stood in his window singing "La Marseillaise" and shouting "Long live Socialism!" while watching members of Kurnatovsky's secret circle being led from the Metekh prison courtyard and herded to a train to Siberia.[83] Perhaps loneliness and the feeling of guilt had inspired him to prove that he was a true revolutionary. In any case, his life glowed most brightly after he had sacrificed it. (Years later, Stalin would point to Ketskhoveli's portrait in his Kremlin office, saying that Ketskhoveli was his first mentor. He claimed that Ketskhoveli was a greater revolutionary than even Lenin.)[84]

Koba was transferred to the Kutais prison, where the Kutais Okhrana hoped to use his information to apprehend Kamo, who at that time was distributing leaflets in Kutais. Koba offered to find Kamo if he was released. The Okhrana usually arranged "escapes" from places of exile, where there was only token police surveillance and escapes were common. Toward the end of September 1903, Koba was sent under guard to the village of Novaya Uda, near Irkutsk, in eastern Siberia. A telegram from the Kutais Okhrana addressed to the Irkutsk Okhrana stated:

I. V. Dzhugashvili plans to leave. Do not stop him. Render assistance.[85]

Toward the end of October, Koba left Novaya Uda with a document that identified him as an Okhrana agent. He arrived at Batum in mid-November 1903[86] and told a story of how he had "fabricated an identity document in the name of an agent of one of the Siberian policemen."[87] He sent Kamo a message asking him to come to Batum. On November 26, 1903, Kamo stepped off the train at the Batum railway station, where an Okhrana officer with an arrest warrant was waiting for him. Kamo offered money to the officer to let him go, but to no avail.[88] This was Kamo's first (but by no means his last) arrest.

At the end of December 1903, Koba arrived in Tiflis, and met for the first time a young Social Democrat, Lev Kamenev, whom party leader V. I. Lenin had sent to Tiflis to take the place of the arrested Kurnatovsky. Kamenev had become Lenin's disciple at the Second Social Democratic Party Congress in London in the summer of 1903, where the party had split into Mensheviks and Bolsheviks. The meeting with Kamenev was the first time Koba had heard about Lenin. On January 5, 1904, shortly after meeting Koba, Kamenev was arrested.[89] That day a Tiflis Okhrana officer made an entry in Koba's file:

On January 5, 1904, Dzhugashvili disappeared from his place of exile.[90]

This officer wanted to hide the fact that he had failed to arrest the "escaped" exile. The 1901 scandal in the Tiflis Okhrana was still fresh in the memory of the Okhrana officers. This officer knew that Koba was connected with Kamo, whose case was being considered on the highest level in St. Petersburg. Prime Minister Plehve fired Zubatov, accusing him of recruiting an Okhrana agent, Dr. Shaevich, who had organized a bloody demonstration of Jewish workers in Odessa.[91] Plehve told Zubatov, "You and your *Zhiduga* [kike-boy] Shaevich!" and ordered Zubatov to get out his office. Although Zubatov was fired and his network of Okhrana agents purged, *zubatovshchina* survived. Plehve was soon assassinated in a terrorist act directed by Evno Azef, a top Okhrana agent and a Jew.

The new Tiflis Okhrana chief, Colonel N. A. Zasypkin, received a warrant for the arrest of Iosif Dzhugashvili, which had been issued by the Department of Police, on May 1, 1904.[92] Koba learned about the warrant and escaped to Gori. On June 21, 1904, he married Katerina (Keke) Svanidze in one of Gori's eight churches.[93] The couple made their home in Didi-Lilo because Koba's wife wanted to stay close to her family. Koba soon left and rarely visited his wife. He was involved in robberies, but the Okhrana protected him from criminal prosecution in exchange for secret information about the revolutionary underground. He led a double life punctuated by the betrayals of fellow revolutionaries. Koba met Lenin for the first time at the 1905 Tammerfors Party Conference, which he attended replacing Peter Montin, the elected delegate from Baku. Montin was killed before his departure to

11

Tammerfors. Sergey Alliluev, Stalin's future father-in-law, was suspected in the murder. In conversation with Lenin during the Tammerfors Conference, Koba promised to organize bank robberies to provide Lenin with money.[94]

After his return to Tiflis, Koba was arrested and released by the chief of the Tiflis Okhrana, Colonel N. A. Zasypkin, to whom Koba announced that he had liquidated the underground, Tiflis-based Avlabar Press in March 1906.[95] The Avlabar press was liquidated by the Okhrana in April 1906. Zasypkin allowed Koba to attend the Stockholm Party Congress. On his way there, Koba visited the St. Petersburg Okhrana headquarters, and offered to provide information about the Congress. The St. Petersburg Okhrana reported Koba's offer to Arkady Garting, the chief of the Okhrana Foreign Agency, whose duty it was to gather information about Russian revolutionaries in Western Europe. Koba arrived in Stockholm with a passport bearing the name of "Ivan Ivanovich Vissarionovich."[96] The Swedish border police recorded his arrival and stated, "Ivan Ivanovich Vissarionovich, a journalist intended to reside at the Hotel Bristol during his stay in Stockholm." The Stockholm police checked the hotel later, recording that "Vissarionovich was not registered in this hotel."[97]

Garting was born Avraam Gekkelman to a well-to-do Jewish family in the town of Pinsk, near the Russian-Polish border.[98] Garting recruited Koba in April 1906. The Stockholm Fourth (Unity) Party Congress opened in Stockholm on April 11; Koba was registered under the alias "X."[99] On his way back to Russia, Koba visited Kamo, who was planning bank hold-ups and assassinations with the Bolshevik-Maximalist group in St. Petersburg.[100] Koba reported these plans to the St. Petersburg Okhrana, using the code-name "Ivanov."[101] While Koba was in St. Petersburg, Kamo murdered "Volodka," one of the members of the Bolshevik-Maximalist group, claiming that "Volodka" was an "Okhrana informer." Kamo struck "Volodka" with an axe and threw his body into the Neva River. It has never been formally established if "Volodka" was an informer.[102] Koba habitually accused others of what he himself was guilty, and Kamo blindly believed everything Koba told him.

Late in March 1907, Koba went to Copenhagen to take part in a Party congress, but he and his fellow delegates were refused entry and had to go to Sweden; then to Oslo, Norway; and finally to London, where the British Socialists secured permission for their Russian comrades to hold their congress. Garting went there too. He provided Koba with 500 rubles for these trips.[103] Koba again used the alias "Ivanovich" when he registered at the London congress.[104] Garting sent Koba's report to St. Petersburg, describing him as a "Social Democrat" who had performed "quite valuable services." Garting also recommended an award for his agent of 1,500 rubles, a large sum at the time.[105]

Among the participants at the London congress were two Okhrana agents: Dr. Yakov Zhitomirsky, Lenin's close friend, who headed the Bolshevik émigré organization in Europe; and Koba, who was one of the non-delegates. Also in attendance were L. B. Krassin, A. S. Bogdanov, and Maxim Litvinov, who were admitted to the congress at Lenin's insistence. They were all members of Lenin's secret group that was planning new expropriations. Lenin proposed a resolution granting these four non-delegates "advisory status." The Mensheviks did not want to quarrel over what seemed a minor point, and granted Lenin's request. In London, Koba first met Maxim Litvinov, a Jew from Bialystok, who was mentioned in Okhrana documents by his real name, Meer Vallakh, and several aliases: "Papasha" [Daddy], "Finkelstein," "Felix," and "Maxim Litvinov." This last moniker was to become his name for the rest of his life. After the London congress, Litvinov, Krassin, Bogdanov, and Koba went to Berlin for a secret meeting with Lenin. They discussed a large bank robbery to be carried out by Kamo's gang in Tiflis.[106] Koba did not tell Garting about the planned robbery. This was the second and last encounter Koba had with Garting.[107]

Koba and Litvinov traveled to Tiflis, and Kamo joined them there. Koba promised his handler, Tiflis Okhrana officer Mukhtarov, that he would keep him informed about the pending expropriations. On the morning of June 13, 1907, Kamo carried out a daring bank robbery in Yerevan Square in Tiflis, turning the place into an inferno. The total take was over 341,000 rubles, but only 91,000 rubles of this amount were in small, untraceable bills. Kamo delivered the money to Lenin in Finland, and Litvinov smuggled it to Europe.[108] Later in the day, Mukhtarov and several other officers brought Koba to one of their secret apartments on the outskirts of Tiflis. Mukhtarov accused Koba of deliberately deceiving him, but Koba insisted that he had told Mukhtarov about the planned heist. Toward the end of November 1907, "the case of Mukhtarov and Dzhugashvili " was sent to the Department of Police in St. Petersburg, and then submitted for the "Administrative Decision" of the "Special Council of the Interior Ministry."[109] Colonel Zasypkin was ordered to establish the identities of the thieves and the location of the stolen money. He ordered Koba to go to Europe to gather this information. Zasypkin provided Koba with a passport bearing the name "Gaioz Vissarionov Nizheradze." One of the Tiflis Okhrana officers said, "Dzhugashvili shows some improvement.

We'll watch what happens next. If he misleads us again, we'll have to seal him in an envelope,"[110] which meant exile.

As Koba traveled to Europe in December 1907, Kamo was arrested in Berlin. Having learned about Kamo's arrest, Lenin and his wife, Nadezhda Krupskaya, fled from Finland, and arrived in Berlin on December 22, 1907.[111] Several of Lenin's followers, among them Koba, met him there. Lenin stayed in Berlin for three days and then he and his wife Krupskaya left for Switzerland, having ordered his followers to cash the stolen banknotes. Koba avoided taking part in the cashing of these notes. On January 4, 1908, several of Lenin's followers were arrested in Munich, Stockholm, Geneva, Sofia, Copenhagen, and Rotterdam. Litvinov was arrested in Paris.[112] While others were being caught in the police dragnet, Koba was on his way to Tiflis. He arrived there in the middle of January 1908 and was summoned by Colonel Alexander Mikhailovich Eremin, who had replaced Colonel Zasypkin as chief of the Tiflis Okhrana.[113] Eremin was thirty-five years old at that time. Before being transferred to Tiflis, he had worked in the Special Section of the Department of Police in St. Petersburg, where he had been involved in the investigation of a Tiflis bank robbery.

By January 1908, the Tiflis Okhrana received the administrative decision in the Dzhugashvili-Mukhtarov case: Koba was to be exiled for two years to northern-European Russia; Mukhtarov was to be exiled for three years to eastern Siberia.[114] Eremin decided to delay Koba's exile, probably because Eremin needed Koba's information. Koba's personal circumstances may also have played a role in Eremin's decision: Koba's wife Keke was in her last months of pregnancy. Eremin ordered Koba to move to Baku and to provide information to him via Captain P. I. Martynov, the chief of the Baku Okhrana. On March 16, 1908, Keke gave birth to a boy named "Koba" (or "Yakobi") in Russian. Koba was arrested nine days later, on March 25, 1908. For the next six months, he remained in Baku's Bailov Prison, waiting to be shipped to his next place of exile.[115] Keke and little Yakobi left Baku and returned to her family in Didi-Lilo.

During his half-year of incarceration in the Bailov Prison, Koba wrote several reports to Captain Martynov, who relayed them to Eremin.[116] Koba identified Kamo in a photograph, which the Germans sent to Russia. On April 22, 1909, Eremin wired a telegram to St. Petersburg stating, "The man in the photograph is Kamo Ter-Petrosian, a native of Gori."[117] While in prison, Koba accused two of his cellmates of being Okhrana agents.[118] Social-Revolutionary Semen Vereshchak, who shared a prison cell with Koba, stated, "Koba revealed an absolutely peculiar hatred of the Mensheviks, calling them scoundrels."[119] Koba frequently made statements such as:

> The Mensheviks are mostly Jews, and Lenin is exasperated that God sent him comrades such as the Mensheviks. Really, what kinds of people are these Martov, Dan, and Axelrod!? Nothing but circumcised kikes! They won't fight and there is no rejoicing at their feasting, cowards and shopkeepers![120]

In a newspaper article that he wrote in 1907, Koba stated:

> Somebody among the Bolsheviks remarked in jest that since the Mensheviks were the faction of the Jews and the Bolsheviks that of the native Russians, it would become us to have a pogrom in the party.[121]

This "somebody" was Koba himself, and he was not joking. Koba's hatred of the Mensheviks was at the bottom of his "absolutely peculiar hatred" of the Jews.

Koba was exiled to the town of Solvychegodsk in "northern European" Russia, where he stayed until the end of June 1909. He then "escaped" with a passport that had been issued by the Tiflis chief of police on May 12, 1909, and that was valid for one year.[122] When this passport expired in May 1910, Captain A. P. Martynov, the chief of the Baku Okhrana, supplied Koba with another passport in the Armenian name of "Zakhar Grigorian Melikanz."[123] On October 19, 1909, Kamo, handcuffed and dragging his shackles and chains, arrived at the Tiflis prison.[124] The same day, Captain Martynov sent Eremin a secret cable, stating:

> Dzhugashvili has departed for Tiflis to participate in the conference, after which he must return to Baku and be involved at once in technical matters. Telegraph of his departure from Tiflis and provide the train number.[125]

Eremin summoned Koba to identify Kamo. Koba stayed in Tiflis for two days, living in a "secret apartment." A friend visited him when Eremin was there. "What do you have to do with this gendarme? Why was this gendarme here?" asked the friend. Koba replied, "He's helping us in the gendarmerie."[126] Eremin was helping Koba avoid exile while Koba was helping Eremin tighten the noose around Kamo's neck. Kamo's case was heard in the Tiflis military tribunal. Each of his six indictment articles called for the death penalty. But Kamo was placed in the psychiatric ward of the Tiflis Metekh prison.[127]

In 1909, Koba's wife Keke committed suicide. She left a year-and-a-half-old son. "I promised Keke that she would be buried in accordance with Orthodox rites, and I shall keep my promise," said Koba. The Svanidze family, too, "insisted on a church burial."[128] In Georgia, as well as in the whole of the Russian Empire, cemeteries were under the jurisdiction of various religious communities, which did not allow a burial without the appropriate rites. Only if Keke had committed suicide could she been denied such a burial. When Koba returned to Baku after the funeral, he was accused of cooperating with the Okhrana.[129] On March 23, 1910, a secret meeting took place at which a worker, Zharinov, accused Koba of having instigated a lethal attack on him.[130] Okhrana officers surrounded the house where the meeting was occurring. All the members of the "court" were arrested. The trial was postponed.[131]

On January 21, 1910, Eremin was appointed Chief of the Special Section of the Department of Police, the third highest post in the department.[132] Because the Special Section did not have its own agents, Eremin did not transfer Koba to St. Petersburg. Captain Martynov had also been transferred from the Caucasus.[133] Eremin "sanitized" Koba's file in the Tiflis Okhrana, removing from it all documents that could point to Koba's employment as an agent.[134] This was the usual procedure for an Okhrana handler, whose responsibility was to protect the cover of his agents and informers. Only the handler who recruited an agent was supposed to know his identity. Koba was exiled to Solvychegodsk in northern Russia to complete the remaining six months of his previous two-year term. Koba's checkered Okhrana career in the Caucasus ended, and memory of him began to fade among the local revolutionaries.[135]

After Koba's arrival in Solvychegodsk, he lived in the house of a widow, Maria Kuzakova, who became pregnant and accused Koba of having raped her. Koba convinced her to settle the case and withdraw her charges.[136] Toward the end of 1911, Kuzakova gave birth to a son, Konstantin Kuzakov. In the late twenties, Maria Kuzakova brought Konstantin, then a teenager, to Moscow, and asked Stalin to help her and the boy.[137] (In 1995, Konstantin Kuzakov, by then an elderly man, allowed publication of his story and a 1935 photograph of himself, his mother, and his three-year-old son.[138]) On his arrival in Solvychegodsk, Koba initiated an elaborate scheme to reinstate himself as an Okhrana agent. When his term of exile expired, he obtained the Okhrana's permission to settle in Vologda. On September 6, 1911, Koba left

Vologda for St. Petersburg, where he contacted Eremin, who was then handling the case of Dmitry Bogrov. Bogrov was an Okhrana agent and a member of the Social Revolutionary Party (Esers). The Okhrana was in turmoil because Bogrov had assassinated Prime Minister Stolypin on September 5, 1911. Various "hidden hand" theories abounded, including the suggestion that the Okhrana was involved, or that the murder had been a Jewish conspiracy in which "the Jew Bogrov" had killed to protest Stolypin's "anti-Semitism."[139]

Eremin was also concerned with the case of Kamo who on August 15, 1911, escaped from the psychiatric ward of the Tiflis Metekh prison. The rope on which Kamo had lowered himself from his prison window snapped, and he was badly injured. He recovered and escaped abroad with the help of friends. His bones not yet fully mended, Kamo knocked at the door of Lenin's apartment in Paris. Lenin advised him to restore his health and then to go to the Caucasus as soon as possible to organize a bank robbery. As always, Lenin needed money.[140] Eremin feared that Kamo's escape might activate the Tiflis bank-robbery case and expose his ties to Koba. But his immediate reason for ordering Koba's arrest was the request by the chief of the Moscow Okhrana, Colonel P. P. Zavarzin who feared that Koba might interfere with Zavarzin's scheme to promote his agent, Roman Malinovsky, to the top of Bolshevik organization in Moscow. Eremin ordered Koba's arrest and exile to Vologda for three years under open police surveillance.[141] Koba's brief sojourn in Vologda had delayed his fateful encounter with Roman Malinovsky.[142]

The Bolshevik conference in Prague opened on January 6, 1912. Lenin's proposal to select Malinovsky as the Bolshevik candidate who could represent the workers of the Moscow Gubernia in the Fourth *Duma* elections was accepted.[143] Lenin also "co-opted" Koba as an "agent of the Central Committee." The hidden meaning of this appointment was to direct Koba to meet Kamo in the Caucasus, and help him carry out an expropriation. Koba arrived in Moscow early in April 1912, and he was introduced to Roman Malinovsky. Koba noticed some obvious similarities between himself and Malinovsky: a heavily pockmarked face and a strong non-Russian accent. But soon Koba made another discovery: he realized that Malinovsky was an Okhrana agent. On the surface, they became close friends.[144]

A complicated Okhrana scheme to promote Malinovsky's election to the State Duma, including fraud and falsification of documents, was carried out in secret.[145] Colonel Eremin told his superiors, Director of the Department of Police S. P. Beletsky and Vice-Director Vissarionov, that it was illegal to interfere in the Duma electoral process, and that it was too dangerous because

Malinovsky's criminal background and ties to the Okhrana might be exposed, creating a "great state scandal."[146] Despite Eremin's objection, Beletsky approved the election scheme and requested approval from the Assistant Minister of the Interior, I. M. Zolotarev who personally informed the Minister of the Interior A. A. Makarov, who gave his consent. For the sake of secrecy, it was decided that only Beletsky and Vissarionov would have contact with Malinovsky.[147]

Koba was arrested on April 22, 1912. While in prison, Koba submitted his handwritten report to the Okhrana, providing information on the revolutionary parties and their leaders. He also complained that Malinovsky was an untrustworthy Okhrana agent. Eremin deposited the original of Koba's report in Koba's file, which was placed in a top secret safe in a "Special Section" of the Okhrana. On June 11, 1912, Eremin sent abbreviated copies of Koba's unsigned report to the chief of the Foreign Agency in Paris and to the St. Petersburg Okhrana Section, omitting Koba's complaint about Malinovsky, and identifying those copies only as "*Spravka bez* No." (Reference without number). Eremin did not mention Koba's complaint about Malinovsky in these two copies. One of the officers in the Special Section, Lieutenant-Colonel Ivan Petrovich Vasiliev, read Koba's original report and decided to expose Malinovsky, expecting that the ensuing scandal would topple his superiors, thus creating a vacancy for his own promotion. The man Vasiliev hoped to replace was his immediate superior, Colonel Eremin. Vasiliev understood that Koba was trying to unmask Malinovsky in order to replace him as Lenin's right-hand man in the Bolshevik organization and as the top Okhrana agent in the Okhrana.[148] The unmasking of Malinovsky served the mutual interests of Koba and Vasiliev, who was associated with the anti-Semitic group "Black Hundreds," and was involved in instigating Jewish pogroms and printing anti-Semitic pamphlets, like the infamous *Protocols of the Elders of Zion*.[149] Vasiliev was also known as a "drunkard and intriguer."[150]

On July 2, 1912, Koba was exiled to the town of Narym in Western Siberia, where he infuriated his fellow exiles, who summoned him to a comradely court. One of the exiles, a Georgian Jew, protested Koba's demagoguery. Koba angrily snapped back in Georgian, "*Uria mamatskhali*" (stinking Jew). Another Georgian Menshevik commented, "Bolsheviks are Bolsheviks . . . now they suddenly turn into anti-Semites as well."[151] Semeon Surin, one of the Jewish exiles in Narym, whom Koba had met in Solvychegodsk, asked Koba how his rape affair with the widow Maria Kuzakova had ended.[152] Koba told him that this affair had been settled. Surin told Koba about a plan to assassinate the Tsar during the forthcoming celebration of the three-hundred-year anniversary of the House of Romanov. Koba decided to use this information to reinstate himself in the Okhrana, and sent letters to Lieutenant-Colonel I. P. Vasiliev, asking him to arrange a meeting with a high official responsible for the security of the Tsar so that he could help thwart this assassination.[153] Semen Surin "escaped" with an Okhrana officer posing as a journalist.[154] Koba received a passport in the name of "Ivanov" and also "escaped" from Narym on September 1, 1912. Surin became an Okhrana agent that same month, when he was threatened with a death sentence for his role in the conspiracy against the Tsar. Having arrived in St. Petersburg, Koba met Assistant Minister of the Interior I. M. Zolotarev in the private room of a restaurant.[155] Koba offered to help the Okhrana foil the plot to assassinate the Tsar, saying: "I can provide you with information—a terrorist act is being hatched, but I haven't yet fully uncovered it, I need some time, and for this I need money."[156] Zolotarev agreed to Koba's request and arranged Koba's employment by the St. Petersburg Okhrana.[157]

On October 26, 1912, Malinovsky was elected to the Duma. In addition to his lucrative Duma salary, Malinovsky was given the status of a "special agent of the Department of Police" with the code-name "X" and an Okhrana salary of 500 rubles. Beletsky and Vissarionov called Malinovsky a "pride of the Okhrana."[158] But dark clouds began to appear over this Okhrana-Bolshevik symbiosis. Lieutenant-Colonel I. P. Vasiliev started a secret campaign, attempting to expose Malinovsky's ties to the Okhrana. He sent a number of anonymous letters to the Menshevik newspaper *Luch*, stating that Malinovsky was an Okhrana agent. Koba went to Krakow in early November 1912, where he attempted to inform Lenin of Malinovsky's Okhrana ties, but ultimately recognized the futility of his attempt, because Lenin refused to believe that Malinovsky was an Okhrana agent. At the end of November, Koba informed Lenin that he had chosen a new alias, "Vasiliev." From this point on Lenin and other party members referred to him as "Vasiliev," or its derivatives "Vasily" and "Vaska." The choice of the alias "Vasiliev" points to Koba's identification with his Okhrana ally I. P. Vasiliev. Both Koba and I. P. Vasiliev had a common interest in exposing Malinovsky.

Lenin needed a non-Russian to publicize his views on the nationalities' problems. Under Lenin's guidance, Koba wrote a short article, which was published in Paris in the Russian-language newspaper *Sotzial-Demokrat* on January 12, 1913. Koba signed this article "K. Stalin." This was the first time he used the name Stalin.[159] Early in January 1913, Koba went to Vienna and wrote an essay titled "Marxism and the Nationalities Problem." In Vienna Koba met Lev Trotsky, who barely paid attention to him. Years later, Trotsky was able to recall a "glint of animosity" in Koba's "yellow eyes."[160] Lenin edited Koba's essay. The most striking feature of Koba's essay were the 174 hostile comments about the Jews and the Jewish Bund. Koba again signed his writing "K. Stalin."[161] Also early in 1912, Koba wrote to Zolotarev, reminding him that he had had the honor of being introduced to him in the private room of a restaurant and stating that he had observed Malinovsky closely and concluded that Malinovsky was not a reliable agent. Koba then offered himself as the main Okhrana agent in the Bolshevik organization.[162] On the margin of Koba's letter, Zolotarev wrote that it was not permissible for an agent to go "over the heads of his superiors," adding, "This agent should be deported to Siberia for good. He is asking for it."[163] On January 25, 1913, Zolotarev resigned and was transferred to another post. Two years later he was appointed a senator.

Early in January 1913, Lenin asked one of his supporters, Elena Rozmirovich, to go to Tiflis to help Kamo organize a large expropriation. At the same time, Koba sent an anonymous message to the Okhrana, revealing the time and purpose of Rozmirovich's trip to Tiflis. When she crossed the Russian border, Rozmirovich came under the observation of Okhrana agents, who assigned her the code-name "Tiflisskaya."[164] Kamo was finally arrested in Tiflis on January 10, 1913.[165] Ten days later, on January 20, 1913, Rozmirovich was arrested in St. Petersburg. The Okhrana had found "highly incriminating material evidence"—Lenin's message to Kamo and the stolen Tiflis banknotes. A long-term prison sentence seemed unavoidable. In a letter to her parents, Troyanovsky threatened to expose an "important party leader" as an Okhrana agent.[166] Malinovsky told Beletsky that he had nothing to do with Rozmirovich's arrest, and Beletsky ordered Rozmirovich released.[167] Malinovsky and Beletsky were at a loss as to who had engineered the "Rozmirovich provocation."

Koba arrived in St. Petersburg on February 16, 1913.[168] Malinovsky reported Koba's arrival to Beletsky, who ordered Koba's Okhrana file to be brought to him. He found Koba's letter to Zolotarev in which Koba accused Malinovsky of being an untrustworthy Okhrana agent. Beletsky realized that Koba's motive in provoking Rozmirovich's arrest was his rivalry with Malinovsky. Koba was arrested on February 23, 1913. "Dzhugashvili, we have finally got you!" said the arresting officer. Koba angrily replied, "I am not Dzhugashvili, my name is Ivanov." The officer laughed, "Tell these stories to your grandmother," and ordered Koba to follow him.[169] Malinovsky walked next to Koba, protesting his arrest and promising to take all necessary measures to free him. Beletsky asked Colonel Eremin to submit a letter describing Koba's Okhrana career. Eremin wrote:

Secret, Personal
Benevolent Sir Stephan Petrovich!
Iosif Vissarionov Dzhugashvili, who has been exiled by Administrative Decree to the Turukhansk region, provided the Chief of Tiflis GGA [Gubernia Gendarmerie Administration] with valuable intelligence information when he was arrested in 1906.
In 1908, the Chief of the Baku Okhrana Section received a series of intelligence reports from Dzhugashvili, and afterwards, upon his arrival in St. Petersburg, Dzhugashvili became an agent of the St. Petersburg Okhrana Section.
Dzhugashvili's work was distinguished by its accuracy, but was fragmentary. After the election of Dzhugashvili to the Central Committee of the Party in the city of Prague, he (having returned to St. Petersburg) went over to the government, into open opposition, and broke completely his connection to the Okhrana.
I am informing you of the above, dear sir, for your personal consideration in the conduct of operational work.
With assurance of my high esteem,

A. Eremin[170]

Beletsky obtained a "Decision of the Highest Authority" to exile Koba to a remote Siberian village for four years.[171] Beletsky placed Eremin's letter and all Okhrana reports on Koba in Koba's file, which contained intercepted letters from and to Koba; the letter to Zolotarev; Koba's prison photographs; his reports to the Okhrana; his signed depositions; and his signed receipts for money he had been paid by the Okhrana. This file was sealed and placed in a large iron safe located in a secret room of the Special Section of the Department of Police, together with all the files of former Okhrana agents who were no longer active because they had either retired, were deceased, or had been dismissed. These files had the warning: NOT TO BE OPENED WITHOUT THE PERMISSION OF THE HIGHEST AUTHORITY, which was a reference to the Tsar.[172]

While writing his report, Eremin already knew that he had been appointed

Chief of the Gendarmerie Administration in Finland. Beletsky suspected Eremin of protecting Koba, basing his suspicion on the fact that Eremin was against the Okhrana's meddling in Malinovsky's election to the Duma, and had said at the time that this interference might result in a "great state scandal." Beletsky also knew that some highly placed Okhrana officer had sent anonymous letters to the Menshevik newspaper *Luch*, trying to expose Malinovsky. Beletsky suspected the wrong man. The treacherous high Okhrana officer was not Eremin, but Eremin's assistant, I. P. Vasiliev.

On July 2, 1913, Koba was transported by train to the Siberian town of Krasnoyarsk. It was from here, at the end of September 1913, that he and his fellow exile Yakov Sverdlov were shipped by a barge down the Yenisey River to the village of Turukhansk. Malinovsky reported Lenin's request to Director Beletsky to arrange their escapes. Beletsky ordered the chief of the Yeniseisk Okhrana, Captain V. F. Zhelezniakov, to transfer Koba and Sverdlov to Kureika, a small settlement near the Arctic Circle. An escape from Kureika was considered impossible. At first, Koba and Sverdlov, a Jew, lived together in a small hut, but Sverdlov complained that Koba was a difficult man to live with, and moved to another hut. As with all political exiles, Koba was receiving a monthly stipend that was sufficient for modest living. He wrote letters to Sergey Alliluev, who sent him parcels through the Red Cross. The outbreak of World War I in August 1914 did not affect the exiles' life in this remote settlement.[173]

In October 1913, Malinovsky went to Paris and visited Vladimir Burtsev, a member of the Social Revolutionary Party who specialized in exposing Okhrana agents. Burtsev revealed to Malinovsky that Syrkin, an officer in the Moscow Okhrana, had told him:

> There is a provocateur, not yet exposed, a man who plays an active role, a man with blood on his hands, who was involved in the affair with the Tiflis banknotes and in the smuggling of arms.[174]

Malinovsky reported this information to Beletsky. Syrkin was arrested and sentenced to hard labor in Siberia.[175]

On January 14, 1914, Beletsky resigned and was appointed Senator.[176] Vice-Director Vissarionov also resigned.[177] Lieutenant-Colonel I. P. Vasiliev, who never gave up trying to expose Malinovsky, informed the Assistant Minister of the Interior General V. F. Dzhunkovsky about Malinovsky's Okhrana ties and about the Okhrana's manipulation of his election to the

Duma. Dzhunkovsky found the Okhrana's meddling in the Duma elections "intolerable," and ordered the termination of all relations with Malinovsky.[178] The chief of the St. Petersburg Okhrana, P. K. Popov, gave Malinovsky 6,000 rubles, and relayed Dzhunkovsky's orders to resign from the Duma and leave the country.[179] Malinovsky resigned the next day, saying to Duma chairman M. V. Rodzianko, "Excuse me, I am leaving the Duma. I have no time. Excuse me."[180] Lenin wrote that he was "convinced without a doubt of Malinovsky's political honesty."[181] The Mensheviks set up a commission of inquiry to investigate the rumors of Malinovsky's treachery. The outbreak of the First World War made it impossible to complete the investigation.

When the war started, Malinovsky was arrested in Germany as a Russian citizen, and placed in a prisoner-of-war camp. On September 16, 1914, it was erroneously reported that he had been drafted and killed in action.[182] Lenin wrote an obituary, which appeared in the Bolshevik émigré journal *Sotzial-Demokrat*, stating:

> Roman Malinovsky was an honest man, and accusations of political dishonesty were filthy fabrications.[183]

Somewhat later, Lenin received a letter from Malinovsky from the prisoner-of-war camp in which Malinovsky pledged personal loyalty to Lenin and devotion to socialism.[184] Lenin decided to use him in defeatist propaganda against the Russian government. In early 1915, Lenin secretly met in Zurich with Alexander Parvus, an agent of the German Foreign Ministry and the General Staff whose real name was Alexander Helfand.[185] Parvus had played an active role in the revolutionary movement as a Jewish socialist during his youth. After the suppression of the 1905 Revolution, Parvus escaped to Germany and become a German intelligence agent. With the start of the war in August 1914, Parvus, in a proposal to the German General Staff, pointed out that Lenin would welcome Russian military defeat and that Germany would be well-advised to use Lenin's organization for his anti-Russian defeatist propaganda. The Germans accepted this idea. Parvus promised to channel German money to Lenin through intermediaries whom Lenin would designate. Malinovsky became one of the most ardent agents of this commission, advocating the defeat of the Russian army.[186] Lenin began to correspond regularly with Malinovsky, sending him parcels of clothing and food.[187] Parvus set up a "research institute" in Copenhagen, where Russian followers of Lenin did "scientific projects." Russian military intelligence reported that the institute was engaged in espionage. The propaganda Malinovsky was peddling to the prisoners-of-war also came to the attention of Russian military intelligence.[188]

On February 27, 1915, Koba, not knowing that Garting had retired in 1909, sent a letter to the Okhrana Foreign Agency's old Paris address at 79 rue de Grenelle. But in May 1910, Eremin had requested that the Foreign Agency's address be changed.[189] The new chief of the Okhrana Foreign Agency, A. A. Krasilnikov, reported that this letter fell into Lenin's hands, and that the author of the letter reported "erroneous information about the opinions of certain members of the Jewish Bund. According to Lenin's opinion, the author is a Bolshevik."[190] The reason Lenin thought that "the author was a Bolshevik" was because he remembered Koba's hostility toward the Jews and the Jewish Bund. In a July 1915 letter to Zinoviev, Lenin asked, "Do you remember Koba's last name?" And in a letter to V. A. Karpinsky, a Bolshevik, Lenin wrote:

> Do me a big favor: find out from Stepko Spandarian, or Mikha Tskhakaya, or someone the last name of Koba. Iosif Dzhu—? We have forgotten. It is very important.[191]

At the end of December 1916, Koba, with a group of exiles, arrived in Krasnoyarsk, where the local military board rejected him for service in the army. Some exiles learned of trips Koba had taken to the Okhrana office in Eniseisk, near Krasnoyarsk, and thought that he had avoided the draft with the help of the Okhrana.[192] Koba was allowed to spend the remaining several months of his four-year term in the little town of Achinsk, where he often visited Lev Kamenev, also in exile, and his wife Olga. Some of the exiles accused Koba of having ties to the Okhrana.[193]

On March 8, 1917 (February 23, Old Style), crowds surged into the Petrograd streets, rioting in protest against the bread shortage. Three days later, the Tsar ordered the Fourth Duma suspended. His order was ignored. Duma deputies elected a Provisional Committee. On the same day, March 12, 1917 (February 27, Old Style), a group of workers proclaimed themselves the "Petrograd Soviets of Workers' Deputies." It was the beginning of the February 1917 Revolution.[194] The Tsar decided to abdicate in favor of his twelve-year-old son, Alexey, who had inherited hemophilia. Tsar Nicholas had resolved to abdicate in favor of his brother, the Grand Duke Mikhail, but at the same time the Provisional Committee of the Duma proclaimed itself the Provisional Government of Russia. The Grand Duke Mikhail refused to ascend to the throne. The three-hundred-year-old dynasty of the House of Romanovs came to an end. The Duma deputies did not foresee the vacuum of power and legitimacy that was to result from the Tsar's abdication.

During the first days of the February Revolution, street mobs stormed the Department of Police buildings in Petrograd and Moscow. Bonfires burned day and night, consuming reference books, files, and loose documents in the courtyard. Much of the Okhrana archives perished, but the Special Section of the Department of Police lost virtually nothing. The safe containing the top-secret files, among them the "dead" files of Okhrana agents Roman Malinovsky and Iosif Dzhugashvili, remained intact.[195] The news of the February Revolution reached Eremin in Finland, where, having been promoted to the rank of major-general, he was the head of the Finnish Okhrana Section. He hurriedly destroyed documents that could have exposed his secret agents.[196] Then he, his wife, and two daughters fled abroad. He and his family lived anonymously in Chile for many years.[197]

Shortly before the February Revolution, I. P. Vasiliev was appointed Chief of the Special Section; on March 1, 1917, he went to the Duma and was placed under arrest. On March 6, Vasiliev submitted his report, accusing top police officials of sponsoring numerous Okhrana provocations, to the Provisional Government. He described these provocations in great detail, and provided the names of the Okhrana agents (and their handlers) who had participated in them.[198] Vasiliev described himself as an "honest and progressive" Okhrana officer who was on the side of the Revolution. Vasiliev's report was patently self-serving. He offered his services to the Provisional Government, and was released from detention.[199]

On March 8, 1917, a group of exiles, among them Koba, boarded a train and headed for Petrograd. The returning Bolshevik exiles sent a telegram to Lenin:

Fraternal greetings. Starting today for Petrograd. Kamenev, Muranov, Stalin.[200]

At this point, the pen name "Stalin" replaced all other aliases, code-names, and nicknames that Iosif Dzhugashvili had used in the past. The government set up the Extraordinary Investigative Commission of the Provisional Government, headed by the prominent attorney N. E. Muraviev, to investigate officials of the Tsarist regime who might have been involved in Okhrana provocations. The commission became known as the "Muraviev Commission." It compiled a number of lists of the Okhrana's secret collaborators, which were published in 1917 by the Ministry of Justice of the Provisional Government.[201] The members of the Muraviev Commission were primarily interested in investigating the criminal meddling of top government and Department of Police officials in Roman Malinovsky's election to the Duma. Stalin's name did not appear on a published list of exposed Okhrana agents.[202] Lenin complained that the enemies of the Bolsheviks were using the issue of Okhrana agents provocateurs "in an attempt to drown our party in slander and filth."[203]

On June 23, 1917, the Muraviev Commission indicted six former Tsarist government and police officials: Minister of the Interior A. A. Makarov; Assistant Minister of the Interior I. M. Zolotarev; Director of the Department of Police S. P. Beletsky; Vice-Director of the Department of Police S. E. Vissarionov; Moscow Okhrana Chief A. P. Martynov; and a Moscow Okhrana officer, V. G. Ivanov.

Malinovsky was not indicted, but a special investigator was appointed to collect information about him. *Pravda* appealed to its readers to submit all the information they knew about Malinovsky to the Muraviev Commission.[204] The Provisional Government ordered the arrest of Lenin and Zinoviev as German agents. Stalin used this opportunity to prove his loyalty to Lenin by offering to hide him at a "safer place," which turned out to be Sergey Alliluev's apartment, a hangout for members of Kamo's old gang at that time and other hardcore criminals who had been set free by the February Revolution. Artillery Colonel B. V. Nikitin would recall years later:

> Criminals formed the vanguard of countless hordes that came from the convict prisons and penal settlements of Siberia and other places of banishment. . . . The old criminal fraternity . . . swelled the ranks of the scum of the population, which boiled over in the tragic upheaval.[205]

Elena Stasova, Lenin's confidante, came to Alliluev's apartment and said that a rumor had been spread that, "according to the documents of the police department, Lenin was an Okhrana provocateur." This announcement "made an incredibly strong impression on Lenin. A nervous shudder ran over his face, and he declared with the utmost determination that he must go to jail."[206] Lenin's determination was short-lived. He decided to go into hiding. He put on a wig, while Zinoviev shaved his head and glued on a mustache. Stalin led them to the small village of Razliv, near Petrograd, where a worker, N. A. Emelianov, and his three sons had built a makeshift hut in a forest for their summer outings. Lenin and Zinoviev stayed in this hut for a month before escaping to Finland.[207]

The German offensive, which Parvus had advocated in his memoranda, began in August 1917. Prime Minister Alexander Kerensky, fearing that Petrograd might fall into German hands, ordered the evacuation of the State Treasury and all archives. The Okhrana files were placed in bags and boxes and transported to various places: to the Moscow State Archive, to Kremlin basements, and to a monastery in the north. Some parts of the archives remained in Petrograd, stored and ready for transportation.[208] In 1917, the name "Iosif Dzhugashvili," meant nothing to the people who searched the archives. His file did not attract the attention of the members of the Muraviev Commission.[209] In April 1918, after the Bolsheviks came to power, the "Moscow Commission for the Investigation of Archives" published a book, *Bolsheviki*, which listed the twelve most important Okhrana agents in the Bolshevik Party:

M. I. Briandinsky, I. A. Zhitomirsky, I. G. Krivov, A. I. Lobov, R. V. Malinovsky, A. K. Marakushev, A. A. Poliakov, A. S. Romanov, I. P. Sesitsky, M. E. Chernomazov, V. E. Shurkhanov, and one thus far unidentified, who had the party alias "Vasily."[210]

Strangely enough, no one in 1918 recalled that in 1913, shortly before Stalin's last arrest and exile, he had assumed "the party alias 'Vasily.'"[211] The researchers at the Moscow Commission for the Investigation of Archives stated:

The twelve mentioned Okhrana agents comprise only a small segment of all the provocateurs and ordinary informers who had worked in the Social Democratic Party.[212]

The complete list of Okhrana agents was never published. Even the Bolshevik party history, which was published in 1926 (when Stalin was already a prominent member of Soviet government), did not mention Stalin even once—even though this tome contained some 500 names of the most prominent party members. The index mentions "Ivanovich," who was present at the Tammerfors conference, but the identity of the person hiding behind this alias remained a mystery to the party historians as late as 1926.[213]

Whoever placed the file of Iosif Dzhugashvili into one of the boxes to be evacuated from Petrograd before the October Revolution had no inkling that it would become a time-bomb of giant destructive power to play a pivotal role in the history of the Soviet Union.[214]

Chapter 2

The Jewish Origins

Stalin did not participate in the October Revolution, which in Lenin's own words had been "easier than lifting a feather."[215] The historian N. N. Sukhanov notes that before and during the October Revolution, Stalin left "the impression of a gray blur, looming up now and then dimly, not leaving any trace."[216] There was a short-lived skirmish in the Winter Palace, where the Provisional Government was defended by a throng of young cadets and a women's battalion. The first session of the Bolshevik government took place in Lenin's office in Smolny Palace on October 26, 1917; it was here that Trotsky, who had organized the military takeover the previous day, met Stalin, who attempted to strike up a friendly conversation. Trotsky felt Stalin's "advances were out of place and unendurably vulgar." He cut him short. Stalin's face changed and in "his yellow eyes appeared the same glint of animosity" that Trotsky had noticed during their first encounter in Vienna in 1913.[217] For the next few years, Trotsky failed to recognize in Stalin's "animosity" toward him the same "peculiar hatred" that Stalin had expressed during the pre-Revolution period toward the Mensheviks whom he had had perceived to be Jews. Stalin felt "peculiar hatred" for the Jews long before 1913. It was well known that Trotsky was a Jew and that his real name was Leiba Bronstein. His face had typical Semitic features.

On October 26, 1917, Lenin announced the creation of the "Council of People's Commissars." He rejected the traditional title of "minister" as being too "bourgeois," naming himself the "Chairman of the Council." At the bottom of the list was the name of I. V. Dzhugashvili, "the Commissar of National Affairs." Lenin saw in Stalin a "non-Russian" spokesman on the nationalities problem, an important issue given the animosies between various ethnic groups in the Russian Empire.[218]

In the years immediately following the October Revolution, when the murder of the Tsar and his family and the trial and execution of Malinovsky took place, Stalin played only a minor role in government affairs.[219] In 1919, Lenin appointed Stalin to the post of chairman of the "Workers' and Peasants' Inspection." This post gave Stalin the power to prosecute people for economic crimes, and to appoint his cronies to important positions in a country suffering from severe shortages of every commodity—at a time when appointments meant precious access to means of survival. At the Eleventh Party Congress, which opened on March 27, 1922, Lenin proposed to create the post of General Secretary to improve the effectiveness of party bureaucracy. Zinoviev suggested Stalin for the post. There were no objections, and the proposal was accepted.

On July 14, 1922, Kamo was run over by a truck as he rode his bicycle. Stalin did not come to the funeral of his old friend. Suspicion arose that Kamo's murder had been ordered by Stalin. The Georgian Bolsheviks made an attempt to bring Stalin to trial, but the case was dropped. Lenin continued to maintain friendly relations with Stalin until September 1922, when he learned that on Stalin's instruction the journal *Proletarskaya revolutsiya* (Proletarian Revolution) had published two telegrams, found in the Tsarist archives, confirming the accusation that Lenin had been receiving German money.[220] Lenin had always denied that accusation.[221] The publication of the telegrams confirmed the Provisional Government's charges that he had been a "German agent." Lenin interpreted the publication of these telegrams as a brazen attempt by Stalin to blackmail him. "That cook will prepare nothing but peppery dishes," Lenin told Trotsky, informing him of his decision to remove Stalin from his post of General Secretary.[222] In October 1922, Krupskaya, pointing at Stalin's Kremlin apartment, told Trotsky in a hushed voice that Lenin considered Stalin "devoid of the most elementary honesty, the simplest human honesty."[223] On January 4, 1923, Lenin dictated a short message, advising the Central Committee to remove Stalin from the post of General Secretary, stating that "Stalin is too rude, and this defect . . . becomes intolerable in a General Secretary. This is why I suggest that the comrades think about a way to remove Stalin from that post."[224] Removing Stalin from his post was no longer an easy task.

Zinoviev and Kamenev sided with Stalin in the ensuing struggle. They feared that Trotsky would remove them from the ranks of the party leadership. They formed the "triumvirate" of Zinoviev, Kamenev, and Stalin. Lenin identified Stalin as one of the "Great Russian chauvinists who pinned labels on Mensheviks, accusing them of the very sins of which he himself was guilty." On February 14, 1923, Lenin dictated a note, stating, "For the label 'deviationist' to be applied to both chauvinistic deviation and Menshevism indicates the existence of an identical deviation coursing through the Great Russian chauvinists."[225] During the month of February, Stalin appeared at Politburo meetings "morose, his pipe firmly clenched between his teeth, a sinister gleam in his jaundiced eyes, snarling back instead of answering. Stalin knew that his fate was at stake, and he was resolved to overcome all obstacles."[226]

After a Politburo meeting at the end of February 1923, Stalin told Trotsky, Zinoviev, and Kamenev that Lenin had asked to have poison brought to him. "Naturally, we cannot even consider carrying out this request!" exclaimed Trotsky. "Lenin can still recover," Stalin replied with a touch of annoyance. "But he won't listen. The Old Man is suffering. He says he wants to have the poison at hand . . . he'll use it only when he is convinced that his condition is hopeless." Trotsky was struck by how Stalin's face, a sickly smile transfixed upon it as though a mask, was inconsistent with the circumstances of the request, and extraordinarily upsetting. This time Trotsky found the discrepancy between Stalin's facial expression and his words insufferable. The horror of it was magnified by Stalin's refusal to express any opinion about Lenin's request, as if he were expecting others to respond and wanted to catch their reaction without having committed himself. Kamenev stood pale and silent while Zinoviev appeared bewildered. Trotsky wondered whether Stalin's two allies had known about Lenin's request beforehand, or whether Stalin's announcement was as great a surprise to them as it had been to him. "Anyway, it is out of the question," insisted Trotsky. "The Old Man is suffering," repeated Stalin, staring vaguely past them and, as before, not committing himself one way or the other. This was an informal conference and no vote was taken. Trotsky was left baffled by Stalin's behavior, sensing that Stalin's true thoughts were not commensurate with the words that he had spoken.[227]

On January 21, 1924, Lenin's health suddenly deteriorated. He called his cook Gavril Volkov and scribbled a note:

> Gavrilushka, I have been poisoned . . . Go fetch Nadia (Krupskaya) at once . . . Tell Trotsky . . . Tell everyone you can.[228]

Lenin died on January 21, 1924. The funeral took place six days later, due to difficulties in arranging the embalming. His mummified body was enclosed in a glass catafalque and was placed on display in the House of Columns. Stalin delivered a strange oration, an odd litany in which overtones of a Byzantine invocation mixed with his Marxist idiom. At that moment he may indeed have been overwhelmed by a deep need for identification with Lenin. Almost two decades earlier he had felt a strong emotional need to identify with his dead father, Vissarion, whose murder he had instigated. Stalin intuitively understood the emotional need of the Russian masses to identify with their dead leader. The great majority of the Russian people were deeply religious, illiterate peasants. The liturgical style of the invocation, delivered by a seminary dropout, aroused their consciousness and evoked in them the memory of centuries-old religious traditions—responses that, for those who had felt trapped in a spiritual vacuum since the murder of the *Tsar batiushka* (Tsar, the Father), were greatly uplifting. Stalin sensed the need to fill this vacuum, and he at once set out to create a Lenin cult in which he would assume the role of Lenin's heir. Zinoviev was the most active in nourishing this cult.[229]

The official communiqué attributed Lenin's death to arterial sclerosis. When Trotsky asked Kremlin doctors about the cause of Lenin's death, they were at a loss to explain it. Trotsky asked Kamenev and Zinoviev about the circumstances under which Lenin had died; they answered in monosyllables, avoided his eyes, and were unwilling to discuss the matter. Trotsky began to suspect that they knew something that they did not want to reveal. Fifteen years later, he wrote:

> Stalin may have feared that I would connect Lenin's death with last year's conversation about poison; that I would ask the doctors whether poisoning had been involved and demand a special autopsy. It was, therefore, safer in all respects to keep me away until after the body had been embalmed, the viscera cremated, and a postmortem examination inspired by such suspicions no longer feasible.[230]

Boris Bazhanov, Stalin's secretary (who would flee abroad in 1926), wrote in his memoirs:

Stalin made a certain amount of progress since the days of Caesar Borgia by using poison.[231]

Trotsky wrote:

Bazhanov suggested that Stalin used a culture of Koch bacilli, mixed into food and systematically administered, which would gradually lead to galloping consumption and sudden death.[232]

After Lenin's death, rumors that Stalin had poisoned him began to circulate.[233] But some Old Bolsheviks thought that he had died of inherited or acquired syphilis. They would point at Lenin's portrait, which traditionally hung on a wall in their homes, and say, "That *sifilitik*" (syphilitic). Their grandchildren would paraphrase it into, "This is Uncle Titi-Liti."[234] In the mid-1980s, KGB researchers established that Stalin had poisoned Lenin. Yulian Semenov, the author of many stories chronicling the daring exploits of the Soviet secret service, enjoyed the trust of KGB officers and the head of the KGB Yuri Andropov. Semenov stated that the KGB did not reveal Stalin's role in the poisoning of Lenin because this was a "very sensitive subject."[235]

Shortly after Lenin's funeral, the question of who would succeed him as chairman of the Council of the Peoples' Commissars was raised at a Politburo meeting. During Lenin's illness, Kamenev had been the acting chairman; in effect, Lenin's deputy. His appointment as Lenin's successor appeared certain, but Stalin said:

We must consider the peasant character of Russia. The Russian peasants, the great majority of the country, will resent having a Jew as the head of their government.[236]

Stalin exaggerated Kamenev's "Jewish origin." Kamenev's father was indeed a Jew (his name was Rosenfeld), which in the eyes of many people also made Kamenev Jewish, even though his mother was a member of the Russian nobility. Zinoviev was unsuitable as Lenin's successor for the same reason—he was Jewish and his real name was Radomyslevsky. Trotsky's Jewish origin was also common knowledge. The unspoken assumption was that, despite the party's major doctrine supposedly being "internationalism," the "Jewish origin" of Trotsky, Zinoviev, and Kamenev ruled them out as leaders of Russia. The

Politburo members silently accepted Stalin's argument. It was not common knowledge at the time that Lenin was closeting the existence of his maternal grandfather, Alexander Blank, who was a baptized Jew. Responding to a census questionnaire in 1922, Lenin answered a question about his maternal grandfather by saying, "I do not know."[237]

It is tempting to interpret Stalin's use of the issue of "Jewish Origin" as a cynical tool in his drive for power. But this does not explain why he continued to instigate the anti-Jewish campaign and long after his Jewish rivals had been defeated. Toward the end of Stalin's life, when he was utterly secure in his role of Soviet dictator, his hatred of the Jews assumed its most deadly form. It was at this time that he instigated his "anti-cosmopolitan" campaign, preparing his country for the Jewish pogrom and for the exile of the entire Jewish population to Siberia. No, Stalin's hatred and persecution of the Jews was not a matter of cynical policy in his struggle for power, but a deeply ingrained, emotional state of his whole being.

"Jewish origin" was the hidden issue at the first show trial in Soviet history. Stalin accused a prominent party official, Sultan Galiev, of Crimean Tartar nationalism and of plotting to cede Crimea to Turkey. Sultan Galiev "fully confessed and repented."[238] He was sentenced to a prison term and soon perished. Stalin's secret scheme was to propagate the idea of creating a "Jewish national home in Crimea" which he figured would be attractive to Zinoviev and Kamenev, thus cementing his alliance with them against Lenin and Trotsky. Stalin assigned to Mikhail Kalinin (the future President of the USSR) the task of promoting the idea of a "Jewish Autonomous Region" in the Crimean peninsula. A prominent journalist, Mikhail Koltsov, wrote articles under the slogan, "Give Crimea to the Jews."[239] But Zinoviev and Kamenev were not interested in a "Jewish national home" in Crimea, or Palestine, or anywhere else. Trotsky also ignored Stalin's bait. These three Bolsheviks thought of themselves not as Jews, but as "internationalists." Jewish nationalism was totally foreign to them. A few years later, Zinoviev and Kamenev were to express regret for having supported Stalin in his trumped-up charges against Sultan Galiev.[240]

The Thirteenth Party Congress was held in May 1924, the first to take place without Lenin. Krupskaya wanted "Lenin's Testament" to be read to the delegates. In his "Testament," Lenin criticized Stalin, calling him a "social-nationalist" and a "crude Great Russian *Derzhimorda* (a repulsive, xenophobic character in Gogol's play *The Inspector General*)." Lenin stated that, "Stalin and Dzerzhinsky must be held politically responsible for this entire Great Russian

Nationalist campaign."[241] He added: "The mutual relations of Trotsky and Stalin are a trifle which may acquire decisive importance."[242] Having read a copy of Lenin's Testament, Stalin exploded with obscene swearing at Lenin in the presence of Kamenev and Zinoviev.[243] But Trotsky agreed to have Lenin's Testament read by Kamenev at the closed session of the Central Committee on May 22, 1924. Zinoviev and Kamenev rushed to rescue Stalin, imploring the Central Committee not to remove him from the post of General Secretary. "Lenin's word is sacred," Zinoviev exclaimed. "But Lenin himself, if he could have witnessed, as you all have, Stalin's sincere efforts to mend his ways, would not have urged the Party to remove him."[244] The decision was not to read "Lenin's Testament" to the delegates, and not to enter it into the Party record. Trotsky did not object because he was paralyzed by his "Jewish origin." Two years later, he was to point to this issue at a Politburo meeting, asking with indignation:

Is it true; is it possible that in our party, in Moscow, in workers' cells, anti-Semitic agitation should be carried out with impunity?!

The Politburo members pretended to know nothing of this anti-Semitic agitation. Only Nikolai Bukharin blushed with shame and embarrassment.[245]

In January 1925, the Central Committee removed Trotsky from his powerful position as war commissar and replaced him with Mikhail Frunze. Stalin's slogan of "socialism in one country" was approved by the majority of the delegates to the Fourteenth Party Conference in March 1926. Bukharin, Rykov, and Tomsky joined Stalin. In the spring of 1926, Zinoviev and Kamenev, having parted ways with Stalin, formed a "United Opposition" with Trotsky. Stalin was not impressed. "Ah, they have granted themselves mutual amnesty," he said scornfully.[246] Zinoviev was removed from his post as the head of the Party organization in Leningrad (the new name for Petrograd following Lenin's death), and Sergey Kirov replaced him. After the death of Mikhail Frunze, Stalin appointed Klement Voroshilov to the post of war commissar. Stalin possessed documents found in the old archives that exposed Vorosilov's ties to the Okhrana.[247]

With this appointment, Stalin came close to becoming absolute dictator. Kamenev was demoted to the status of "candidate member" of the Politburo. Stalin added to the Politburo his three cronies: Voroshilov, Kalinin, and Molotov, whom he controlled by threatening to expose their "sins."[248] Usually, he blackmailed people with documents found in the Okhrana archives. By the summer of 1926, Stalin had considerably improved his position within the party apparatus, but his name was still hardly known outside the narrow party circles. The defeat of the "United Opposition" of Trotsky, Zinoviev, and Kamenev, whom Stalin called "Jewish intellectuals," seemed inevitable. Only a miracle could have saved them at the Party Plenum of the Central Committee, which opened on July 14, 1926. Such a miracle almost happened.[249]

Shortly before July 14, "all archival materials of the Petrograd Historic-Revolutionary Archive were transferred to Moscow."[250] An employee of the *Glavarkhiv* (Main Archive Administration) discovered the file of Iosif Dzhugashvili and informed the editor of the Menshevik journal *Sotsialistichesky vestnik* in Berlin, David Shub, about it. The employee stated that Stalin's Okhrana file had been located, and that it contained documents proving that Stalin had for many years been an Okhrana agent. To Shub, the thought that the leader of the Soviet Union might have been a former Okhrana agent was bordering on fantasy. For all his hostility toward Stalin, Shub could hardly imagine that Stalin could be a creature of the despicable Okhrana. Shub felt that this information could not be made public without supporting documentation, which his informant did not provide.[251] But Shub confided this information to his trusted friend, the prominent American journalist Isaac Don Levine.[252]

This was the file that the director of the Department of Police, S. P. Beletsky, had placed in the "top-secret" safe in the Special Section of the Department of Police. Stalin's Okhrana file was brought to Dzerzhinsky. On July 18, 1926, Dzerzhinsky stayed in his Lubyanka office late and remained there until the next day, going home at 3:00 in the morning on July 20. Later that morning, he went to his Lubyanka office again and stayed there briefly, leaving Stalin's Okhrana file hidden amongst his personal papers. Dzerzhinsky knew that the leaders of the "United Opposition"—Trotsky, Zinoviev, and Kamenev—considered him a narrow-minded fanatic whose career depended upon Stalin's victory over the Opposition. Dzerzhinsky's behavior at the plenary session was frantic and bizarre.[253] His two-hour-long speech was a disjointed outburst, punctuated by hysterical diatribes against the leaders of the United Opposition and complaints of dubious meaning. He was repeatedly interrupted. At one point he shouted:

> You know perfectly well what my power consists of! I do not spare myself . . . and because of this you all here love me, <u>because you trust me</u> . . . I have never twisted my soul! It is difficult for me alone to tackle this

problem, and, therefore, I beg your help.[254]

Dzerzhinsky was twisting his soul: Stalin's Okhrana file posed a dreadful problem for him because victory by the United Opposition meant that he would be removed from all of his posts. He also knew that Stalin would destroy anyone who knew of the file's discovery. Dzerzhinsky drank several glasses of water during his long speech. At one point, he suddenly turned pale, lost consciousness, and fell off the podium. He was carried to the lobby, where he died in the presence of the delegates who had gathered around him.[255] Rumors that Dzerzhinsky had been poisoned immediately started to spread in Party circles in Moscow.[256]

Stalin ordered Abram Belenky he head of the Kremlin bodyguards, and Stanislav Redens, Dzerzhinsky's assistant, to carry the corpse to Dzerzhinsky's home because Stalin wanted to avoid an autopsy. Dzerzhinsky's body was cremated, and his ashes were immured in the Kremlin Wall. (Belenky was to perish during the purges in the thirties.[257]) Redens was married to a sister of Stalin's wife, Nadezhda Allilueva, so Stalin and Dzerzhinsky were remote relatives. (Redens was later shot during the purges.) According to Stalin's fraudulent version, Dzerzhinsky had died of a heart attack "suddenly, instantly, in a single moment, upon returning home after his speech."[258] Numerous Soviet authors enlivened these lies with other fantastic inventions, occasionally mixing in some surviving particles of truth.[259] Dzerzhinsky was the first casualty of Stalin's Okhrana file upon its emergence from the archives.[260]

Dzerzhinsky used the Okhrana documents to blackmail and recruit former Okhrana officers, agents, and informants. He also gave Stalin several documents that contained compromising information about Soviet officials. Stalin gathered these documents in his personal archive and used them to blackmail people by threatening to expose their past. One of the first victims of such blackmail was Trotsky's secretary Glazman, whose Okhrana file fell into Stalin's hands. Glazman committed suicide, which shocked many party members.[261]

Stalin learned that his informers had found his file, and feared that these sensitive documents might have fallen into the hands of his enemies. His behavior changed markedly. Members of his family began to suffer from his angry outbursts. His wife took their six-month-old baby daughter Svetlana and their seven-year-old son Vasily to Leningrad to live with her parents. Yakov Dzhugashvili, Stalin's son from his first marriage, attempted suicide by shooting himself in the chest. "He can't even shoot straight," was Stalin's comment. Nadezhda came back to Stalin after he pleaded with her for some time. Stalin's injured arm periodically bothered him, and he sought the help of V. M. Bekhterev, the eminent Russian specialist in neuropathology. On December 22, 1927, Bekhterev was invited to visit Stalin in the Kremlin. After seeing Stalin, Bekhterev told his colleagues, "I have examined one short-armed paranoiac."[262] According to another version, Bekhterev said, "The diagnosis is clear. This is a typical case of heavy paranoia." Bekhterev also said that Stalin suffered from a "severe case of split personality, paranoia, and schizophrenia."[263] Sigmund Freud wrote:

> The most striking characteristic of symptom formation in paranoia is the process, which deserves the name of projection. An internal perception is suppressed, and, indeed, its content, after undergoing a certain degree of distortion, enters consciousness in the form of an external perception.[264]

Bekhterev's diagnosis was reported to Stalin. The next day Bekhterev was poisoned but it was reported that he had died of "heart paralysis."[265] Bekhterev's son insisted that his father had been poisoned by his Jewish stepmother. He was arrested and sentenced to "ten years in prison without the right to correspondence," which meant that he was to be executed. His wife died in a prison camp. Their three children were sent to orphanages.

Stalin began to stage show trials, in which he paraded a large number of Jewish defendants. The "Shakhty" show trial was held in the Moscow Hall of Columns in 1929. Many Soviet citizens (including fifty engineers), as well as three foreigners, were all forced to "confess." During the proceedings, a twelve-year-old boy, the son of one of the defendants, rose from his seat in the audience and proclaimed that his father, engineer Kolodub, was "a traitor and enemy of the working class."

> My father is a traitor and enemy of the working class. I reject him and the name he bears. From now on I shall not call myself Kolodub, but Shakhtin.[266]

Similar scenes, in which sons denounced their fathers and demanded their execution, were to take place frequently during subsequent show trials. Stalin was continually restaging his own court testimony of 1890 against his father Vissarion.

One of the Shakhty trial defendants, as the judge explained, had "gone mad in his cell." Another defendant, an eighty-year-old Jew denied his guilt and asked one of the defendants, "Why do you lie, eh? Who told you to lie?" Another Jewish defendant shouted, "One day another Zola will arise and will write *J'Accuse* to restore our name to honor."[267] The defendants were sentenced to various prison terms.

Stalin reenacted the events of his past not only on the stages of his show trials, but in "real life" as well. In 1927, he ordered V. R. Menzhinsky, who had replaced Dzerzhinsky as the head of the GPU (Soviet Secret Police), to use an agent, Stroilov, to set up an "underground Trotskyite printing press" and to plant leaflets at the press in order to incriminate the Opposition leaders. This press was "liquidated," and Stroilov was declared a "White Guard officer."[268] Menzhinsky did not know that a similar provocation had been engineered by Okhrana informer Iosif Dzhugashvili in Tiflis in 1900.

Trotsky, Kamenev, and Zinoviev were expelled from the party at the Twenty-Fifth Party Congress in December 1927. Trotsky was exiled to Alma-Ata, the capital of Kazakhstan. Trotsky's supporters were exiled to various parts of the country. Stalin labeled the opposition "Trotskyite deviation," and called its members "a castrated force of Jewish intellectuals." Zinoviev and Kamenev renounced their views and Stalin benevolently allowed them to be readmitted to the party.

In April 1927, Chiang Kai-shek's troops massacred Communists in Shanghai; and in December 1927, they brutally suppressed the "Canton commune." The chief of the GPU Operations Department, Karl Pauker, arrested all of the Chinese in Moscow. Stalin laughed boisterously when Pauker mimicked the frightened Chinese and imitated their accent. Pauker, a Hungarian Jew, was a talented clown. Stalin relished his antics, especially the "Jewish anecdotes" which Pauker told with a Yiddish accent. Stalin's fear of the Chinese threat led him to concoct a scheme to use the Soviet Jews as a buffer against China. By that time Stalin had long abandoned his 1923 idea to create the "Jewish Crimean Autonomous Republic." Instead, he issued a decree in March 1928 to create a "Jewish Autonomous Region in Biro-Bidzhan," and to designate this region for the "settlement of the toiling Jewish masses."[269] The Biro-Bidzhan region was located along the Soviet-Chinese border. Stalin intended to use this "Jewish Autonomous Region," as a Jewish buffer zone in the event of military conflict with China. Mikhail Kalinin, who by 1928 had become Chairman of the Supreme Soviet, proclaimed:

As a nation, the Jews are most vital and politically influential. That is why the creation of the Jewish republic would have enormous significance. . . . I proposed Biro-Bidzhan a long time ago, despite the fact that it is located near China. . . . There were some cries: "Only not under China!" The Jewry, which in the USSR consists of about three million, should have at least a little republic. And then everybody would know that this nationality has its own "state title" on our territory, if I may say so.[270]

In 1911, the Tsarist government surveyed the Biro-Bidzhan area, and determined that it was "unsuitable for colonization" because of

permanently frozen subsoil; marsh-ridden terrain made uninhabitable by gnus (bloodsucking insects: gnats, horseflies, midges); floods and prolonged below-forty-degree frosts; cultural isolation; located more than a thousand verst (about 700 miles) from the sea; unbearable intensity of labor; short growing period under unfavorable seasonal distribution of precipitation.[271]

Stalin intended to eventually turn Biro-Bidzhan into a graveyard and place of exile for the Jews. Besides using it as a "Jewish buffer" against the Chinese threat, Stalin's hatred of the Jews was the hidden motive behind his Biro-Bidzhan scheme. Yan Sten, a prominent Party official, told his friends:

Koba will do things that will make the trials of Dreyfus and Beilis pale in comparison.[272]

For a long time Trotsky denied that Stalin was a Jew-hater, but finally, outraged by the anti-Semitic cartoons in the Party's press (which were received with sly snickers), he said:

Stalin and his henchmen even stooped to fish in the muddied waters of anti-Semitism.

In response to Trotsky's remark, Stalin glibly replied:

We are fighting Trotsky, Zinoviev, and Kamenev not because they are Jews, but because they are oppositionists.

Trotsky recognized the true meaning of Stalin's denial and stated:

It was a reminder to all not to forget that the leaders of the opposition were Jews.[273]

On January 21, 1929, Stalin ordered the celebration of the fifth anniversary of Lenin's death. Lenin's birthday had never been celebrated during Stalin's rule. On that day, the Politburo approved Stalin's recommendation to exile Trotsky from the Soviet Union. Only Bukharin abstained from voting. The only country that agreed to accept Trotsky was Turkey, where he enjoyed the status of an "honorary citizen," which the Turkish leader Kemal Atatürk bestowed upon him for cooperating with Turkey during the Russian Civil War. On February 12, 1929, Trotsky, his wife Natalia Sedova, his older son Lev Sedov, Sedov's wife Anna Riabukhina, and their baby son were brought to the heavily guarded port of Odessa, where the freighter *Ilyich*—named after Lenin—was waiting for them. Stalin liked such symbolic "coincidences" and used them to mark important events in his life. Trotsky's younger son Sergey Sedov refused to go abroad, saying that he had nothing to do with the political activities of his father. (Sergey was later executed.) Trotsky and his wife went aboard first, followed by Lev Sedov, but Sedov's wife Anna and their baby son were prevented from boarding and were led away. Trotsky, his wife, and Lev Sedov protested, but the guards ignored them. The *Ilyich* left Odessa and headed for Istanbul.[274]

In October 1929, Yakov Blumkin, a GPU resident in Turkey, was on his way to visit Trotsky (who had rented a house on the island of Prinkipo in the Sea of Marmora, near Istanbul) when he was ordered to return to Moscow. Stalin counted on Blumkin's ability to "win Trotsky's confidence, and kill him."[275] Stalin believed that Blumkin was able to accomplish this deed because in July 1918, as a young officer of *Cheka* (the original Soviet secret police), Blumkin made history by taking part in the assassination of Count von Mirbach, the German ambassador in Moscow. Trotsky saved Blumkin from the death sentence.[276] Trotsky did not suspect that Stalin might use Blumkin to assassinate him. Trotsky was extraordinarily naïve, not unlike many diehard leftists. Trotsky treated Blumkin as an old friend and a committed party member. He asked Blumkin to deliver a personal letter to David Riazanov, who used to provide Trotsky with translation work during Trotsky's exile in Alma-Ata.

Upon his arrival in Moscow, Blumkin reported to his superiors in the GPU about his visit to Trotsky, and received permission to forward Trotsky's letter to Riazanov. Menzhinsky and the Chief of the GPU Foreign Department,

Meer Trilisser, planned to send Blumkin on a new European assignment in December 1929.[277] Shortly before Blumkin returned to Moscow, his friend Grigory Rabinovich, who was the Assistant Chief of the Secret Political Department of the GPU and had access to the documents and personal papers of secret-police chiefs, happened upon Stalin's Okhrana file.[278] Rabinovich decided to ask Blumkin to deliver the file to Trotsky. Blumkin felt it was his revolutionary duty to save the country by exposing the entrenched Okhrana agent. In December 1929, Stalin was preparing for a pomp-and-splendor celebration by the entire country of his fiftieth birthday. The official slogan proclaimed, "Stalin is the Lenin of today."

Blumkin did not keep his mouth shut. In talking to Karl Radek, a former close friend and ally of Trotsky, Blumkin hinted at Stalin's file. What exactly Blumkin told Radek about the file is not known, but Radek promptly reported the exchange to Stalin. The dictator at once resolved to recover the file and to arrest Blumkin the moment he was to leave Moscow for his new assignment abroad. Stalin also decreed the arrest of anyone with whom Blumkin had established contacts.[279] Blumkin's departure abroad was scheduled for December 21, 1929, the day the country was to celebrate Stalin's fiftieth birthday. Stalin intended to give himself a good birthday present. Blumkin was arrested. Stalin's Okhrana file was in his suitcase, which was delivered to the chief of the GPU, Menzhinsky. Stalin trusted Menzhinsky; the head of state had blackmailed him with the anti-Lenin statements. Menzhinsky before the Revolution published a number of biting articles in the Russian émigré press, criticizing Lenin as an "illegitimate child of Russian autocracy" and a "political Jesuit." Menzhinsky also called Lenin a "political manipulator," and a con artist like Chichikov in Gogol's *Dead Souls*. Stalin called Menzhinsky "my amiable but watchful Polish bear" and thought that he had Menzhinsky on the "hook."

This assessment proved to be wrong.[280] Menzhinsky decided not to tell Stalin about the file and hid it among his personal papers.[281] He feared that Blumkin could reveal that the file was in the suitcase, and immediately carried out Stalin's order to execute Blumkin, Rabinovich, and Silov, who were arrested the same day. They were accused of having had contact with Blumkin. Menzhinsky thus denied Stalin the opportunity to find out what had happened to the file.[282] Blumkin and Rabinovich were the first two Jews whom Stalin had identified as enemies who were planning to destroy him by using his file. He did not know what had happened to his file, and decided to discredit the documents it contained by "proving" that they were forgeries.

Immediately after the murder of Blumkin, Stalin decided to stage a show trial for former Tsarist Army General A. P. Kutepov, who was the chairman of the ROVS (Russian Union of Army Veterans), a Parisian émigré organization of White Guard officers. Stalin decided to force Kutepov, to confess that he had overseen the forgery of documents aimed at discrediting Soviet leaders. Kutepov was kidnapped in Paris on January 26, 1930, and brought to the Lubyanka prison in Moscow. But Stalin abandoned the idea of parading General Kutepov at a show trial, because the French government would assuredly have protested the kidnapping within its borders. Although the testimonies had been prepared and the defendants had "confessed," Stalin canceled this show trial and ordered all of the defendants, including Kutepov, to be "liquidated administratively."[283] After these executions, Stalin ordered the preparation of another show trial of "saboteurs and spies," which was scheduled to take place in autumn 1930. But Stalin also suddenly canceled this show trial and ordered all forty-six defendants secretly shot.[284]

The "Industrial Party" show trial opened in the Moscow Hall of Columns on November 25, 1930. The chief defendant was Professor Leonid Ramzin, an Old Bolshevik and a leading specialist on thermodynamics. He was forced to "confess" that he had met Lawrence of Arabia in London, and that he had been a "wrecker" of the Soviet economy and the head of the 2,000-member "Industrial Party." Ramzin also "confessed" that he had received "wrecking instructions" from two wealthy Russian émigrés, Riabushinsky and Vishnegradsky, although it later turned out that both of them had died long before their alleged meeting with Ramzin had occurred. Ramzin also "confessed" that he had received "wrecking instructions" from Lawrence of Arabia. As it turned out, Lawrence was not in England at the time. Finally, Ramzin "confessed" to having met with French president Raymond Poincaré and discussing with him plans for an invasion of the USSR. Poincaré denied this.[285] The other seven accused officials also "confessed" various imaginary "crimes." Stalin's mind, gripped by fear, was producing fantasies which the GPU investigators did not dare question. The prosecutor Nikolai Krylenko noted his puzzlement over the defendants' signed depositions, which prominently mentioned "documents, circular letters, reports, and records," which they could not produce in court. He wondered:

What evidence can there be? Are there, let us say, any documents? I inquired about that. It seems that where the documents existed, they were destroyed . . . . But, I ask, perhaps one of them has accidentally survived? It would be futile to hope for that.[286]

During the closing session, the young son of one of the defendants rose from his seat in the spectators' gallery and demanded that his father be shot, declaring, "To me, my father is a class enemy, nothing more!" The press glorified him as a model for Soviet youth.[287]

Stalin's Okhrana file made a baffling appearance at the March 1931 show trial conducted on the mythical "Union Bureau of the Central Committee of the Menshevik Party." The only Menshevik among all of the Jewish defendants was Nikolai Sukhanov, a Jew and a prominent historian whom Lenin had extensively praised for his *Memoirs of the Revolution*, but whom Stalin hated because the book had described him as a "gray blur," hardly noticeable during the Revolutionary period. Sukhanov was forced to "recall" that in 1928 he had had a meeting with Rafael Abramovich, an émigré, who had allegedly come to Russia secretly to organize an anti-Soviet plot. Abramovich issued a statement, declaring that he had been attending the International Socialist Congress in Brussels at the time.[288] I. I. Rubin, another Jewish defendant, was a forty-five-year-old economist accused of having given a "sealed file of documents for safekeeping" to David Riazanov. Riazonov, a Jew, was the director of the Marx-Engels-Lenin Institute, to whom Blumkin had delivered Trotsky's letter in 1929.[289] Stalin suspected Rubin of harboring his Okhrana file. He was put through horrible torture and was finally forced to admit that he had given the "sealed file" to Riazanov.[290] Rubin was sentenced to five years in prison. Riazanov was arrested after the show trial and was shot a few years later for "aiding the Menshevik traitors."[291] Rubin was released in 1935, but was again arrested in the fall of 1937, not long before his death.

Shortly after the Menshevik show trial, Stalin published a book, *Provokator Anna Serebriakova*. He used the pseudonym "I. V. Alekseev" (the initials I. V. stood for Iosif Vissarionovich).[292] The book consists mostly of reports, circular letters, receipts, and other documents reproduced from the file of the Okhrana agent Anna Serebriakova, who had been thrown into a Moscow prison in 1925. She died shortly thereafter. In the preface to the book, Stalin wrote:

Professor Ramzin and writer Sukhanov are people of the same kind. . . . And there, in history, we find the ancestral father of the present-day wrecker—the provocateur of the tsarist Okhrana.[293]

Stalin further stated:

The life story of the provocateur Serebriakova is, undoubtedly, instructive.

Her story represents the history of the revolutionary movement, reflected in the cross-section of the life of one extraordinary person.[294]

No one in the Soviet Union, except for Stalin, would have dared characterize an Okhrana agent as an "extraordinary person."

In the conclusion of this book, Stalin provided a psychological profile of Serebriakova. He actually projected himself onto her without realizing it. He mentioned *psikhologicheskuyu razdvoennost* (psychological duality), the "two natures" ("split personality") of the Okhrana agent; as well as the ability to "separate the thoughts from the words," as well as the "gigantic willpower," and "steel-hardened stamina to control the speech" of such an agent."[295] He also cited the habit of accusing others of what the agent was guilty of, a habit that Stalin quite appropriately called a "false target."[296] Stalin was habitually "projecting" his guilt on "false targets"—the psychological mechanism of freeing oneself from guilt by projecting it onto others. He probably never recognized himself in his projections.[297] The unmistakable praise that Stalin bestowed upon Okhrana agents suggests that, on some level, Stalin was aware of his own "two personalities" and of his need to employ "false targets." But he noted coyly:

> We repeat, we will not take upon ourselves the mission to unwrap the mystery of this person. If it is true that "man's soul is darkness," then the "soul" of any provocateur is indeed a gloomy night, and Serebriakova's soul is three times gloomier.[298]

Stalin had an obsessive need for the falsification of historical records, which he performed through the forgery of documents and the deliberate omission of facts.

Such revisionist history first surfaced in 1930 with the publication of the book *Okhranniki i avanturisty* (*Okhrana Officers and Adventurers*), which quoted Colonel I. P. Vasiliev's March 21, 1917, report to the Provisional Government. P. E. Shchegolev, the author of this book, states that Vasiliev "presented himself as a progressive Okhrana officer" and an "enemy of provocations." There was no mention in this book of Okhrana agent Roman Malinovsky, whom I. P. Vasiliev had tried to expose. Vasiliev's report did not appear in the record of the "Muraviev Commission," which was published in 1924. "I quote Vasiliev's report in its entirety," states Shchegolev. But he quotes it very selectively. He also omits any mention of Okhrana agent "Vasily," with whom

Vasiliev had conspired to expose Malinovsky.[299] Several of Stalin's Okhrana files were found in the old Caucasian Okhrana archives, and delivered to him.[300] He ordered his brother-in-law Alexander Svanidze to doctor these documents to glorify Stalin's revolutionary past. In 1936 he placed these forgeries in Soviet archives, and ordered Lavrenty Beria to publish them. The real documents found in the old Okhrana archives Stalin called "Kutepov documents."

In 1930, Stalin ordered the forced collectivization of the peasantry, which resulted in a disruption of the economy and an outbreak of famine. At a Politburo meeting on March 5, 1930, Stalin blamed Commissar of Finance Nikolai Brukhanov for the "catastrophic condition" of the country. He drew a caricature of Brukhanov hanged by his genitals and explained:

> Commissar of Finances on the second day of the test: "To Politburo members: For all present and future sins, hang Brukhanov by his balls; if his balls can stand it, consider him acquitted by the court. If not, drown him in the river. I. Stalin."[301]

In May 1930 Stalin ordered all institutions of higher education purged of members of the "rights opposition" led by Bukharin, Rykov, and Tomsky. Lazar Kaganovich, a Jew and one of Stalin's most trusted aides, mentioned to him the name of Nikita Khrushchev, a first-year student at the Industrial Academy. Stalin needed such a student to sign a letter that he had fabricated. On May 29, 1930, Khrushchev was summoned by Lev Mekhlis, Stalin's Jewish assistant, who had read a letter about "political machinations being used for the oppression of human rights" and believed that it had come from the Industrial Academy. "Are you in agreement with the contents of this letter? Would you be willing to put your signature on it?" asked Mekhlis. Khrushchev agreed to sign the letter.[302] This was the beginning of Khrushchev's career. He was appointed secretary of the Party organization in the Industrial Academy, where Stalin's wife, Nadezhda Allilueva, was a student. Stalin noticed that Khrushchev was looking at him with adoration.[303] Years later, other people, too, were to express their belief that Khrushchev was "receptive," with a tendency to submit to strong personalities.

In the summer of 1932, Stalin learned about a peasant boy, Pavlik Morozov, who had testified in court that his father was resisting the drive for collectivization. This report again reminded Stalin of how, as a ten-year-old in 1890, he had testified in Tiflis against his own father Vissarion. Stalin glorified this boy as a martyr and a hero for the Soviet youth to emulate. By glorifying Pavlik he was glorifying himself, but at the time he said glibly: "What a little swine, denouncing his own father!"[304] During the following half-century, a plethora of streets, squares, pioneer houses, and factories were named after Pavlik Morozov. Numerous books, articles, songs, and poems were published about him. In the opera *Pavlik Morozov*, the subject's father sang remorsefully, "Why did I let Pavlik join the Pioneers?" A Soviet writer stated in 1982 that the life of Pavlik "still awaits its Shakespeare."

Nadezhda Allilueva, Stalin's wife, committed suicide on November 7, 1932. This day was the fiftieth anniversary of the October Revolution. Family friends found Nadezhda's letter, and gave it to Stalin. He read it in silence over and over again.[305] Stalin's daughter Svetlana was to reveal:

> It was a terrible letter, full of reproaches and accusations. It was not purely personal; it was partly political as well . . . at times Stalin was gripped by anger, rage. This was because my mother had left this letter for him.[306]

Nadezhda knew of Stalin's Okhrana past. She often quarreled with Stalin, accusing him of torturing Russian people, and shouting, "I know what kind of revolutionary you are!" She knew that he was afraid of people harboring his Okhrana file. He dismissed her accusations as "Trotskyite rumors," and castigated her for spreading "anti-Soviet propaganda."[307] A brief official announcement of her death read:

> Party member and Stalin's comrade-in-arms Nadezhda Allilueva died suddenly and prematurely.[308]

Stalin did not walk in the funeral procession to the Novodevichy Convent.[309] A marble sculpture still marks Nadezhda's grave.[310]

The party's new recruits disliked Old Bolsheviks, whom Stalin suspected of knowing about his Okhrana file. At the time of Blumkin's execution, and for a few years thereafter, rumors of this file circulated throughout Moscow. They reached Isaac Don Levine, an American journalist and the author of the first Western biographies of Stalin.[311] An Old Bolshevik, A. P. Shirin, the secretary of Moscow's Bauman district party committee, was arrested in January 1931 and secretly executed. M. N. Riutin, the secretary of Moscow's *Krasnaya Presnia* District Party committee, accused Stalin of being a "great agent-provocateur" and the "gravedigger of the Revolution."[312] Riutin wrote a pamphlet, "Stalin and the Crisis of Proletarian Dictatorship," and a long article "Appeal to All Party Members," stating:

> Even the most daring, genius-like provocateur could not have invented anything better than what Stalin and his clique did . . . We must put an end to Stalin's rule as soon as possible.[313]

Riutin was arrested in July 1931, and Khrushchev was appointed in his place. Menzhinsky refused to execute Riutin, which alarmed Stalin. Menzhinsky also resisted Stalin's demands to confiscate all copies of the "Riutin Platform."[314] Having this document in one's home became a serious crime.

Stalin suspected that Menzhinsky was plotting against him and he was not mistaken: Menzhinsky indeed intended to depose Stalin.[315] He resisted Stalin's attempts to transform the GPU into his "private power base."[316] But Menzhinsky was gravely ill: he was suffering from *sukhotka* (the progressive disease *tabes dorsalis*), spending most of his time on a sofa in his office while the GPU was managed by his deputy, Genrikh Yagoda. Riutin and his friends distributed the "Riutin Platform" amongst the Party members with an attached short note, "Having read this, pass it on to another person. Multiply and distribute."[317] This was the first attempt in the Soviet Union to distribute *samizdat* ("self-publications"). Several people who had discussed the Riutin Platform were arrested on September 23, 1931—among them Peter Petrovsky, a son of the former *Duma* deputy Grigory Petrovsky, to whom Stalin had said:

> We know everything about you. In 1905 you caroused with the chief of police in Pavlograd. Look out, this might prove unpleasant![318]

Stalin showed the Okhrana file to Petrovsky and shouted, "We shoot people like you, but I will have mercy on you."[319] Petrovsky outlived Stalin. His son Peter was accused of having not reported the discussion of the "Riutin Platform." He was sentenced to ten years in prison in 1931 and released in 1941. He was arrested again shortly after his release in 1941, and executed.

At the beginning of November 1932, the Central Control Commission ruled to expel all involved in the Riutin case from the Party as "degenerates and traitors," among them Zinoviev and Kamenev.[320] Menzhinsky refused to execute the arrested people. Politburo members Kirov, Kuibyshev, and Ordzhonikidze objected to Stalin's demand to execute Riutin, who had been sentenced in court to ten years in prison (although the sentence was later lengthened to fifteen years).[321] Riutin was incarcerated in the infamous "Susdal Isolator." A few years later, Riutin and all the members of his family, except for his daughter Luba, were executed.

At the Seventeenth Party Congress in 1934, Menzhinsky was removed from the Central Committee. Stalin appointed the Genrikh Yagoda, a Jew, to head the GPU. Meer Trilisser, the Chief of the GPU Foreign Department, also a Jew, found the file of Okhrana informer Genrikh Yagoda in the old archives and gave it to Stalin, who kept Yagoda on the "hook."[322] Sergey Kirov was murdered on December 1, 1934.[323] On January 26, 1935, it was announced that Valerian Kuibyshev had died of heart disease. (Three years later, his secretary Maximov-Dikovsky was accused of poisoning him.) Kuibyshev's body was cremated, and the ashes placed in the Kremlin Wall to the left of Kirov's urn. In a secret letter to the Party organizations entitled "The Lessons of the Evil Murder of Comrade Kirov," Stalin called for the arrests and executions of jailed members of the opposition. Mass arrests took place in Moscow and Leningrad.[324] On December 16, 1934, Zinoviev and Kamenev were brought to the Lubyanka from their places of imprisonment, where they had been serving terms for "not reporting about the 'Riutin Platform.'" They were now accused of instigating the murder of Kirov. Kamenev and Zinoviev were sentenced to five- and ten-year prison terms, respectively.[325] On July 27, 1935, Kamenev was secretly sentenced to an additional ten-year prison term for having plotted to poison Stalin.[326]

Stalin provoked the murder of Kirov.[327] Menzhinsky was poisoned and died on May 10, 1934.[328] Stalin's Okhrana file remained hidden among Menzhinsky's personal papers.[329] Sergey Kirov was murdered on December 1, 1934.[330] On January 26, 1935, it was announced that Valerian Kuibyshev had died of heart disease. (Three years later, his secretary Maximov-Dikovsky was accused of poisoning him.) Kuibyshev's body was cremated, and the ashes placed in the Kremlin Wall to the left of Kirov's urn. In a secret letter to the Party organizations entitled "The Lessons of the Evil Murder of Comrade Kirov," Stalin called for the arrests and executions of jailed members of the opposition. Mass arrests took place in Moscow and Leningrad.[331] On December 16, 1934, Zinoviev and Kamenev were brought to the Lubyanka from their places of imprisonment, where they had been serving terms for "not reporting about the 'Riutin Platform.'" They were now accused of instigating the murder of Kirov. Kamenev and Zinoviev were sentenced to five- and ten-year prison terms, respectively.[332] On July 27, 1935, Kamenev was secretly sentenced to an additional ten-year prison term for having plotted to poison

Stalin.[333]

In 1935, the journal *Krasny Arkhiv* (Red Archive) published a lead article titled "Revolutionary Vigilance" that had been written by Stalin. The dictator castigated "archival rats" that "dig out accidentally selected documents," stating:

> We know that wicked dvurishniki [double-dealers] and contrabandists do not shrink from committing fraud and falsification.[334]

Stalin ordered Beria, with whom Stalin shared many of his secrets, to purge the old Okhrana archives of "Kutepov documents," which Stalin claimed had been forged by "enemies" to defame him. Stalin's Okhrana files were discovered in Tiflis, Baku, Batum, and Kutais archives, and were delivered to Stalin.[335] Stalin realized that it was his St. Petersburg Okhrana file which Blumkin had attempted to smuggle abroad. Starting in July 1935, *Pravda* began publishing Beria's articles praising Stalin's "leading role in the Revolution." The journal *Krasny arkhiv* published doctored Okhrana documents, from which Stalin had erased embarrassing data and had inserted flattering statements. These adulterated Okhrana documents contained crude absurdities that reveal the blatant fraudulent nature of these forgeries. But some parts of the original text were left intact, which helps to ascertain the truth. The documents were doctored in a secret Kremlin press headed by Alexander Svanidze, the brother of Stalin's first wife.[336] Karl Radek wrote a book entitled *The Architect of Socialist Society*, in which he described the future of the USSR at the end of the twentieth century and the essay "Great Stalin: The Genius of All Humanity." Stalin ordered millions of copies published.[337] Trotsky wrote:

> I do not think that any single entity in all of human history could be found that even remotely resembles the gigantic factory of lies that the Kremlin—under the leadership of Stalin—has organized. And one of the principal purposes of this factory is to manufacture a new biography of Stalin.[338]

In 1935, Stalin began planning a show trial of Kamenev and Zinoviev that was to be staged in the summer of 1936. Kamenev was a longtime friend of Maxim Gorky, whom Kamenev had proclaimed the "great proletarian writer." Gorky strongly objected to the trial and demanded a passport that would allow him to travel abroad. His request was refused. In a letter to French Communist writer Romain Rolland, Gorky complained that he was trapped and felt like an "old bear with a ring in my nose."[339] Maria Kudasheva, Rolland's wife and a Soviet agent, agreed to visit Gorky in Moscow with her husband. Gorky also tried to hasten the arrival in Moscow of French writers André Gide and Louis Aragon. Stalin ordered Aragon's wife Elsa Triolet (Elizaveta Kagan), who was also a Soviet agent, to prevent Aragon's journey. But, scheduling a boat to Leningrad, she managed to arrange their travel to Russia, explaining that she wanted to visit her sister Lilia Brik, the former lover of the late poet Vladimir Mayakovsky. Lilia Brik became a mistress of Vitaly Primakov, the Commander of the Leningrad Military District, who in 1934 abandoned his Jewish wife Anna Yakovlevna Kirshenblat and their six-year-old son Evgeny Primakov— who later became a KGB operative in Arab countries and an anti-Israel propagandist. (After the collapse of the Soviet Empire, Evgeny Primakov became chief of the Russian Intelligence Service, and was later appointed Russian Foreign Minister. On September 10, 1998, President Boris Yeltsin appointed him Russian prime minister.)[340]

Elsa Triolet stated:

My husband is a Communist because of me. I am a tool of Soviet power. I love to wear jewelry, I am a society woman, and I am a dirty whore.[341]

Elsa Triolet delayed Aragon's visit until June 18.[342] That day Gorky died at 11:10 a.m. His house was surrounded by security troops and the gates were closed. The next day, *Pravda* reported that Gorky had died of "paralysis of the heart."[343] But the rumor that Gorky had been poisoned spread.[344]

Stalin appointed Andrey Vyshinsky state prosecutor in June 1935, and gave him the leading role in the show trial, which took place in the summer of 1936. It was there that Kamenev and Zinoviev were branded *podlye dvurushniki* (vile double-dealers). Stalin ordered Yagoda to prepare documentary "proof" that Kamenev and Zinoviev had been Okhrana agents.[345] This show trial revealed a great number of Jewish defendants. Jewish interrogators G. A. Molchanov, Abram Slutsky, Mikhail Shpigelglas, Y. D. Agranov, and many others, took part in this trial. When the interrogators dared to suggest to Stalin that many people would not believe the accusations against the Old Bolsheviks, Stalin replied, "Never mind, they'll swallow everything!"[346] The show-trial scenarios revealed several true events in Stalin's own life that kept cropping up in the "confessions" of the defendants upon whom he projected his own crimes.

One of the Jewish defendants, E. S. Holtzman, "confessed" that in 1932 he had met Trotsky's son, Lev Sedov, in Berlin, and had arranged to go with him to Copenhagen for a conference with Trotsky. Holtzman testified, "I arranged with Sedov to be in Copenhagen within two or three days, to be put up at the Hotel Bristol, and to meet him there. I went to the hotel straight from the station, and met Sedov in the lounge. At about 10 a.m. we went to Trotsky." Holtzman further testified that Trotsky had told him that "it was necessary to remove Stalin and to choose cadres of responsible people fit for the task."[347] When Holtzman's testimony was published, Danish newspapers declared the material a fabrication, informing their readers that the Hotel Bristol in Copenhagen had been demolished in 1917; that is, fifteen years before Holtzman's alleged meeting there with Trotsky's son Sedov. Trotsky declared that Holtzman's testimony was entirely false. It was actually Iosif Dzhugashvili who had gone to the Hotel Bristol in 1906 to meet an Okhrana officer, who had introduced Dzhugashvili to Arkady Garting, the Chief of the Okhrana Foreign Agency.[348] The John Dewey Commission of Inquiry stated in its published report that:

> The fact that there was not a Hotel Bristol in Copenhagen in 1932 is now a matter of common knowledge. It would, therefore, have obviously been impossible for Holtzman to have met Sedov in the lobby of the Hotel Bristol.[349]

Stalin shouted at the NKVD chiefs:

> What the devil did you need a hotel for? You ought to have said that they had met at the railway station. A railway station is always there![350]

One of the defendants, Sergey Mrachkovsky, was reluctant to testify against the Jewish defendants. Stalin told him:

> Part ways with them. What is binding you, a famous worker, to this Jewish Sanhedrin?[351]

Stalin was familiar with the Okhrana forgery, *Protocols of the Elders of Zion*, which his Okhrana handler, I. P. Vasiliev, had begun printing and distributing in 1905. "Jewish Sanhedrin" was prominently mentioned in this forgery.

Sometime in July 1936 Stalin ordered Yagoda to find "proof" of Zinoviev's and Kamenev's Okhrana ties. Yagoda commanded the Assistant

Chief of the NKVD Secret Political Department, Isaac Lvovich Stein, to search for such incriminating evidence among the documents and personal papers that had been kept in Menzhinsky's old office and had been sealed since his death. While perusing Menzhinsky's papers, Stein discovered the file of "Iosif Dzhugashvili." His first impulse was to report immediately to Yagoda that he had found documentary proof of Stalin's glorious revolutionary past. As he began to read the contents of the file, his elation turned to horror. He realized that these documents identified Stalin as an Okhrana agent. He read the letter of the Chief of the Okhrana Special Section Colonel A. M. Eremin to the Director of the Department of Police S. P. Beletsky, in which Eremin described the major points of Stalin's Okhrana career.[352]

Stein realized that Stalin was an Okhrana imposter, a despicable traitor. The purges, show trials, and executions of the Old Bolsheviks now took on the most sinister meaning. Stein's best friends, with whom he had enjoyed a close bond since the days of the civil war and whom he trusted, were V. A. Balitsky, a Pole, who was NKVD chief in the Ukraine, and Zinovy Katsnelson, his Jewish deputy. With Stalin's Okhrana file in his briefcase, Stein took a train to Kiev. Balitsky and Katsnelson put the documents through the tests and came to the conclusion that they were genuine. They decided to do what they could to save the country from the entrenched Okhrana agent. The only force in the USSR that stood any chance to depose Stalin was the Red Army, where Balitsky had close friends: Marshal M. Tukhachevsky, the First Deputy Commissar of Defense, and Yan Gamarnik, the head of the Political Administration of the Red Army. Gamarnik was also a full member of the Central Committee. Balitsky gave Stalin's Okhrana file to Tukhachevsky and Gamarnik, who together decided to overthrow Stalin.[353]

A conspiracy, headed by Tukhachevsky, came into being. A delay would risk the exposure of the plot. "Don't you see where all of this is leading to?" asked one of the conspirators. General B. M. Feldman. "He will strangle all of us, one by one, like baby chicks. We must act." Tukhachevsky objected. He refused to participate in a coup d'état.[354] He and Gamarnik insisted that a secret Party court should judge Stalin. The plotters made numerous photocopies of Colonel Eremin's report, which included a concise summary of Stalin's Okhrana career.[355]

Meanwhile, sixteen of the defendants at the 1936 show trial had heard Vyshinsky shouting in his closing speech:

These mad dogs of capitalism. They killed our Kirov, they wounded our hearts. I demand that these dogs gone mad should be shot—every one of them!"[356]

Stalin crossed off from the list of defendants a scientist named Ioffe, a Jew, saying, "Release him. He might be useful to us."[357] All the other defendants were executed after they had read their "final words," which had been approved by Stalin.[358] Yagoda and Karl Pauker watched as the doomed men were led to the cellar. Kamenev walked as if in a dream. He was shot from behind. He fell, moaning. "Finish him off!" shouted an officer, kicking Kamenev with his tall boot. Zinoviev could not walk. The guards threw a pail of water on his face and he fell to the floor. An officer, Evangulov, ordered the guards to push Zinoviev into the nearest empty cell; and grabbing his bushy hair and jerking his head down, shot him point-blank. Evangulov received a citation for having acted expeditiously under difficult conditions.[359]

On December 20, 1936, Stalin invited top NKVD chiefs to his Kuntsevo *dacha* to celebrate his fifty-seventh birthday, as well as the eighteenth anniversary of the founding of *Cheka*, the original Soviet secret police. The newspapers published the usual congratulations from the "toiling people" and from Stalin's admirers abroad, where Stalin had many admirers in so-called "progressive circles." As usual, the guests soon got drunk. They pleaded with Karl Pauker to perform the scene of Zinoviev's execution. They knew Stalin would relish it. Stalin enjoyed Pauker's performances. Pauker, who prior to World War I had played the part of a barber in the Budapest Operetta, liked to perform "comical" scenes and tell Jewish anecdotes with a Yiddish accent. Stalin liked this very much. That night Pauker performed the execution of "Zinoviev." Two NKVD officers dragged in a third officer who played the role of "Zinoviev," who, moaning and rolling his eyes in terror, hung helplessly off their hands. Stalin roared with laughter. "Zinoviev" fell to his knees in the middle of the room, and, embracing the boots of the "guard," cried, "Please, comrades, for God's sake, call up Iosif Vissarionovich!" Stalin was enjoying the scene, so the guests demanded that Pauker repeat the performance. He was happy to oblige, but this time he enriched his "shtick" with a new detail: he dropped to his knees and raised his hands to Heaven, crying in Hebrew, "*Shema Yisrael, Adonai Eloheinu, Adonai Ehad!*" (Hear, Israel, the Lord is our God, the Lord is one!) This Hebrew prayer threw Stalin into uncontrollable hilarity. He bent over, holding his belly with both hands and choking with laughter, motioned to Pauker to stop the performance.[360]

After the execution of Zinoviev and Kamenev, Stalin ordered the NKVD to prepare for a new show trial.

Toward the end of 1936, the country faced a bizarre situation when two files—the Okhrana file with genuine documents, exposing Stalin as an Okhrana agent, and the fabricated "Tukhachevsky Dossier," containing fraudulent accusations of Tukhachevsky's treason—were at the center of two conspiracies whose outcome depended on which one of Stalin or Tukhachevsky would strike first. Stalin did not suspect that his Okhrana file was in the hands of Tukhachevsky, while Tukhachevsky did not know that he had been selected by Stalin as his next victim.[361] Stalin was annoyed by Yagoda's failure to "prove" that Kamenev and Zinoviev had ties to the Okhrana. On September 25, 1936, he sent a telegram to members of the Politburo (signed also by Andrey Zhdanov, his new *soratnik* [comrade-in-arms]) demanding the replacement of Yagoda with Nikolai I. Yezhov, who ultimately became the head of the NKVD.[362] Yagoda was demoted to the post of Commissar of Communications.

The next show trial of the "Anti-Soviet Trotskyite Center" opened on January 23, 1937. The main defendant Grigory Piatakov was forced to "confess" that in December 1935 he took a flight to Oslo where he met with Trotsky. Soon thereafter the Norwegian newspaper *Aftenposten* reported:

> Piatakov's conference with Trotsky in Oslo was quite improbable, because no airplanes had landed at the Oslo airport during December 1935, when Piatakov supposedly traveled there.[363]

Actually it was Stalin who had ventured to Oslo in 1907 to meet Arkady Garting, the chief of the Okhrana Foreign Agency.

Thirteen defendants, many of them Jewish, were sentenced to death and four, among them Radek, received prison terms.[364] Radek's face lit up when he heard his ten-year prison sentence pronounced. He turned to his fellow defendants, shrugged, and flashed a guilty smile. The execution of Piatakov was a great blow to Ordzhonikidze, who accused Stalin of falsely promising him to spare Piatakov's life.[365] On February 18, 1937, Stalin ordered Poskrebyshev, the chief of his personal secretary, to go to Ordzhonikidze's apartment and shoot him.[366] At 5:30 p.m., Ordzhonikidze's wife, Zinaida, heard a shot. When she looked out the window, she saw a man running across the Kremlin lawn. She went into her husband's study and found him dead. She called Stalin, whose apartment was nearby. Stalin arrived and sardonically exclaimed:

Heavens, what a tricky illness! The man lies down to have a rest, and the result is a seizure and a heart attack![367]

The official medical report stated that the death had resulted from "paralysis of the heart." Khrushchev delivered an emotional oration in which, choking with tears and anger, he referred to the "enemies," stating:

It was they who struck a blow at thy noble heart. Piatakov—the spy, the murderer, the enemy of the working people—was caught red-handed, caught and condemned, crushed like a reptile.[368]

Stalin planned the next show trial of Marshal Tukhachevsky, against whom Stalin had nursed a grudge since the days of the civil war. Stalin accumulated "evidence of Tukhachevsky's crimes" in a file that became known to history as the "Tukhachevsky Dossier." Tukhachevsky did not know that Stalin was secretly approaching Hitler to form an alliance with Nazi Germany while Commissar of Foreign Affairs Maxim Litvinov was trying to unite European countries against German fascism.[369] On March 31, 1935, *Pravda* published Tukhachevsky's article, in which he predicted that Hitler would start a war by attacking the Soviet Union and much of Europe. This article sparked a storm of protests in Berlin. It also annoyed Stalin.

In February 1937, Zinovy Katsnelson, the Deputy Chief of the Ukrainian NKVD, visited his cousin Alexander Orlov, an NKVD general stationed in Europe, in a Paris hospital. He told Orlov about the discovery by I. L. Stein of Stalin's Okhrana file, and about the contents of its documents as well as about the conspiracy of military officers to depose Stalin. Orlov and Katsnelson were hoping that the plot headed by Tukhachevsky to depose Stalin would succeed.[370] A March 18, 1937 speech by Yezhov focused upon the liquidation of "Yagoda's nest," stating that Yagoda had been exposed as an "Okhrana agent" who had wormed his way into the Soviet secret police to mastermind a network of spies in the NKVD, and had attempted to escape abroad "with a suitcase full of *valuta* [foreign currency]." Stalin projected upon Yagoda not only his own Okhrana past, but also Blumkin's attempt to flee with a suitcase full of foreign currency. Yagoda was arrested on April 3, 1937. He told Abram Slutsky:

There must be a God after all! From Stalin I deserve nothing but gratitude for my faithful service. From God I deserve the most severe punishment for having broken his commandments one thousand times. Now look where I am, and judge for yourself whether there is a God or not![371]

In March 1937, Yezhov ordered all the chiefs of the NKVD departments (besides Slutsky and Pauker) to go on "inspection tours." At the first stop outside Moscow they were arrested and shot. Their deputies, too, were executed. Some 3,000 NKVD officers were murdered in total, with many suicides as well. According to Stalin's scenario, Yagoda and Tukhachevsky were to appear as chief defendants at the next show trial, which was to expose "German spies" and "Okhrana agents."

Stalin was delaying Tukhachevsky's arrest while waiting for additional "criminal evidence" against him that he was expecting to receive from Hitler's secret police. Soviet agent General Nikolai Skoblin provided such "information" to the "Guchkov Circle," a Russian émigré group in Berlin who had been infiltrated by several NKVD agents including Guchkov's own daughter.[372] Using Skoblin's "information," Reinhardt Heydrich, the head of *Sicherheitsdienst* ("SD"), a German intelligence service, suggested to Hitler a plan to fabricate "evidence" of a conspiracy between the "Red Bonaparte" Tukhachevsky and the German High Command. Hitler agreed. Heydrich ordered SD forger Franz Putzig to add Tukhachevsky's signature to documents that had been stolen from the German General Staff.[373] Putzig fabricated fifteen such documents.[374] Heydrich ordered his assistant, Behrens, to go to Prague to offer these forgeries to Czech president Edvard Beneš, who referred Behrens to the Soviet embassy in Berlin. Leonid Zakovsky, who represented Yezhov, agreed to pay three million rubles for these forgeries, which reached Stalin at the beginning of May 1937.[375] (The three million rubles proved to be of no use to the Germans—they were in large banknotes and the serial numbers were known to the NKVD. The German agents who did use them were arrested.)[376] The "Tukhachevsky Dossier" was complete by the beginning of May 1937. It had some fifteen Soviet and fifteen German forgeries. But Stalin no longer had the slightest interest in using these fabrications.

On May 19, 1937, during a nightly routine search of the apartment of one of the arrested Red Army officers, NKVD operatives happened upon a photocopy of Colonel Eremin's report to the director of the Department of Police, S. P. Beletsky. The photocopy was handed over to Karl Pauker, the chief of the NKVD Operations Department, who had a poor knowledge of the Russian language. Pauker, a drinking companion of Stalin, entertained him by telling Jewish jokes with a Yiddish accent. Pauker did not understand the significance of this document and brought it to Stalin. Stalin immediately realized that his St. Petersburg Okhrana file was in the hands of plotters who intended to destroy him. He ordered Yezhov to declare a state of emergency; surround his office and living quarters with NKVD troops and a cadre of bodyguards; and cancel all passes into the Kremlin.[377] He said that the extraordinary security measures were needed because he had uncovered a vast conspiracy to murder Yezhov.[378] Stalin, as usual, had pointed at a "false target" in order to divert attention from himself. He ordered Yezhov to execute Karl Pauker and his deputy Volovich, stating that they were "Polish and German spies."[379] By murdering Pauker, Stalin denied himself the opportunity to determine where exactly the photocopy of Eremin's report had been found, and to be able to trace the threads of the conspiracy from there. He had made the same mistake in 1930 by ordering Blumkin's execution.[380]

On May 22, 1937, Walter Krivitsky, head of Soviet military intelligence in Europe, paid a visit to Mikhail Frinovsky, Yezhov's deputy. "Tell me, what's going on? What's going on in the country?" asked Krivitsky, wondering what had caused such a "succession of arrests and executions that it seemed as if the Russian roof were falling and the whole Soviet edifice tumbling." Frinovsky said that the worst of this extremely dangerous situation was over, adding:

> We've just uncovered a gigantic conspiracy in the Army, a conspiracy such as history has never known. And we've just now learned of a plot to kill Nikolai Ivanovich Yezhov himself! But we have got them all. We have got everything under control.[381]

Krivitsky left Moscow for The Hague the same day, feeling as if he were departing a severely earthquake-ravaged city.

On May 19, 1937, an NKVD interrogator, Ushakov, a notorious sadist, accused General Feldman of taking part in a military conspiracy. Ushakov later testified:

> I summoned Feldman to my office, and locked him and myself up; on the evening of May 19, Feldman wrote his testimony about the conspiracy involving Tukhachevsky, Yakir, Eideman, and others. [382]

Ushakov insisted that it was he who had uncovered the Red Army conspiracy and made history by forcing Feldman to confess.

Stalin did not suspect Tukhachevsky when the arrests began. He appointed him Commander of the Volga Military District. On May 25, 1937,

Tukhachevsky went to see Yan Gamarnik to say goodbye.[383] The following day, Tukhachevsky was arrested during a meeting at the Kuibyshev Party headquarters. An express train delivered him to Moscow. Tukhachevsky, bandaged and being carried on a stretcher, was brought to the Kremlin for personal interrogation by Stalin.[384] He was then taken to the Lubyanka prison and interrogated by Ushakov, who would testify about the matter two decades later:

Tukhachevsky was given to me. I already had him confessing on May 26.[385]

On May 28, a detachment of NKVD troops surrounded the Department of Defense. On May 30, 1937, A. S. Bulin, the newly appointed chief of the Cadre Administration of the Red Army, and his deputy, I. V. Smorodnikov, went to Gamarnik's apartment and took from him the keys to the safe in his office at the Department of Defense. There they found Stalin's Okhrana file, and gave it to Stalin.[386] At 5 p.m. on May 31, Bulin and Smorodnikov returned to Gamarnik's apartment. His wife showed them the door the bedroom, and went to the kitchen. She heard two shots and saw Bulin and Smorodnikov getting ready to leave. They pretended to be surprised by the shots, and the three of them went back into the bedroom. Gamarnik was dead. Blood was seeping from two bullet wounds.[387]

On June 1, 1937, a report in *Pravda* announced:

Former member of the Central Committee Y. B. Gamarnik, having been entangled with anti-Soviet elements and fearing that he would be unmasked, has committed suicide.[388]

Rumors about "two gunshots" were spreading. Some NKVD officers were convinced that Gamarnik had been murdered.[389] (Bulin and Smorodnikov were later shot as "Japanese spies."[390]) The army commanders I. P. Uborevich and Iona Yakir were arrested at the end of May 1937. From June 1 to June 4, 1937, the Military Council, presided over by Voroshilov, who castigated the "counterrevolutionary Fascist military organization."

The Okhrana file, which Stalin worried about for many years, was finally in his hands. Mass arrests and executions followed. The detained generals were tortured and forced to sign their testimonies while blood dripped from their wounds. (Two decades later, during Khrushchev's reign, the brownish spots on their "confessions" were determined to be blood.)[391] On June 11, 1937, *Pravda* reported:

> The case of Tukhachevsky, M. N.; Yakir, I. P.; Uborevich, I. P.; Kork, A. I.; Eideman, R. P.; Feldman, B. M.; Primakov, V., and B. K. Putna, arrested by the organs of the NKVD at different times, has been brought to investigative conclusion and transferred to the court.[392]

The only surviving record of the generals' last words is in the archives of Vitaly Primakov. It is not known whether he actually delivered this long speech, but its style of questions and answers, peculiar logic, and repetition of the same idea leaves no doubt that it was penned by Stalin. The record reads:

> Of whom did this plot consist? Whom did the fascist banner of Trotsky unite? It united all the counterrevolutionary elements . . . treason, betrayal, defeat of one's country, wreckage, espionage, terror. I named more than seventy people to the investigation.

The central theme of this record was to portray the defendants as being not Russians, but Jews, Poles, Latvians, and Lithuanians.[393] All of the defendants, including Primakov, were shot immediately after the trial. That same day, June 11, 1937, thousands of Gulag inmates (mostly common criminals who had built the Moscow-Volga Canal) celebrated their release from prison camp in the ancient town of Dmitrov, not far from Moscow. They were awarded *udarniki* (shock-worker) citations, dated June 11, 1937, which were signed by Zinovy Katsnelson, who had earlier been appointed chief of the Gulag.[394] At this point Stalin still did not know that Katsnelson was involved in the conspiracy.

At the party plenum that started on June 23, Stalin provided "extraordinary emergency powers" to Yezhov. Osip Piatnitsky, a Jew, objected, saying that he had information about the illegal methods of investigation employed by NKVD officers under Yezhov's leadership. The next day, Yezhov said that the NKVD possessed "undeniable data proving that before the Revolution, Piatnitsky had been an informer of the Okhrana section of the Department of Police."[395] Stalin's Okhrana file contained Stalin's report, in which he listed the names and aliases of the most important Bolsheviks, among them Piatnitsky, of whom he wrote, "Transport: in Leipzig in the hands of Tarshis (Piatnitsa)."[396] (Tarshis was the real family name of Piatnitsky.) Krupskaya, Lenin's widow, tried to defend Piatnitsky, but Stalin warned her that if she did not stop bothering him, the Party would proclaim that Lenin's wife was not Krupskaya but Elena Stasova, the Old Bolshevik who was Lenin's friend. "Yes, the Party can do anything," Stalin said.[397] Piatnitsky was arrested on July 7, 1937, and shot. His wife perished in a prison camp. Only his daughter Yulia survived.[398]

Stalin decided to fabricate an almost identical "Eremin Letter," in which were inserted several easily detectable "mistakes" to convince skeptics, and probably, most importantly, also himself, that all the documents in his Okhrana file were forgeries that had been fabricated by Stalin's enemies. He intended to exhibit these forgeries at a gigantic show trial that was planned for the end of 1937. Stalin ordered the kidnapping of General E. K. Miller, the chairman of the Russian White Guard officers' organization in Paris—the ploy strongly resembled the earlier kidnapping of the White Guard general Kutepov in Paris in 1930. Stalin intended to parade Miller at the planned show trial, and force him to "confess" that he had organized the fabrication of Okhrana forgeries, including the "Eremin Letter." This was an ingenious cover-up scheme. On September 22, 1937, General Miller was kidnapped in Paris and delivered to Moscow.

The second and more complicated part of Stalin's scheme began in July 1937, when Stalin summoned Genrikh Lyushkov, the deputy chief of the NKVD Secret Political Department who had just replaced I. L. Stein who had committed suicide. Lyushkov, a former member of Odessa's Jewish criminal underworld, was known among NKVD officers for his extensive use of provocations. Lyushkov was described by a fellow NKVD officer as an "arrogant, arbitrary, and sadistic bully."[399] Stalin assigned to him the most important missions during the preparations for the Zinoviev-Kamenev trial. Lyushkov headed a team of interrogators who tortured the defendants, among them Riutin. In July 1937, Stalin appointed Lyushkov chief of the Far Eastern NKVD, and gave him four fabricated Okhrana forgeries, among them the "Eremin Letter." Stalin ordered Lyushkov to deliver these forgeries to M. D. Golovachev a Soviet agent in China, for publication in the Russian émigré newspapers there.[400]

Toward the end of July 1937, Lyushkov arrived in Khabarovsk and arrested V. A. Balitsky, who had been appointed chief of the Far Eastern NKVD in 1936. In the early thirties Lyushkov worked together with Balitsky, Katsnelson, and Stein in the Kharkov GPU.[401] Lyushkov, after arresting Balitsky, sent him to Moscow under guard of several soldiers. Lyushkov had a list of army men whom Stalin had ordered arrested and shot.[402]

In July 1937, Lyushkov traveled to Shanghai under an assumed name and gave the "Eremin Letter" and three other forgeries to M. D. Golovachev, whom he instructed to publish the documents in the Russian émigré newspapers, stating that the origin of these documents was the former Okhrana officer and Shanghai resident V. N. Russianov. Amongst the Russian émigrés in China, Golovachev had the reputation of being a shady character. He was suspected of being a Soviet agent who had set up various "institutes" that were actually fronts for Soviet intelligence.[403] Golovachev misrepresented himself as "Professor Golovachev"; Golovachev planted a package with Okhrana stationeries, rubber stamps, and other Okhrana paraphernalia, as well as photos of Stalin, Trotsky, and Malinovsky, in Russianov's home.[404] Stalin's plan was to provoke the Chinese police to search Russianov's home for "evidence" to "prove" that Russianov had been involved in the fabrication of the "Eremin Letter" and other forgeries. Stalin remembered Russianov from the time of his last exile in Kureika when Russianov had been appointed chief of the Eniseysk Okhrana section shortly before the Revolution.[405] Russianov escaped to China in 1937. He lived in Shanghai and worked as a chauffeur for a wealthy American family.

In July 1937, Ignaz Reiss, a NKVD resident in Switzerland, wrote a letter to the Soviet Party central committee, declaring his opposition to Stalin and calling for a "return to Lenin, his teachings, and his cause."[406] Reiss a Hungarian Jew, had learned about Stalin's Okhrana file from Zinovy Katsnelson, who visited him and Alexander Orlov in February 1937. Katsnelson also then told Trotsky's son Lev Sedov about the discovery of Stalin's Okhrana file. Mark Zborovsky, a NKVD agent, penetrated Lev Sedov's Trotskyite circle in Paris and reported this information to Moscow. Stalin ordered the murders of Reiss, Lev Sedov, and two of Trotsky's aides, Erwin Wolf and Rudolf Klement, who also had learned about the file from Reiss.[407] In the early morning of September 4, 1937, Swiss police found the body of Ignaz Reiss riddled with bullets. The murder of Reiss was carried out by a mobile group of killers under the command of Mikhail Shpigelglas, the deputy chief of the NKVD Foreign Department.

On February 16, 1937, after the murder of Reiss, Mark Zborovsky brought Trotsky's son Lev Sedov to a Paris hospital for an appendectomy. He tipped off the NKVD killers, who murdered Sedov in his hospital bed. Zborovsky also guided the slayers to Trotsky's secretaries Erwin Wolf and Rudolf Klement. Wolf was murdered in Spain. The decapitated body of Klement was found floating in the Seine. (After the German occupation of France, Zborovsky went to the United States and was arrested as a Soviet agent. He helped the FBI expose a large Soviet espionage network and struck a deal with the prosecutors, pleading guilty to a perjury charge in exchange for a short prison term. He worked in various hospitals and universities after completing his sentence.)[408]

Renate Steiner, another NKVD agent, was arrested in Switzerland. She led the Swiss authorities to Reiss' assassins, but by the time the police got there, the killers had left. In their rooms, the police found luggage containing a box of poisoned chocolates, Stalin's "present," which Gertrude Shildbach, another NKVD agent, had for some reason failed to give to Reiss' wife and daughter. The investigation of Reiss' murder by the French police threatened to expose a large network of Soviet agents in Europe, and lead the police to the Soviet embassy in Paris, the center of this network. (Like the Okhrana Foreign Agency before it, the main branch of NKVD Foreign Department was located in the Paris Soviet embassy.) Soon after the murder of Reiss, the president of Soviet military intelligence in Europe, Walter Krivitsky, defected to the West. He had learned from Reiss about the discovery of Stalin's Okhrana file, and realized that he was on Stalin's list of people to be eliminated. After escaping to the United States and writing his book in 1941, Krivitsky was murdered in a Washington hotel.[409] Shortly before his murder, Krivitsky had complained to David Shub that he feared that Stalin would order his assassination. Shub replied, "You have nothing to be afraid of. You have revealed of all Stalin's secrets in your book and statements." Krivitsky disagreed, "I did not reveal his most important secret." The most important secret that Krivitsky did not reveal was his knowledge of Stalin's Okhrana file.

By October 1937, most of the Soviet agents in Europe had been recalled to Moscow, and executed. Some of them returned to save the lives of the wives, children, and relatives they had left in the Soviet Union. According to a June 8, 1934, decree, all the relatives of military personnel who had escaped abroad or refused to return to Russia were to be exiled to Siberia for ten years. By a secret addition to this law, all relatives of NKVD "traitors" were to be executed if the traitors revealed "state secrets." Dr. Max Eitingon, an NKVD resident in Vienna who was the handler of General Skoblin and his wife Nadezhda Plevitskaya, also defected.[410] Eitingon settled in Jerusalem and opened a psychiatric clinic. He died under mysterious circumstances in 1944.[411] Sergey Efron, a literary critic and the husband of the Great Russian poet Marina Tsvetaeva (who did not know of her husband's ties to the NKVD), complied with the order to return to the USSR. Their daughter went to Moscow to find out what had happened to her father, and was arrested.

Tsvetaeva herself went to Moscow in 1939 in search of her daughter and husband. She was exiled to the Siberian village of Elabug, where she hanged herself on August 31, 1941. Efron was shot in prison in October 1941. Their daughter spent sixteen years in the Gulag, emerging after Stalin's death as an emotional and physical cripple.[412]

Stalin realized that to use General Miller as a defendant at a show trial would confirm that the Soviets had engaged in criminal kidnapping on French territory, and lead to a break in diplomatic relations with France. He drastically curtailed his plan for a new show trial. On December 15, 1937, many prospective defendants were executed. The names of some of them were later made public.[413] Generals Miller and Skoblin, who had facilitated the kidnapping of Miller, were secretly executed. But the story of the "Eremin Letter" forgery, like a genie let out of a bottle, acquired a life of its own.[414]

On February 16, 1938, Abram Slutsky, the chief of the NKVD Foreign Department, was poisoned by Yezhov's deputy Mikhail Frinovsky. *Pravda* published an obituary signed by a "group of friends." Stalin was clearly destroying the people who "knew too much." Mass arrests and murders made foreign diplomats in Moscow wonder about the "sick man in the Kremlin." But Alexander Orlov, who had escaped to the United States, wrote:

> The almighty dictator was not a lunatic. When all the facts connected with the case of Tukhachevsky become known, the world will understand: Stalin knew what he was doing.[415]

The "Bukharin show trial" opened on March 2, 1938. On March 3, American journalist Isaac Don Levine published the article "Stalin Suspected of Forcing Trials to Cover His Past." Levine wrote:

> Is Stalin a former agent of the Tsar's Okhrana, trying to wipe out in blood the preserved traces of his past career in the secret service of the Romanovs? As the author of the first biography of Stalin, this writer has long been familiar with reports that some of the Old Bolsheviks had possessed a secret file from the archives of the Okhrana that could prove that Stalin had been a super spy for the Tsar when he joined forces with Lenin. So incredible did this charge initially appear, in spite of the fact that there had been suspicious circumstances throughout Stalin's career that one did not dare to make it public without further substantiation.[416]

Levine's article was widely dismissed as an exercise in sensationalism. All of Stalin's biographers had rejected the notion that Stalin had been an Okhrana agent. Levine had received information about Stalin's Okhrana file from Lev Sedov's assistants Erwin Wolf and Rudolf Klement, who had gotten it from Ignaz Reiss.[417] Their murder convinced Levine that these executions had been ordered by Stalin to silence people who knew anything about the file.

As usual, all defendants at the "Bukharin show trial" admitted their guilt and described crimes they had never committed. Stalin's friend Avel Enukidze, who had been executed on December 15, 1937, was presented as the mastermind of a huge anti-Soviet conspiracy. Two "Okhrana agents" testified that they had been agents prior to the revolution. I. A. Zelensky, a Jew who before his arrest had been Director of Cooperative Organizations; and V. I. Ivanov, formerly the People's Commissar of the Timber Industry, cited events from Stalin's Okhrana career in their testimonies.

Stalin's aliases "Vasily" and "Vasiliev" were mentioned by another accused "Okhrana agent," P. T. Zubarev, an official in the Agriculture Commissariat. Zubarev, who described how he had been recruited by a police officer "Vasiliev," who had told him, "If you, Zubarev, want to escape punishment, the only way you can do so is to accept my proposal that you become an agent of the police." Zubarev, said that he had agreed to this proposal, and that his codename was "Paren." Vyshinsky then asked, "This was your second pseudonym?" Zubarev replied, "Yes, Vasily was my first one." When Zubarev, began to speak of the espionage he had committed "for the benefit of Fascist Germany," but Vyshinsky interrupted him: "I request that Inspector Vasiliev, who enlisted Zubarev, be called as a witness." An elderly man was led into the courtroom. He said that his name was Dmitry Nikolaevich Vasiliev, that he was born in 1870, and that he had served as police inspector from 1906 to 1917. He was greeted with a stir of approving whispers and laughter from the audience, and even extracted the semblance of a good-natured smile from Vyshinsky.

Ulrikh asked, "In particular, did you enlist Zubarev?" to which "Inspector Vasiliev" replied, "Zubarev . . . yes." Ulrikh then said, "Tell us in a few words how you did this." Vasiliev recounted how he had recruited Zubarev some thirty years earlier and had gotten a signed pledge from him. "What was the nature of the pledge?" asked Ulrikh. "To the effect that he agreed to supply the police with information. In making the pledge, he said that his pseudonym would be 'Vasily.'" "Did he say that?" asked Ulrikh. Vasiliev readily responded, "Yes. I remember it very well." Vyshinsky interjected, "How is it that you remember him so well? Much time has elapsed since then, and yet you remember this Zubarev quite well." To which Vasiliev replied, "I have not set eyes on him since 1909." Vyshinsky then asked Zubarev, "Do you remember? Was Vasiliev the inspector at that time?" Zubarev was uncertain what he was supposed to say. "Thirty years have elapsed since then and it's hard for me to remember, but I think that is the man . . . I don't deny it." Vyshinsky probed further. "Does he resemble him?" he asked. "Yes," said Zubarev. "He was younger then," Vyshinsky said. "Of course," answered Zubarev. Then Vyshinsky asked, "Did you yourself choose the pseudonym 'Vasily?'" Zubarev replied, "I don't remember whether I adopted it myself, or whether he proposed it; I don't remember, and I wouldn't deny that he gave it to me, or that I chose it myself. But the event occurred."[418]

Stalin's Okhrana file suddenly made its appearance in the guise of the mysterious "secret Rykov file." Yagoda's assistant, Bulanov, testified:

I know from what Yagoda told me that the decision to assassinate Nikolai Ivanovich Yezhov...

Vyshinsky interrupted, "Did you know where Rykov's secret file was kept?" Bulanov immediately replied, "Yagoda had it." Vyshinsky persisted, "The conspiratorial file?" Bulanov replied:

If it was not conspiratorial, Rykov would hardly have sought such a reliable place for it. I will now address the attempt on the life of Nikolai Ivanovich Yezhov. According to Yagoda . . .

Vyshinsky allowed Bulanov to proceed with a fantastic story about vast conspiracies, poisonings, and murders that had been directed by "Enukidze, who was acting on behalf of Trotsky." But Alexei Rykov interrupted:

Bulanov spoke here about my archives, which were located in Yagoda's possession. I should like him to tell us about what was found; where those archives came from, what their contents are, and how he knows about them.

Bulanov answered:

Unfortunately, I have no such information at my disposal . . . when

Yagoda was moving to different premises during the renovation of the building . . . I found a file of documents among some of the things which had been sitting for a long time in the safe. I asked Yagoda about it. He said: "Don't unpack them, these are Rykov's archives."

During the next session, Yagoda described the poisoning of Menzhinsky, Kuibyshev, Gorky, and Gorky's son Peshkov, as well as the murder of Kirov. He said that he had committed these crimes on the "orders of Enukidze." Rykov used the first opportunity to ask:

I have a question to ask Yagoda regarding the archives about which Bulanov spoke.

Yagoda replied, "I had no archives of Rykov." Vyshinsky pursued the issue further. "I have a question to Bulanov. What archives of Rykov's did you say were in Yagoda's keeping?" Bulanov replied:

It was clear that they were personal documents of Alexei Ivanovich Rykov. Yagoda confirmed my opinion, but as to what was there, and how much of it, I have said and say now that I do not know.

Turning to Bulanov, Yagoda said:

Allow me to raise a question. Perhaps you will recall one document, at least, and will say what it was?

Bulanov answered, "Had I remembered, I would already have said it." Yagoda persisted:

Rather strange. He establishes that this was Rykov's archive, but by what documents? Just by name, or what?

Yagoda had the final word:

In any case, even if the archives had really existed, the Rykov archives are a trifle in comparison with the other crimes.[419]

This "trifle" was the essence of all of Stalin's show trials. In the original script, which Stalin had considerably altered, Rykov was accused of having been an

Okhrana agent while Bulanov was to state that "Rykov's Okhrana file" had been found in Menzhinsky's office "during a change of premises." Fragments of this original version survive. "Rykov's secret file" was one such fragment.

As usual, a disproportionately large number of defendants at the "Bukharin show trials" were Jews. Vyshinsky asked defendant Arkady Rosengolts why a Jewish prayer had been found in his pocket. He read translations of eight verses of the Psalms—"Let God arise, let his enemies be scattered . . ." Rosengolts said that his wife, a religious woman, had put it in his pocket for good luck. Vyshinsky "winked to the crowd, which roared with laughter."[420]

The Bukharin show trial came to its predictable end on March 12, 1938. In their final pleas, the defendants demanded punishment for their "heinous crimes." Bukharin delivered his last plea, in which he mentioned "some of the Western European and American intellectuals who do not understand that in our country the enemy has a divided, dual mind." He said that in the Soviet Union, Dostoyevsky's characters were a thing of the remote past, and "such types exist perhaps only on the outskirts of small provincial towns, if even there. On the contrary, such psychology is to be found [in abundance] in Western Europe."[421] Stalin pointed Bukharin's finger at a "false target" far away from himself.[422]

On March 13, 1938, Ulrikh read death sentences to Bukharin, Yagoda, Rykov, and all of the "exposed Okhrana agents." The others received long sentences that none of them survived. The death sentences were carried out immediately. Walter Duranty, the *New York Times* Moscow correspondent, in a book he published in 1942, described Ulrikh as a "hard judge, but a just one."[423] He also stated that the suicide of Gamarnik "proved that he had been engaged in some deal with the Germans."[424] Joseph Davies, the American ambassador to the Soviet Union, in his March 7, 1938, report to Washington, wrote that the show trials offered proof "beyond a reasonable doubt to justify the verdict of guilty of treason."[425] Davies drew laughter in his lectures before American audiences in his reply to questions about a fifth column in Russia; he used to crack the joke, "There aren't any, they shot them all."[426]

Stalin did not destroy all of the documents in his St. Petersburg Okhrana file. In 1941, Stalin for the first time published two Okhrana circular reports, which he had found in his Okhrana file and placed them in the Soviet archives. One report, dated March 7, 1913, mentions Stalin as "having assumed the Party aliases of 'Koba' and 'Vasily.'" The other report, dated April 19, 1913, also mentions these two aliases.[427] The "yet-unidentified Okhrana agent Vasily" whom the 1918 book *Bolsheviki* had listed was finally identified by Stalin himself.

In the summer of 1938, Stalin commissioned two films, *Lenin in October* and *Lenin in 1918*, in which the leading role was assigned neither to Lenin nor Stalin, but to a mysterious "Worker Vasily" who had no last name and appeared larger than life. In the movies, Lenin looked like a babe lost in the woods that had no idea what to do without the wise advice of the "Worker Vasily." Critics were certain that this towering figure represented the wisdom of the masses. The film's story of "Worker Vasily" had a familiar ring: in July 1917, worker Vasily leads Lenin to a makeshift hut in a forest near Petrograd, from where Lenin later escapes to Finland. Actually, it was Stalin who, had led Lenin and Zinoviev to a makeshift hut near the village of Razliv to hide them from the "bloodhounds of the Provisional Government." No one in 1939 was in a position to challenge Stalin's fraudulent version. "Worker Vasily" was Stalin's idealized double. In Stalin's mind, truth and fiction merged in a bewildering tangle. Petrograd worker Emelianov, the owner of this makeshift hut, had been arrested in 1935 along with his wife and their three sons. All of them perished.[428] Krupskaya, who knew Emelianov, died just before "Worker Vasily"" appeared on the screen. Rumors spread that she had been poisoned.[429]

In May 1938, Stalin sent his personal assistant, Lev Mekhlis, and Yezhov's deputy Mikhail Frinovsky to the Far East to "liquidate" the Red Army's "Gamarnik-Bulin gang" and the "Balitsky nest" in the NKVD. Trucks with arrested NKVD and Red Army officers were delivering their human cargo to Khabarovsk prisons. Frinovsky personally shot sixteen top NKVD officers.[430] The chief of the Far Eastern NKVD, Genrikh Lyushkov, was not among the executed officers, but he knew that the "Eremin Letter" and the other forgeries that he had delivered to Golovachev had been fabricated by Stalin, and that sooner or later Stalin would liquidate him as well.

On June 9, 1938, Lyushkov escaped across the Soviet-Manchurian border. A major from a Japanese military-intelligence organization, who was also a linguist, promptly reported to the Japanese Army headquarters in Seoul, Korea, that he had encountered the "escapee of the century." A report about Lyushkov's defection was released on July 1, 1938. By this time, Soviet diplomats had been instructed to insist that the real Lyushkov was still in Russia, and that the one in Tokyo was an "imposter."[431] A July 4, 1938, *New York Times* editorial, titled "Diary of a Japanese Schoolboy," depicted Lyushkov's defection as an "anti-Soviet invention." Richard Sorge, the top Soviet agent in Tokyo, who was posing as a correspondent for a German newspaper, was ordered by Moscow to relate all available information on

Lyushkov.[432]

Lyushkov was very selective in what he told the Japanese. He did not expose Soviet agents in China or Japan.[433] He kept quiet about his own role in the mass purges. Nor did he talk about the deportation of Koreans from the Soviet Far East, which he had directed in December 1937 and for which he was awarded a citation.[434] The Japanese would have had a special interest in this deportation, since Korea was under their occupation. Nor did Lyushkov mention the forged Okhrana documents which Stalin had assigned him to plant in China. He had no desire to discredit the Soviet system, which had elevated him, a common criminal, to one of the top positions in the Soviet secret police. Despite Lyushkov's silence on these matters, there was a report that the Soviet embassy in Tokyo had directed the Japanese Communist Party to assassinate Lyushkov.[435]

After Lyushkov's escape, Marshal Vasily Bliukher, the commander of the Far Eastern forces, was arrested, taken to the Lubyanka, tortured, and shot. Twenty-two NKVD officers were executed, among them Lyushkov's deputy, Grigory Osinin-Vinnitsky, who was declared a Japanese spy.[436] Special troops replaced the frontier guards. They opened artillery fire on Japanese positions across the border. The Japanese responded by attacking the area of Hal Kin Gol and Lake Khasan. There were substantial losses on both sides in the ensuing battles. Stalin ordered Yezhov's deputy Frinovsky to go to a border crossing to capture "a dangerous spy. Frinovsky was arrested and executed for trying to "flee abroad."[437]

Golovachev, the NKVD informer to whom Lyushkov had given the "Eremin Letter" and other forgeries, remained in possession of the material, not knowing what to do with it—his NKVD handlers had been recalled to Moscow and executed.[438] Soon after Lyushkov's defection, Colonel Russianov, from whom Golovachev had supposedly received the "Eremin Letter" and other forgeries, suddenly died. He was fifty-nine years old. Russianov's family suspected that he had either been poisoned or committed suicide. His family wanted to bury him in the Russian Orthodox cemetery and feared that they could be turned away if it were established that the cause of death was suicide by poisoning. His son found a strange package in their home; it contained Okhrana stationery, rubber stamps, and a number of photographs of Stalin, Trotsky, and Malinovsky. He could not explain the package's origin and decided to preserve it. Russianov's family had left Shanghai before the capture of the city by the Chinese Communists, and moved to Australia. In 1956, his son sent the package with the Okhrana paraphernalia still intact to Isaac Don

Levine, the American journalist who was investigating the origin of the "Eremin Letter."[439] In 1941, Golovachev attempted to sell the letter to the Germans. The Germans refused to buy it. [440]

When Alexander Orlov, the chief Soviet intelligence adviser to the government of Spain, went to Paris in the summer of 1937 he met with Pavel Alliluev, the brother of Stalin's late wife Nadezhda. Pavel complained that NKVD agents were following him everywhere. Orlov asked him what was behind the execution of Tukhachevsky and other generals. Alliluev fell silent and then said:

> Alexander, don't ever inquire about the Tukhachevsky affair. Knowing about it is like inhaling poison gas.[441]

A few months later, Orlov read in a Soviet newspaper that "Pavel Alliluev died while carrying out his official duties." Orlov grimly concluded that Stalin had had him murdered.[442] (Ten years later, Stalin would accuse Pavel Alliluev's wife Evgenia of having poisoned her husband.)[443] Orlov himself "inhaled" this "poison gas" in February 1937 when his cousin, Zinovy Katsnelson, told him about the discovery by Stein of Stalin's Okhrana file. Orlov knew that Katsnelson had been executed and that Stein had committed suicide. On July 9, 1938, Orlov received Yezhov's order to return to Moscow.[444] He knew that this would be the end of him and his family. Orlov drove across the border to France, and together with his wife and daughter boarded a ship to Canada and then applied for political asylum in the United States. For fifteen years he and his family lived anonymously in the United States. He believed that American authorities were unable to protect him from the long arm of the NKVD. In 1953, the year of Stalin's death, Orlov wrote a book entitled *The Secret History of Stalin's Crimes*. He hinted therein at the truth behind the execution of Tukhachevsky and other generals:

> I am making this assertion because I know from an absolutely unimpeachable and authoritative source that the case of Marshal Tukhachevsky was tied up with one of Stalin's most horrible secrets which, when disclosed, will throw light on many things that seemed so incomprehensible about Stalin's behavior.[445]

In 1956 Orlov published an article in *Life* magazine, telling what he knew about the Tukhachevsky plot.[446]

Yezhov was removed from the post of NKVD chief in December 1938, and Lavrenty Beria was appointed in his place. Stalin ordered him to destroy "Yezhov's nest." Yezhov was arrested and executed. Stalin exclaimed to Aleksander Yakovlev, a leading airplane designer:

> That scoundrel Yezhov! He finished off some of our finest people. He was utterly rotten. That's why we shot him.[447]

The purge in the Ukraine, where the Tukhachevsky conspiracy had taken root, was directed by Nikita Khrushchev, who in January 1938 was appointed First Secretary of the Ukrainian Party. Khrushchev arrested the entire Ukrainian government, and executed every member of the Ukrainian Politburo.[448]

Soon after the murder of Ignaz Reiss, Stalin ordered the NKVD to assassinate Trotsky.[449] The first attempt on Trotsky's life was made in January 1938, shortly before the murder of Sedov. Trotsky escaped unharmed. Stalin provided detailed instructions to Leonid Eitingon and Gaik Ovakimian, the NKVD resident and Soviet General Consul in New York, to order NKVD agent Ramon Mercader to murder Trotsky by striking him on the head with an "axe wrapped in a wet quilted jacket." Stalin's instruction made no sense—to wear a quilted jacket in the hot Mexican summer weather appeared absurd, but it was impossible to argue with "Ivan Vasilievich." Stalin was reenacting a traumatic event in his life—the murder of his father Vissarion. (In January 1948, he was to order his secret police to murder Solomon Mikhoels by striking him on the head with an "axe wrapped in a wet quilted jacket.")[450]

On August 20, 1940, Mercader came to Trotsky's villa wearing a hat and hugging a black overcoat. Trotsky invited him into his office. Mercader took the axe out of his overcoat and brought it down on Trotsky's head. He planned to kill Trotsky on the spot, and to leave the villa unnoticed. Eitingon was waiting for him in a car parked not far from Trotsky's villa. But Trotsky leapt to his feet and flung everything he could lay his hands on at Mercader. Then he bit Mercader's hand and yanked the axe out of his grip. Trotsky's wife Nataliya and the guards rushed in. Afraid his guards might kill Mercader, Trotsky murmured slowly, "He must not be killed . . . he must talk." Mercader shouted, "They made me do it. They're holding my mother; they will put my mother in jail!"[451] Trotsky died the next day. When Trotsky's death was confirmed, Stalin wrote a *Pravda* article entitled "The Death of an International Spy," declaring that Trotsky "had been finished off by the same terrorists whom he had taught to murder from behind a corner," and that he had "worked for the intelligence services and general staffs of England, France, Germany, and Japan; and organized the villainous murders of Kirov, Kuibyshev, and Gorky; and become the victim of his own intrigues, betrayals, treason, and evil deeds."[452] Stalin murdered not only Trotsky and his sons, but also all of Trotsky's relatives.[453] Ramon Mercader was sentenced by a Mexican court to twenty years in jail. Stalin paid for his silence by arranging for the most comfortable prison conditions possible.[454] In August 1960, Mercader walked out of prison and was greeted by representatives from the Czechoslovakian embassy, who handed him a passport. Mercader lived in Prague until the "Prague Spring" of 1968. He was spirited off to Moscow after the Soviet invasion.[455] The name on his gravestone in a Moscow cemetery was engraved as "Raymond Lopez."[456]

Before his death, Trotsky finally revealed his true feelings about Stalin, writing prophetically:

Stalin seeks to strike not at the ideas of his opponent, but at his skull. . . . With his monstrous trials, Stalin proved much more than he had wanted to; rather, he failed to prove what he had set out to. He merely disclosed his secret laboratory; he forced 150 people to confess to crimes they had never committed. But the totality of these confessions turned into Stalin's own confession.[457]

Trotsky also commented:

Fascism goes from victory to victory and finds its main ally in Stalinism. Terrible military threats knock at the door of the Soviet Union, but Stalin chooses this moment to undermine the army. The time will come when not he, but history, will put him on trial.[458]

Chapter 3

The Stalin-Hitler Alliance
and the "Eastern Question"

By 1939, Stalin knew the names of people who had taken part in the plots to expose and destroy him using his Okhrana file. He learned that many Poles and Jews had played major roles in these plots. Roman Malinovsky, his hated rival in the Okhrana, was a Pole. The Director of the Department of Police, S. P. Beletsky, came from a Russified Polish gentry. The chiefs of the Soviet secret police, Felix Dzerzhinsky and V. P. Menzhinsky, were Poles. Marshal Mikhail Nikolaievich Tukhachevsky traced his ancestry to the Polish gentry.[459] V. A. Balitsky, S. V. Kossior, Stanislav Redens, the NKVD chief in Moscow, and Dzerzhinsky's nephew, were all Poles. Stalin came to feel an intense hatred of Polish people"[460] Stalin ordered executions of the families and relatives of Dzerzhinsky, Menzhinsky, Tukhachevsky, and all four Kossior brothers.

Stalin's lifelong, deep-seated anti-Semitism was further heightened when he learned that in 1929, Rabinovich, a Jew found Stalin's Okhrana file among Dzerzhinsky's papers and that Yakov Blumkin, also a Jew, had attempted to smuggle the file abroad. He also learned that I. L. Stein, a Jew, found the file among Menzhinsky's papers in 1936 and that Zinovy Katsnelson; Generals Y.

B. Gamarnik, Yona Yakir, and B. M. Feldman; and several other Jews had taken part in the Tukhachevsky conspiracy. Soviet intelligence officers Alexander Orlov, Walter Krivitsky, Ignaz Reiss, and Genrikh S. Lyushkov, all of them Jewish, escaped abroad after they learned of the discovery of his Okhrana file. Stalin also nourished deep hatred toward the large number of defendants at the Jewish Show Trials, even though he knew that they had no connections to his Okhrana file. Stalin lived in a state of constant fear that his shameful past would be exposed by his Jewish enemies.

Stalin became obsessed with the idea of destroying not only the individual Poles and Jews whom he had identified as his enemies, but with annihilating all of Poland and its large Jewish population. It might appear incredible that this obsession was at the root of the conflict that led to the Second World War, yet these irrational motives played an important as the source of the conflict. Stalin knew about Hitler's hatred for the Jews and decided to provoke Hitler to attack Poland and convince him to partition the Polish state between Germany and the Soviet Union. He decided to enter into an alliance with Nazi Germany, using Poland as the bait. The Munich agreement to partition Czechoslovakia, signed by the Western democracies with Hitler on September 30, 1938, was interpreted by Stalin as a capitulation by England and France. Munich strengthened both his respect for Hitler and his contempt for the "decadent" European democracies. Shortly after the end of the Munich conference, Assistant Commissar of Foreign Affairs Vladimir Potemkin told Robert Coulondre, the French ambassador to Moscow:

> My friend, what have you done? I don't see any conclusion other than a fourth partition of Poland.[461]

The three partitions of Poland in 1772, 1793, and 1795 by Russia, Austria, and Prussia (Germany) had been part of an intricate arrangement between the three great European powers of the time, who wanted to avoid military conflict among themselves over their claims to the inheritance of the decaying Ottoman Empire (which was retreating from the European continent, North Africa, and the Near East). This rivalry became known to history as the "Eastern Question." The great European powers treated all of Polish territory as an exchangeable commodity with which they could compensate each other to avoid a war. As the result of the three partitions, the Russian Empire absorbed eastern Poland, with its large Ukrainian, Byelorussian, and Jewish populations. But Stalin's scheme of the "fourth partition" of Poland was not motivated by the geopolitical considerations that had been at the heart of the three previous partitions of Poland. Stalin decided to destroy Poland by using Hitler as his "hit man." This scheme was consistent with Stalin's habit of committing a crime by setting up other people to do the dirty work for him.

In his March 10, 1939, speech to the Eighteenth Party Congress, Stalin stated that the British, French, and American press was trying to "incense the Soviet Union against Germany, to poison the atmosphere, and to provoke a conflict when no sensible reasons for such a conflict exist." He warned "warmongers who are accustomed to having others pull chestnuts out of the fire for them." These declarations were received favorably in Berlin.[462] On March 15, 1939, the German army began its occupation of Czechoslovakia. On April 3, Hitler ordered the *Wehrmacht* to prepare for an attack on Poland, and on April 28, he renounced the Polish-German peace treaty. On April 17, 1939, Soviet ambassador to Berlin Alexei Merekalov encouraged the German foreign ministry to start a process of improvement in Soviet-German relations.[463] Commissar of Foreign Affairs Maxim Litvinov was unsuitable for negotiation with Hitler because he was a Jew and was known in Berlin as a supporter of rapprochement with the Western democracies. On May 1, 1939, Litvinov was dismissed and Molotov was appointed in his place. Thirty diplomats on Litvinov's staff were arrested, and only one of them, Evgeny Gnedin (the illegitimate son of Alexander Parvus), survived the torture they were subjected to. (He was to be released after Stalin's death.) From May to August 1939, Lubyanka interrogators were preparing a show trial of the "Litvinov case," but then Stalin decided to call off the trial and keep Litvinov alive for a while.

The Soviet chargé d'affaires in Berlin, Grigory Astakhov, reported that Hitler was pleased by the fact that Molotov was not Jewish. (Schulenburg, the German ambassador in Moscow, was an ardent supporter of improvement in Soviet-German relations and did not report to Hitler that Molotov's wife, Polina Zhemchuzhina, was Jewish). Hitler said that the dismissal of Litvinov was the "decisive factor" in his decision to start negotiations with Stalin.[464] On May 23, 1939, Hitler told top German generals that he intended to attack Poland even if Britain and France came to Poland's defense. The generals objected, saying that Russia might be one of the intervening nations. Hitler replied that Russia would be interested in the destruction of Poland.[465] He did not suspect that the destruction of Poland was Stalin's main motive in improving relations with Germany. The German foreign minister, Joachim von Ribbentrop, predicted that a friendly agreement with Stalin to maintain neutrality in the German-Polish conflict would prevent Britain and France from declaring war on Germany. Hitler set the end of August 1939 as the date for the invasion of Poland. He sent Stalin a personal letter, urging him to have Ribbentrop sign the Non-Aggression Pact by August 23, 1939. When Stalin's positive reply was presented to Hitler, he pounded on the wall with his fists and shouted: "I have the world in my pocket!"[466]

Ribbentrop arrived in Moscow on the 23rd and signed the pact that same evening. The partition of Poland was spelled out in a secret protocol, stating that Poland was to be divided between Germany and the Soviet Union by a line that ran through the middle of the country along the Vistula River. Stalin put his signature on the map on which the line was drawn. (More than fifty years later, the secret protocol, with this map and Stalin's signature, was found in the Soviet Communist Party archive and published.[467]) The protocol also stated that Estonia, Latvia, and Finland were within the Soviet sphere of interest, while Lithuania was relegated to the German sphere. Stalin also expressed his interest in the Bessarabian part of Romania, and the Germans took note of this. A reception and a banquet followed the signing ceremony. "I know how much the German nation loves its Führer," Stalin said in his toast. "I should therefore like to drink to his health." Ribbentrop then toasted Stalin and Molotov.[468] When the German delegation was leaving the Kremlin, Stalin took Ribbentrop's arm and said, "The Soviet government takes the pact very seriously. I can guarantee on my word of honor that the Soviet Union will not betray its partner."[469] On his return to Berlin, Ribbentrop said that being part of Stalin's entourage had made him feel as though he were among his old Nazi comrades. Henry Picker, Hitler's senior stenographer, provided his recollection:

> Stalin, in his conversation with Ribbentrop, did not hide his intention to wait for the moment when the USSR would have enough of its own intelligentsia to completely obliterate the predominant number of Jews in leadership positions—Jews we still value today.[470]

A jubilant Hitler called Ribbentrop the "new Bismarck." Hitler intended to order the German army to march into Poland on August 26, 1939, but on August 25 the British repeated their pledge to come to Poland's defense. Hitler was furious. "What now?" he shouted at the "new Bismarck." He then rescinded the invasion order.[471] The next several days were filled with anxiety for both Hitler and Stalin. Hitler's top-secret memorandum of 1936 had envisioned that the German economy would be able to support a major war in

1940, but he was now risking such a war a year earlier. Stalin, eager to see Hitler crush Poland, was afraid that the threat of a larger war might force Hitler to abandon his plans to attack Poland. The Supreme Soviet ratified the Pact with Germany on August 31, 1939. The next morning, German troops crossed the Polish frontier. "Let us not have another war of flowers," said Hitler, having in mind his previous easy victories in Austria and Czechoslovakia.[472]

Britain and France declared war on Germany on September 3, 1939. On September 6 a Polish request for help arrived in Moscow, but Molotov told the Polish ambassador that the Soviet government had no intention of helping Poland. Outnumbered and lacking in modern equipment, the Polish army was, for all its gallantry, no match for the highly mechanized German divisions. The *Wehrmacht* rolled over Poland, approaching the secretly agreed upon Soviet-German border along the Vistula River. Stalin was aware that, in the eyes of the civilized world, his partnership with Hitler regarding the partition of Poland would be seen as a criminal act. As usual, he was looking for ways to escape responsibility and to create the impression that he had nothing to do with the destruction of the Polish state. "Of course, it's all a game to see who can fool whom," he said. "I know what Hitler's up to. He thinks he's outsmarted me, but it's actually I who has tricked him."[473]

Stalin finally ordered the Red Army to cross the Polish border on September 17, 1939. The Soviet propaganda machine presented the move as an innocent act of extending a "brotherly hand" to the Ukrainian and Byelorussian peoples living in Polish territory. Polish general Mecheslav Smoravinsky ordered his troops not to fight the advancing Soviet units. Soviet planes dropped leaflets with appeals to Polish soldiers to kill their officers and government officials. Many Polish officers were murdered by Soviet troops. Some fifteen thousand Polish officers were taken prisoner and transported to three separate camps in Kozelsk, Starobelsk, and Ostashkovo. Most of the Polish officers were reservists who had been called to active duty at the onset of the war. In December 1939, they were granted permission to send Christmas cards to their families.

Stalin acquired the strange habit of going to the Bolshoi Theater for the performance of Mikhail Glinka's opera *Ivan Susanin*. He never stayed to the end, always leaving abruptly in the middle of the second act after a scene depicting the death of Polish soldiers in a forest near Moscow; an episode that, according to popular tradition, took place in 1613 at the time of the Polish invasion of Russia when Ivan Susanin, a peasant from a village near Moscow, volunteered to lead a detachment of Polish soldiers to Moscow but instead lured them into a dense virgin forest where they all perished. Susanin's heroic deed gave birth to many poems and songs, including a poem by K. F. Ryleev, which Glinka adopted into the libretto for his opera. Stalin avidly watched the scene of the dying Polish soldiers. A large plate with hard-boiled eggs was placed in front of him in his secret box. From time to time he would take an egg and eat it, all the while keeping his eyes fixed on what was taking place on the stage.[474] (In 1898, a Russian psychiatrist, Bekhterev, was assigned by a court to examine a Russian country squire named Shebalin, who was accused of murder. Bekhterev's diagnosis was paranoia and persecution-mania combined with megalomania, and he concluded that the lives of others had no value for Shebalin, who lived in constant fear of assassination. Shebalin's diet consisted mostly of hard-boiled eggs because he thought it was impossible to inject them with poison.[475])

Stalin convened a Politburo meeting on March 5, 1940. He proposed to execute the 14,700 Polish officers being held in camps in Kozelsk, Starobelsk, and Ostashkovo, as well as 11,000 arrested Polish factory owners, landlords, government officials, and priests being held in various prisons in territories that had been incorporated into the Soviet Union. Stalin put his signature on the record of this decision. (This paper was found in October 1992 in the personal archive of M. S. Gorbachev, and published by the Yeltsin government.[476]) The chiefs of the NKVD in the annexed Polish territories were ordered to direct the executions.[477] A special system was instituted in the three camps for the slaying of the Polish officers. The massacre went on for many days. 180,000 Poles were immediately deported to Siberia, and another 1,200,000 were sent there in the course of the next two years.

After the partition of Poland, relations between Stalin and Hitler continued to be good for several months, but signs of trouble later began to appear. The Soviet-German communiqué stated that since the disappearance of Poland from the political map of Europe was a fact of life, there was no need for the continuation of the war, and declared that Britain and France had been the aggressors and were fully responsible for the hostilities. It also stated that the Soviet Union and Germany intended "to engage in mutual consultations in regard to necessary measures" in case the war should continue.[478] Stalin also agreed to a mutual exchange of citizens with Germany. The NKVD handed over to the Gestapo a large number of German refugees, most of them German Jews who had sought safety in the USSR. The agreement included a provision allowing for consultations in the coordination of police measures to combat Polish nationalist agitation. In October 1939, Stalin forced Latvia and

Estonia to sign a "mutual assistance" pact that allowed Soviet bases on their territories. He attempted to coerce Finland into a similar arrangement, but the Finns balked. On November 29, 1939, Stalin accused Finland of shelling the Leningrad area, and the Red Army invaded Finland. Otto Kuusinen, a Finnish Communist whose son was imprisoned in Moscow, was made the head of the newly installed puppet government in Finland.

The Finns put up strong resistance. The Red Army suffered 250,000 casualties: 50,000 dead and 200,000 wounded. The number exceeded that of the entire Finnish Army. The heroic Finnish resistance inspired an outpouring of sympathy from the Western democracies as well as from Germany. Great Britain and France were urgently debating sending military help to the Finns. The Soviet Union was expelled from the League of Nations; and in March 1940, Stalin sued for peace, settling for minor mutual land concessions with Finland. Following the Finnish war and the failure of the Tukhachevsky plot, the impotence of the Red Army, whose officers were being arrested and executed en masse, was painfully evident. Stalin, as usual, did not blame himself. In March 1940 he ordered the NKVD to prepare a new show trial of "not-yet-exposed participants of the Tukhachevsky conspiracy." A new wave of arrests swept the Red Army.[479]

Stalin's show trials made a strong impression on Hitler, convincing him that Stalin was an enemy of "Jewish Bolshevism" and that Stalin's personal dictatorship was quite compatible with German fascism. Hitler openly expressed his admiration for Stalin. He called him "the cunning Caucasian" and stated that Stalin commanded his "unconditional respect" and was "in his own way, just one hell of a fellow! He knows his models, Genghis Khan and the others, very well." Hitler described Stalin as "one of the most extraordinary figures in world history."[480] Hitler also considered Stalin a "worthy rival."[481] He felt that in Stalin he had found a "kindred soul."[482] Stalin, too, considered Hitler a kindred soul, especially because of their shared hatred of the Jews. On this issue, Stalin could not help but envy the openness with which Hitler preached and practiced his anti-Semitism.

Events did not unfold the way the two dictators had planned. On May 10, 1940, Winston Churchill became the prime minister of England. On the same day, Hitler ordered the German army to attack France, the Netherlands, Luxembourg, and Belgium. On May 21, the German army advanced to the English Channel, forcing British troops to escape from Dunkirk. The French army was crushed. On June 10, 1940, Italy declared war on Britain and France. French prime minister Paul Reynaud, who had earlier replaced Daladier, resigned. The new French prime minister, Marshal Pétain, a World War I hero, promptly sued for peace. Britain faced the Germans alone. The fall of France had led Stalin to believe that German victory was near. He promptly ordered the occupation of Estonia, Lithuania, and Latvia, and in July 1940 these Baltic States were "admitted" into the USSR as constituent republics. In late June 1940, Stalin annexed Bessarabia and northern Bukovina, proclaiming this formerly Romanian territory part of the Moldavian Soviet Socialist Republic. Hitler decided not to wait for Stalin to swallow what was left of Romania. In August and September 1940 the German army moved into Romania, and Hitler assigned part of its Transylvanian province to Hungary and the province of Dobrudja to Bulgaria. The dark shadow of the "Eastern Question" fell on German-Soviet relations. Territories that once were part of the Ottoman Empire became bones of contention between Germany and Russia, as had happened in the late eighteenth century in the relations between Prussia, Russia, and Austria.

But by this time Poland had already been partitioned, and parts of it could not be used to satisfy the territorial aspirations of both Stalin and Hitler. In September 1940 the Tripartite Pact of Germany, Italy, and Japan was signed. The purpose of Molotov's visit to Berlin in November 1940 was to reach an agreement with Hitler on the conditions under which the Soviet Union would join the Berlin-Rome-Tokyo Axis. Hitler greeted Molotov warmly on his arrival to Berlin on November 12, 1940. After a few words of welcome, he went into a long presentation of his plans for the division of the world between Germany and her allies. The same day, Ribbentrop told Molotov that the Germany's aspirations were limited to the former German colonies in central Africa, while the interests of Italy were focused on northern and eastern Africa. Ribbentrop suggested that Russia might turn to the south, "in the direction of the Persian Gulf and the Arabian Sea, for a natural outlet to the open water."

Hitler did not mention the Persian Gulf or the Arabian Sea the next day when he spoke of the future partition of the British Empire, suggesting that the Soviet Union should extend its sphere of influence in the direction of India. Hitler declared that according to a Soviet-German oral agreement, the former Austrian territories were to fall within the German sphere of influence.[483] This meant that the Balkan states, which at one time belonged to the Ottoman Empire and were later part of the Austrian Empire, were within the German sphere of interest. Hitler pointed out that the underlying rationale of the secret protocol of the August 1939 Soviet-German Pact was the agreement to restore the territorial possessions of the two empires that he and Stalin had inherited.

Hitler viewed himself as the heir of the old German and Austrian empires. He said that Stalin should restore the Old Russian Empire. It was unavoidable that the two dictators would also inherit the bitter rivalries that had in the past divided these empires over the "Eastern Question."

Hitler was not present at the final discussion, which was conducted in an air raid shelter on the evening of November 13, 1940, during the British bombing of Berlin. Ribbentrop said that the decisive question was whether the Soviet Union was "prepared and in a position to cooperate with us in the great liquidation of the British Empire." He offered the German draft of a new secret protocol, expressing the hope that "an agreement could be reached on possible Soviet aspirations in the direction of British India, if an understanding was also reached between the Soviet Union and the Tripartite Pact."[484] Molotov insisted on Soviet interest in the Near East; in Turkey, Bulgaria, Romania, Hungary, Yugoslavia, and Greece. Ribbentrop asked Molotov to sign another secret protocol with the statement:

> The focal point of the Soviet Union's territorial aspirations would presumably be centered south of the Soviet territory, in the direction of the Indian Ocean.[485]

Molotov said that he could not take a "definite stand" on this question without Stalin's concurrence.[486]

But before the last conversation between Molotov and Ribbentrop on the previous day, November 11, 1940, Ivan Maisky, the Soviet ambassador to Great Britain, reported to Stalin in a coded massage that Germany had lost the air war over England. This message and the British air raid on Berlin led Stalin to believe that Hitler was in a weak position, and that the time was right to extract concessions from him. On November 25, 1940, Stalin sent Hitler a note stating:

> The Soviet Union is prepared to accept the draft of the Four Powers Pact with a modification: that the area south of Batum and Baku, in the general direction of the Persian Gulf, be officially recognized as the center of the Soviet Union's aspirations.[487]

Stalin proposed this idea twice in his note. He also demanded the establishment of a Soviet naval base on the Bosphorus and the Dardanelles, and stated that in case of Turkish resistance, "the Soviet Union agrees to work out and carry through the required military and diplomatic measures."[488] Gustav Hilger, the German foreign ministry's expert on Soviet affairs, wrote:

> The conflicting aims of the partners in the negotiations became so obvious that it was clear even then that there was little hope for the possibility of reaching an understanding.[489]

After his conversation with Molotov on November 12, Hitler told Göring of his decision to crush the Soviet Union.[490] Hitler had not expressed much interest in the Near East prior to November 1940, but by the time of Molotov's visit to Berlin, his strategic thinking had undergone a drastic change: he had decided to make the Near East a zone of German interest. This decision was dictated by the German defeat in the air war over England, which threatened to prolong the conflict. Since Germany had no oil resources of its own, German dependency on oil supplies from abroad became an important factor in Hitler's August 1940 decision to occupy Romania to secure that nation's oil-producing Ploesti fields for Germany. Hitler was also attracted to the vast oil resources of Iran and Iraq, where his agents were enflaming anti-British rebellions and where various organizations sympathetic to Germany were active. Stalin's claims to the "territory south of the Batum-Baku line" (meaning Iran, Iraq, and Palestine) were in direct conflict with Hitler's plans.

Hitler was also driven by his pathological hatred of the Jews. The Jewish population of Palestine appeared to Hitler as a major "Jewish threat." Hitler cultivated pro-German feelings among the Arab nationalists who were antagonized by Britain's efforts to create a "national home" for the Jews in Palestine. In 1939, Arab fanatics in Palestine set up a shadow cabinet under the leadership of Hajj Amin al-Husseini, the Grand Mufti of Jerusalem, who had incited the riots that led to a bloody Jewish pogrom and the Arab rebellion that year. The Grand Mufti openly sided with Hitler and spread hate propaganda about Britain and the Jews. He appealed to Hitler to destroy the Jews in Palestine and free the Muslims from the "the Jewish and British yoke." When the pro-German groups in Palestine were crushed by the British in May 1941, Hajj Amin al-Husseini fled to Germany.[491]

In 1939, the Germans seized control from the Italians of the Arabic-language broadcasting station that had been spreading the anti-Jewish and anti-British propaganda.[492] Hitler viewed all these activities as indications of Germany's favorable prospects in the Near East, and decided that Stalin's claims to this area were not compatible with German interests. He did not answer the Soviet note of November 25, 1940. On December 18, he signed a secret order to the German high command, code-named "Operation Barbarossa," stating: "The German *Wehrmacht* must be prepared to crush Soviet Russia in a quick campaign."[493] The date of the invasion was set for May 15, 1941.

Events in Yugoslavia prevented Hitler from attacking the Soviet Union on May 15 as he had originally planned, because on March 20, Serbian officers, who were opposed to any alliance with Germany, had overthrown the Yugoslav government, which had joined the Axis. Hitler ordered German troops, who had been moving into Poland, to divert into Yugoslavia to suppress the rebellion.[494] This development postponed the invasion of the Soviet Union by more than one month. On April 3, 1941, Churchill informed Stalin of Hitler's intention to invade the Soviet Union.[495] Stalin was receiving similar warnings from various sources, but he shrugged them off as attempts by Great Britain to sow discord between Hitler and himself. A number of alerts of the impending German attack came from Richard Sorge, the Soviet master spy in Japan. Stalin also disregarded Sorge's information. (The Japanese later arrested Sorge, and executed him in 1943.) In the spring of 1940, Stalin unleashed a new wave of arrests of officers, many of them Jewish, whom he suspected of plotting against him. They were forced to sign depositions accusing General K. A. Meretskov, the Deputy Commissar of Defense, of heading this conspiracy. Approximately forty such depositions had been signed by the end of spring 1941. Stalin planned to arrest Meretskov in June and to stage his show trial soon thereafter.[496]

On May 1, 1941, Stalin appeared (as he often had) atop the Lenin mausoleum, reviewing the military parade and civilian demonstration. Next to him stood Beria's assistant, V. G. Dekanozov, the newly appointed ambassador to Germany. On May 6, 1941, Stalin assumed the post of Chairman of the Council of People's Commissars; that is, a position equivalent to that of prime minister. Schulenburg reported to Berlin that, in his opinion, Stalin wanted to correct the recent mistakes of Molotov's foreign policy, which had led to the cooling of Soviet-German relations.[497] On June 18, 1941, the Soviet ambassador to Great Britain, Ivan Maysky, told Stalin of the transfer of 147 German divisions to areas along the Soviet border. Maysky had learned of the transfers from British Foreign Secretary Anthony Eden. Despite this, on the day he left for his annual vacation in the Caucasus, Stalin issued an order to avoid "provocations" along the Soviet-German border. He instructed Molotov to start a diplomatic offensive through Schulenburg to repair ties with Hitler.

At 9 p.m. on June 21, 1941, Molotov met with Schulenburg, who promised to do his best to improve relations between their countries. Early next morning, German troops attacked along the entire Soviet-German border, from the Baltic to the Black Sea. Motorized divisions of the *Wehrmacht* moved rapidly inside Soviet territory, easily breaking the Red Army's resistance and taking a large number of prisoners. Schulenburg returned to Molotov's office early in the morning and read the declaration of war. "I know it is war," said Molotov. "Your aircraft have just bombarded some ten open villages. Did we really deserve that?"[498]

At noon, Soviet radio transmitted Molotov's announcement that, with the sudden attack of the "fascist brigands," the war had begun. For the next ten days, Stalin issued not a single statement to the Soviet people, who expected him to rally them for the defense of the country. War with Germany did not fit into Stalin's plans, and he did not want to part with his cherished vision of an alliance with Hitler. Stalin had the tendency to mistake wishful thinking for reality. He refused to accept the fact that his alliance with Hitler was a thing of the past. He clung to the notion that the attack had been a "provocation" by some undisciplined German units.[499] His attention was fixed on the imaginary plot of General K. A. Meretskov, whom he intended to parade at the planned show trial.

During the first week of war, Stalin refused to see any Politburo members except Beria, with whom he discussed the depositions of Meretskov and other "plotters" in preparation for the planned show trial. But on June 30, 1941, a group of Politburo members went to Stalin, pleading with him to take immediate steps to improve the situation at the front.[500] Stalin appointed himself supreme commander-in-chief and head of the *stavka* (military headquarters). His radio address was tape-recorded in Sochi, and the tape was broadcast several times during July 3, while Stalin was on his way to Moscow. He spoke in a nervous, halting voice with the familiar Georgian accent. His train made frequent stops along the way while the track was being checked for mines. (Stalin chose to travel by train because he was afraid of planes.[501])

Upon his arrival in Moscow, Stalin ordered Beria to force several arrested men to sign depositions stating that Mikhail Kaganovich, the younger brother of Politburo member Lazar Kaganovich, was Hitler's agent and that Hitler had intended to appoint him "vice president of Russia" after German victory. Hitler earlier suggested that after victory over Russia he would entrust the administration of the country to Stalin—under German supervision—because "Stalin was the best man to handle the Russians."[502] Mikhail Kaganovich had been the People's Commissar of the aviation industry before the war. Stalin also accused him of ordering aircraft factories to be built near the border so that the Germans would capture them in the event of war. It was Stalin who had ordered the construction of airplane factories near the German border because he had considered Hitler an ally and did not foresee a war against him. When Stalin informed the Politburo members of the charges against Mikhail Kaganovich, his brother Lazar Kaganovich said, "Well, so what? If it's necessary, arrest him!" Stalin praised Lazar for being a "man of principles." Mikhail Kaganovich was taken to Anastas Mikoyan's office for a face-to-face confrontation with a prisoner who had been ordered to repeat the accusations. Mikhail asked permission to go to the toilet, from where a shot was heard moments later.[503] Stalin's bodyguards shot Mikhail Kaganovich, who was buried at the Novodevichy cemetery, near the grave of Stalin's wife.[504]

The rapid advance of the German army inside the Soviet Union forced Stalin to seek help from the Western democracies. On July 11, 1941, Britain and the Soviet Union signed the "Agreement for Joint Action." It took effect immediately.[505] Among those present at the signing was Maxim Litvinov, the former Commissar of Foreign Affairs, whom Stalin immediately appointed ambassador to the United States. By the end of July, Harry Hopkins, President Roosevelt's special emissary, had arrived in Moscow. Litvinov translated the conversation. Litvinov's sudden reappearance in the Kremlin reminded Hopkins of "a morning coat which had been laid away in mothballs when Russia retreated into isolation from the West, but which had now been brought out, dusted off, and aired as a symbol of changed conditions." Of the Russian leader he said, "Talking to Stalin was like talking to a perfectly coordinated machine." Stalin asked Hopkins to relate to Roosevelt that the Soviet government "would welcome American troops on any part of the Russian front under the command of the Americans."[506]

On July 16, 1941, the Germans captured hundreds of thousands of Red Army soldiers and officers near Vitebsk. Among them was thirty-three-year-old Yakov Dzhugashvili, Stalin's older son by his first wife. German planes dropped leaflets with a photo of Yakov and an appeal to Soviet soldiers to follow his example. When one of the leaflets was brought to Stalin, he ordered the arrest of Yakov's Jewish wife, Yulia Meltser, accusing her of being a German spy and of "tricking Yakov into German hands." Yakov's and Yulia's daughter, Gulia Dzhugashvili, was four years old. Yakov refused to cooperate with the Germans. One of the German interrogators recorded:

Good, clever face of a typical Georgian. Behaved properly. Spoke to his father by phone for the last time before going to the front. Categorically rejected a compromise between capitalism and communism. Did not believe in German final victory.[507]

In the autumn of 1941, Hitler ordered to extend preferred treatment to Yakov.[508] Georgian immigrants in Germany were allowed to visit him, but Yakov refused to cooperate with either them or the Germans. In April 1942 he was transferred to a prisoner-of-war camp near Lubek, where his bunkmate in the barrack was René Blum, son of the former prime minister of France, Léon Blum. Hitler offered Stalin a trade: Yakov for the captured Field Marshal von Paulus, but Stalin sent a reply through Count Bernadotte, the Swedish chairman of the Red Cross, stating, "I do not trade marshals for soldiers." Yakov often felt depressed and refused to eat. He was especially hurt by Stalin's slogan: "There are no prisoners-of-war, only traitors," which was often transmitted over the camp radio. After several attempts at escape, Yakov was transferred to the Sachsenhausen death camp. Ironically, his close friends in the camp were Polish officers who were captured by the Germans in 1939. They, like the British and French officers, were receiving parcels and money transfers from their relatives through the Red Cross, and the Poles received aid from the Polish government in exile in London. Soviet prisoners received nothing. Polish officers allotted Yakov a monthly portion of their parcels of food. On several occasions, he and these officers attempted to escape.[509] On the night of April 14, 1943, a scuffle broke out between Yakov and some British officers, who accused him of not cleaning up after himself. One of them hit Yakov in the face. Yakov ran out of the barrack and threw himself on the electrified barbed wire. A guard on duty fired his gun. Yakov was killed, and his body was burned in the camp crematorium.[510] Upon learning about Yakov's refusal to collaborate with the Germans and his death in a prisoner-of-war camp; Stalin ordered Yakov's wife Yulia released from solitary confinement in Lefortovo prison. Yulia left the prison a cripple, and died shortly thereafter.[511] Their daughter Gulia survived.[512]

William Bullitt, who had been the American ambassador to the Soviet Union in the early 1930s, warned Roosevelt of Stalin's imperialistic claims, which he felt could only be checked if Stalin renounced Soviet territorial acquisitions in Poland, the Baltic States, and Romania. Roosevelt disagreed:

I just have a hunch that Stalin is not that kind of man. Harry says he's not and I think that if I give him everything I possibly can and ask nothing from him in return, noblesse oblige, he won't try to annex anything and will work with me for a world of democracy and peace.[513]

Bullitt replied that when Roosevelt "talked of *noblesse oblige*, he was not speaking of the Duke of Norfolk, but of a Caucasian bandit whose only thought when he got something for nothing was that the other fellow was an ass." Roosevelt was annoyed and ended the conversation by saying, "It is my responsibility, not yours, and I am going to play my hunch."[514]

German tanks broke through Red Army defenses on September 28, 1941, and were rapidly advancing toward Moscow. Stalin requested the landing of some thirty British divisions in the port of Archangel, or their transfer to the Soviet Union through Iran. Churchill had great difficulty rallying even two divisions for the defense of the Middle East. He commented:

> It is almost incredible that the head of the Russian government, with all the advice of their military experts, could have committed him to such absurdities . . . It seemed hopeless to argue with a man thinking in terms of utter unreality.[515]

During a meeting with Stalin on September 30, 1941, Minister of Supply Lord Beaverbrook noticed that Stalin was doodling numerous wolves.[516] He did not know that, for Stalin, the wolf symbolized an "enemy."

At this moment, Stalin's wolves represented the military "plotters," whom he intended to execute. Stalin, however, decided to release some of the accused "plotters" from prison when he realized that they would be more useful to him alive than dead. He ordered the release of General Meretskov, whom he invited to visit him in the Kremlin. When Meretskov entered his office, Stalin took several steps toward him, saying, "Good day, Comrade Meretskov! How do you feel?" People's Commissar of the Defense Industry B. L. Vannikov, a Jew, was expecting execution when he received Stalin's order "to describe in writing your proposals in regard to the development of the production of armaments under the condition of commenced military actions." Vannikov, was released and reinstated to his post. A different fate awaited other arrested military men. Most were evacuated from Moscow on October 15, 1941. On October 18, Stalin ordered the termination of the investigation and the immediate execution of twenty-five "plotters." The wives and children of Gamarnik, Kork, Uborevich, and other Red Army generals were executed in the city of Orel the same day.[517]

Also in October 1941, Stalin ordered Beria to execute Alexander Svanidze, the brother of his first wife, but to spare his life if he asked forgiveness for having fabricated Okhrana documents designed to discredit Stalin. "For what should I ask forgiveness?" Svanidze replied. "I have committed no crime." Following his execution Stalin said, "See how proud he is! He died without asking for forgiveness."[518] The execution of Svanidze was connected with events in far away Shanghai. When German troops reached the suburbs of Moscow in October 1941, M. D. Golovachev thought that Stalin's regime was about to be destroyed, and decided to sell the "Eremin Letter" to the German embassy in Shanghai. On November 26, 1941, a cable with Golovachev's offer was sent to the German foreign office in Berlin. A request for additional information about the origin of the "Eremin Letter" went from Berlin to Shanghai. On January 5, 1942, the German embassy in Shanghai sent a secret cable to Berlin, stating that Golovachev's document "had been hidden at the time by tsarist police officers," and that it had been "smuggled out only in 1934."[519] Gustav Hilger, at that time a specialist in Russian affairs at the German foreign office in Berlin, took part in the discussion of what to do about Golovachev's offer. It was decided not to follow up on this offer because German officials felt that because of the war they would be unable to put the "Eremin Letter" through the "necessary external tests."[520] Stalin knew from the Soviet intelligence reports of Golovachev's attempt to sell the forgery to the Germans, and decided to execute Svanidze, who on Stalin's order had forged the "Eremin Letter."

Richard Sorge, the Soviet master spy in Japan, assured Stalin that the eastern Soviet borders were safe because the Japanese were preparing to attack an American base in the South Pacific. Stalin did not transfer this information to the Americans. He appointed General G. K. Zhukov Commander of the Western Front on October 7, 1941, and ordered him to defend Moscow.[521] Zhukov transferred some 400,000 troops from Siberia and the Far East, and deployed them in Moscow's defense. Because of the arrival of the Siberian reinforcements and the unusually early onset of a bitterly cold winter, for which the German troops were woefully unprepared, the German offensive came to a halt. In November 1941, Soviet troops under the command of Zhukov rolled the German units back from the suburbs of Moscow.

On December 7, 1941, the Japanese attacked Pearl Harbor. General Rodion Malinovsky would command one of the Soviet army corps. General Malinovsky's name was mentioned during a meeting in Stalin's office. Stalin was alarmed and several times asked Khrushchev:

> Who is this Malinovsky? When you return to the front, you'd better keep a
> close watch on him. Check up on all his orders and decisions. Follow his
> every move.

Khrushchev replied, "Very well, Comrade Stalin, I won't let Malinovsky out of
my sight." Khrushchev was puzzled. He did not know that the name
"Malinovsky" reminded Stalin of his Okhrana rival Roman Malinovsky.
Khrushchev wrote in his memoirs:

> When I got back to the front, I had to spy on Malinovsky every hour of
> the day. I had to watch him even when he went to bed to see if he closed
> his eyes and really went to sleep. I did not like having to do this one bit.[522]

Khrushchev added that in General Malinovsky's case, "perhaps the practical
demands of wartime reality compelled Stalin to hold his anger and
suspiciousness in check."[523]

Paradoxically, the war years were the most normal time during Stalin's rule.
For once, the country was fighting real enemies. The threat of defeat forced
Stalin to seek help even from those he most hated, among them the Polish
people. He agreed to allow the formation of a Polish army on Soviet territory.
At the end of July 1941, General Wladislaw Sikorsky, the head of the Polish
government in exile in London, and Ivan Maisky, the Soviet ambassador to
Great Britain, signed an agreement that all Polish citizens and prisoners-of-war
would be released from Soviet camps and jails and allowed to join the Polish
army. The agreement stated that all the Nazi-Soviet treaties of 1939 had "lost
their validity." The existence of the secret protocols detailing the partition of
Poland was not known at the time.

In October 1941, when German troops were threatening Moscow, Beria
summoned Polish general Zygmunt Berling, who had been released from
prison following the Soviet-Polish agreement and was one of the few surviving
Polish officers, to discuss a plan for organizing the Polish Army. General
Berling, said that, according to information he had received, there were many
Polish officers in three camps (Kozelsk, Starobelsk, and Ostashkovo), and they
would be enough to organize the Polish Army. Beria's assistant V. N.
Merkulov dropped an alarming hint: "No, not these. We made a big mistake in
regard to these."[524]

On November 14, Stalin received the Polish ambassador to the Soviet Union, Stanislav Kot, who asked Stalin to "ensure" that all Polish officers and citizens would be released from detention. "Are there Poles not yet released?" asked Stalin, pretending to be surprised. "We have names and lists," said Kot. "Are the lists exact?" asked Stalin. Kot explained that the Polish government knew the names of all the officers taken prisoner by the Soviet army. Stalin pretended to be incredulous. He picked up the telephone. "NKVD?" he said into the receiver. "This is Stalin. Have all the Poles been released from prison?" Stalin waited for a few seconds, as if listening to a reply, and then said, "Because I have the Polish ambassador with me, and he tells me that they haven't all been released." Again, Stalin pretended to be listening for a few moments. Then he put down the receiver and turned to Kot, muttering as though confused, "They say they've been released."[525]

Two weeks later, Ambassador Kot, General Sikorsky, and General Wladislaw Anders, who had been appointed commander of the Polish forces on Soviet soil, asked again for the release of the 15,000 Polish officers who were not in German prisoner-of-war camps and had not returned to their homes in Poland. Stalin feigned extreme surprise. "That's impossible," he said. "They've fled." General Anders asked, "But where could they flee to?" Stalin said, "Well, for instance, to Manchuria," recalling Lyushkov's defection. "It isn't possible that they have all fled," General Anders protested. "They must have been released, only they haven't arrived yet," insisted Stalin. "Please understand that the Soviet government has no reason whatsoever to detain a single Pole."[526]

Stalin used to say about people he had sent to their death:

There is no need to remember the victims, because they were all "odnim mirom mazany" [tarred by the same chrism brush].[527]

The silence of mass graves seemed to assure Stalin that his victims were forgotten. However, the case of the murdered Polish officers began to haunt him soon after the Germans found the secret mass grave in the Katyn Forest near Smolensk, which contained the remains of thousands executed Polish officers. Exhumation began a year later, and the first report regarding the Katyn Massacre of thousands of Polish officers by the NKVD was broadcast on Berlin radio on April 13, 1943. Two days thereafter, Soviet radio accused the Germans of the massacre of Polish officers in the Katyn Forest that, the Soviets insisted, had occurred in the summer of 1941, after the Soviet troops retreated from the area. After the Soviet army recaptured the Katyn area in January 1944, a column of covered trucks delivered wooden boxes containing the bodies of 925 Polish officers from Katyn to the Moscow Institute of Judicial Medicine, where the NKVD manipulated the remains and inserted newspaper articles and forged diaries as "material proof" of Stalin's assertion that the executions had taken place *after* the German occupation of the Smolensk area. The next night these trucks carried the remains back to Katyn. On Stalin's order, a small stone monument was erected at Katyn. The inscription read:

> Here are buried prisoners—officers of the Polish Army, who perished in horrible torment at the hands of German-Fascist occupiers in the fall of 1941.[528]

(After the war, Stalin attempted to include the Katyn massacre in the record of the Nuremberg Nazi War Crimes tribunal; but early in July 1946, the tribunal decided not to list Katyn massacre among the Nazi crimes.)

During the Teheran Conference, which started on November 27, 1943, Stalin suddenly suggested to Roosevelt and Churchill that 50,000 German officers should be executed at the end of the war. Churchill objected:

> The British Parliament and the public will never tolerate mass executions. The Soviets must be under no delusion on this point. I would rather be taken out into the garden and shot here and now than sully my own and my country's honor by such infamy.[529]

But Stalin insisted, saying, "50,000 must be shot. The general staff must go." Roosevelt intervened, jesting, "I have a compromise to propose. Not 50,000, but only 49,000 should be shot." His son Elliott Roosevelt, who was invited to the dinner, said that he agreed with Marshal Stalin's plan and was sure that the United States Army would support it. Churchill, greatly annoyed, left the table, saying that he resented "this intrusion." Stalin followed him, claiming that everything he had said was a "joke."[530]

During the Teheran Conference, Roosevelt was eager to establish a close personal relationship with Stalin, trying to please him by teasing Churchill. Roosevelt later recalled Stalin's reaction to his teasing:

A vague smile passed over Stalin's eyes, and I decided I was on the right track . . . I began to tease Churchill about his Britishness, about John Bull, about his cigars, about his habits . . . I kept it up until Stalin was laughing with me. . . . The ice was broken and we talked like men and brothers.[531]

Sir Alan Brooke, the British Chief of the Imperial General Staff, wrote in his diary:

This conference is over when it has only just begun. Stalin has got the President in his pocket. [532]

Brooke wrote that Stalin intended to bring the Balkans, Turkey, and the entire eastern Mediterranean into the Soviet sphere of influence. What Brooke did not know was that Stalin's disagreement with Hitler over these areas had led to the war between Germany and the Soviet Union. The perennial "Eastern Question," was now threatening relations between Stalin and his Western allies. Churchill was annoyed and saw a threat to British interests in the Roosevelt-Stalin cozy relations.

By the time of the Teheran Conference, Stalin felt confident of victory. The German army had suffered defeat at Stalingrad and had been driven from the Caucasus, which opened the route for the delivery of aid through Iran by her Western allies. On March 6, 1943, Stalin bestowed upon himself the rank of "Marshal of the Soviet Union," and proclaimed him "the greatest strategist of all times and all peoples." In June, Stalin received a report that British and American troops had landed on the shores of Normandy, opening the second front. On June 20, 1944, a group of German officers attempted to assassinate Hitler, hoping that with him out of the way Germany would be able to end the obviously hopeless war. The plotters were executed. Goebbels expressed a hatred toward them that was reminiscent of Vyshinsky's oratory at the Moscow show trials. He stated:

Degenerates to their very bones, blue-blooded to the point of idiocy, nauseatingly corrupt, and cowardly like all nasty creatures—such is the aristocratic clique which the Jew has thrust upon National Socialism . . . We must exterminate this filth, extirpate it root and branch.[533]

The attempt on Hitler's life reminded him of Stalin's mass purge by the military in the years of 1937–38. Hitler stated that the assassination attempt had made him finally realize that in trying Tukhachevsky, Stalin had taken the decisive step toward a successful conclusion of the war. This new interpretation of the Tukhachevsky case inspired Hitler's belief that he had reached the great turning point in the war. "The days of treason are over," he exclaimed. "New and better generals will assume command."[534]

By the end of July, the Soviet army had reached the Vistula River. Stalin ordered General K. K. Rokossovsky not to cross it. He wanted to enable the Germans to crush the underground Polish army, which was fighting under the command of General Tadeusz Bor-Komorovsky. The Polish uprising continued for two agonizing months. When the Germans finally obliterated the Polish resistance, some 15,000 Polish fighters had been killed, and 250,000 inhabitants of Warsaw had met their deaths under the debris of their city. On January 17, 1945, three months after the surrender of General Bor-Komorovsky and his fighters, the Soviet army entered Warsaw. Churchill bitterly complained that the Russians found "little but shattered streets and the unburied dead" there.[535]

In January 1945, when the Soviet army captured Budapest, Stalin received a secret report that a Swedish diplomat, Raoul Wallenberg, who had helped to save a large number of Hungarian Jews, was taken prisoner. A group of American Jews asked the thirty-three-year-old Wallenberg to join the Swedish embassy in Budapest in order to save Jews from death in the Nazi concentration camps. On his arrival in Budapest in July 1944, Wallenberg issued 20,000 Swedish passports to Hungarian Jews and placed thirteen thousand more of them in Swedish-owned houses. Stalin had earlier opposed the Allies' plans to bomb crematoriums in the Nazi concentration camps. He did not want to stop the murder of the Jews.[536] When on January 17, 1945, Soviet troops entered Budapest, V. S. Abakumov, the head of the Soviet counterintelligence agency SMERSH (Death to Spies), arrested Wallenberg. The Swedish foreign ministry received a report informing it that Wallenberg was under Soviet "protection," but later inquiries by the Wallenberg family, the Swedish government, and various Jewish organizations met with denial by Soviet authorities of any knowledge of Wallenberg's fate. Molotov told the Minister of State Security V. S. Abakumov of Stalin's decision to quietly liquidate "this spy." Abakumov ordered the head of the Lubyanka prison hospital, Dr. A. L. Smoltsov, to poison Wallenberg. On July 17, 1947, Smoltsov, reported to Abakumov, stating:

I report that the prisoner Wallenberg, of whom you know, suddenly died at night in his cell, apparently of myocardial infarction. In view of your command to personally observe Wallenberg's condition, I request your instruction as to whom to assign the autopsy.[537]

Smoltsov, returned to his office and wrote:

I personally reported to the minister. His order was to cremate the body without autopsy.[538]

The same day, Abakumov sent a report to the Minister of Foreign Affairs, V. M. Molotov, notifying him about the termination of the "Wallenberg case" in view of his "sudden death."[539] The body was cremated, and the cremation recorded under a secret number by the registrar of the Moscow crematorium.[540]

Churchill did not know about the existence of the secret Soviet-German protocol that detailed the partition of Poland. He agreed to an unspecified percentage of Soviet hegemony over Poland in exchange for Stalin's promise to endorse Britain's control over Hong Kong and the British possessions in the Middle East. (The record of Churchill's negotiations with Stalin in Moscow in October 1944 were made public in 1973 by the British wartime archives, but the section dealing with the "political conversations" between Stalin and Churchill was found in complete disarray, with many documents missing. Officials said they were at loss to explain the papers' disappearance.)[541] The "Eastern Question" and the fate of Poland were again discussed on February 5, 1945, at the Yalta Conference. Stalin declared that the Polish territories that had been taken over by the Soviet Union in September 1939 would not be returned to Poland, but that Poland would be compensated by German Silesia, which was rich in mineral resources. Churchill objected, saying that Poland would not be able to absorb the large German population of Silesia, but Stalin countered, "When our troops come in, the Germans run away." Stalin demanded most of East Prussia with the large city of Königsberg as compensation for the Soviet Union's sufferings during the war. He promised to declare war on Japan within three months of victory over Germany in exchange for several large Soviet territorial acquisitions at Japanese expense: the Kuril Islands, the southern part of Sakhalin Island, access to the port of Dairen, the lease of Port Arthur for use as a Soviet naval base, and joint Sino-Soviet operation of the Manchurian railroads. Roosevelt took it upon himself to secure Marshal Chiang Kai-shek's acceptance of these agreements, which were spelled out in secret protocols signed by Roosevelt and Stalin. Churchill, for the sake of unity, reluctantly added his signature. British foreign secretary Anthony Eden called these secret protocols "a discreditable by-product of the conference."[542]

On April 12, 1945, Stalin learned of Roosevelt's death and sent a letter of condolence to the new American president, Harry S. Truman, describing the late president as a "great statesman of world stature and champion of post-war peace and security."[543] Soon thereafter, Stalin sent a letter to General Dwight D. Eisenhower, asking him to restrain his armies to allow Soviet troops to enter Berlin before the Western Allies, as he explained, "in accordance with the "agreement with Roosevelt and in view of the amount of blood our people have shed." Eisenhower halted his offensive.[544] Stalin's aim was for Soviet forces to capture the German foreign ministry archive to prevent any chance of discovery of the secret protocols, which detailed Stalin's 1939 agreement with Hitler about the partition Poland and the absorption of the Baltic States by the Soviet Union. On April 30, 1945, Hitler and his mistress Eva Braun committed suicide. On May 1, General Hans Krebs reported the deaths of Hitler and Braun to the Soviet headquarters and presented the new German government's offer to start capitulation talks. Zhukov called Stalin, who said, "It's a pity that we couldn't capture Hitler alive. Where is Hitler's body?" Zhukov replied that according to General Krebs, Hitler's body had been burned.[545]

On the morning of May 2, 1945, Soviet troops broke into the courtyard of Hitler's chancellery, where they found two badly burned bodies wrapped in still-smoldering rugs and buried in a shallow grave. The bodies were not completely destroyed because the gasoline that had been splashed on them had been partially absorbed by the freshly dug earth. Hitler's dentist confirmed that the jaw and teeth matched those on Hitler's X-rays.[546] Hitler's body was flown to Moscow for an autopsy, which was performed on May 8, 1945. Soviet deputy foreign minister Vyshinsky came to Berlin the same day, with Stalin's instructions to Zhukov to suppress information about Hitler's death. At a press conference, Zhukov declared:

> The circumstances are very mysterious. We have not identified the body of Hitler. I can say nothing about his fate. He could have flown out of Berlin at the very last moment.[547]

(In 1965, long after Stalin's death, Zhukov stated publicly: "Hitler and Goebbels, seeing no other way out, ended their lives by suicide."[548])

In his statements to the Allies, Stalin insisted that Hitler had fled in a large submarine to Japan; but on other occasions, he mentioned South America as the place from where Hitler continued to threaten the human race. As usual, Stalin pointed at a "false target" to deflect attention from him. Stalin wanted to imply that the Western powers were Hitler's protectors and had inherited Hitler's mantle as the enemies of all mankind. On May 9, 1945, Stalin, standing atop Lenin's mausoleum, reviewed the victory parade being staged by Red Army units. He used this occasion to bestow upon himself the rank of "Generalissimo"; a medal for being the "Hero of the Soviet Union"; and an honorary commendation, the "Order of Victory." In July 1945, Stalin, who was afraid to fly, arrived at the Potsdam Conference in a special train of eleven cars, which included four luxury cars that once had belonged to the Tsar's family and were taken from a museum. Truman invited Stalin to stay for lunch before the start of Potsdam Conference. Fearing poisoning, Stalin said that he could not stay. "You could, if you wanted to," replied Truman. Stalin, persuaded by Truman's bluntness, decided to stay. During lunch, Stalin baffled Truman by insisting that Hitler was alive and hiding somewhere in Spain or Argentina. But the previous day, while waiting for Stalin's arrival, Truman and Churchill had gone on a tour of Berlin ruins. Soviet soldiers had shown them the spot where they had found the severely charred bodies of Hitler and Eva Braun.[549]

The evening before Stalin's arrival, Truman received a report about the successful test of the first atom bomb at the Alamogordo Air Force Base in the New Mexico desert. He passed the news on to Churchill, noting that, in view of America's new weapon, the Soviet entry into the war with Japan would not matter much. Churchill said that this weapon meant a speedy end to the Second World War and perhaps much else besides.[550] They decided to inform Stalin about the bomb. Stalin displayed no interest in it, saying, "That's fine. I hope you make good use of it against the Japanese."[551] In fact, Stalin was not surprised by the news, since Soviet intelligence had been giving him progress reports on America's development of the atom bomb. He tried to downplay the bomb's importance in order to elicit concessions from the Allies. Stalin had a sizable list of demands, all of them related to the "Eastern Question." He wanted to absorb Iran and Libya into the Soviet sphere of interest, and claimed the Soviet right to participate in the administration of Tangier. His most insistent demands were for the establishment of a Soviet naval base in the Bosphorus. Truman and Churchill rejected all of these demands. Churchill realized that Stalin had established tight control over the Eastern European countries, thus breaking their October 1944 agreement. Pointing to the Soviet secret police's reign of terror in these countries, Churchill, in Truman's presence, said, "An iron curtain has descended across the Continent." Stalin retorted, "All fairy tales."552

During the Potsdam Conference, the Labor Party's landslide victory led to the replacement of Churchill with Clement Attlee as British prime minister. Churchill's defeat gave Stalin no advantage, since at this point Truman had assumed the role of guardian of Western interests. Less than a week after Stalin had returned from Potsdam, the first atom bomb was dropped on Hiroshima. On August 6, 1945, Stalin's daughter Svetlana came to the Kuntsevo *dacha* with her three-month-old son, Iosif. No one paid attention to her because all of the Politburo members were absorbed in the news of the Hiroshima bombing. Stalin realized that Japan's surrender was imminent and that he had to enter the war at once if he was to claim his share of the spoils. He declared war on Japan on August 8, and Soviet troops crossed the border into Manchuria. The second atom bomb was dropped on Nagasaki, and Japan's unconditional surrender followed, but Soviet troops continued their advance.

When Soviet troops moved into Manchuria, Genrikh Lyushkov was in the city of Port Arthur, having been sent there from Tokyo as a "consultant on Russian affairs." Fearing capture by the Soviet troops, Lyushkov escaped to the headquarters of the Japanese Kwantung Army in Dairen and demanded to be immediately evacuated to Tokyo. General Yanagito Gendzo, the chief of staff of the Kwantung Army, decided that if Lyushkov refused to commit suicide, he should be shot to prevent his falling into Stalin's hands. At 9 p.m. on August 19, 1945, General Takeoka invited Lyushkov to his office and for two hours tried to convince him to commit suicide. Lyushkov kept refusing and insisting that his escape to Tokyo be arranged. Pretending that he was taking Lyushkov to the Dairen port to locate a suitable boat, General Takeoka led him downstairs into the courtyard. There, he shot Lyushkov in the chest. Lyushkov's body was cremated, and the urn with his ashes was placed in a Buddhist temple in Dairen under the name of a Japanese officer. Lyushkov's urn is still in the Dairen temple.553 General Takeoka recounted the story of Lyushkov's death to Soviet interrogators and later told it to the inmates of a Kolyma prison camp. With Lyushkov's death, Stalin was the only person alive who knew the truth behind the "Eremin Letter."

Winston Churchill was the first to sound the alarm over Stalin's aggressive designs. In a March 5, 1946, speech at Westminster College in Fulton, Missouri, Churchill said:

From Stettin in the Baltic to Trieste in the Adriatic an iron curtain has descended upon the Continent. Behind that line lie all the capitals of the states of Central and Eastern Europe—Warsaw, Berlin, Prague, Vienna, Budapest, Belgrade, Bucharest, and Sofia . . .[554]

Stalin's angry response appeared in an interview in which he compared Churchill with Hitler, calling him "the warmonger of the Third World War."[555] Alice Bacon, a left-wing member of British Parliament, visited Moscow and declared:

> Stalin is a very humane man, a man with a fine sense of humor and a keen intellect.[556]

Lord Montgomery of Alamein recalled in his memoirs that Stalin had once asked him, "Have you seen Lenin?" Baffled by the question, Montgomery answered, "I thought the man was dead." Stalin agreed, "So he is. But all the same, you ought to go and see him in the mausoleum in Red Square." Montgomery wrote that Lenin looked to him "pretty waxen and yellow." He also recalled that Stalin looked much older than he had two years earlier, when they had met at the Potsdam Conference.[557]

When the British Labor government announced its decision to withdraw its assistance to Greece, Stalin instigated a civil war there. He wanted to absorb Greece into the Soviet sphere of interest and force Turkey to acquiesce to the establishment of a Soviet military base in the Bosphorus. On March 12, 1947, President Truman declared America's intention to take "immediate and resolute action" in support of any nation resisting Communist aggression. In a speech proclaiming what became known as the "Truman Doctrine," Truman stated:

> I believe that it *must* be the policy of the United States to support free peoples who are resisting attempted subjugation by armed minorities or outside pressures. I believe that we *must* assist free peoples to work out their own destinies in their own way.[558]

In July 1947 Stalin rejected the Marshall Plan, which was aimed at pressing forward the peaceful economic development of all countries ravaged by war. The Cold War had started. Yugoslav Politburo member Milovan Djilas visited Stalin in January 1948. He was invited to Kuntsevo *dacha* for dinner. Djilas noticed that Stalin had aged. He was surprised that Stalin laughed at the stupid jokes being cracked by Politburo members. At the end of the dinner Stalin proposed a toast: "To the memory of Vladimir Ilyich [Lenin], our leader, our teacher, our all!" Djilas was wondering whether Stalin was being serious or joking. During the dinner Stalin asked Djilas whether there were many Jews in the Yugoslav Politburo, noting that there were none in the Soviet Politburo. He suddenly shouted at Djilas: "You are an anti-Semite, an anti-Semite!" Then Stalin turned on a record player and tried to dance a Caucasian *lizginka*, but soon stopped, saying, "Age has crept up on me and I'm already an old man!" Politburo members began to chant, "No, no, nonsense. You look fine. You're holding up marvelously." As the guests were about to leave, Stalin played a loud, cacophonous record of wolves yowling, barking, and howling. He kept laughing until he noticed that Djilas was baffled. "Well, still, it's clever, devilishly clever," said Stalin.[559] Djilas did not realize that for Stalin the wolves represented the Jews. At the time of Djilas's visit, Stalin was already planning the mass deportation of Jews, a scheme that, had he lived, would have rivaled the Holocaust.

Chapter 4

"Murderers in White Gowns"

Shortly after Ribbentrop's visit to Moscow in August 1939, Stalin told A. M. Kollontai, the Soviet ambassador to Sweden:

> Zionism strives for world domination; it will take revenge for all our successes and achievements . . . international Zionism with all its power will strive to destroy our union so that Russia would never recover.[560]

Both Hitler and Stalin believed in the myth of a "Jewish conspiracy for world domination." They both accepted the *Protocols of the Elders of Zion* as the proof of such conspiracy. This notorious canard was a forgery, which Stalin's Okhrana handler I. P. Vasiliev had promoted at the turn of the century. Stalin ordered a Russian translation of Hitler's *Mein Kampf*, arranging for all of the Fuhrer's anti-Jewish ravings to be distributed amongst the Soviet officials.[561] However, when Hitler's army attacked the Soviet Union, Stalin decided to form an alliance with the Jews.[562]

On August 24, 1941, he ordered the formation of the "Jewish Anti-Fascist Committee" (JAFC).[563] Initially, Stalin intended to make the JAFC an international Jewish organization with the aim of mobilizing Jewish worldwide support for the Soviet war effort, especially in the United States. He believed that the Jews had great political and financial power, and would use it to help Soviet Union.[564] He ordered Beria to release from prison two prominent Polish Jews, Henryk Erlich and Victor Alter, who, as leaders of the Polish Jewish Bund, were arrested in the Soviet-occupied part of Poland in September 1939. They were awaiting execution as "spies." Their death sentences were annulled, and on September 24, 1941, they appealed to Polish Jews to enlist in the Polish army, which was being organized in the USSR.

Meanwhile, Stanislaw Kot, the Polish ambassador in Moscow, was trying to find out what was happening to the fifteen thousand Polish officers held in Soviet prisoners-of-war camps. Among these officers were many Polish Jews. The Polish government-in-exile in London, through Ambassador Kot, asked Erlich and Alter to help locate the missing officers. When in October 1941 the German Army advanced close to the Moscow suburbs, Erlich and Alter, were evacuated to Kuibyshev (formerly Samara) and lodged in a hotel. They kept asking what had happened to the Polish officers. In the privacy of their rooms, they discussed what could have happened to them. Their conversations were recorded and reported to Stalin. On December 3, 1941, NKVD Colonel L. F. Raikhman, a Jew, served them with warrants for their arrests, signed by Beria. They were incarcerated in solitary cells numbers 41 and 42 of the NKVD Internal Prison in Kuibyshev. On April 13, 1943, German radio reported the discovery of thousands of executed Polish officers in the Katyn Forest. The broadcast stated, "Jewish commissars murdered the Polish officers." On May 14, 1942, Erlich, sixty years old at the time, committed suicide in his cell by hanging himself from the window bars. Victor Alter was executed on February 17, 1943. NKVD Major S. I. Ogoltsov reported Alter's execution to Beria's deputy, V. N. Merkulov, stating:

> All documents and notes relating to the arrested number 41 have been destroyed, and his belongings burned.[565]

American Jewish trade union leaders David Dubinsky and U. Green inquired about the fate of Erlich and Alter. The Soviet report put an end to such queries by announcing:

> In October and November 1941, Erlich and Alter, waged systematically treasonous activities, appealing to the troops to stop bloodletting and to generate peace with fascist Germany immediately. . . . By the decision of the Military Collegium of the Supreme Court of the USSR, dated December 23, 1941, they were executed by firing squad.[566]

Stalin abandoned the notion of making the JAFC an "international" organization and appointed Solomon Mikhoels the Chairman of JAFC. Mikhoels traveled to the United States where he met in New York with the Zionist leader Dr. Chaim Weizman, the future President of Israel. When Weizman and Mikhoels were alone for a few moments, Weizman asked in Yiddish, "How do the Jews fare in Russia?" Mikhoels, looking around fearfully and raising his hands to Heaven, whispered in horror, "Gevalt!" Weizman recorded this episode in his diary.[567] Palestinian Jews read the reports about Mikhoels' fundraising in the United States and his appeal found an enthusiastic response in the Jewish community in Palestine, which sent money and medical supplies to the Soviet Union. Stalin became interested in the Palestine Jews and sent a number of agents to explore the possibility of using the strong pro-Soviet sentiment in the Palestine Jewish community to advance his plan of turning the "progressive nature and socialist economy" of the Jewish community there to Soviet advantage. Stalin decided to support the future Jewish state, hoping to turn it into a Soviet satellite with the help of the communist and other leftist parties in Palestine. He was impressed with the struggle of the Palestinian Jews against the British, who had prevented Jewish immigration from the camps for displaced persons in Germany and other European countries.[568] Early in 1946, the resident of Soviet intelligence in London, Viktor Kukin, told Mordechai Oren, one of the leaders of the Jewish leftist party MAPAM, that a "socialist" Jewish state would have Soviet support if it followed a pro-Soviet policy in international relations. "We are going to help you," said Kukin.[569]

Stalin believed that he would be able to expand the Soviet sphere of influence in the Middle East by converting Palestine into a Soviet satellite. His 1939 alliance with Hitler had failed to achieve this goal of expanding the Soviet sphere of influence "to the south of the Baku-Batum line, in the general direction of the Persian Gulf." He hoped to achieve the same goal in a partnership with the leftist Jews in Palestine. The "Eastern Question" had emerged again in Stalin's scheme to dominate the Middle East. Stalin's scheme was born out of his profound contempt for leftist Jews like Trotsky, Zinoviev, Kamenev, and others, whom Stalin had manipulated and then destroyed. Stalin intended to create not a Jewish, but an "Arab-Jewish socialist state" similar to the "Popular Democracies" that he was establishing in Eastern Europe. At the same time, he planned to unleash a Jewish pogrom in the Soviet Empire. These two policies formed a bizarre contradictory mix during the last years of Stalin's life when his hatred of the Jews exploded precisely at the time when he actively pursued the policy of support for the State of Israel.

Two representatives from the Soviet embassy in Ankara, Mikhailov, the First Secretary, and Petrenko, the Press Secretary there, were the first of Stalin's emissaries to arrive in Palestine. They established contacts with leftist Jews, who bragged about their "Zionist-Socialist undertaking in the land of Israel."[570] The next to arrive was Polish-Jewish journalist and Soviet agent Samuel Volkovich, who promoted pro-Soviet policy "in view of Moscow's future leading role in the international scene after the war."[571] At the end of 1942, a "Soviet trade representative" arrived in Palestine and inquired about the strength of *Hagana* (the underground Jewish army in Palestine). Hagana's second-in-command, Israel Bar-Yehuda, revealed to him that Hagana had some 90,000 soldiers.[572] Baroyan, the head of the Soviet Red Cross in Iran, informed the delegation of the pro-Soviet "Victory League " in Palestine that "a new era in Soviet relations with the Zionists" was about to begin.[573] In October 1943, Ivan Maisky, the Soviet ambassador to London, visited Palestine and reported to Stalin that a future Jewish state had "socialist potential." Harold Lasky, a prominent left-wing member of British Parliament, read Maisky's report and told David Ben-Gurion, the future prime minister of Israel, that this report made him an "ardent Zionist."[574]

The British Labor government ordered the blockade of the coast of Palestine, which was under British mandate, to prevent the immigration of Holocaust survivors from war-ravaged Europe. The Palestinian Arabs insisted upon the blockade.[575] It was this Jewish-Arab conflict which Roosevelt had in mind when, at the end of the Teheran Conference in 1943, he told Stalin that he intended "to review the entire Palestine question with the King of Saudi Arabia." Stalin then said:

> The Jewish problem has been extremely difficult. The Soviet Union tried to establish a national home for the Jews, but they had stayed there only two or three years before returning to the cities. The Jews are natural traders, only small groups of them were willing to settle in agricultural areas.[576]

By "a national home for the Jews," Stalin meant his pet project, the "Jewish Autonomous Area of Biro-Bidzhan" in the far eastern sector of Siberia. Before that, in 1923, he promoted the "Jewish Crimean Autonomous Republic." However, in 1944, after Stalin had ordered the mass deportation of all Crimean Tartars to Siberia and central Asia, he decided to blame the Jews for this crime.

He instructed Solomon Lozovsky, the Chairman of the Soviet Information Bureau, to suggest the idea of "Crimea for the Jews" to members of the JAFC, and to tell them to write a petition, addressed to Stalin, suggesting this slogan. This idea first originated in Stalin's mind early in 1923, when he decided to "bribe" Zinoviev and Kamenev, at the time his Jewish partners in the "Triumvirate" they had formed against Lenin and Trotsky. Three years later, after he had defeated Zinoviev, Kamenev, and Trotsky, he decided to create a "Jewish Autonomous Area of Biro-Bidzhan" in the far eastern region of Siberia. On February 15, 1944, Lozovsky told Solomon Mikhoels, Sakhno Epstein, and Izhak Fefer to send Stalin a letter proposing the creation of a "Jewish Crimean Autonomous Republic." Rumor of this proposal briefly circulated among the Jews in the camps for displaced persons in European counties. Stalin soon dropped the idea, but he did not forget it.

On October 12, 1946, Stalin ordered the MGB to send a report to the Council of Ministers entitled "On the Nationalistic Manifestations of Some Members of the Jewish Anti-Fascist Committee," accusing them of plotting to create an "anti-Soviet base in Crimea." On November 26, 1946, M. A. Suslov, a Secretary of the Central Committee and its ideological watchdog, sent a similar report to Stalin, in whose mind the scenario for a "Crimean case" had already crystallized.[577] At the end of November 1947, Solomon Mikhoels delivered a speech at the Polytechnic Museum in Moscow. He stated that Andrey Gromyko, the Soviet representative to the United Nations, had declared Soviet support for the creation of a Jewish state in Palestine and thus "pointed out the road to the land of Israel." Stalin ordered the arrest of anyone who had any contacts with Mikhoels.[578] I. I. Goldstein, an economist, was arrested on December 19, 1947; as was Z. G. Grinberg, a literary critic, arrested on December 28, 1947. On January 10, 1948, Minister of State Security V. S. Abakumov gave Stalin the depositions of Goldstein and Grinberg, who had "confessed" that Mikhoels was an "American and Zionist agent."[579] Stalin summoned the Politburo members and, choking with rage, shouted that Mikhoels was a traitor who "must be struck on the head with an axe wrapped up in a wet *telogreika* [quilted cotton jacket] and run over by a truck."[580] The Politburo members were puzzled by Stalin's bizarre instructions. They did not know that Stalin was reenacting two earlier murders: the murder of his father Vissarion in 1906 by Kamo, who had used an axe wrapped in a rain-soaked quilted jacket; and the murder, on Stalin's order, of Kamo, who in 1922 was run over by a truck. Immediately after this meeting, Stalin ordered Abakumov to "liquidate Mikhoels." In his deposition, dated April 2, 1953, Abakumov wrote:

> As I recall, the head of the Soviet government, I. V. Stalin, gave me an
> urgent order: to organize immediately the liquidation of Mikhoels by MGB
> USSR personnel, assigning it to special persons."[581]

Abakumov further revealed that he had assigned MGB officers Shubnikov and
Ogoltsov to carry out the assassination of Mikhoels and to make the murder
look like a car accident. Abakumov ordered Lavrenty Tsanava, the Minister of
State Security of Byelorussia and a nephew of Beria, to take part in the murder
of Mikhoels.[582]

Mikhoels and his companion, literary critic and MGB agent V. Golubov-
Potapov, were driven to Tsanava's *dacha* outside of Minsk. At midnight, their
mutilated bodies were taken a deserted snow-covered street and dumped there.
Then the bodies were run over by a truck. The next morning their corpses
were found by passers-by. On the evening of Mikhoels's murder, Stalin's
daughter Svetlana Allilueva visited her father. As she walked into his office, the
telephone rang. Stalin listened and then quietly, as if he were making a
suggestion, said, "Well, it's an automobile accident." He hung up and greeted
Svetlana. After a while he said, "Mikhoels was killed in an automobile
accident." Svetlana realized that her father had received the report of
Mikhoels's murder, and invented the automobile accident to cover up the
crime. "I knew my father's obsession with 'Zionist' plots around every corner
only too well," she was to recall.[583] The newspapers reported that Mikhoels and
Golubov-Potapov, had died in a car accident. Mikhoels's body was placed on
the stage of the Moscow Jewish Theater. Deep wounds left by the axe blows
were clearly visible despite the heavy makeup. A large crowd gathered inside
and outside the theater. Although Mikhoels was buried with full official
honors, the rumor spread that MGB agents had murdered him.[584]

Several of Stalin's relatives had been arrested shortly before the murder of
Mikhoels. Among them were Anna Redens, the sister of Stalin's second wife
Nadezhda Allilueva; and Olga Allilueva, the widow of Nadezhda's brother
Pavel Alliluev. Anna's husband Stanislav Redens had been executed in 1938.
Pavel Alliluev's sudden death was reported that same year. Pavel's wife Olga
remarried, and her second husband, a Jew, was arrested with her. Stalin
explained to his daughter Svetlana the reason for her aunts': arrests "They
knew too much. They blabbed a lot. It played into the hands of our
enemies."[585] Other arrestees include Lev Tumerman and his wife Lidia

Shatunovskaya, the Jewish neighbors of Olga Allilueva. Initially all of them were accused of taking part in an anti-Soviet conspiracy headed by "Zionist and American agent Mikhoels," but soon after the murder of Mikhoels their interrogation records were suddenly rewritten, and the name of Mikhoels removed. A few months later, the MGB Special Council sentenced all the defendants to long prison terms in the Vladimir Central Prison.[586] Soon after Mikhoels's murder, Stalin ordered one of his agents to poison Sakhno Epstein, the secretary of the JAFC. This agent ordered two glasses of tea and then spoke with Epstein for a few minutes. Leaving the office, he announced that Epstein had died of a heart attack.[587] The members of the JAFC were arrested one by one and accused of plotting to turn the Crimean peninsula into an "American-Zionist base for an attack on the Soviet Union."[588]

When the creation of the State of Israel was proclaimed on May 14, 1948, Soviet and American recognition followed almost immediately. After the armies of seven Arab countries attacked Israel, Stalin ordered his agents to supply Israel with weapons. The Communist coup in Czechoslovakia in February 1948 led to the murder of Czech foreign minister Jan Masaryk, whose body was found in the courtyard of the Foreign Ministry with a bullet hole behind his ear, indicating that he had been shot and thrown out of a window.[589] Many Israeli Jews were disturbed by recent events: the conflict between Stalin and the president of Yugoslavia, Marshal Josip Tito, in the summer of 1948; the Soviet blockade of Berlin the same year; and the problems with the "Popular Democracies" that Stalin had installed in Poland and in other East European countries. Israeli President Chaim Weizman opposed the Jewish leftists, who worshiped Stalin. Prime Minister David Ben-Gurion had no illusions. In 1938, he had protested against the Moscow show trials, calling Stalin a *Kham ha-Gruzini* (coarse Georgian bully).[590]

Stalin planned to replace Ben-Gurion with Moshe Sneh, the second-in-command of *Hagana*, who was an effective public speaker and who had fiercely pro-Soviet views. "Sneh headed the intelligence service of MAPAM (a left-wing Israeli Party), and reported to the Soviet MGB residents about infiltration into the Communist Party of Israel by Israeli intelligence."[591] In 1946, Hagana's intelligence agents spotted Sneh secretly boarding a Soviet plane at the Teheran airport, from where he flew to Moscow. He was removed from the Hagana command. Later he joined the Communist party.[592] Chaim Weizman, the first president of Israel, noticed Sneh during a visit to the Soviet embassy in Tel-Aviv, and, pointing him out to his aides, said in Yiddish, "*Unzerer Azefel* [our little Azef], the infamous agent-provocateur of the Tsarist *Okhrana*."[593] The leader of the Israeli Communist Party, Samuel Mikunis, said, "In 1948, our party advocated the creation of an Arab-Jewish socialist state in Palestine."[594] Stalin entertained the idea of building a canal through the Negev desert to connect the Mediterranean and Red Seas.[595] But according to the United Nations resolution to partition Palestine, Negev would have been allotted to the proposed Arab State. On Stalin's instruction, Semyon K. Tsarapkin, a Soviet representative in the UN, told Abba Eban, the Israeli UN delegate, that the Israeli army should occupy Negev and "plant some trees and bushes, and settle some people so that everyone could see that Jews live there."[596] Count Bernadotte, a Swedish diplomat who had been appointed UN mediator in the Arab-Israeli conflict, insisted on Negev being retained by the Arabs. On September 17, 1948, Bernadotte was assassinated by terrorists of the extreme Jewish leftist group *Lehi*, which maintained close contact with Soviet intelligence officers, who had approved of the assassination. The Soviet explanation for the assassination was: "Bernadotte was murdered by the terrorists because he attempted to exclude Negev from the borders of the Israeli territory."[597] The Lehi terrorists murdered Bernadotte because he supported the "internationalization of Jerusalem," an idea unacceptable even to leftist Jews.[598] Because Stalin intended to build a canal to the Red See he, shortly before the Arab-Israeli armistice agreement of 1949 was signed, ordered Semyon Tsarapkin to instruct Israeli foreign minister Moshe Sharet to have the Israeli army occupy a part of the Red Sea coast. An Israeli motorized column seized a stretch of land on which Israel later built the port of Eilat. A British Army unit landed in the nearby harbor, where the Jordanian port of Aqaba is now located. With these two military operations, the first Arab-Israeli War came to an end.[599]

In September 1948, Israeli ambassador Golda Meir arrived in Moscow. A large crowd of Jews greeted her outside the Moscow central synagogue. An elderly Jew, Abram Goldman, dropped to his knees and kissed her skirt as she and her daughter passed by him. An MGB agent recorded this scene in a photo, which was made a part of "Zionist Goldman's case" when this old man was arrested a couple of years later.[600] Another photograph was taken by David Khavkin, a Moscow Jew, who stood on a balcony overlooking the crowd, in the midst of which was Golda Meir. This photo was passed from person to person and wound up in many MGB "Zionist cases," including Khavkin's case. Eventually Khavkin brought the negative to Israel, where it was reproduced on ten-shekel banknotes (which are no longer in circulation). Khavkin's slogan was "People, don't be afraid!" (These are words from a song by his beloved bard Alexander Galich.)[601] Vitaly Svechinsky wrote, "Galich gave all his life to the Jewish national struggle."[602]

Molotov's wife, Polina Zhemchuzhina, said a few words in Yiddish to Golda Meir at a reception in the Kremlin. Stalin noticed this and ordered Zhemchuzhina, arrested. At the beginning of November 1948, Suslov summoned all the members of the JAFC to his office and said:

> The time to act has arrived. In the opinion of the Central Committee, all the Jews living in the territory of the Soviet Union must be resettled to the Jewish Autonomous Region in Biro-Bidzhan.[603]

Yiddish poet Peretz Markish objected, stating, "I cannot stab my people in the back."[604] On November 20, 1948, Stalin submitted Resolution 81 to the Politburo. It read:

> The Bureau of the Council of Ministers of the USSR orders the Ministry of State Security of the USSR to liquidate the Jewish Anti-Fascist Committee. In connection with this decision, the newspapers of this committee must be closed and the files confiscated. For the time being, do not arrest anybody.[605]

On January 13, 1949, the first anniversary of the murder of Mikhoels, Malenkov summoned Lozovsky and demanded that he confess his role in the conspiracy to separate the Crimea from the Soviet Union and turn it into an "American and Zionist base." Malenkov confronted Lozovsky with the "criminal evidence," the letter, dated February 15, 1944, signed by Mikhoels, Epstein, and Fefer, in which they proposed the idea of creating a "Jewish Autonomous Republic in the Crimea." On January 18, 1949, Lozovsky was expelled from the Party. He was arrested eight days later. By then, all the other members of the JAFC had also been arrested.[606] The idea of creating a "Jewish Autonomous Republic in Crimea" was Stalin's monstrous provocation. As usual, Stalin projected his own ideas onto the "false target," accusing the Jews of what he himself was guilty.

On December 30, 1949, all the Jews living in the towns of Kuntsevo and Davydkovo, which were close to Stalin's dacha, were evicted. Having learned that "the Jews were being exiled," their Russian neighbors helped themselves to the belongings of the expelled Jewish residents.[607]At the same time, Stalin started a campaign against "cosmopolitans, rootless parasites, people without kith and kin, and wanderers without passports," whose obviously Jewish names were supplied in parentheses in newspaper articles. The mass arrests of "cosmopolitan, Jewish bourgeois nationalists and Zionists" were unleashed amidst the celebration in the Soviet press of Stalin's seventieth birthday on December 21, 1949. Gifts from all over the world were placed in a special museum. The Jewish tailors of New York's garment district donated a fur coat to Stalin. Prominent writer Leonid Leonov predicted in a *Pravda* article that the new calendar would begin not with the birth of Christ, but with Stalin's birthday, which would soon be celebrated by people all over the world.

On May 25, 1950, the North Korean communists attacked the Republic of South Korea. Stalin was outraged when the Israeli delegation voted with the United States for the UN resolution, condemning the aggression. President Truman ordered American troops to land on the Korean peninsula. The Soviet press kept silent about the retreat of the North Korean troops. Stalin realized that his attempt to use Israel as a Soviet satellite in the Middle East had suffered defeat. His hatred of the Jews was further enflamed. In May 1950, he told A. I. Likhachev, the director of the Automobile Factory in Moscow, that the Jewish engineers working there were involved in sabotage. Likhachev told one of his assistants, Georgy Meerson, "Take my advice, Georgy, quit your job at once. Otherwise, I will have to fire you in order to save you. Don't ask questions."[608] Meerson was the only one to survive; all the other Jewish factory engineers were arrested and secretly executed. The guards unleashed their dogs and ordered them to run. The chief engineer, Edinov, died first. Weakened by torture, he could not run.[609] Stalin's daughter Svetlana wrote that her father would "express his hatred of the Jews openly; he started doing so only later, after the war."[610] Svetlana's personal life was affected. Stalin exiled her first love, the screenwriter Alexei Kapler, a Jew, and refused to meet her Jewish husband, Grigory Moroz. Khrushchev wrote that during the last five "crazy" years of his life, Stalin "couldn't keep his anti-Semitism hidden."[611]

Israeli leaders besieged Soviet representatives with appeals to allow Soviet Jews to go to Israel. In conversation with Israeli leftists, a Soviet embassy official, Fedorin, said:

> The emigration is not a big problem. We are not against it. The big problem is the policy of your state, and whether or not you would allow Israel to drift into the American sphere of influence. The decisive questions are: How do you see the role of the Soviet Union in this region? What stand would Israel take in the Big Power conflict?[612]

He slightly paraphrased Stalin's maxim, "Who is not with me, is against me."[613] Stalin's anti-Semitism affected the behavior of the staff of the Soviet embassy in Israel. Before their departure from Moscow, Molotov instructed them:

> You must remember that the Jews are a nation with worldwide ties, especially in some important countries, and because of this, you must always be vigilant.[614]

Soviet intelligence agents forbid their Israeli informers to address them as "comrades," which often made Israeli admirers of Stalin feel uneasy and estranged.[615]

During the summer of 1950, when the Korean War was raging, *Pravda* published Stalin's "Questions of Linguistics," an article which attacked the prominent Soviet linguist, the academician Niko Marr, who died sixteen years earlier, in 1934. Stalin became interested in "linguistics" by accident, when he spotted a brief entry under "Georgian Language" in the *Jewish Encyclopedia*, sixteen volumes of which were published in 1913. MGB agents used to confiscate these volumes during searches in the homes of many of the arrested Jews. The entry under "Georgian Language" stated that a young linguist, Niko Marr, in an article in 1896 in a 1907 pamphlet in the Georgian journal *Iveria,* had postulated a theory on the Semitic origin of the Georgian language.[616] Marr cited the word *Iveria* (the ancient and poetic name for Georgia in the Old Georgian language) as partial proof of the Semitic origin of the Georgian language. In 1949, Stalin ordered the Georgian magazine *Iveria* renamed *Sakartvelo,* which means "Georgia" in the contemporary Georgian language. Stalin even purged the word *Iveria* from his own childhood poem. Marr's disciples were fired from their jobs, many were arrested, their dissertations proscribed their lives and careers ruined. Marr's many disciples were not even aware that in his youth he had postulated his theory of the Semitic origin of the Georgian language. Stalin found Marr's theory most offensive.[617] For Stalin the most insulting implication of this theory was that the Georgians were Semites and were "related" to the Jews.[618] Stalin ordered the chief of his secretariat, A. N. Poskrebyshev, to find pre-revolutionary publications on linguistics.[619] Stalin never revealed the real reason why he had attacked Marr. For him, Marr's crime was unspeakable.

Late in 1951, Stalin invited his personal physician, Professor V. N. Vinogradov, for a regular checkup. During the examination, Stalin said that several Kremlin doctors had poisoned Politburo members A. S. Shcherbakov and A. A. Zhdanov. Vinogradov knew these doctors well and said that he had absolute trust in their honesty and professional competence. He advised Stalin to rest more and to work less. To Stalin this advice had a familiar ring. Three decades earlier, he plotted to hasten Lenin's death and, pretending to worry about Lenin's health, advised him to work less. Stalin immediately suspected Vinogradov and ordered his arrest. Vinogradov, who came from a family of prominent Russian physicians, was accused along with a group of Jewish Kremlin doctors of having poisoned Shcherbakov and Zhdanov.

In May 1951, half a year before Vinogradov's arrest, Stalin began to gather "evidence" against the Jewish Kremlin doctors. He ordered the chief of the MGB Special Investigative Department, Lieutenant-Colonel M. D. Riumin, who had earlier worked in Stalin's personal secretariat, to induce Lidia Timashuk, an X-ray technician in the Kremlin hospital and an MGB "unofficial collaborator," to write a report accusing Jewish doctors of poisoning Zhdanov and Shcherbakov.[620] Using her letter, Riumin fabricated the "case of the Kremlin doctors" and submitted it for approval to Minister of State Security V. S. Abakumov, who in turn reported it to Beria. Abakumov and Beria realized that the "case of the Kremlin doctors" was a monstrous anti-Semitic provocation and that it might explode into an international scandal. They told Riumin to terminate the case of Kremlin doctors. Riumin complained to Stalin, who in November 1950 had ordered Riumin to arrest Dr. Yakov G. Etinger and accuse him of being a "Jewish nationalist" and of shortening the life of Politburo member A. S. Sherbakov. Abakumov ordered Riumin to limit Etinger's case to the accusation of "anti-Soviet activities." and accused Riumin of being a "stupid adventurer." Riumin disagreed. Abakumov arrested him, but Riumin complained to Stalin that Abakumov and Beria had obstructed the investigation of Dr. Etinger.[621] Stalin decided not to react immediately and went on vacation to Georgia.

Stalin spent the summer of 1951 at his dacha at the Barzhomi mineral-waters resort. Before leaving Moscow, Stalin ordered his daughter Svetlana not to talk to Beria, saying, "I don't trust that man!"[622] Stalin decided to first arrest the Mingrelian generals, whom he considered Beria's men and issued a secret decree, accusing the whole Mingrelian population of treason.[623] Stalin summoned the chief of the Georgian MGB, Nikolai Rukhadze, to the Barzhomi dacha, ordering him to arrest "all the Mingrelian generals" and to prepare for the exile of the entire Mingrelian population from Georgia to Siberia. On the way back to Tbilisi, Rukhadze smoked one cigarette after another. "Is anything wrong?" asked his driver, Colonel Samson Parulava.

"Bad, very bad," said Rukhadze.[624]

After his return from Barzhomi on July 12, 1951, Stalin summoned Abakumov to his office in the Kremlin. As Abakumov entered the elevator to Stalin's second-floor office, he was frisked and arrested by General Vlasik, the head of Stalin's bodyguards, who removed Abakumov's belt, ripped off his shoulder boards, and drove him to the Lubyanka prison. Stalin had ordered Abakumov's arrest because he had brought the interrogations of Dr. Etinger to a halt. The chief of the prison, Colonel Mironov, "could not believe his eyes" when he saw the new prisoner, the Minister of State Security, to whom he had submitted his routine report a few hours earlier, in shackles. Pointing at Abakumov, Vlasik said, "Take him!"[625] Abakumov wound up in the same cell from which Riumin had walked out a few minutes earlier. Stalin had ordered him to continue the investigation of the "Kremlin doctors' case." and specifically to continue the interrogation of Dr. Etinger.[626]

Stalin also ordered the new Minister of State Security, S. D. Ignatiev, to "renew the investigation into the case of the terrorist activities of Etinger."[627] Soon thereafter, Dr. Etinger died after succumbing to interrogators' torture. Medical expert P. I. Semenovsky signed the autopsy report, stating, "Death took place as a result of heart paralysis." Several years earlier, Semenovsky had signed a similar report after the execution of Marshal Blucher.[628] Documents in Etinger's case do not mention if his body was cremated, or where it was buried.[629] Dr. Etinger proved to be the central figure in the Kremlin doctors' case, and the focus of Stalin's personal attention.

On February 7, 1953, the MGB arrested thirty-seven persons, among them twenty-eight doctors and members of their families.[630] Among those detained was Maria E. Weizman, a sister of Chaim Weizman, the first president of Israel. Her case started in 1948, when Abakumov reported to Stalin that "Maria Weizman has expressed a desire to go to Palestine." Maria Weizman was by then sixty years old. She admitted that she had seen her brother forty years earlier, in Berlin in 1913, soon after she had graduated from Zurich University and was about to return to Russia. Chaim Weizman died in November 1952. Interrogator A. Ivanov told her:

> The investigation knows everything. Mikhoels, while in the U.S.A. in 1943, met your brother. We know that he received from him enemy directives. ... Tell us what these directives were.[631]

In accordance with the first post-Stalin amnesty, Maria Weizman was released from prison following Stalin's death.

In February 1953, Stalin received Krishna P. S. Menon, the Indian ambassador to Moscow. Menon was the last foreigner to see him. While they talked, Stalin kept doodling wolves in various aggressive postures, in pairs and in packs, as he often used to do during his conversations with visitors. Having noticed that Menon was looking at his doodling, Stalin suddenly said:

> The Russian peasant is a very simple man but a very wise one. When the wolf attacks him, he does not attempt to teach it morals, but tries to kill it. And the wolf knows this and behaves accordingly.[632]

Menon understood that the wolves symbolized enemies for Stalin, but he did not know that Stalin considered the Jews his enemies and was preparing their destruction similar to the Holocaust. Stalin and Hitler had some common personality traits, among them their pathological hatred for the Jews. Menon was very surprised when Stalin unexpectedly asked about the impurity of the languages spoken by people in India. Menon did not know about Niko Marr's theory of the Semitic origin of the Georgian language, and could not have imagined what dangerous implications this theory held for Stalin.

The obsessions with Jews and wolves were common to both Hitler and Stalin. While Stalin was incensed by Niko Marr's theory of the Semitic origin of the Georgian language, Hitler dreaded the thought that he had a Jewish ancestor. Hitler ordered his lawyer Hans Frank to investigate his lineage. Frank discovered that Hitler's grandmother Maria Anna Schickelgruber had become pregnant while working as a house cleaner in a Jewish household in Graz, Austria. She gave birth to a son, whom she named Alois, leaving the father's name blank on Alois's birth certificate. Hitler's grandmother later married Johann Georg Hitler, who adopted Alois, Adolf Hitler's father.[633] The possibility that a Jew had fathered Alois haunted Hitler his whole life. Percy Ernest Schramm, an authority on Hitler, wrote that anti-Semitism had run "like a red thread" through Hitler's entire life; Schramm, deduced that "we must be satisfied with the realization that there is about Hitler's anti-Semitism an unknown factor." He added that "psychology and psychiatry, in spite of all their refinements, are confronted by an 'X.'"[634] German historian Karl D. Bracher suggested that anti-Semitism was "the only 'genuine' fanatically held and realized conviction of Hitler's entire life," and that "Hitler's fanatical hatred of the Jews defies all rational explanation; it cannot be measured by political and practical gauges." Bracher felt it represented "the inexplicable dynamics of one man."[635] The same is true of Stalin. But when the dynamics of one man defy all rational explanations and cause the suffering and death of millions of innocent people, one must not be satisfied with the realization that there is an unknown factor about Hitler's or Stalin's anti-Semitism. An attempt should be made to explain such a fanatical hatred by probing the irrational motives behind it.

At the turn of the century, Sigmund Freud treated his most famous patient, a Russian noble, who was suffering from a severe obsession with wolves and who became known in psychiatry as the "Wolf-Man." Freud traced this obsession to a traumatic event in the early childhood of the Wolf-Man, who, as a year-and-a-half or two-year-old child, had awakened and seen his parents engaged in a sex act, without understanding its meaning. The boy was petrified, having seen his father standing upright and "wearing white underwear, like a wolf in the fairy-tale 'The Wolf and the Seven Little Goats,' with one foot forward, his claws outstretched, and his ears pricked," while his mother was "bending down like an animal." Freud concluded that the boy had "witnessed *coitus a tergo*" and had been able to see "his mother's genitals, as well as his father's organ." Freud suggested that the result of this life-altering experience was a "fear of castration," which became "the motivational power for the transformation of the affect." Freud believed that the "wolf became the boy's first father-surrogate"[636] and that the fear of the father ("or wolf") was at the root of the fear of castration.[637]

In his psychological analyses of Hitler, Walter C. Langer stated that as a little boy "Hitler must have discovered his parents during intercourse. Examination of the data makes this conclusion almost inescapable, and from our knowledge of his father's character and past history, it is not at all improbable."[638] In his autobiography *Mein Kampf*, Hitler described his childhood miseries, the "brutal attacks on the part of my father toward my mother, or assaults due to drunkenness" in which the brutality of the father "left nothing to the imagination." He wrote, "I witnessed this personally in hundreds of scenes from the beginning with both disgust and indignation."[639] Robert Waite, in his biography of Hitler, attributed great significance to Hitler's physical abnormality, which Soviet pathologists had discovered while performing the autopsy of Hitler's body:

> Hitler's left testicle could not be found either in the scrotum, or on the spermatic cord inside the inguinal canal, or in the small pelvis.[640]

Waite singled out this anomaly as the major cause of Hitler's castration fantasies.[641]

Stalin never mentioned any recollections about what he saw waking up in the large "ancestral Georgian bed," which occupied most of the space in the one-room house where he was born and grew up. This bed "served as the only resting place for the entire family."[642] The Okhrana records mention only Stalin's webbed toes which, like the missing testicles, are among the abnormalities that scientists believe are common to certain types of psychopathic personalities.[643] Stalin's obsessions with genitals, and the MGB interrogators' practice of genital mutilation, suggest that during his early childhood Stalin, like Hitler, may have witnessed the sex act of his parents. The dissident writer Vladimir Maksimov related his conversation with a former MGB officer, who had once said, indignantly: "Why was it necessary to castrate people? They could as well have shot them. It would have been more humane."[644] Stalin had a peculiar interest in the mutilation of genitalia. He used to complain that the oppositionists were a "castrated force of Jewish intellectuals." During a Politburo meeting on March 5, 1930, Stalin drew a caricature of Commissar of Finance Nikolai Briukhanov depicting him hanged by his genitals. Under this drawing, Stalin wrote:

> To the Politburo members: For all the present and future sins to hang Briukhanov by his balls; if the balls withstand it, consider him exonerated by the court; if not, drown him in the river.[645]

One victim of torture survived. Yakov Etinger, the stepson of Dr. Etinger, wrote:

> The MGB colonel forced a pupil of Dr. Etinger, a woman in her early forties, into a gynecological chair and inserted a bottle into her vagina. A heavy bleeding ensued and a doctor was called, who said that if the torture continued, "the woman will die." This saved her. After her release, she met this doctor in the Moscow subway. He said that he remembered her, and that many arrested women had been treated the same way. He said that he had quit the prison medical service after Stalin's death. One of the arrested Kremlin doctors related how his "interrogator had squeezed his genitals with some type of pliers." He lost consciousness several times. The guards helped him to recover, and the "procedure" was repeated again during other interrogations. Soon after his release, the professor died.[646]

Sigmund Freud wrote:

There must, of course, be more than one reason for a phenomenon of such intensity and lasting strength as the popular hatred of Jews... some of the reasons are obvious, while others lie deeper and spring from secret sources, which one would regard as the specific motives."[647]

Freud pointed to several reproaches often directed against Jews: that they are foreigners; that Jews, as an outside minority living among other people, invite suppression; that they are "different" from the people among whom they live, thus inspiring intolerance; that they defy oppression and cruel persecution and have a "capacity for holding their own in practical life." He added:

The deeper motives of anti-Semitism have their roots in times long past; they come from the unconscious, and I am quite prepared to hear that what I am going to say will at first appear incredible.[648]

Freud suggested that the primeval father used to castrate his sons, whom he perceived as sexual rivals, and this long-forgotten custom is at the root of the castration complex.[649] British psychiatrist Ernest Jones, in his description of the "God complex," stated:

People with this type of disorder are unable to tolerate any authority, which they distort into the imago of the wicked father; and that with this disorder there invariably goes also an anti-Semitic tendency. The castration complex is, if possible, even more pronounced in this variety than in the main type."[650]

On January 12, 1931, Stalin stated:

Anti-Semitism, as the extreme form of racial chauvinism, is the most dangerous vestige of cannibalism.[651]

On the surface, this statement appeared to be a very strong condemnation of anti-Semitism, and was accepted as such by some of Stalin's biographers. Isaac Deutscher, for instance, stated that Stalin was not an anti-Semite, "because nobody had been blunter than Koba in the condemnation of racial hatred."[652]

Actually, Stalin's condemnation of anti-Semitism was too strong to be real, and, if anything, had all the earmarks of a reaction-formation; that is, his strong hatred of the Jews was hidden behind an equally strong condemnation of anti-Semitism. He traced anti-Semitism to cannibalism without acknowledging the cannibal in himself. Stalin dealt with his "enemies" the way he feared they intended to deal with him.

The trial of the members of the Jewish Anti-Fascist Committee took place from May 8 to July 18, 1952, at the military tribunal of the Soviet Supreme Court. The accused, among them Jewish writers, poets, and actors, were forced to confess of conspiring to turn the Crimea into a "Zionist and American base." Thirteen defendants were sentenced to death by shooting. Lina Stern, a leading expert on longevity (a subject of great interest to Stalin), was sentenced to a three-year prison term. One of the accused died during interrogation. Another group of 110 Jewish intellectuals, arrested in connection with the "Crimean case," were secretly tried later. Ten of them were executed; five died during interrogation; and the others were sentenced to prison terms ranging from five to twenty-five years.[653]

During the Nineteenth Party Congress in October 1952, the first since 1939, Stalin renamed the Politburo the "Presidium," and expanded it from nine to twenty-five members. (Years later, Khrushchev wrote that by replacing the old Politburo with the Presidium, Stalin intended to "annihilate the old Politburo members and, in this way, to cover up all of his shameful acts.")[654] By 1952, Stalin was the only surviving member of the original Politburo, which had been set up by Lenin in great secrecy in May 1917 to deal with the scandal created by the exposure of the Okhrana agent Roman Malinovsky. At the congress, Stalin made a brief statement about the "struggle for the preservation of peace." In a photograph taken during the 1952 congress, Stalin appears in a generalissimo uniform in the midst of a large group of marshals, generals, and admirals. He ordered them to speed up the production of long-range jets and rockets capable of delivering nuclear weapons to America.[655] "We will show this Jewish shopkeeper how to attack us!" Stalin said, having convinced himself that President Truman was a Jew. Stalin's speech was greeted with a roar of applause.

During November 1952, Stalin's attention was fixed on the show trial that was being staged in the "People's Court" in Prague. Most of the defendants were Jews. Several of the accused, including chief defendant Rudolf Slansky (the secretary general of the Czechoslovak Communist party), were charged with having provided Israel with weapons during the Arab-Israeli War of

118

1948–49. They were actually opposed to Stalin's support for a Jewish State, because they considered themselves not Jews but "internationalists." Stalin, as usual, blamed them for the failed policy that he had ordered them to implement. Mordechai Oren, one of the leaders of the Israeli leftist party MAPAM, was arrested as he crossed the Czech-German border. Five years earlier, in 1946, Oren had told a Soviet intelligence officer in London that the Palestinian Jews would create a pro-Soviet state. M. T. Likhachev, the deputy chief of the MGB Investigations Department for Especially Important Cases, who had been assigned to Prague, asked Oren, "Why did you fool us?"[656] Stalin was outraged that the leftist Jews in Israel had "fooled" him by failing to carry out their pledge to turn Israel into a Soviet satellite. "So they thought they could fool Stalin! Just look at them, its Stalin they tried to fool!" was his angry response to the Jewish "betrayal."[657] Stalin told members of the Presidium of the Central Committee:

> It is time to finish off these Israeli traitors. We helped them in 1948. We thought then that the most effective way to assist the Jews was to create a Jewish state in Palestine. We, of course, figured that the majority of Zionist leaders—who are originally from Russia—called themselves socialists, but it turned out that they were liars, and instead of creating a socialist state they went for close relations with the U.S.A. They should be severely punished.[658]

Stalin ordered the MGB to spread a rumor in Georgia that "the Jews were killing Christian children for the purpose of using their blood in the making of matzoth." On his prompting, the Georgian secret police induced a woman, Natalia Kavtaradze, to scream hysterically through the streets of Tbilisi that the Jews had been caught "murdering Christian children and rolling them in wooden barrels studded with nails in order to drain their blood for use as an ingredient in matzos."[659] The Russian police had first made such an accusation in Georgia during Stalin's early childhood.[660]

Stalin commissioned the play *Pavlik Morozov*, in which Pavlik accuses his father saying: "He was a beast, and remains a beast!"[661] Stalin ordered Pavlik's remains placed in the center of Pavlik's native village below a two-yard-deep concrete foundation under Pavlik's monument. The transfer of Pavlik's remains was done at night.[662] Toward the end of his life, Stalin decided to destroy the evidence of his mass murders. He focused upon the "burial grounds" that contained the remains of millions of his victims in mass graves all over the Soviet Union. It was a major undertaking. A number of these "burial grounds" were excavated, and the skeletons destroyed.[663] In January and February 1953, *Komsomol* (Communist Youth) and some Party members were mobilized to peruse newspapers and magazines in Soviet libraries and archives, and to remove articles containing negative references to Stalin or positive statements about "enemies of the people," such as Trotsky and other members of the opposition.[664] Stalin also was urgently trying to ensure his immortality by having numerous statues of himself erected, some of them consuming hundreds of tons of bronze.[665]

In February 1951, Stalin told D. I. Chesnokov, a lecturer on Marxism-Leninism at Moscow University, to develop a thesis for the deportation of Jews from central Russia to Siberia. By the beginning of February 1953, millions of copies of Chesnokov's pamphlet, "Why It Was Necessary to Transfer the Jews from Industrial Centers to the Interior," had been printed by the Ministry of Internal Affairs.[666] The Gulag prisoners built barracks in Biro-Bidzhan and other areas of Siberia to which the deported Jews were to be sent.[667] Stalin created a special "Deportation Commission," and appointed M. A. Suslov its chairman and N. N. Poliakov its secretary. As Poliakov was to reveal years later, the deportation was scheduled to begin in the middle of February 1953, but the lists of Jews to be exiled were incomplete. There were two lists: one containing the names of "pure-blooded" Jews, who were to be deported first; and one with the names of *polukrovki* ("half-breeds," or Jews with only one Jewish parent), who were to be deported later. The delay in compiling the lists forced Stalin to order the trial of the Kremlin doctors to be held on March 5–7, 1953. Their executions by hanging were to take place on March 11–12 at the *Lobnoe Mesto* ("Forehead Place") in the center of Red Square, where beheadings had taken place centuries earlier during the reign of Ivan the Terrible.[668] According to Stalin's plan, the public hanging of the Kremlin doctors, in plain view of the incensed populace, was to serve as the signal for the start of a Jewish pogrom. Stalin intended to use this pogrom to justify the exile of the Jews by transporting the Jews to "safe places" and by playing the role of "savior" and "protector" from the "justifiably enraged Russian populace."[669]

On January 9, 1953, the new presidium adopted the decision to "approve the press report about the arrest of the group of doctors-wreckers, and publish it together with the article in *Pravda*." Poskrebyshev wrote a letter to the editor of *Pravda*, stating:

Comrade Mikhailov: I am sending you one copy of the chronicle "Arrest of Doctors-Wreckers" so that you may place it in the papers in the fourth column to the right.[670]

On January 13, 1953, the fifth anniversary of the murder of Mikhoels, *Pravda* published the first report regarding the arrests of a group of Kremlin doctors, stating that "having been agents of the Jewish Joint Distribution Committee and of American intelligence, they carried out orders that had been passed on to them by the well-known bourgeois nationalist Solomon Mikhoels."[671] The doctors were accused of shortening the lives of the Politburo members Zhdanov and Shcherbakov, as well as of harming the health of Soviet marshals, generals, and admirals. Dr. Vinogradov was accused of being an agent of British intelligence. *Pravda*'s front-page editorial, entitled "Foul Spies and Murderers under the Mask of Doctors and Professors," accused the Kremlin doctors of being a "gang of doctors-poisoners" directed by American and British "bosses" who were "feverishly preparing for a new world war." The editorial also blamed the "organs of state security" for their "lack of vigilance." It reminded its readers that the doctors Levin and Pletnev had "killed the great Russian writer A. M. Gorky and the great Soviet statesmen V. V. Kuibyshev and V. R. Menzhinsky."[672]

The charge of "lack of vigilance" had been directed against Beria and Abakumov. In the beginning of 1953, Stalin spread the rumor that Beria was a Jew and ordered the arrests of MGB generals, mostly Mingrelians, who had been accused of a plot to separate the West Georgian province of Mingrelia from the Soviet Union. They were forced to sign confessions confirming their guilt and implicating Beria. Stalin thought that the Jews and the Mingrelians were related.[673] The connection was probably the fact that the old Mingrelian dialect had many Hebrew words. There were villages in Mingrelia with large numbers of Jews who spoke the old Mingrelian dialect. The files with "confessions" of the Mingrelian generals were brought to Stalin, who wrote on them in red pencil, "Death to the Mingrelian bandits," and instructed interrogators not to forget "the chief Mingrelian"; that is, Beria.[674] The houses and apartments of Mingrelians in Tbilisi and other Georgian cities were placed on special lists in expectation of the order to exile them to Siberia, which was to take place at the same time as the exile of the Jewish population. Cossack troops with sabers and whips arrived in Mingrelian cities and villages to carry out the exile order. Their pre-revolutionary uniforms startled the local population.[675] Stalin accused "Abakumov and Vlasik of surrendering Lidia Timashuk to foreign spies and terrorists."[676] The daily barrage of statements against the "murderers in white gowns" created a pogrom-like atmosphere in the country. The Gulag administration was ordered to incite the inmates into murdering Jewish prisoners.[677]

On February 9, 1953, a bomb exploded in the courtyard of the Soviet embassy in Tel-Aviv, causing minor damages. Stalin used this incident to break diplomatic ties with Israel. No culprits were ever found. A former Soviet diplomat stated:

> Our side lent its hand to the explosion in the Soviet mission in Israel in February 1953; this was a classical provocation in order to once again accuse Israel and break its relations with Moscow.[678]

Oleg Kalugin, former Major-General of Soviet intelligence, wrote that MGB agents had "defiled Jewish cemeteries in the West." He added, "As a matter of fact, they did it in New York."[679] At the beginning of 1953, Stalin invited Khrushchev and two Ukrainian high officials, Melnikov and Korotchenko, to a dinner, telling them to organize pogroms in the Ukraine. He said, "The good workers at the factory should be given clubs so they can beat the hell out of those Jews."[680] Leonid Brezhnev, a protégé of Khrushchev, was elevated to Candidate-Member of the Presidium in October 1952. Stalin sent him to Moldavia to supervise the deportation of the Jewish population from there. Some of Stalin's *saratniki* (comrades-in-arms) had Jewish wives who became objects of Stalin's suspicion. Stalin, a seminary student, was familiar with the Biblical story of Esther. He also knew that at the end of February and beginning of March 1953 the Jews would celebrate Purim, thanking God for the miracle of Esther, a Jewish concubine of an ancient Persian king. According to the Bible story, Esther had saved the Persian Jews from their enemy Haman, who had plotted to destroy them more than two millennia earlier. Stalin planned to start the pogrom during the days of Purim to prove to the Jews that this time they would not be saved. Stalin feared that among the Jewish wives of his *saratniki* was another "Esther," who might prevent him from executing his plan. Molotov's wife, Polina Zhemchuzhina, had earlier been exiled to Kustanai, Kazakhstan, where she was kept under the code name "Object Number 12," until January 1953, when she was transferred to Moscow's Lubyanka prison and included in the Kremlin doctors' case.[681] Stalin accused Molotov of being an American spy. Then General A. V. Khrulev's Jewish wife was imprisoned in Vladimir Central, the top security prison. Voroshilov's Jewish wife was exiled, and Stalin also called Voroshilov a

"British spy." He ordered the arrest of Dora Khazan, Andreyev's Jewish wife. Andreyev was expelled from the Politburo and lived in fear of arrest.[682]

Stalin suspected Marshal Zhukov of being Jewish.[683] Before exiling Zhukov to the Urals, Stalin showed him a report, signed by Beria, stating:

> We established that Marshal G. K. Zhukov has been an agent of British intelligence for more than fifteen years and has continuously informed the hostile power about the defense secrets of the Soviet Union.[684]

Lieutenant General N. Vlasik, the chief of Stalin's bodyguards for many years, was arrested on December 15, 1952, and accused of "loss of vigilance" for having maintained friendly relations with his Jewish neighbor, to whom he allegedly passed secret information.[685] Early in January 1953, Stalin fired Alexander Poskrebyshev, the chief of his personal secretariat, who was his closest assistant for years. His Jewish wife, Bronislava Metallikova, who was a sister of Lev Sedov's wife, was poisoned by Beria in 1940 on Stalin's order. Poskrebyshev expected the arrest.[686]

By the end of January 1953, *Pravda* had already begun typesetting the appeal "To All the Jews of the Soviet Union," asking them to cooperate in their "relocation to safe areas."[687] It was signed by fifty-nine prominent Soviet Jews. The appeal stated:

> Dear brothers and sisters! Jews and Jewesses! We, the workers in science and technology, literature and the arts—Jews by nationality—appeal to you at this difficult period in our life.[688]

The appeal went on to remind the readers about the exposure "by the organs of State Security of a group of doctors, evildoers, spies, and traitors, who turned out to be in the service of American and English intelligence and international Zionism under the cover of a subversive organization." The appeal further stated:

> The horrible shadow of the murderers in white gowns covered the whole Jewish population of the USSR. . . . Under these conditions, in places where the party, government, and the great Vozhd (Leader) of the Soviet people I. V. Stalin will send us, there will be only self-denying labor. . . . This is why we approve completely the justifiable measures of the party and government that were directed toward the cultivation of the open

areas of eastern Siberia, the Far East, and the remote north by the Jews. Only by honest, self-denying labor will the Jews be able to prove their devotion to the motherland and to the great and adored Comrade Stalin, and reestablish their good names in the eyes of the entire Soviet populace.[689]

(The typewritten copy of this appeal was found among the papers of a deceased typist who had worked at *Pravda*. Her daughter discovered the "yellowing pages" among her mother's papers, and brought them to Iakov Etinger, the stepson of the murdered Kremlin doctor Yakov G. Etinger.)

Stalin ordered Yakov S. Khavinson, the General Director of TASS (Telegraph Agency of the Soviet Union), and M. B. Mitin, the chief of the Party Propaganda Department, to sign this appeal and ask other prominent Jews to do the same. They enlisted journalist David Zaslavsky and historian Isaac Mintz, who signed this appeal and promised to convince other Jews to cooperate with the authorities. Some Jews refused to sign, among them General Yakov Kreizer, singer Mark Reizen, writer Veniamin Kaverin, and Arkady Ierusalimsky, Svetlana's teacher. After Stalin's death, Ilya Ehrenburg said that he had not signed the appeal.[690] But on January 27, 1953, two weeks after the publication of the Kremlin doctors' arrests, Ehrenburg was present at the pompous reception in the Kremlin at which he was awarded the "Stalin Prize." Ehrenburg's signature on the appeal was the most prominent one on the document.[691] During the January 27, 1953, reception, Stalin said, "We have anti-Semites in our Central Committee. This is a profanation." Composer T. N. Khrenikov, present at the reception, was surprised by this statement and wrote it down.[692]

The rumor that Lazar Kaganovich had refused to sign the appeal and in protest had thrown his Party card on Stalin's desk circulated years later. Actually, Stalin crossed out Kaganovich's name on the list of Jews who were required to sign it.[693] He had appointed Kaganovich to direct the deportation of the Jews. Stalin saw in Kaganovich not a Jew, but a fellow criminal who had even approved the murder of his own brother. Khrushchev found it difficult to believe that, as he wrote in his memoirs, "Kaganovich a Jew himself, was against the Jews!"[694] Kaganovich was not merely an anti-Semitic Jew, but an utterly depraved, amoral creature who helped Stalin exterminate countless innocent people. Yet rumors often contain particles of truth. Someone in Stalin's entourage refused to sign the appeal. This event took place around February 13, 1953. On February 14, *Pravda* announced that Lev Mekhlis, "one of the prominent leaders of the Communist Party and the Soviet Union, and a member of the Central Committee, died of heart failure."[695]

Party and government circles were openly discussing the "liberation of the Soviet Union from the Jewish yoke."[696] An old Bolshevik, O. I. Goloborodko, who was working at the Council of Ministers, years later recalled, "I thought I would go crazy when I learned about the transportation of Jews to Biro-Bidzhan."[697] The problems of relocating Jews to Biro-Bidzhan were discussed in the Council of Ministers. When Stalin was told about the difficulty of transporting a large number of Jews to the remote area, he replied, "Half of them will die on the way there."[698] Some ten years earlier, hundreds of thousands of Chechens, Crimean Tartars, Kabardins, and Volga Germans were sent in cattle trains to places of exile in Siberia, Central Asia, and the Far East. Half of them perished en route. Stalin ordered his defense minister, Nikolai A. Bulganin, to dispatch "several hundred military railway trains" to Moscow and other large cities. A large number of cattle trains were concentrated on reserved lines. According to Bulganin, Stalin planned to organize assaults on the trains with the deported Jews by "people's avengers."[699] By the estimate of a Soviet historian, 30–40 percent of the deported Jews would not have reached their destination.[700] Years later Stalin's daughter Svetlana wrote: "During the last days of February 1953, everything grew quiet, as before a storm."[701] The trial of the Kremlin doctors was scheduled to take place early in March 1953. That year Purim was to start at sundown on Saturday, February 28. According to the Jewish lunar calendar, it was the fourteenth day of the month, Adar, 5713.

Chapter 5

The Murder of "Dr. Moreau" and the Cover-Up

Stalin spent the last days of February 1953 in his Kuntsevo *dacha*. On Saturday, February 28, 1953, at about 4 a.m., Stalin went to sleep in his three-room bedroom suite. On Sunday morning, March 1, Gogi Zautashvili, a native of Gori and one of Stalin's Georgian bodyguards, noticed that a bulb on the control panel had lit up and not turned off. It meant that Stalin had opened a door in one of his rooms and it had not closed automatically behind him. Zautashvili notified M. Starostin, the chief bodyguard on duty that night. Starostin tried to call Stalin, but there was no response. After several more attempts to reach Stalin by phone, Starostin ordered the guards to break through the steel-plated door. They found Stalin lying on the floor in the doorway between the second and third rooms, his head resting on his arm, his body curled in a fetal position. The right side of his body was paralyzed. The guards and Stalin's maid placed him on a couch.[702]

Starostin reported Stalin's condition to Minister of State Security S. D. Ignatiev, who told Starostin to call Politburo members Beria and Malenkov. Beria did not answer his phone. Malenkov called back thirty minutes later and said, "I couldn't find Beria. Try to track him down yourself." When Beria finally called the Kuntsevo dacha, he said, "Don't tell anybody about Stalin's illness, and don't call anybody!" Beria and Malenkov arrived in Kuntsevo Monday morning, March 2. Malenkov took off his squeaky shoes and tiptoed toward Stalin. Beria was already looking intently at Stalin's face. Turning to the bodyguards, he snapped, "Don't raise a fuss, and don't disturb Comrade Stalin." He cursed them in unprintable Kremlin slang, basically saying: "Who appointed you, idiots, to serve Comrade Stalin?" Beria and Malenkov left, saying that doctors would get there soon. They arrived around 9 a.m.

Without waiting for doctors, Beria left for the Lubyanka and took over the MGB headquarters, while Ignatiev switched immediately to Beria's side. His men prevented all communications with Kuntsevo and the Kremlin.[703] Beria then arrested Riumin and all of Riumin's assistants and locked them ip in Lubyanka cells. He released the arrested Mingrelian generals and gave them back their belts so they could hold up their pants. Beria showed them their interrogation files, on which Stalin had written in red pencil, "Death to the Mingrelian bandits." He said, "The *gotferan* [pederast, in Georgian] is dying. We have no time to lose. Go back to your offices and resume your duties."[704]

Beria also set free Vardo Mikhailovna Maximilishvili, a trusted Beria aide and one of his former lovers. Beria met Vardo when she was a student at Tbilisi Medical Institute while he was a high secret police official in Georgia. He raped her and she gave birth to a child. On Beria's instruction his assistants delivered the baby to an orphanage.[705] A high-ranking Soviet intelligence chief, Pavel Sudoplatov writes that after his transfer to Moscow, Beria had Vardo working in his secretariat, and then arranged that she marry a rank-and-file officer of NKVD, also a Georgian. Beria gave Vardo the Moscow apartment of Vsevolod Meyerhold after Meyerhold's arrest and execution on June 20, 1939. Because of Meyerhold's Jewish-sounding name, Stalin assumed, as many people did at that time, that Meyerhold was Jewish, although he was not. Meyerhold's wife, Zinaida Raikh, was Jewish. She had earlier been married to the Russian poet Sergey Esenin. A few days after Meyerhold's arrest, Zinaida Raikh was murdered in their apartment. She had seventeen knife wounds, and her eyes were cut out. The only things taken from the apartment were documents. In his NKVD file under the joint name "Meyerhold-Raikh," Meyerhold was accused of being a "Japanese spy" and an "Okhrana agent" with a code name "Semenych."[706] On January 13, 1940, three days before his trial, Meyerhold wrote to Vyshinsky, not knowing that by then Vyshinsky had been promoted to the position of Deputy Commissar of Foreign Affairs. Meyerhold wrote:

Interrogator Boris Rodos broke my left hand but left my right one unbroken so that I could sign my depositions with it. My statements are false; I could not withstand the torture and denigration. He forced me to drink his urine, to crawl—me, an old man.[707]

Meyerhold went before Judge Vasily Ulrikh, who hurriedly asked him a few formal questions. Meyerhold denied all the accusations and was taken to the Lubyanka cellars and shot.

Vardo received intelligence training with the wife of Pavel Sudoplatov. Pavel Sudoplatov writes:

I was invited to Vardo's wedding to observe her and her husband and to determine their manner of behavior (for example, whether they drink too much). This information was needed because the intention was to send the newlyweds to Paris to work with the Georgian community there. After one or two years of work in Paris, Vardo returned to Moscow where she worked in intelligence till 1952, In 1952 she was arrested and accused of having, participated in a conspiracy against the Soviet state while working in Paris. [708]

Vardo was arrested as a part of the "Mingrelian bandits' case." She provided "evidence" to MGB interrogators against the "chief Mingrelian" that is, Beria and other "Mingrelian bandits." Having released Vardo Beria from her cell in Lubyanka prison, Beria drove her to the Kuntsevo dacha. After they arrived at Kuntsevo Beria pretended to do all he could to save Stalin's life. He summoned several prominent physicians, including the heart specialist P. E. Lukomsky, without telling them who their patient would be. When the physicians saw Stalin, they were frightened and began to shake with fear. Beria scared them even more with the grim question, "Do you guarantee Comrade Stalin's life?"[709] V. A. Negovsky, the Soviet pioneer of reanimation science, and Galina Chesnokova, his assistant, were brought to Kuntsevo. Chesnokova later recalled, "We immediately felt that Beria was the foremost boss here."[710] They were led into a large living room where Stalin was lying on a sofa. Next to him sat his daughter, Svetlana.

On March 1, 1953, Svetlana had tried unsuccessfully to telephone her father. On the morning of March 2 she was told that Stalin was ill and that she should go to Kuntsevo. There she met Khrushchev and Bulganin, who had just arrived. "Let's go in, Malenkov will tell you everything," they informed her.

Years later, Svetlana described the scene of her father's last moments:

> Everything was dying in front of my eyes. They all felt that something portentous, something almost majestic, was going on in the room. There was only one person who was behaving almost obscenely. That was Beria . . . He was trying so hard, at this moment of crisis, to strike the right balance, to be cunning yet not too cunning. It was written all over him.[711]

Stalin was dying a horrible death. His face darkened, his lips blackened. Then something very strange happened:

> The agony was awful. He literally choked to death. At what seemed like the very last moment, he suddenly opened his eyes and cast a glance over everybody in the room. It was a horrible glance, insane or perhaps angry, and full of fear of death. . . . Then something incomprehensible happened ... He suddenly lifted his left hand as though he was pointing to something above and bringing down a curse upon us all. . . . The next moment, after a final effort, the spirit wrenched itself free from the flesh.[712]

Stalin lifted his crippled left arm as if he was cursing his enemies, the "wolves" and their prototype: his father Vissarion, who had caused him so much suffering.

Svetlana noticed a female doctor in her mid-thirties who looked familiar, but she could not recall the woman's name. The woman doctor was Vardo Maximilishvili.[713] Svetlana watched her with suspicion. And for good reason—this woman doctor was about to poison her father. The type of poison Vardo Maximilishvili administered to Stalin, and exactly how she did it—has remained a mystery. A prominent Russian writer and Hero of the Soviet Union, Vladimir Karpov, stated that Molotov had told him:

> There are many reasons to believe that the hunches that Beria poisoned Stalin are true. On May 1, 1953, Beria told Khrushchev and Malenkov: "I got rid of Stalin in a very timely manner . . ." Beria poisoned Stalin. Perhaps he personally did not do it, but used his Chekists or doctors. My medical conclusion supports this.... One of the medics, Professor Miasnikov, later recalled that Stalin had all the symptoms of poisoning by venom. However, under the sharp and cold stare of Beria, the medics compiled an opinion that he had dictated.[714]

When Stalin breathed his last, his son Vasily, drunk as usual, shouted, "Scoundrels, you murdered my father!" He was led out of the room. Then Beria ordered: "Take Svetlana away!" No one paid attention. Svetlana recalled:

> Beria could hardly restrain his joy. Not only I, but also many people there, understood that. But my father was much feared, and they all knew that at the moment of his death, no one in Russia had as much power as this horrible person.[715]

Seeing that Stalin was dead, Beria triumphantly ordered Stalin's chief bodyguard, "Khrustalev, get my car!" Other close associates of Stalin's were crying. Khrushchev, in the old peasant tradition, dropped to his knees next to Stalin, loudly sobbing. One after the other, the servants and guards came close to the body of their *khoziain* (boss), whom they had venerated for many years, to pay their respects. Tears rolled down their faces. All soon left, except for Svetlana, Bulganin, and Mikoyan.

On the morning of March 5, Stalin's body was removed, embalmed, and placed in the Hall of Columns, the hall where Stalin had for years held his show trials and forced thousands of defendants to confess to crimes they hadn't committed.[716] Stalin's *soratniki* (comrades-in-arms) stood in the "honor guard," headed by Beria. Past them moved grief-stricken mourners in a long line stretching for many streets. Thousands of mounted militiamen, security police, and soldiers tried to maintain order, but they could not stop the human avalanche. Large crowds surged into the Moscow streets, stampeding and crushing under their feet thousands of crazed worshipers, whom Stalin was dragging along with him into the grave. The death toll was especially high near Trubnaya Square.[717]

A similar frenzy had seized the Muscovites more than half a century earlier, in 1896, when they had rushed to Khodynka Field to celebrate the coronation of Tsar Nicholas II. Then the crowd crushed hundreds of people to death. One difference was that in 1896 they were celebrating the accession to the Russian throne of the scion of a 300-year-old dynasty, while in March 1953 they lamented the death of the greatest criminal in history, whose appalling carnage they could not even comprehend. Stalin's unmitigated brutality was something many Russians would not be able to fathom (or even acknowledge) for decades after his death. Stalin's body was entered into the Lenin-Stalin mausoleum to be worshiped with the same veneration as Lenin's mummified remains. In having embalmed Stalin's body, Beria obliterated any traces of the deadly poison in Stalin's body. He treated the body of the dead dictator with the same veneration that had been afforded to Lenin's remains. In the circle of the Mingrelian generals, whom he had set free, Beria bragged that he had poisoned Stalin and thus saved not only them, but also the entire Jewish and Mingrelian populations from deportation to Siberia and certain death.[718]

A Russian historian, Vladimir P. Naumov, and a Yale University scholar, Jonathan Brent, coauthored the book *Stalin's Last Crime*, stating that Lavrenty Beria had poisoned Stalin during a dinner in the Kuntsevo dacha using *"warfarin,* a tasteless and colorless blood-thinner also used to kill rats."[719] They based their opinion upon recollections, published in Khrushchev's 1970 memoirs in which he had stated that two months after Stalin's death Beria had told Molotov: "I did him in! I saved all of us." The two authors also used excerpts from an early draft of the medical report, which stated that Stalin had suffered "extensive stomach hemorrhaging during his death throes." Naumov and Brent noted that "significant references to stomach bleeding were excised from the twenty-page official medical record, which was not issued until June 1953," more than three months after Stalin's death.[720] Stalin could not be poisoned during a dinner at his dacha—his bodyguards tightly controlled his food and he usually asked his guests to first taste every dish at his table. He was poisoned while he was paralyzed and was under Beria's control in Kuntsevo. It was well known that Beria kept many varieties of toxins in the Soviet Secret Police arsenal.

Years later, in 1979, the author asked an Israeli rabbi when Purim had fallen in 1953. The rabbi looked it up in the Hebrew calendar, and said that Purim that year had begun on the night of February 28, 1953. When the author told him that Stalin had suffered a stroke that night, the rabbi raised his hands to Heaven and declared that God had struck down another Haman to save the Jewish people from destruction. Religious Jews might also honor Vardo as a modern Esther and say that Stalin's stroke was a proof of God's "miracle." However, Stalin's stroke could have been caused by the excitement of the avid anticipation of the pogrom he was about to unleash on his lifelong enemies, the Jews.

Shortly before his death Stalin ordered the translation into Russian of the H. G. Wells' science-fiction novel *The Island of Dr. Moreau.* In Wells' tale, the deranged Dr. Moreau craved to create ideal human beings by exploring the "extreme limit of plasticity in a living shape." He performs plastic surgery and organ transplanting on oxen, wolves, apes, pigs, and other animals that, having survived his experiments, were forced to chant commandments, known as

"The Law." Finally, while Dr. Moreau was performing an operation on a puma, the animal broke its fetters and ran away. Dr. Moreau pursued the terrified and bleeding puma and was killed in the ensuing struggle with the terrified animal. The dread the mad doctor had instilled eventually faded from the memories of the tormented creatures, and they slowly began to revert to their original animal state.[721] This masterpiece of the macabre was first published in 1896, when Wells could not have foretold the emergence of the mad Soviet dictator. Wells did not recognize Dr. Moreau in Stalin when he interviewed him in 1934, or when he described Stalin as a very kind man who "owes his position to the fact that no one is afraid of him and everyone trusts him."[722] Stalin also did not realize that Wells' horror story would someday be seen as an allegory for Stalin's own atrocities.

After Stalin's death, millions of gulag prisoners sensed that the end to their misery was in sight. A few victims of the Great Purge were still alive then, and some of them sincerely cried, lamenting Stalin's demise.[723] However, the great majority rejoiced. A Ukrainian prisoner, Roman Romanyuk, struggling against the Norylsk black blizzard, shouted joyfully to a fellow prisoner, "The mustachioed scum either got sick or has already dropped dead."[724] Like Dr. Moreau's tortured animals, the Soviet people, paralyzed by fear, needed time to shed it. Beria was the first of Stalin's *soratniki* to defy Stalin's legacy. He began the process of erasing the "personality cult." He rescinded Stalin's order to deport the Jewish and Mingrelian people to Siberia and terminated the "case of the Kremlin doctors." Those doctors who had survived torture were in appalling physical condition. He provided them with medical help. On April 3, 1953, a month after Stalin's death, the doctors were released. They were unable to climb even a few stairs without the help of guards.

The next day, April 4, 1953, an event unprecedented in Soviet history took place when *Pravda* announced:

> The former Ministry of State security of USSR had acted incorrectly and without any lawful basis when it had arrested the Kremlin doctors. All of the accused in this case have been completely exonerated of the accusations against them, and released. The persons accused of incorrect conduct in the investigation have been arrested, and criminal charges have been brought against them."[725]

Beria abolished Stalin's Presidium and reinstated the old Politburo, in its pre-October 1952 composition. He also merged the Ministry of State Security with the Ministry of Internal Affairs to concentrate these organs of power in his own hands.

Soon after Stalin's death, Beria invited Molotov to his office. Beria stood behind his desk, smiling, while Molotov and his wife Polina Zhemchuzhina embraced and kissed each other. Beria released all the other imprisoned Jewish wives, as well as Stalin's relatives Anna Redens and Olga Allilueva and their neighbors and friends. Among the released prisoners was Svetlana's first love, the screenwriter Aleksei Kapler.[726] The overcrowded cells of the Lubyanka and other prisons were almost empty. On March 27, 1953, three weeks after Stalin's death, an amnesty for millions of prison camp inmates was issued, which also applied to "political prisoners" with sentences of up to five years.[727] On April 6, 1953, *Pravda* published an editorial, entitled "Soviet-Socialist Legality Should Not Be Violated," which accused "despicable adventurers of the Riumin type" of enflaming national antagonism and slandering the Soviet people. The article stated that "careful investigation has established, for example, that an honest public figure, the People's Artist of the USSR, Solomon Mikhoels, was slandered in this way."[728] Stalin's close associates kept silent. The process of dismantling the "personality cult" was only in its initial stage. The veneration of the dead dictator as "the greatest genius of all mankind" was prevalent among Politburo members and common citizens alike. Beria was an exception.

The millions of released Gulag prisoners were the first to shed their fear of the dead dictator. In May 1953, "special regime" camps in Norilsk, Vorkuta, Karaganda, and other areas of the Gulag were swept by uprisings. Such disobedience would have been unthinkable during Stalin's reign; the uprisings would have ended with mass executions. The uprising in the Norilsk camp began on May 3, 1953. On May 7, a special commission arrived from Moscow, informing the inmates that "Lavrenty Pavlovich Beria himself sent us to discuss your demands." A committee of the inmates submitted a prisoner's appeal with a list of demands, which included the review of all sentences, removal of numbers from prisoners' garb, and permission to correspond with relatives. During the 1953 May First parade, standing on the mausoleum with Khrushchev, Molotov, and Bulganin, Beria told them that he had had Stalin poisoned. The Politburo members worshiped Stalin and considered the very thought of murdering him an unspeakable blasphemy. It was then that they began to fear Beria and to plot his removal.

In June 1953, workers in Soviet-occupied East Berlin began their revolt, which scared Soviet leaders. Zhukov shared this resentment against Beria with Bulganin and Khrushchev. Although Beria brought Zhukov back to Moscow from exile, Zhukov held a grudge against Beria because he thought that the reason he had been sent away was Beria's fabricated espionage charge against him. Marshal Zhukov was ordered to suppress the revolt of East Berlin workers. He shared his resentment against Beria with Bulganin and Khrushchev. The plotters feared that Beria intended to change Stalin's domestic and foreign policies. Beria revoked Stalin's order to appoint Russian officials to all top positions in the non-Russian republics. Khrushchev, Bulganin, and Zhukov saw in this change a sign of Beria's Mingrelian nationalism. They were against the revocation by Beria of Stalin's policy of "Russification" of all the ethnic republics. Their hostility toward Beria was a natural reaction to what they perceived as his "Mingrelian nationalism." They were incensed at the thought that the destiny of the Soviet Union might be in the hands of a non-Russian, for Beria remained, in their eyes, a "Mingrelian bandit." They were also opposed to Beria's intention to ease international tension by withdrawing Soviet forces from Austria and East Germany.[729] To Khrushchev, Bulganin, and Zhukov, Beria's policy meant the betrayal of Stalin's legacy, which was still very dear to them.

On the morning of June 26, 1953, Bulganin secretly summoned to his office Colonel-General K. Moskalenko, Major-General A. Baksov, Lieutenant-General P. Batitsky, Lieutenant-Colonel V. Yuferov, and Colonel I. Zub (all of whom had been recommended by Zhukov). Riding in two cars, together with Zhukov and Bulganin, the group was admitted to the Kremlin under the pretext of attending a conference. They entered a small room next to Stalin's former office. Khrushchev and Bulganin walked in. "Do you know why we invited you?" Khrushchev asked. They did not. "You are assigned to arrest Beria," Khrushchev said, and warned them that in the event that the operation failed, they would be declared "enemies of the people." Zhukov and the five officers entered Stalin's former office, where Politburo members were gathered for a conference. "Comrades, don't worry!" Zhukov said to the Politburo members, most of whom did not know what was happening. Turning to Beria, he snapped, "Get up! Follow me!" and ordered the officers, "Shoot him on the spot if he tries to escape." Beria was placed in the underground shelter of the Moscow military district headquarters. Bulganin told the five officers, "Forget all you know and all you've seen." He promised to award them with Hero of the Soviet Union medals if they continued to carry out this operation. He kept his word.[730]

On July 10, 1953, two weeks after Beria's arrest, *Pravda* announced that Beria was "an enemy of the Communist Party and the Soviet people" and had been detained to face trial. That day, Beria's "personal representative," Colonel Kuznetsov, and his group, whom Beria had sent to negotiate the end of the prison camp uprising at the Norilsk Gulag, disappeared from the camp. In the beginning of August, all six special political camps at Norilsk were surrounded by troops of the Ministry of Internal Affairs. The uprising was suppressed, leaving many dead and wounded. The uprising in Vorkuta and other areas of the Gulag were also suppressed. Stalin was dead, but his methods were very much alive. The most active participants in the prison camp uprisings were sent to punishment camps.

Among the inmates in the punishment camp, which was located 101 kilometers from Norilsk, was Chabuk Amiragibi, a scion of Georgian grand dukes. He had co-authored a prisoners' appeal at the Norilsk camp number 4. Shortly before Beria's arrest, Amiragibi received a message from his sister Rodam, a close friend of Beria and the wife of the poet Mikhail Svetlov. Rodam wrote that Chabuk would soon be released; and that Beria would empty the Gulag, increase the production of goods in the Soviet Union, and improve relations with the West by the withdrawal of Russian troops from East Germany and Austria.[731] Beria's arrest stopped the de-Stalinization process. Khrushchev and Bulganin, supported by Zhukov and the army, assumed power. In September 1953, the "security organs" were renamed the KGB (Committee of State Security). In October, the Soviet hydrogen bomb was successfully tested, which emboldened Khrushchev into believing in the eventual victory of the Soviet Union in the Cold War. He and Bulganin made their first trip abroad as the new Soviet leaders, and numerous pictures of them exposing their protruding bellies received wide publicity.

Meanwhile, the officers who had arrested and interrogated Beria forbade him from mentioning Stalin's name in his testimony, insisting that he replace references to the dictator with the euphemism *instantsiya* (higher authority). One of the officers, I. Zub, who had been elevated to the rank of general for his role in Beria's arrest, wrote years later:

> Three and a half months after Stalin's death, nobody had yet whispered a word about the cult [of personality]. For everybody in the country, Stalin still remained Stalin—the great, the infallible, the indisputable. At that time, the sorrow of his death had not yet settled into the hearts of the people.[732]

"Beria's case" grew into nineteen volumes. More than 200 women, among them Vardo Maksimilishvili, who was rearrested together with the Minglelian generals after Beria's arrest, testified that he had raped her.[733] Beria did not deny these charges, but when he was accused of murder, he repeatedly stated that he had only carried out "the orders of *instantsiya*." When he was accused of collaborating with British intelligence and the Mussavatist government in Azerbaijan in 1918, he replied that Stalin had been an Okhrana agent. The interrogators ordered him to stop mentioning this. When he was accused of fabricating false charges against innocent people, including Marshal Zhukov, Beria replied that *instantsiya* had fabricated these charges and forced him to sign them. He stated that Stalin had intended to destroy every Politburo member, including him, and that Stalin's death had prevented the deportation of the Jewish and Mingrelian populations.[734] Politburo members read Beria's testimony, and it might have been then that Khrushchev began to surmise that "the greatest genius of all mankind" had been the greatest evil genius; and that Beria, by shortening Stalin's life, had saved himself, Khrushchev, and millions of others from death. However, at that time Khrushchev was still very far from challenging Stalin's "personality cult." He placed all responsibility for Stalin's crimes upon Beria.

Beria had intended to honor Vardo Maximilishvili with a prestigious award, but it was withdrawn when Beria was arrested. Maximilishvili, along with the Mingrelian generals, was again detained. Beria's secret trial took place on December 18–23, 1953, in the Moscow military district headquarters. His six close assistants, Dekanozov, Vlodzimersky, Merkulov, Meshik, Goglidze, and Kobulov and Peter Sharia were tried at the same time. The chairman of the court was Marshal Konev, and the state prosecutor was Rudenko. All the defendants, except for Peter Sharia and Vardo Maximilishvili, were sentenced to death by shooting. Sharia was sentenced to ten years in Vladimir Central Prison, which he served in full. Vardo was released from prison after serving two years. She was not charged with poisoning of Stalin because the Soviet leaders did not want to disclose that the dictator had been poisoned. They spared her life also because they used her testimony against Beria, where she accused him of raping her. She "returned to her medical profession" and went back to the apartment near Nikitskie Vorota, which Beria gave her after the execution of Vsevolod Meyerhold. During Gorbachev's *glasnost* and *pereastroika period*, Vardo Maximilishvili was pressured to vacate the apartment, but she objected, arguing that she had been a victim of "repression" during Stalin's rule. The KGB, wishing to avoid a scandal, found a similar apartment for her.[735] Meyerhold's apartment was turned into the only Meyerhold museum in

Russia. For many years after Stalin's death, Maximilishvili worked as chief physician at Polyclinic number 112 in the Krasnopresnensky district of Moscow, and after her retirement moved to Tbilisi to live with her daughter.[736] Later on, in the 1990s, Vardo moved back to Moscow after the death of her daughter and lived in the Arbat area with some Georgian attendants, because, as an elderly invalid, she needed help and medical treatment.[737]

Beria was executed first. His hands were tied behind his back and he was taken to the bomb shelter, where he was tied to a large wooden board to keep bullets from ricocheting and striking the executioners. Marshal Konev and all the officers who had taken part in Beria's arrest, except for Marshal Zhukov, witnessed the execution. Prosecutor Rudenko read the sentence. "Allow me to say," Beria began, but Rudenko interrupted him: "You have already said enough. Plug his mouth with a towel. Carry out the sentence." General Batitsky volunteered to do the shooting. He took out his pistol and pulled the trigger. Beria's body slumped. It was wrapped in a bed sheet and delivered to the crematorium. Beria's six close assistants were also executed the same day.[738]

After Beria's execution, Ogoltsov, who in 1948 had murdered Mikhoels and had been arrested by Beria after Stalin's death, was released from prison and was proclaimed "completely rehabilitated." He continued to work in various privileged positions for years thereafter. In 1959 he was fired from the Party and denied his general rank and all citations for his "serious breach of socialist legality in his conduct of the Leningrad affair." Lavrenty Tsanava, who had helped Ogoltsov murder Solomon Mikhoels, committed suicide in his prison cell in 1955. The same year, A. G. Leonov, V. I. Komarov, and M. T. Likhachev who had tortured the Kremlin doctors and members of the Jewish Anti-Fascist Committee, were executed together with the former Ministry of State Security Abakumov. They had all been accused of crimes in the "Leningrad case." Their executions were part of the gigantic cover-up of Stalin's anti-Jewish policies. The Politburo members continued to hide Stalin's role in his crimes.

Soon after Beria's execution Khrushchev and the Party Presidium assigned Secretary of the Central Committee P. N. Pospelov to write a report on Beria's crimes.[739] A chance discovery changed Khrushchev's mind. Construction workers, who were converting Stalin's Kremlin apartment into a museum, found a secret safe inserted into a wall. The safe was brought to Khrushchev, who opened it. Years later, he mentioned only one of the documents he had found there: the letter in which Lenin threatened to break off all relations with Stalin. Khrushchev wrote in his memoirs, "I was astonished that this note had been preserved. Stalin had probably forgotten all about it."[740] Khrushchev did not reveal what other documents he had found in this safe because his colleagues in the Politburo objected to the publicizing of any negative information about Stalin.[741]

This discovery started to erode Khrushchev's veneration of Stalin. Despite the objections of Politburo members, Khrushchev, on February 24, 1956, at the Twentieth Party Congress, delivered a "secret speech" condemning Stalin's "personality cult" and reminding the Soviet people of the dictator's heartless persecution of many Party members. Khrushchev's "secret speech" was read mostly to Party members at various jobsites all over the Soviet Union.[742] Leaders of the Communist party in Eastern Europe also received the text of Khrushchev's secret speech, which was then leaked to the West and published.[743] This "secret speech" did not mention the Kremlin doctors' case, or Stalin's anti-Jewish campaign, or his Okhrana career and the part the Okhrana file had played in Soviet history.

The denial of Stalin's plan to deport the Jews to Siberia and the cover-up of his Okhrana past started during Khrushchev's rule.[744] Russian historian G. V. Kostyrchenko wrote a very informative book, *Stalin's Secret Policy*, in which he cited numerous documents that he had found in Soviet archives, revealing many facts about Stalin's anti-Semitic policies. Yet Kostyrchenko, in the chapter "The Myth About the Deportation," denied that Stalin had plans to deport the Soviet Jews.[745] Soviet leaders had destroyed many documents in the Soviet archives so Kostyrchenko couldn't locate any paperwork containing Stalin's deportation orders. He states:

> Only N. A. Bulganin liked (while intoxicated) to tell his guests, naturally "as a big secret," about how Stalin had ordered him to prepare and carry out the deportation of the Jews.[746]

However, Kostyrchenko, to his credit, found a document, which he described:

> At the end of January 1953, fifty-nine prominent Soviet Jews signed a letter to Pravda with an appeal to the Jews to cooperate with the Soviet authorities in their deportation to Siberia. The text was ready, and not only in typed form, but even in the newspaper print.[747]

Kostyrchenko further stated:
In 1990 alone, 186,000 Jews left the country. This was indeed a mass flight

of people from the country, which was disintegrating before their eyes. . . . It was not by accident that it was at precisely this time [Stalin's final months] that the widespread propaganda-myth about how the dictator was supposedly preparing the deportation of the Jews began.[748]

To substantiate his denial, Kostyrchenko stated, "Even a critic as furious of Stalin as Khrushchev did not mention this plan in his memoirs." The Jewish deportation and Stalin's Okhrana ties have remained taboo subjects in Russia to the present day.

Khrushchev attempted to find out the truth behind the veil of secrecy surrounding Stalin's Okhrana story. Alexander Orlov, an NKVD general who had defected to the United States in 1938, read Khrushchev's secret speech and decided to reveal what he knew about the discovery of Stalin's Okhrana file and about the Tukhachevsky conspiracy. Orlov wrote:

> However it happened, it seems certain to me that the documentary proof that Stalin had been a tsarist police agent was placed before the current collective leadership.[749]

Orlov published his revelation in the April 1956 issue of *Life* magazine in an article titled "The Sensational Secret behind the Damnation of Stalin." Khrushchev appointed a group of several surviving Old Bolsheviks to investigate Stalin's crimes, including his Okhrana service. The commission established that Stalin had doctored and fabricated Okhrana documents in order to glorify himself as a "great revolutionary leader," and had inundated Soviet archives with these forgeries. A Soviet historian F. D. Volkov who took part in the inquiry, stated:

> In 1962, O. G. Shatunovskaya, a member of the commission dealing with the rehabilitation of the victims of the personality cult, raised before the Central Committee of the Communist Party the question of making public all the materials exposing Stalin as an Okhrana agent.[750]

The Old Bolsheviks in the commission established that several of Stalin's Okhrana files had been found in the old archives and delivered to him.[751] They also reported to Khrushchev about I. L. Stein's discovery of Stalin's Okhrana file, about the rivalry between Stalin and top Okhrana agent Roman Malinovsky, and about the Tukhachevsky conspiracy.[752] Khrushchev at that time did not dare openly disclose the commission's findings, claiming that to do so "would reveal that for more than thirty years the country was ruled by an agent of the tsarist Okhrana."[753]

In 1957, Politburo members Molotov, Kaganovich, and Malenkov attempted to depose Khrushchev, accusing him of undermining the Soviet system by exposing Stalin's crimes. Marshal Zhukov supported Khrushchev against Kaganovich and Malenkov. Later on Bulganin and Voroshilov were removed from the Politburo. Then Khrushchev accused Marshal Zhukov of harboring "Bonapartist schemes," and dismissed him. The places of Stalin's old cronies in the Politburo were taken over by Khrushchev's protégés, among them Leonid Brezhnev, Alexei Kosygin, Kontantin Chernenko, and Yuri Andropov. This new group of Politburo members did not share Khrushchev's hatred of Stalin, and felt that revealing Stalin as an Okhrana agent would discredit the entire Soviet system, cutting off the branch upon which they all were sitting.

Yet despite the opposition of the new Politburo members, Khrushchev in 1962 decided to expose Stalin's Okhrana past. On Khrushchev's order, the "Eremin Letter" was stolen from the Tolstoy Foundation archive in the United States and delivered to Moscow where several Party historians, assigned by Khrushchev to research Stalin's Okhrana past, examined it.[754] A sinister picture of a tsarist spy haunted by fear of exposure, a mass murderer bent on shrouding his ignoble Okhrana past, began to emerge in Khrushchev's mind. He was gradually consumed by the emotional need to avenge the humiliations to which Stalin had subjected him personally. Stalin used to clean his smoking pipe by knocking it against Khrushchev's balding head, saying, *"Durachok ty, Nikitushka, durachok!"* (You're a little fool, Nicky boy! A little fool!), while Khrushchev, cringing with pain and smiling, had to act apologetic and endure the abuse. He recalled how Stalin used to force him, an overweight and aging man, to drink many glasses of vodka and dance the Ukrainian *gapak*, causing him excruciating pain.[755] Stalin also liked to place burning paper between the fingers of Politburo members, and watch how long they tolerated this torture. Khrushchev recalled with shame how he, in boundless devotion and gratitude to Stalin, had cried as he kneeled next to the body of the dead dictator, kissing his hand.[756]

Similar memories filled Khrushchev with rage and regret. He was driven by the urge to expose the tyrant, this despicable creature of the Okhrana and avenge his own humiliation. Khrushchev's anti-Stalin drive created a rift in the Communist camp. Chinese leader Mao Tse-tung and Albania's staunch Stalinist ally Enver Hoxha refused to attend the 22nd Party Congress, which opened in Moscow in October 1961. In his speech, Khrushchev said that all he was trying to accomplish by criticizing Stalin was the prevention of a similar "personality cult." He accused Hoxha of using Stalin's methods of repression against his own people.[757] Because of the opposition of the majority of Politburo members, Khrushchev decided not to deliver his prepared speech, where he intended to accuse Stalin of organizing the murder of Kirov.[758] However, on the night of October 31, 1961, Khrushchev delivered a blow to Stalin by other means—by removing his embalmed body from the mausoleum and secretly burying it near the Kremlin wall. The burial of Stalin's embalmed body was carried out by a detachment of soldiers working under the headlights of military vehicles.[759] A black granite plate with the inscription "I. V. Stalin, 1879–1953" was placed atop the grave. Stalin's name was removed from the mausoleum. Lenin's body again became the sole occupant of this shrine.

In the summer of 1962 the remains of the Tsar Ivan the Terrible, who had been idolized by Stalin as one of Russia's greatest statesmen, were removed from the Tsar's tomb in the Kremlin's Cathedral of Archangel Mikhail. Tsar Ivan had been buried there since his death in 1584. The skeleton revealed the presence of a considerable amount of arsenic, raising the possibility that the Tsar Ivan had been poisoned. Mikhail Gerasimov, a prominent Soviet anthropologist who had earlier reconstructed the facial features of the prehistoric Java and Peking men, sculpted a bust of Ivan the Terrible. Gerasimov determined that Tsar Ivan had been six-feet-three-inches tall, a giant by sixteenth-century standards.[760] Not content with merely demythologizing Tsar Ivan, Khrushchev called for the condemnation of all books that praised him.[761]

Politburo members began noticing signs of irrational behavior in Khrushchev. During a reception in the Yugoslav embassy, Khrushchev got drunk and dropped on all fours, declaring that he was the "locomotive of history." He began to tell Soviet generals that under his leadership the Soviet Union would achieve greater victories in a future war with "imperialist countries" than Stalin had achieved in the war with Hitler's Germany. Khrushchev visited the United States, declaring that he would show the West "where the crayfish spends winter" (roughly equivalent to the threat of teaching someone a lesson) and boasting, "We will bury you!" During a speech at the United Nations, he took off his shoe and banged the podium with it. Americans were intrigued by this odd way of making a point, and tried to analyze the meaning of the Russian proverbs Khrushchev had used. The explanations varied, indicating the great chasm between the world Khrushchev came from and the West. Khrushchev could not understand why John Kennedy had allowed the Cuban exiles to be routed during the Bay of Pigs invasion after having promised them American military support. Khrushchev convinced himself that Kennedy was an easy pushover and decided to blackmail him by placing Soviet rockets with nuclear warheads in Cuba. But Kennedy proved to be less of a pushover than Khrushchev had imagined and Khrushchev was forced to withdraw the rockets.

In 1962 Khrushchev sponsored the publication of Alexander Solzhenitsyn's *One Day in the Life of Ivan Denisovich*. The prison-camp jargon, developed by generations of Gulag inmates, poured into the Russian language. Dissident groups secretly distributed anti-Soviet *samizdat* (self-publishing). The fear of Stalin's era was slowly fading away from the Soviet "Island of Doctor Moreau."

Early in March 1963, Khrushchev delivered a speech in which he mentioned Stalin several times. At one point, he said:

> There has been more than one case of betrayal and treason to the cause of the Revolution in the history of the Bolshevik Party; for example, the activities of the double agent Malinovsky, a member of the Bolshevik faction of the State Duma.[762]

Khrushchev's hint of "more than one case of betrayal" was not lost on those who knew of Khrushchev's intention to reveal Stalin's Okhrana ties. In the summer of 1964, Khrushchev decided to make public the history of Stalin's rivalry with Malinovsky. Politburo members were against such a revelation.[763] On July 19, 1964, Khrushchev delivered a speech at a Moscow reception honoring a Hungarian party delegation. At one point he shouted in a high-pitched voice:

> In vain are the attempts of those who want to alter the leadership in our country and take under their protection all the evil deeds that Stalin committed. No one can whitewash him. You can't whitewash a black dog.[764]

Khrushchev also hinted publicly for the first time that Stalin had been murdered. He said:

> In human history, there have been many cruel tyrants, but all of them met

their death by an axe, the same axe with which they had maintained their power.[765]

This part of his speech was cut from the published version, but it had been broadcast over the radio and recorded. A statement made by Enver Hoxha on May 24, 1964, alarmed the Soviet leaders:

> The Soviet leaders are plotters who have the impudence to say openly, as Mikoyan has been doing, that they secretly hatched a conspiracy to murder Stalin.[766]

Brezhnev and his Politburo allies were against any radical rewriting of Soviet history. They decided that Khrushchev was behaving irrationally and that he should be removed from power. In October 1964, while Khrushchev was vacationing at the Black Sea resort of Pitsunda, they removed him from power, accusing him of recklessness and of harboring "harebrained ideas." Brezhnev suppressed the story of the Stalin-Malinovsky rivalry that was about to be published. Only the part relating to Malinovsky's Okhrana story was printed in 1965, with no mention of Stalin at all.[767] Brezhnev attempted to restore Stalin's prestige as a "great leader," but Khrushchev's "secret speech" had tarnished Stalin's halo beyond repair. The speech was no longer secret after its publication by Khrushchev in the Soviet Union in 1959.[768] Millions of prisoners were released from the Gulag during Khrushchev's rule and told their stories to the world.

Chapter 6

A Dangerous Enemy and the Six-Day War

Khrushchev set the stage for the ongoing Soviet Middle East policy of exploiting the Arab-Israeli conflict and manipulating the "Palestinian issue" to Soviet advantage. Khrushchev endorsed "Arab rights in Palestine," which became the focus of Soviet propaganda. He declared:

> The State of Israel deserves of condemnation . . . from the first days of its existence it began to threaten its neighbor.

Khrushchev accused Israel of "plotting, with imperialism, to savagely ravage the natural treasures of the region." By "natural treasures" he meant the Middle East oil. The United States and Great Britain launched the "Baghdad Pact," an alliance of "Northern Tier states," which included Iran, Iraq, Turkey, Pakistan, and their Arab neighbors. Soon it became clear that the Arab-Israeli conflict posed a danger to the unity of this alliance. Americans came up with a "secret peace initiative" code-named "Alpha Plan," which was designed to coerce Israel into conceding large chunks of territory to the Arabs in return for an Arab pledge of no "belligerency." It was assumed that Colonel Gamal Abdel Nasser, who had come to power in Egypt as the result of a CIA-assisted coup, would be a "moderate" leader. The hope was that Nasser would cooperate with the West in exchange for "American arms and Egypt's long-coveted land bridge across the Negev."

However, by 1953, Nasser had begun sponsoring attacks by so-called *fida'iyyun* (self-sacrifice fighters), who attacked the Israeli Negev region from Egyptian Sinai bases. He launched a propaganda campaign for a "second round" in the war to extinguish Israel and nationalized the Suez Canal. On September 24, 1956, Israeli, British, and French representatives signed a secret protocol allowing Israeli forces to recapture the Suez Canal, thereby providing Israel's European allies with a justification to "protect" it. On October 29, 1956, Israeli paratroopers landed in the Mitla Pass in Sinai, twenty-four miles east of the canal. British and French troops landed in Suez on November 4, 1956.

The timing of the British-French-Israeli operations distracted attention from the 1956 Hungarian uprising, which started precisely at the same time and was brutally crushed by Soviet troops. President Eisenhower was annoyed by this Israeli, British, and French "adventure." For him, the operation appeared to be a return to the European colonialism which he abhorred. At the Teheran conference, Roosevelt, in conversation with Stalin, had made fun of Churchill's "reactionary" devotion to British "colonial imperialism." Eisenhower shared President Roosevelt's "anti-colonialist" point of view, which was the prevailing liberal ideology of that period.

Khrushchev threatened to retaliate against any American support of the Hungarian rebels. The threat of a nuclear confrontation with the Soviets appeared to be real. Eisenhower pressured the Israeli, British, and French governments to withdraw from Suez. With the Hungarian uprising crushed and the Soviet grip on Hungary restored, Khrushchev ordered his satellite Czechoslovakia to supply large quantities of Soviet arms to Nasser. Egypt was turning into a Soviet base in the Middle East, threatening Israel and conservative Arab regimes. Eisenhower disliked both Cairo's "nonalignment policies" and the presence of Soviet military specialists in Egypt. He therefore abandoned the "Alpha secret peace initiative." Eisenhower's personal emissary Robert B. Anderson, a Texas oilman and former secretary of the treasury, delivered another secret proposal (code-named "Gamma") to Nasser, which again offered Israeli land in exchange for Nasser's promise of "non-belligerency." Ben-Gurion rejected the idea. Nasser refused to even meet Anderson. As Czechoslovakia began delivering large quantities of Soviet arms to Nasser, Eisenhower approved yet another top-secret project, code-named "Omega," to topple Nasser "by all means except assassination."[769]

Despite the enormous pressure from the United States and Russia, Israel was not in a hurry to retreat from Sinai, Gaza, or the Straits of Tiran. Ben-Gurion insisted on guarantees for free passage through the Straits of Tiran and for protection against terrorist attacks across Egypt's borders. Canadian Foreign Minister Lester Pearson negotiated the agreement between Nasser and UN Secretary General Dag Hammarskjöld to install the UN Emergency Force (UNEF) to supervise the evacuation of Anglo-French forces from Egypt. Pearson also arranged for UNEF troops to be deployed at Sharm al-Shekh and the areas surrounding the Straits of Tiran and the Egyptian-Israeli border in Gaza. American Secretary of State John Foster Dulles pledged to Israel's Foreign Minister Golda Meir that the U.S. would regard any Egyptian attempt to blockade the Straits of Tiran as an act of war under Article 51 of the UN Charter. Ben-Gurion agreed, and by March 11, 1957, the last Israeli soldier had left Sinai.

In the summer of 1957, Nasser and Khrushchev sailed on a Soviet battleship into the Black Sea port of Sukhumi and rode in a motorcade through its streets, waving to the adoring crowds.[770] The Soviet press praised Nasser as a hero of the "war of national liberation" and bragged about the role of the USSR in building the Aswan Dam, "the greatest engineering feat in the Middle East since the pyramids." Nasserism, the radical blend of socialism and Arab nationalism, was on the march in the Middle East. Egypt's unification with Syria in the "United Arab Republic" followed, as well as coups, assassinations, the Iraqi revolution of 1958, and attempts to overthrow the Lebanese and Jordanian governments. Eisenhower tried to counter this trend by issuing the "Eisenhower Doctrine," which led to the landing of American Marines in Lebanon. The "Arab street" and the Arab press were urging a war to "liberate Palestine." The next decade was marked by turmoil in the Arab world and a steadily growing Soviet-Egyptian friendship. Evgeny Primakov, now a KGB operative masquerading as a *Pravda* correspondent, kept publishing articles about "Israeli aggressors" and "Zionist agents of American imperialism" while praising Nasser as a "progressive Arab leader." A writer named Yuri Ivanov published a booklet entitled *Danger, Zionism!* His mother, like Primakov's mother, was Jewish.[771]

The triumvirate of Prime Minister Alexei Kosygin, President Nikolai Podgorny, and Communist Party Secretary-General L. I. Brezhnev continued Khrushchev's "anti-Zionist" policy. When top Egyptian general and Nasser's confidant Abd al-Hakim Amer came for a state visit to Moscow, they told him, "We will give you everything, even secret weapons"; to which Amer replied,

"We will keep those secret."[772]

At this point, a new key player, Yasir Arafat, entered the Middle East scene as head of the militant group Al-Fatah ("The Conquest"), also known as the "Movement for the Liberation of Palestine." On the night of December 31, 1964, this group, armed with Soviet-made explosives, crossed from Lebanon into northern Israel and attempted to blow up a water-pump station. They intended to provoke an Israeli retaliation and to ignite an all-Arab war against the "Zionist entity." The explosives failed to detonate. Despite the fiasco of this first terrorist raid, Arafat proclaimed victory in the "Jihad [holy war], the dream of revolutionary Arabs from the Atlantic to the Gulf." Several years later, Arafat, after having eliminated all of his rivals, proclaimed himself the leader of the "Movement for Liberation of Palestine."

In January 1964, Nasser convened a large gathering of Arab leaders in Cairo that approved a $17,500,000 plan to reduce Israel's water supply by diverting the Jordan River at its source. It also approved the creation of the United Arab Command to counter any Israeli military response. During the Arab summits in Alexandria, Egypt, in September 1964, and at Casablanca, Morocco, one year later, the delegates approved the establishment of the PLO under Ahmad al-Shuqayri, a lawyer and Nasser protégé. It was decided to deploy the Palestinian Liberation Organization along Israel's borders. Arab leaders agreed to cease interfering in each other's internal affairs and to concentrate on "Palestine's redemption."

After Khrushchev's downfall in 1964, Brezhnev decided to establish a Soviet sphere of interest in the Middle East by forming an alliance with the Arabs, promising to defeat Israel and deliver Palestine to them. The centuries-old "Eastern Question," the struggle for control of the strategically placed Middle East, was renewed in earnest. However, the "Eastern Question" was not the only motive behind Soviet pro-Arab policy. Not far from the surface, there lurked a deep streak of anti-Semitism, which Stalin had cultivated among his entourage and among Communist party members, as well as the Soviet people. There also was the upsetting awareness that a great number of Soviet Jews would want to immigrate to Israel, not because they were ardent Zionists, but because many wanted to escape from the misery of Soviet life. The Soviet leaders feared that a Jewish exodus to Israel would threaten the survival of the Soviet system by encouraging other ethnic groups to emigrate. The need for self-preservation motivated Brezhnev and other Soviet leaders in their quest for the destruction of Israel.

Soviet secret police archives contain numerous reports with the requests of

Soviet Jews at the time of the Arab-Israeli war in 1948–49 to allow Jewish emigration to Israel. The Jewish Anti-Fascist Committee received thousands of such requests and reported them to the MGB and to the Party Central Committee. The petitioners were arrested on Stalin's orders. Among these petitioners were Colonel D. A. Dragunsky, the hero of the Soviet Union, and an engineer, I. G. Pogachevsky. They offered to organize a "special Jewish division" to fight in the war for Israeli independence. Izhak Fefer reported this offer to the MGB and Pogachevsky was arrested.[773] Colonel Dragunsky, on the other hand, "came to his senses" after he was summoned to MGB headquarters. He later rose to the rank of general and was appointed head of the Soviet school for Palestinian terrorists. They were trained for combat against Israel. Later, Dragunsky headed the Soviet anti-Zionist propaganda campaign for many years. He was in the good graces of the Soviet government when he died, and his descendants were showered with privileges.

By 1967, a new Soviet scheme to destroy Israel had emerged in the minds of Soviet leaders, who decided to use Soviet Jews as an instrument of their anti-Israel policies. On December 3, 1966, during a state visit to Switzerland, Soviet premier Alexei Kosygin delivered a speech in which he promised to allow emigration from the USSR for the "reunification of Jewish families." The new Soviet proposal was seen as a liberal trend toward a more humanitarian Soviet policy. Shortly after, the relatives of Israeli prime minister Levi Eshkol, and several hundred other Soviet Jews, arrived in Israel. They were at a loss to explain why the Soviets had suddenly bestowed upon them such incredible good fortune.[774]

But this change in Soviet emigration policy had nothing to do with humanitarian motives but rather the intention to convince Israeli leaders, and particularly Premier Eshkol, that there was hope that the Soviets might one day allow Jewish emigration to Israel, the dream of the Israeli Zionist leaders. The Soviets intended to use this leverage to encourage Eshkol to be more receptive to Soviet advice during the coming Arab-Israeli war that the Soviets were planning to provoke.

Early in May 1967, the Soviet press began publishing reports about "40,000 Israeli soldiers and 3,000 vehicles massing along the Syrian border and preparing to attack Damascus." Eshkol invited Sergei Chuvakhin, the Soviet ambassador to Israel, to inspect the border area, but Chuvakhin twice refused to go there, saying that his mission was to deliver the truth, not to verify it. Chuvakhin warned, "You will be punished for your alliance with imperialism, and you will lose your access to the Red Sea."[775] The Soviet press continued to condemn America's bombing of Hanoi and to denounce the "Israeli plots" to conquer Syria. Soviet diplomats professed their commitment to averting violence against Israel. When Nasser announced the blockade of the Straits of Tiran on May 22, 1967, Chuvakhin insisted that there was a big difference between the "principle of free passage and Egypt's unassailable sovereignty over the Straits of Tiran." *Pravda* warned:

> Should anyone try to unleash aggression in the Near East, he would be met not only with the united strength of the Arab countries, but also with strong opposition from the Soviet Union and all peace-loving people.[776]

When the Egyptian minister of war, Shams al-Din Badran, assured Kosygin that the Egyptian army was ready and able to defeat Israel, Kosygin brushed aside this bravado and said that he was not certain that Americans would watch passively if Israel were attacked, even though conventional American forces were tied up in Vietnam. He said that the U.S. might react in the Middle East, using their only remaining means, namely, nuclear weapons. Kosygin advised Badran, to compromise with Israel, saying:

> We will back you, but you have made your point and win a political victory. It is better to sit at the negotiating table than to wage a battle by the sword.[777]

Badran was not convinced, and asked for more weapons.[778] Kosygin promised to "consider" additional requests, but ruled out any delivery of arms for the PLO. Kosygin warned:

> We want no part of the PLO or its army. You are free to give them what you want, but think carefully about what you're doing lest they lead you into a war.[779]

On May 30, 1967, Jordan's King Hussein secretly flew to Egypt. Nasser welcomed him at the Al-Maza military airport with the words, "Since your visit is a secret, what would happen if we arrested you?" Hussein smiled, "The possibility never crossed my mind." Nasser assured the King that Arab armies would defeat the Israelis in a matter of days, adding, "If the Americans intervene, I will be quite prepared to ask for Soviet assistance." Hussein said that he was willing to sign the Egyptian-Syrian defense treaty. He agreed to admit Iraqi, Saudi, Syrian, and Egyptian troops to his territory and to reopen the PLO offices in Amman. PLO Chairman Ahmad al-Shuqayri, who had previously threatened to lead the Palestinian army into Amman to overthrow Hussein, now strode up to Hussein declaring his readiness to visit Jordan. "If he gives you any trouble, throw him into one of your towers and rid me of him!" Nasser told the King.[780]

The problem of Jewish emigration from Russia to Israel played a major role in the calculations of Soviet leaders as they tried to influence Eshkol's decisions. Eshkol temporized, trying to determine the intentions of various countries. Israeli commanders complained that the delays were a gamble with Israel's survival. A paratroop platoon commander, Yoni Nataniyahu, wrote to his girlfriend, "What are we waiting for?" After a thirty-hour absence, Chief of Staff Yitzhak Rabin appeared in Eshkol's office and tendered his resignation. He had a nervous breakdown. Eshkol merely said, "Forget it," waving him off. Years later, Rabin wrote:

> Eshkol was a warm, wise man. Perhaps he had long known, and I had just then been forced to face the frightening depth of man's vulnerability.[781]

At this point, word arrived that four Egyptian MiG-21s had flown over Dimona and photographed the nuclear reactor. Eshkol asked Yitzhak Rabin and Ezer Weizman point-blank:

> Am I to understand that you both want to attack today?[782]

Weizman replied:

> All the signs indicate that the Egyptians are ready to strike. We have no option but to attack at once.[783]

Rabin said that the danger was obvious but that all of the diplomatic options had not yet been exhausted. Eshkol wanted to send Golda Meir to Washington, but she fell ill and Abba Eban went instead, with the instructions to secure American support. "We will wait until Eban's meeting with Johnson," said Rabin.[784] Eban had been deeply involved in the history of Israel since its birth. He held important diplomatic positions such as ambassador to the UN and to Washington from 1947 to 1950. He was elected to the Knesset and became education minister under Ben-Gurion, and then deputy prime minister under Eshkol. Cambridge-educated, polyglot, author of many books and a great orator, Eban was widely admired by American and European Jews, although in Israel he continued to be known as Aubrey Solomon, a South African Jew from Cape Town, an outsider among the Hebrew and Yiddish-speaking Russian-Jewish establishment.

The last days of May 1967 were extremely tense with anticipation of the impending outbreak of hostilities. *Pravda* declared, "There should be no doubt about the Soviet Union's commitment to give political and material aid to the Arabs." Kosygin ordered the Soviet ambassador to Israel, Chuvakhin, to immediately contact Eshkol and instruct him to prevent the outbreak of hostilities. On May 27, 1967, Chuvakhin rushed to the Dan Hotel in Tel-Aviv with Kosygin's letter, and demanded to know if Israel intended to attack Egyptian forces. Eshkol, dressed in pajamas, replied, "The Egyptians, sir, have already fired the first shot in this war." Chuvakhin left the Dan Hotel two hours later, convinced that his mission had failed.

Eban's first stop was in Paris. "Do not make war," Charles de Gaulle told him. "Do not be the first to shoot." Eban reminded de Gaulle that Israel had agreed to withdraw from Sharm al-Sheikh in 1957 largely because of the French commitment to free passage though the Straits of Tiran. "That was 1957. This is 1967," replied de Gaulle. At his press conference on December 2, 1967, de Gaulle said that the Jews were "an elite people, sure of themselves and dominating." The next day, December 3, 1967, the French newspaper *Le Monde* mocked de Gaulle's remark in a cartoon that depicted a man dressed in the striped prison garb of a Nazi concentration camp, his jacket emblazoned with the Star of David, his head lifted in a Napoleonic gesture of supremacy, and his foot rested on barbed wire. The heading "*Une libre opinion*" was followed by the caption, "Sure of himself and dominating." *Le Monde* mentioned that leading French Jews were accusing de Gaulle of anti-Semitism and that Israeli prime minister Levi Eshkol had expressed "profound regret over President de Gaulle's comment."[785]

Eban's stop in London was more promising. Prime Minister Harold Wilson was "warm, almost fraternal; a long-time admirer of Israel," where his son had volunteered to work on a kibbutz. Wilson assured Eban of his commitment to reopen the Straits through action "inside or outside the UN." He also said that Nasser had altered the balance of power in the Middle East in Soviet favor, and to not respond to this provocation would "be like 1938." He had Munich's 1938 appeasement of Hitler in mind. Wilson promised that Britain would do everything to fulfill its promises from 1957, and pledged to send his foreign secretary to Moscow to ascertain where the Soviets stood. Encouraged by his apparent success in London, Eban flew to Washington, hoping to secure strong American support. His first encounter was with American secretary of state Dean Rusk, whom Eban considered somewhat of an "Arabist" in the State Department tradition. Eban knew that Rusk had led the State Department UN desk in 1947–48 and had been strongly opposed to the creation of Israel. Rusk advocated the establishment of a bi-national Jewish-Arab state, an idea then supported by both the Israeli Communist party and the Soviet Union. President Harry Truman rejected Rusk's advice and recognized Israel, despite the fact that Truman on occasion would rant about the "liberal New York Jews" who had supported Henry Wallace, the "Progressive Party" candidate, in the 1948 election. Rusk was also considered to be a "China hand" because of his service in China during World War II. Rusk advised President Lyndon Johnson to pursue "multilateralism, nonintervention, and, above all, prudence."

There were many Jews in the Johnson administration, and some of them were supporters of Israel. Johnson had close ties with Jewish activists in the Democratic Party, especially with its chairman, Hollywood mogul Arthur Krim, whose wife Matilde was a former Israeli. In 1967, many American Jews were opposed to Johnson's Vietnam policy. Abe Feinberg, Johnson's liaison with the Jewish community, told Johnson that the American defense of Saigon served as proof to the Jews that Americans would also defend Israel. "Then why the hell don't the Jews believe that?" asked Johnson, and added that American Jews were ungrateful for his support of Israel and hypocritical for not backing the war against the Vietcong guerillas, who were not unlike the Palestinian guerillas. Johnson was also annoyed by Israel's failure to support his Vietnam policy. "Israel gets more than it's willing to give. It's a one-way street," he complained. Johnson had many Jewish advisers, among them the Rostow brothers, Walter and Eugene, speechwriter Ben Wattenberg, and domestic affairs aide Larry Levinson. He also appointed Supreme Court Justice Arthur Goldberg as ambassador to the UN. He was also especially close to Supreme Court Justice, Abe Fortas. On Friday, May 26, Johnson gathered his advisers for a meeting at which Rusk said, "If Israel fires first, it'll have to forget the U.S." Defense Secretary Robert McNamara was against promising Eban any support.

Eshkol instructed Eban not to insist upon sending an international naval convoy, the "Regatta," to open the Straits of Tiran, but to ask for American support for Israel in case of war. Instead of following Eshkol's instructions,

Eban persisted in asking for the "Regatta." General Wheeler said that to send the "Regatta" would mean to start a war; and one more war besides Vietnam was an anathema to legislators on the Hill. Some of the legislators who were "doves" on Vietnam began to turn "hawks" on Israel. The popular slogan was, "You don't have to be Jewish to be against the war." Rusk compared the idea of Regatta to "Tonkin Gulfitis," mocking the congressional Tonkin Gulf resolution. Senators Mike Mansfield, Albert Gore, and William J. Fulbright (whom President Truman once called "Halfbright") were adamantly against the idea of Regatta. Rusk and McNamara reported to Johnson that an effort to get a meaningful resolution from the Congress on the notion of Regatta would "run the risk of becoming bogged down in acrimonious dispute." Johnson wrote in his diary, "The Canadians and Europeans will not accept responsibility. They say it's not their trouble and they shouldn't get into the Middle East right now." Regatta was dead. Johnson agreed to see Eban on condition of total secrecy (including no press leaks), so as not to upset the Arabs and Soviets, and to delay the meeting until after the Veterans' Day weekend that started on Saturday, May 27, 1967.

Eban began by summarizing the history of U.S. commitments to Israel, and then said, "The question I have to answer is, 'Do you have the will and determination to open the Straits?'" Then he added, "Do we fight alone, or are you with us?" Eban came out of his meeting with Johnson stunned by the image of a "paralyzed president." On the following day Eban met Arthur Goldberg, who gave him the blunt news: "The 'Regatta' plan is dead." Goldberg added, "You owe it to your government, because lives are going to be lost and your security is involved, to tell your Cabinet that the President's statement means a joint resolution of Congress, and the President can't get such a resolution because of the Vietnam War." It was obvious that the conflict in Vietnam and Israel's destiny were deeply entwined

At that time a heated debate among politicians and military officers was raging in Israel. Ariel Sharon said:

> The people of Israel are ready to wage a just war, to fight and to pay the price. The question isn't free passage [through the Straits of Tiran], but the existence of the people of Israel.[786]

Somewhat confused by Eban's report, Eshkol decided to send Meir Amit, the director of the Mossad (the Israeli Intelligence Service), to Washington. Amit had extensive connections in the United States. The massage Amit carried to

Washington was grave: "Israel's blood is on the American conscience."[787] The first man he met in Washington was James Angleton, the CIA head of counterintelligence and the main liaison with the Mossad. Angleton insisted that the Soviets had been planning this crisis for years. CIA chief Richard Helms was of the same opinion. After talking to Angleton and Helms, Amit told McNamara, "I am returning home with a recommendation of war." McNamara replied, "I read you loud and clear."

Johnson came to the conclusion that he could offer Israel diplomatic, but not military, help. He asked his national security adviser Walt Rostow what he thought Israel would do. Rostow replied:

Israel would move like the marshal in *High Noon*, alone, employing the necessary force.[788]

When Amit returned to Israel on Friday, June 2, he found the country different from the one he had left two days earlier. The "Israeli street" erupted in an uproar, demanding the creation of a National Unity government to put an end to political bickering. The National Unity government held its first meeting on Thursday night, June 1. A number of opposition leaders, including Menachem Begin (now Minister without Portfolio), were present. Begin delivered a fiery speech about the destiny of the Jewish nation and the dangerous trial awaiting it, to which Eshkol responded, "Amen, Amen." Only a few years earlier, during the 1961 election campaign, Begin's left-wing opponents had called him a "fascist."[789]

The Unity Government decided to strike. On Monday morning, June 5, Israel's air force attacked Egyptian airfields, decimating most of Egypt's planes. Then IDF units moved into Sinai, breaking through Egyptian defenses and rapidly advancing toward the Suez Canal and Sharm el-Sheik. Meanwhile, Israeli soldiers could hear Arab broadcasts announcing that the Egyptian army was advancing toward Tel-Aviv.[790] Six days later, the Israeli army defeated the combined Egyptian, Syrian, and Jordanian forces and captured all of Sinai, the West Bank, the Old City of Jerusalem, and the Golan Heights.[791] The Soviets feverishly attempted to save whatever remained of the armed forces of Egypt, Syria, and Jordan by arranging for a UN cease-fire resolution. Soviet UN delegate N. T. Federenko threatened that the "Soviet government was prepared to use every available means to make Israel respect the cease-fire resolution." Johnson then ordered the "Sixth Fleet, with its two aircraft carriers and their accompanying ships, to steam eastward to within a hundred miles of

Israel's coast." Richard Helms told Johnson, "The message is going to get back to Moscow in a hurry." Arthur Goldberg confided to the Israelis:

> The United States government does not want the war to end as the result of a Soviet ultimatum. This would be disastrous not only for Israel, but for us all. It is your responsibility to act now.[792]

Eshkol received a cable from Moscow, stating:

> If Israel does not cease its actions immediately, then the USSR, together with other peace-loving nations, will take sanctions, with all the implications thereof.[793]

Chuvakhin entered Eban's office, announcing:

> In light of the continued aggression by Israel against the Arab states, and Israel's flagrant breach of the Security Council's resolutions, the USSR government has decided to end relations with Israel. I have come here to tell you about the rupture in relations.[794]

With these words, Chuvakhin burst into tears. He knew that he would be a scapegoat for the Soviet failure to use the issue of Soviet-Jewish emigration to Israel as leverage to manipulate the Israeli leaders into submission to Soviet dictates. (Chuvakhin was soon ousted from the Foreign Service and sent to Siberia to work in a meaningless position.) Nine other Communist Bloc countries, with the sole exception of Romania, recalled their ambassadors from Israel. The third Arab-Israeli war ended with these acts.

Kosygin wrote to Johnson:

> If all military actions are concluded today, it will be necessary to proceed to the next step of evacuating the territory occupied by Israel, and the return of troops from behind the armistice line . . . I consider that we should maintain contact with you on this matter.[795]

Johnson was thinking in more ambitious terms, which included his hope for Soviet help in getting him out of Vietnam. In his reply, Johnson wrote:

> It now appears that military action in the Middle East is being concluded. I hope our efforts in the days ahead can be devoted to the achievement of a lasting peace throughout the world.[796]

Chapter 7

The Exodus Begins

Johnson was hoping that the Soviets would help him "achieve a lasting peace" in Vietnam, but the Soviets had no intention of helping America extricate itself from that war. They hoped to use the Vietnam War as leverage to force Johnson into pressuring Israel into exchanging the "occupied territories" for a "lasting peace" with the Arabs. But Nasser was unwilling to offer any type of peace to Israel. On August 29, 1967, Nasser arrived in Khartoum, Sudan, and declared that his goal was to regain by force the territories the Arabs had lost in the 1967 war, including Jerusalem. The other Arab heads of state also called for "erasing the traces of aggression," and the return of all the land they had lost in the Six-Day War. Ahmad al-Shuqayri, who then represented the "Palestinian Liberation Organization," declared that the PLO would settle for nothing less than "erasing Israel."

Eshkol arrived at Johnson's Texas ranch in January 1968 and told him:

> My feeling is one of relief that we were saved from disaster in June, and for that I thank God. All my thoughts are now turned toward making peace with our neighbors—a peace of honor and equals.[797]

Eshkol died of heart failure one year later. Moshe Dayan sobbed and cried out

"Eshkol! Eshkol!" The editors of *Ha'aretz*, who had earlier demanded Eshkol's resignation, now praised his "roots as a Jew, an Israeli, and a man experienced in the ways of life far beyond politics." *Ma'ariv* praised his leadership in the 1967 war, stating:

> Perhaps only Eshkol, whose personality combines audacity, obstinacy, and weakness, could have weathered the most serious crises Israel has ever faced.[798]

The Arab press, as was expected, lauded Eshkol's demise. Cairo radio announced the death of the "leader of the gang that built Israel on the body parts of Arab victims." The Iraqi press described Eshkol as a "man who committed crimes in our captured land." In a communiqué issued in Damascus, *Fatah*'s leader Yasir Arafat, having replaced al-Shuqayri as PLO chairman, bragged about having "killed Eshkol with a surface-to-surface missile." He declared: "Our primary goal now is the liberation of Palestine through armed force, even if the struggle continues for tens of years."[799]

The President of the Soviet Union, Nikolai Podgorny, visited Cairo on June 22, 1968, and agreed to Nasser's request for jets, tanks, and advisers; in return for a seaport for the Soviet navy. He suggested a political solution for the Arab-Israeli conflict on the basis of a "'land for non-belligerency' agreement," but Nasser countered that any discussion of political concessions would serve only as a "reward for aggression." Iraqi President Aref and Algerian president Houari Boumedienne arrived in Moscow in July to negotiate on Nasser's behalf. Brezhnev suggested, "Let Israel withdraw and then do whatever you want." The Soviets promised to help the Arabs recover the territories they had lost in the Six-Day War, and agreed to rearm Egypt and Syria. They had a scheme up their sleeves. It was the same master plan to entice Israeli leaders to withdraw from the "occupied territories" by promising them unrestricted Jewish emigration from Russia. The Soviet leaders figured that this promise would serve as an attractive lure for the Israeli leaders. They had tried this scheme before, at the onset of the Six-Day War. This time the Soviets hoped that Israeli leaders would retreat from the "occupied territories" in the expectation of seeing the Soviet Jews being allowed to come to Israel en masse—the perennial dream of all Israeli leaders. The problem was that the Soviet Jews were too scared to apply for exit visas to Israel. One Ukrainian Jew, Dr. Levin, assumed it was a KGB provocation when he was offered an exit visa to Israel. He refused to apply.[800]

On June 10, 1968, Yuri Andropov, the head of the KGB, and Foreign Minister Gromyko dispatched Secret Document 13, addressed to the Central Committee of the Communist Party. It stated:

> The reactionary bourgeois press and radio and the Zionist centers abroad accuse the Soviet Union of anti-Semitism. . . . They demand issuance of exit permits for the Soviet citizens of Jewish origin to Israel. We recommend issuing exit visas to Soviet citizens for permanent residence in Israel for up to 1,500 persons in the current year, which would allow us to free ourselves from nationalistically oriented persons and religious fanatics who exert harmful influence on their neighbors. The Committee of State Security (KGB) would be able to use this channel for operational purposes.[801]

On October 6, 1968, the Central Committee of the Communist Party of the Soviet Union decided:

> The advice of the KGB. . . . Allow the exit of up to 1,500 Soviet citizens for permanent residence in Israel in 1968. Give permits for exit to persons of advanced age who do not have higher or special education. The KGB and MID-USSR [Ministry of Internal Affairs of the USSR] should submit proposals later about the quotas for exit to Israel in 1969 and in forthcoming years, considering the circumstances.[802]

Several Jews in the Baltic republics dared to apply when the KGB offered them exit visas to Israel. To their amazement, they were allowed to leave for Israel at the end of 1968. Efim Spivkovsky, a former Gulag inmate, and his prison-camp friend Vitaly Svechinsky learned that their Latvian friends had departed for Israel. Efim and Vitaly went to the Moscow OVIR (Department of Visas and Registration of Foreigners), where Svechinsky asked Captain Akulova, an OVIR official, whether he could visit his "aunt in Czechoslovakia." Akulova answered, "No, but you may apply for an exit visa to Israel." Svechinsky and Spivkovsky went outside the building, laughing and dancing with joy. The guard on duty that day spotted them, and flashed an amazed stare.

A Latvian Jew, Efim Zal, told Svechinsky that he had an exit visa and a ticket to fly to Israel. Svechinsky gave him a letter addressed to the author's mother, asking her to send him an invitation to come to Israel. Zal could not explain why the Soviets were releasing the Jews. Nechemia Levanon, the head of the Israeli department dealing with Jewish emigration from Russia, did not know either.[803] Svechinsky soon received the official invitation from the author's mother and submitted it to OVIR. He received the standard negative reply: "The intelligence services find your exit to Israel *nezelesoobrazny* [not having a purpose]." Initially, Svechinsky succeeded in convincing ten Moscow Jews to sign an open letter with an appeal for help from the West. Thirty-nine Jews signed the next letter; and others followed. Israeli officials initially attempted to keep secret the flow of Soviet Jews to Israel, fearing that publicity would anger the Soviets, who could halt the exodus. The decisive Israeli victory in the 1967 Six-Day War released a long-suppressed craving of Soviet Jews for the right to free emigration from the Soviet Union. Some Soviet Jews started to greet themselves by paraphrasing the Russian anti-Semitic slogan "Beat the kikes and save Russia" as "Save Israel and beat the Arabs as kikes do." Open letters from Soviet Jews, asking for support for free emigration from the Soviet Union, were published in the American press. It was announced at a press conference in New York in 1971 that the Russian Human Rights Organization, led by Sakharov, Tverdokhlebov, and Chalidze, had joined the International League for Human Rights.[804]

The Soviet leadership feared that other ethnic groups would also demand the right to leave the Soviet Union if they learned about the Jewish exodus. The Soviets also worried that such an exodus would be an embarrassing confirmation of the failure of the Soviet Communist system. The KGB had its own interest in allowing emigration to Israel, which offered the opportunity to use "this channel for operational purposes," that is, to infiltrate Israel with KGB agents. Among the many KGB agents exposed in Israel, a special place belongs to Shabtai Kalmanovich, who immigrated to Israel from Lithuania in 1971. The KGB supplied him with initial capital, which he multiplied in numerous shady financial deals, including cashing two million dollars' worth of forged checks at a Monte Carlo bank. Scotland Yard arrested him. The Israelis learned that the information supplied to the KGB by Kalmanovich was transmitted to Arab countries. In December 1988, Kalmanovich pleaded guilty to spying for the Soviet Union, and was sentenced to nine years' imprisonment. Many Soviet agents ended their contacts with the KGB after relocating to Israel.[805]

In 1968 the Soviets planed to provoke an Egyptian attack on Israel across the Suez Canal. A retired Soviet admiral, Vladimir Cherniavin, revealed that in 1968 Brezhnev had ordered the Soviet nuclear submarine "K-172" to sail to Israeli coastal waters and wait for a signal to strike Israeli cities with eight nuclear rockets onboard.[806] The Israeli press reported that pontoon barges to ferry Egyptian troops across the Suez Canal had been included in Soviet arms deliveries. Moshe Dayan and Yegal Alon declared that "Israel is not Czechoslovakia," and would not submit to Arab and Soviet threats. In November 1968, Hubert Humphrey lost the election to Richard Nixon. *Ma'ariv* published an article, "The Confrontation That Did Not Happen," in which it was reported that in January 1969, during the transition period, Johnson had received Brezhnev's letter with a proposal for joint American-Soviet military intervention should an Israeli-Egyptian war breaks out. Johnson consulted with the president-elect, Richard Nixon, who rejected the Soviet proposal.[807] Brezhnev abandoned his scheme.[808] Richard Nixon's election in 1968 was met with gloom and foreboding in Israel, where many people thought that "Democrats are better for the Jews." Articles with favorable opinions of Nixon's Middle East policy had little chance to be published. But there were a few exceptions.[809]

By September 1970, the Egyptian economy was in shambles. Thousands of Soviet advisers flooded the country. The Soviets were also in direct contact with Yasir Arafat, who staged a revolt against King Hussein of Jordan that same month. Syrian tanks were moving toward Amman. On September 21, King Hussein appealed to Great Britain to ask Israel to attack the Syrian tanks. British prime minister Edward Heath expressed doubts whether it was worth "prolonging, possibly for only a short time, Hussein's increasingly precarious regime." Heath, nevertheless, passed King Hussein's request to Washington. President Nixon asked Yitzhak Rabin, then the Israeli ambassador to the United States, to transmit his advice to Israeli prime minister Golda Meir to move Israeli troops into position to attack the Syrian tanks. Nixon also warned the Soviets to stay out of the conflict and to halt the Syrian intervention. The Soviets complied. Syrian forces withdrew from Jordan, and King Hussein crushed the PLO guerrillas. Nasser negotiated an agreement under which King Hussein expelled both Arafat and the PLO guerillas from Jordan back to Lebanon. These events became known as the "Palestinian Black September."

On September 28, 1970, Nasser returned to Cairo from Jordan. He was utterly drained by the preceding events, by the officers' coup against him, and by the attempted suicide of his lifelong friend, General Abd al-Hakim Amer. Nasser went to bed, never to rise again. After his expulsion from Jordan, Arafat launched guerila raids on northern Israeli towns from Lebanon. In 1972, PLO "Black September" terrorists murdered eleven Israeli athletes during the Munich Olympic games. President Nixon dispatched a military plane to bring the body of an American-Israeli athlete back to his parents in the United States.

During the Nixon presidency, the issue of Soviet-Jewish emigration to Israel entered the American political scene. Jewish organizations, calling for free emigration of Soviet Jews, appeared across the United States. Their slogan was, "Let my people go!" One such organization, the "League for the Repatriation of Soviet Jews," had a fundraising meeting where a young Wall Street money manager, Michael Steinhardt, wrote a check for $20,000 and then hurried back to his busy office. James Buckley, who in 1970 was running for a U.S. Senate seat from New York on the Conservative Party ticket, was the first to raise the Soviet-Jewish emigration issue. Both his Democratic and Republican opponents were silent. Buckley won the election.[810] The beginning of Soviet-American "détente" led to a rapid increase of Jewish emigration. Large groups of Jews gathered at Moscow's airports to see off family members and friends going to Israel. One family carried an elderly woman on a stretcher. She raised her hand, crying, "*Iskhod! Iskhod!* [Exodus! Exodus!] This is a reminder of how we escaped from Egypt!"[811] Among the arrivals in Israel was Vitaly Svechinsky, who was welcomed at the Tel-Aviv airport by Prime Minister Golda Meir and other Israeli officials. Twenty-nine thousand eight hundred Jews left Russia for Israel in 1972; the number increased to 33,500 in 1973. Russian historian G. V. Kostyrchenko stated:

> Because of the rapid development of "détente" between East and West, the Soviet leadership made considerable concessions in the question of Jewish emigration. . . . This became most obvious after the visit of U.S. President R. Nixon to Moscow, and in connection with the passage by the American Congress of the Jackson-Vanick Amendment of October 4, 1972, which tied the status of "most favored nation" to free emigration.[812]

Chapter 8

Watergate and the Yom Kippur War

Nixon's election in 1968 was met with gloom and foreboding in Israel where many believed that "Democrats are better for the Jews." It also was widely known that Nixon was deeply distrustful of the Soviets. Nixon realized that the Soviets used the Arab-Israeli conflict to advance their interests in the Middle East, just as they were using the North Vietnamese to advance their interests in Asia. Nixon understood that Chinese leaders viewed Soviet meddling in Vietnam as an attempt to encircle China. He knew that the Vietnam War and the fate of Israel were entangled.[813]

In September 1970 Yasir Arafat unleashed his PLO guerrillas against King Hussein in Jordan. Syrian tanks moved on Amman to help PLO to defeat Jordanian army. Golda Meir, the Israeli prime minister, consulted President Nixon who advised her to position Israeli tanks to intercept the Syrian columns. Nixon told the Soviets to stop the Syrian aggression and they did. King Hussein crushed the PLO and expelled Arafat and his guerrillas to Lebanon.

Nixon's policy was to confront the USSR as America's real enemy in Vietnam and in the Middle East.[814] Instead of chasing the Vietcong through the muddy fields and along the jungle trails of South Vietnam, he ordered the bombing of the North Vietnamese port of Haiphong while Soviet ships were unloading military supplies there. He also ordered the bombing of Hanoi and denied safe haven to the Vietcong in Cambodia and Laos. Henry Kissinger went to China, thus ending America's obsession with what Dean Rusk, President Johnson's Secretary of State, called the "yellow peril." Nixon then traveled to Moscow, to a red carpet reception, at which there were many wagging Soviet tails. Soviet leaders were impressed with Nixon's decisiveness. Henry Kissinger signed the Paris Peace Treaty with the North Vietnamese, winning him the Nobel Peace Prize. Yet America was ablaze in anti-Vietnam war demonstrations. Jane Fonda went to Hanoi, while John Kerry, a decorated war veteran, threw away his decorations in protest against the war, demanding withdrawal from Vietnam at any price and testifying in Congress about American "atrocities in Vietnam," telling of "rapes, beheadings, torture, and pillaging perpetrated by American soldiers in a fashion reminiscent of Genghis Khan."[815] It became fashionable to burn American flags and dodge the draft.

Such was the political atmosphere during the 1972 election campaign in which Nixon was running against democratic candidate George McGovern, who campaigned on the anti-Vietnam War platform. Nixon won by the greatest landslide in American history, but the dark shadow of the Watergate break-in outcry threatening his presidency. The scandal started on June 17, 1972, when five Cuban-American veterans of the Bay of Pigs fiasco were arrested for breaking into the offices of Democratic National Committee in the Watergate complex in Washington, D.C. The mostly Cuban-Americans became known as "plumbers" after they broke into the office of Lewis Fielding, Daniel Ellsberg's psychiatrist, when it had become a matter of concern to the Nixon administration that Ellsberg was "unstable" and that the Pentagon Papers, which Daniel Ellsberg leaked, had "appeared in Moscow before they were published by the *New York Times*."[816] Although the Watergate break-in was barely mentioned by the media during the 1972 election campaign, it turned into a great national scandal after Nixon's victory. Two *Washington Post* reporters, Bob Woodward and Carl Bernstein, assumed that the burglars intended to install tape-recording equipment on telephones used by Democratic campaign workers, whom they suspected of having ties to Fidel Castro's agents. It was soon revealed that the burglars were connected to the Nixon Reelection Committee. Woodward and Bernstein, encouraged by their superiors at the *Washington Post,* began to highlight the break-in, spicing it up with sensational revelations by what they described as their "very, very deep source" in the Nixon White House. Howard Simmons, Managing Editor at the *Washington Post,* jokingly suggested the code name "Deep Throat" for this "very, very deep source," borrowing this name from the notorious pornographic movie of the same title. The name stuck.

The careers of Woodward and Bernstein eventually skyrocketed into countless articles, books, and movies. The congressional testimony of Watergate "star witness" John Dean, who at the time of the break-in was Counsel to the President in the White House, played the major role in the destruction of Nixon's presidency. The *New York Times* headline, NIXON CANNOT SURVIVE DEAN, pretty much summed up John Dean's central role in President Nixon's eventual downfall. After firing Dean, Nixon appointed Leonard Garment to the post of Counsel to the President. In his book *In Search of Deep Throat—The Greatest Mystery of Our Time*, Garment took the reader on a 280-page tour of his tortured reasoning of why he had selected and then discarded dozens of candidates for the role of Deep Throat.[817] In his review of Garment's book in the *New York Times,* Francis X. Clines wrote that Garment, "after years of amateur sleuthing, without whisper or flinch," identified John Sears as Deep Throat. Sears, a prominent adviser to both the Nixon and Reagan election campaigns, called Garment's accusation "absolute nonsense" and threatened to take a lie detector test and to sue Garment.[818] Garment, in his book, stated that Benjamin Bradlee, the *Washington Post*'s Editor-in-Chief, predicted that when Deep Throat was finally identified, everyone would say, "Why didn't I think of that?" Garment wrote, "Which is precisely what I said to myself when I finally figured it out."[819]

Larry King, in his June 1997 interview with Woodward and Bernstein, asked them whos identity it was they were hiding behind "Deep Throat." They refused to reveal who Deep Throat was and said, "The man is still alive and we have an obligation to protect our source." Benjamin Bradlee in the same interview with Larry King said that Woodward and Bernstein had told him at the time of the Watergate scandal who Deep Throat was, but Bradlee too did not want to reveal his identity. General Alexander Haig, the White House Chief of Staff during the last days of Nixon Administration, in the same interview with Larry King, said that he, after "substantial research," had come to the conclusion that "Deep Throat was some high CIA official." Over the years many candidates have been mentioned for the role of Deep Throat, among them Secretary of State Henry Kissinger; CIA Director Richard Helms; Attorney General Richard Kleindienst; FBI Acting Director L. Patrick Gray; White House lawyer Fred Fielding, and others. Clairvoyant Jeanne Dixon said that she had had a hazy vision in which Deep Throat appeared as a "woman . . . her eyes were light, perhaps blue, gray, or green . . ." Dixon added:

I did not recognize her... Sometimes her voice is almost audible—like the wind in the far end of a long tunnel.... I do know that the day will come when she will be unveiled for the entire world to see.[820]

The identity of Deep Throat has remained hidden for more then thirty years, while most secrets in Washington become public knowledge immediately.

Soon after the "plumbers" were arrested, it was revealed that a man by the name of George Gordon Battle Liddy, who had worked for the Nixon Reelection Committee, took part in the break-in. Nixon first heard of Liddy when his name came up on June 23, 1972, in the course of his inquiry into what the break-in was all about. At one point Nixon asked his chief of staff H. R. (Bob) Haldeman: "Who was the asshole that did it? Is it Liddy? Is that the fellow? He must be a little nuts." Haldeman replied, "He is." Nixon then asked, "I mean he just isn't well screwed on, is he? Isn't that the problem?"[821] This was a huge problem. Liddy refused to talk to the prosecutors and for next thirty years insisted that he knew nothing about the break-in. Liddy was a strange person in the Watergate scandal. In 1980 he published his autobiography, titled *Will*, providing good insight into his confused, bravado-obsessed mind. In his book Liddy introduced himself:

An extraordinary gene pool somehow produced a frail, sickly, little crybaby named George Gordon Battle Liddy.[822]

He further wrote that he was driven by the need to overcompensate for his fears. As a boy he feared rats. To overcome this fear he killed a rat. He wrote:

For the next hour, I roasted the dead rat. Then I removed the burned carcass with a stick and let it cool. I skinned, then cut up and ate the roasted haunches of the rat... from now on rats could fear <u>me</u> as they feared cats; after all, I ate them too.[823]

Liddy's life was punctuated by similar aberrations. His wife, after reading *Will*, said:

Now, everybody will know what I had to put up with for 23 years.[824]

Liddy was briefly employed by the FBI's Denver office. Long after he left the

FBI, Office Chief Scott Wermer was "to shake his finger" at anyone who would suggest an especially crazy scheme and shout, "That's a liddy! That's a liddy." The FBI men in the office would roar with laughter. Assistant Attorney General Henry Peterson described Liddy as a "kind of super patriot who out of a misguided sense of loyalty to the President of the United States was refusing to cooperate." Peterson said:

> Basically this man is crazy . . . He is burning his arm. He showed it to the prosecutor and said, "I will stand up to anything . . . jail will not break me, and what have you."[825]

Judge John Sirica, instead of subjecting Liddy to a psychiatric test, imposed an outrageous sentence of six-to-twenty years in prison and a $40,000 fine for not cooperating with the court. In his autobiography, Liddy stated that he had been a "good soldier" by keeping silent and thus proving his loyalty to his "prince," that is, Nixon. Probably nothing short of Nixon's direct, in-person appeal would have changed Liddy's decision not to tell investigators what he knew about the break-in. Instead of personally ordering Liddy to tell the truth, Nixon transmitted his request through Liddy's lawyer. This did not help. Liddy refused to talk. Years later President Carter was asked at a press conference whether he could persuade Liddy to tell what he knew about the break-in. Carter replied, "According to my reading of Liddy's mind, Liddy would never talk." But in his January 29, 2001, sworn testimony in a Philadelphia court Liddy for the first time stated that the Watergate break-in had been "John Dean's operation." He testified that John W. Dean III, who had recruited Liddy to work for the Nixon "Committee to Reelect," told him at the time:

> An all-out offensive and defensive political operation with a $1 million budget was needed for the 1972 election.[826]

Liddy testified that in 1991 he read the book *The Silent Coup* by Len Colodny, which linked Dean's fiancée Maureen Biner to a call-girl ring that was serving the staff of the Democratic National Committee. Liddy further told the court, "I said to myself, 'Oh, my God!' My eyes opened. This was a John Dean op." Liddy testified that these photographs were located in the desk of Ida Wells, one of the Committee's secretaries. Wells was suing Liddy for defamation, seeking $5.1 million in damages, because he publicly linked her to the prostitution operation. Dean and his wife Maureen also sued St. Martin's Press, which had published *The Silent Coup*, stating that the book's claims that he had masterminded the break-in, was "baloney." The publisher settled the libel suit in 1997. This important revelation was buried in the *New York Times'* back page A19 and ignored by most of the media.[827]

John Dean said that had Liddy revealed the truth about the break-in, he and Liddy would probably have saved Nixon. If Liddy had agreed to Nixon's request to tell the investigators what he knew about the break-in, he would have indeed saved Nixon, but he would have exposed Dean's role in the break-in. Dean, of course, did not tell Liddy that he wanted to retrieve Maureen's photos from the Watergate headquarters desk.

Liddy assumed that the operation was needed to prove that the Democrats had contacts with agents of Fidel Castro and he employed the Cuban anti-Castro "plumbers" for the break-in who also assumed that this was the purpose of the "operation."

L. Patrick Gray III, the acting director of the F.B.I. at the time of the Watergate scandal, was interviewed by George Stephanopoulos on ABC-TV shortly before he died at the age of 88. The interview ended Gray's more than three decades of silence by finally revealing that he had "turned over the raw F.B.I. reports and lead sheets to John W. Dean, Nixon's counsel." He also revealed that Dean prompted him to "burn the files he had been given from the White House safe of E. Howard Hunt in the fireplace of his Connecticut home." Gray said that he had been "justified in burning these files because their content was unrelated to Watergate." He said that one of the files contained "top secret cables implicating the administration of President John F. Kennedy in the assassination of President Ngo Dinh Diem of South Vietnam in 1963." He also said that he "burned the second file which contained letters intended to embarrass Senator Edward M. Kennedy, Democrat of Massachusetts, if he ran for president." Gray also told George Stephanopoulos:

> Everything went up in the air when everybody found out that I was sending FBI files and reports on the investigation to John Dean at the White House, and it was at that point that John Dean exploded over there.[828]

Gray's disclosure turned the White House against him and he resigned in April 1973. When Gray heard Erlichman's saying on the released White House tapes that Gray should be left to "twist slowly in the wind," instead of being appointed Director of FBI, he reacted with anger. He told Stephanopoulos:

Well, what I thought cannot be repeated on television.[829]

The Watergate scandal was not about the break-in. Nixon was not even accused of ordering it. The scandal was not even about the cover-up of which Nixon was accused. It was about invalidation of Nixon's 1972 landslide victory. This was a calamity, which cries out for a close look at the Watergate scandal. Leonard Garment in the *New York Times* op-ed article "Justice Is Not the *Issue*" stated:

Watergate grew out of a dispute about Richard Nixon and his prosecution of the Vietnam War. This dispute was, in political terms, virtually irresolvable.[830]

Garment failed to remind his readers that this "dispute" was resolved by the forced resignation of Richard Nixon, the congressional passage of the "War Powers Act" that tied the hands of President Gerald Ford, and the conquest of South Vietnam by the Communist North. The consequences of the Watergate scandal were the tremendous weakening of American diplomacy and intelligence capabilities, especially following the Church Committee hearings into CIA operations.

President Nixon did not mention Deep Throat in his memoirs. Leon Jaworski, the Watergate Special Prosecutor, in his book *The Right and the Power*, did not inquire into Deep Throat's identity despite the startling fact that this unknown person was the only source of leaks, demonizing President Nixon. But Jaworski noticed with amazement that John Dean "seemed to know something about everything that had occurred in the White House."[831] Indeed, John Dean testified with an impressive grasp and certainty about the whole web of the Watergate break-in and cover-up. But Dean, despite his expert knowledge of the Watergate scandal, failed to reveal the "greatest mystery of our time": the identity of Deep Throat. He did suggest several candidates for this role. His first choice was Robert Bennett, a former CIA official, who denied the charge. In the original version of *Blind Ambition* Dean pointed his finger at David Gergen, then Director of Communications in the Nixon White House. But the published version left the Deep Throat mystery intact. Dean said only that he had been "raking his brains" trying to figure out who Deep

Throat was. The index to his book does not list Deep Throat. When Woodward and Bernstein published their book, *All the President's Men*, Dean said that they had "cooked up Deep Throat just to throw people off." Dean later changed his mind again and said that he knew who Deep Throat was and would reveal him in his next book. So far this promise has remained unfulfilled.

From the day of the break-in on June 17, 1972, to March 21, 1973, Dean insisted that no one in the White House was involved. In 1979, Mr. Felt, a high FBI official, wrote a book called *The FBI Pyramid from the Inside*. He wrote:

> John W. Dean III, who later served four months in prison for his role in the Watergate break-in, demanded to be informed of everything the FBI had learned.[832]

Leon Jaworski, a life-long liberal democrat, in his book, *The Right and the Power*, does not hide his animosity towards Nixon. He stated that Nixon would have never appointed him Special Prosecutor "but for the fact that the public would not have allowed the selection of someone biased in Nixon's favor." But Jaworski admitted that media coverage of Watergate was "pervasive and almost totally adverse to Mr. Nixon." He wrote that if he were asked how long it would be before Mr. Nixon could be afforded his constitutional rights for an impartial jury not influenced by prejudicial publicity he stated:

> I would have to say in fairness that I did not know. The media was totally saturating the American people with Watergate.[833]

There were only a few pro-Nixon Letters to the Editor of the *New York Times*. One such a letter was published in 1974. It pointed at the Watergate "frightening precedent," stating:

> Any future President could be removed from office because some fantastic charges gained wide publicity. The next logical step would be to remove the legally elected head of state by public opinion poll, or by partisan cabal… President Nixon will stand tall in history for his courage and statesmanship in his foreign policy initiatives, in his courageous, if unpopular at the time, decisions on Vietnam and Cambodia, as well as in September 1970 during the Jordanian crisis and in last October [1974] Middle East war, for his remarkable endurance to stay in office and to

169

uphold our constitution despite pressure from his opponents and his friends....[834]

Dick Harwood, an editor at the *Washington Post*, said that Katherine Graham, the paper's owner and publisher, was personally involved in directing "an army of reporters assigned to delve into the Watergate story." Woodward and Bernstein led the pack. Shortly after the Watergate break-in, Stewart Alsop at a dinner with Mrs. Graham and told her that he liked Nixon's foreign policy and suggested that the *Post* should support Nixon's reelection. Mrs. Graham replied angrily:

> I hate him and I'm going to do everything I can to beat him.[835]

The *Post*'s Editor-in-Chief, Benjamin Bradlee, insisted that the Nixon administration was "committed to the destruction of the press." Actually, the opposite was true: Mr. Bradlee and Mrs. Graham were committed to the destruction of Nixon. Bradlee said:

> We don't print the truth. We print what we know, what people tell us. So we print lies.[836]

Printing government officials' leaks without revealing their identity was not the proclaimed policy of the *Post*, which made the following announcement in December 1971:

> No government official would be allowed to talk anonymously on a "source" basis.[837]

Yet Deep Throat's leaks were printed without attribution. He obviously was a government official. Bradlee acknowledged in the interview with Larry King that Woodward had told him at the time of the Watergate scandal who Deep Throat was. Of course Bradlee revealed this information to his boss, Mrs. Graham. Woodward had his last meeting with Deep Throat in the underground garage on May 16, 1973, and wrote down in his notebook:

> Deep Throat was pacing nervously. His lower jaw seemed to quiver. Liddy told Dean that they could shoot him and/or that he would shoot himself, but that he would "never talk and always be a good soldier."[838]

Woodward reported Deep Throat's behavior to his bosses and was ordered by Graham and Bradlee to stop having secret meetings. But Woodward continued to receive Deep Throat's leaks.

After accusing President Nixon of various crimes, Dean pleaded with the Ervin Committee to "forgive" Nixon. It is quite obvious, especially if we recall how persistently Dean bargained for immunity, that he was not at all interested in soliciting forgiveness for Nixon. In a transfigured and projected form he pleaded for forgiveness for himself. Press reports that Dean had pleaded guilty to numerous crimes were buried in the back pages, if mentioned at all. He was assigned an office in the prosecutors' section of the Justice Department with his nameplate on the door as if he was one of the prosecutors. As a result of the plea bargaining his sentence was reduced to four months in a privileged prison facility. The tapes also reveal that Nixon did not order the break-in and was not interested in covering it up. Besides, real criminals do not record their criminal conversations on tape. Before resigning Nixon stated that he had "no knowledge of the cover-up." He did not lie to the nation, nor did he lie under oath.

On June 16, 1973, the *Post* published one of Deep Throat's revelations and the Watergate Special Prosecutor Archibald Cox held a press conference, announcing his intention to indict Nixon. The same day Soviet leader Leonid Brezhnev arrived in Washington for a summit meeting with Nixon. The summit moved to San Clemente, Nixon's California estate. At 10:30 p.m. Nixon received a message from Henry Kissinger: "The Russians want to talk." Brezhnev proposed a Soviet-American deal to jointly force the "withdrawal of Israeli troops from all occupied territories" and "international guarantees for this type of settlement." Nixon wrote in his memoirs:

> Brezhnev was trying to browbeat me into imposing on Israel a settlement based on Arab terms... I refused. My agreement to Brezhnev's demand would amount to our abandoning Israel.... I am confident that the firmness I showed that night reinforced the seriousness of the message I conveyed to the Soviets when I ordered a military alert four months later during the Yom Kippur War.[839]

In October 1973 the Watergate scandal was reaching its climax. The headlines were proclaiming that Nixon was "paralyzed" and NIXON CANNOT SURVIVE DEAN. This prediction convinced Brezhnev that Nixon's weakness would allow the Soviets to provoke an Arab-Israeli war and then to intervene with impunity to "preserve peace." They acted fast. Neither American nor Israeli intelligence had time to evaluate the significance of the massive Soviet deliveries of military hardware suddenly detected to Egypt and Syria. Stewart Steven, in his book *Spymasters of Israel*, provided incisive details concerning the intelligence background prior to the Yom Kippur War and Golda Meir's failure to assess the available intelligence.[840]

When the Yom Kippur War broke out in October 1973 the Israelis were caught unprepared and suffered initial defeats. Israel was almost destroyed. The Broadway show *Golda's Balcony* portrays a panicky Golda Meir, Israeli prime minister at the time, frantically telephoning Simcha Denis, Israeli ambassador in Washington, demanding that he immediately tell Nixon and Kissinger about Israeli planes being loaded with atomic bombs and ready to drop them on Egyptian and Syrian targets. Whether this scenario was based on facts or was just a theatrical embellishment remains unknown. What is known is that Nixon told Kissinger, "Get over there everything that flies," ordering him to provide Israel with badly needed arms. When the Israelis rolled back and then routed the Egyptian and Syrian forces, the Soviets sent Nixon a threatening note, demanding joint Soviet-American military intervention. If the United States refused to join the Soviets, the note warned, Soviet troops would intervene unilaterally to "guarantee peace." Nixon's response was prompt and unequivocal—he proclaimed a military alert and told the Soviets to stay out. They did. The media accused Nixon of proclaiming the military alert in order to "detract public attention from Watergate." The fact of the matter was that Nixon, despite Watergate, prevented Soviet intervention and saved Israel.

The Watergate hysteria reached a boiling point in March 1974 when even some of Nixon's supporters asked for his resignation. In their book, *Silent Coup—The Removal of a President*, Len Colodny and Robert Gettlin suggest that Nixon resigned because Al Haig pressured him, confronting him with some incriminating evidence.[841] Nixon explained his resignation differently. On August 8 1974, he spoke to the nation from the Oval Office, stating:

> I have never been a quitter. To leave office before my term is completed is opposed to every instinct in my body. But as President I must put the interests of America first... Therefore, I shall resign the Presidency effective tomorrow.[842]

Al Haig told Leon Jaworski that the Watergate "road map" was "drawn simply to harm President Nixon and was not the result of the credible testimony of witnesses." Haig could not hide his strong dislike of John Dean. He told

Jaworski:

The tapes after March 21 show Dean to be a subtle but clear liar.[843]

Nixon resigned on August 9, 1974, saving the nation from the agony of an impeachment trial. After his resignation Gerald Ford was sworn in as President of the United States. The Democratic Congress passed the "War Powers Act," which prevented President Ford from deploying American forces in Vietnam, thus, in fact, legislating American defeat and allowing the North Vietnamese to trash the Paris Peace Agreement, negotiated by Nixon and Kissinger with impunity. Millions of South Vietnamese fled from their communist "liberators" and hundreds of thousands of Vietnamese "boat people" perished on high seas in the quest for freedom. The communist Khmer Rouge slaughtered two million Cambodians. America remained submerged in the "Vietnam syndrome" until President Ronald Reagan lifted her spirit from the self-inflicted malaise.

During Gerald Ford's presidency the Soviets did not cause much trouble to Israel beyond their usual complaints about "Zionist aggression." For some time Soviet Jews continued to immigrate to Israel and the United States, encouraged by the Jackson-Vanick amendment of October 4, 1972. In the 1976 election Ford was running against Jimmy Carter, who proclaimed himself an "outsider" and "born again Christian." One of Carter's prominent campaign issues was President Ford's pardon of Nixon and Carter's promise to cleanse the nation of the "Watergate and Vietnam shame." In the following years John Dean was in the news on many occasions. In 1982 Nixon's former aides gathered in Washington's Marriott Hotel for a private dinner to celebrate the tenth anniversary of Nixon's landslide victory in the 1972 elections. A large sign read, "Welcome class of 1972." John Dean was not invited, but he was in the news for the occasion anyway. "I am delighted I wasn't invited to the Nixon dinner," he stated through a Los Angeles public relations firm. "I am just surprised that the school for scoundrels would hold a class reunion." Dean was also in great demand as the "expert on Watergate" on various TV talk shows during the Monica Lewinsky scandal. On September 17, 1998, he was interviewed on Fox News, stating that he was in possession of some "exculpatory information" that could exonerate President Nixon, but he did not say what it was.

Rick Sanchez of MSNBC also interviewed Dean, introducing him as an "expert on Watergate and Nixon." Sanchez sought Dean's opinion about the latest release of some of the White House tapes. Dean stated, "According to my reading of the tapes Nixon was an anti-Semite." Clyde Haberman in an article "No Escape from Degrees of Nixon" wrote:

> Good grief! Is it possible that we New Yorkers still have Nixon to kick around? It seems we do, though it is 31 years since he left the White House in disgrace and 11 years since he died."[844]

The occasion for Mr. Haberman to kick the dead Nixon was Rev. Billy Graham's sermon in Queens, New York, and the reminder of a 1972 tape recording, released three years ago, about which he wrote:

> Rev. Graham was indulging in serious Jew-bashing with his close friend Nixon, who had a blatant anti-Semitic streak. Mr. Graham long denied ever having said anything nasty about Jews.[845]

Since the dead Nixon does not have the luxury of such a denial, one must say something in his defense. President Truman used to rant about "These damn New York progressive Jews," because in the 1948 elections they overwhelmingly voted for the Progressive Party candidate Henry Wallace, despite the fact that in 1948 Truman recognized the State of Israel, ignoring the contrary advice of George Marshall, Dean Rusk, and the "Arabists" of the State Department. Just because someone speaks in a derogatory way doesn't mean he's a racist or an anti-Semite. Verbal abuse simply exists, but it doesn't necessarily mean anything deeper.[846] As for Nixon, who saved Israel from defeat in the Yom Kippur War and who, for the first time in American history, appointed a Jewish refugee from Nazi Germany, Henry Kissinger, to the post of national security adviser and secretary of state, indicates that he of all people was most certainly not an "anti-Semite"!

John Dean cashed in on the Watergate scandal again during the 2004 election campaign. On April 6, 2004, he appeared on TV evening shows, promoting his latest book, *Worse than Watergate: The Secret Presidency of George W. Bush.* This book was also eagerly promoted by the Bush-bashing media. On May 10, 2004, the *New York Times Book Review* published Dean's glowing review of Joseph Wilson's book, *Inside the Lies that Led to War and Betrayed My Wife's CIA Identity: A Diplomat's Memoir.* Dean praised this "riveting and all-engaging book" about Wilson's complaint that Bush "deceived the nation and the world in going to war in Iraq." Dean also wrote that Wilson, "tells captivating stories of his life" and described how Wilson "fell in love with and married a C.I.A. covert operative—a willowy blond, resembling a young Grace Kelly." Dean also wrote a book titled *Unmasking Deep Throat*, in which he stated, "I have little doubt the first person to complete sorting out the facts will have everyone saying—why didn't I think of that?"[847]

Woodward and Bernstein sold their "Watergate papers" to the University of Texas for five million dollars with the stipulation to "keep the identity of Deep Throat secret until their "very, very deep source" dies. They "donated $500,000 to the University of Texas to establish a series of conferences on Watergate." *Washington Post* publisher, Boisfeuillet Jones, Jr., explained that there were reasons why the identity of Deep Throat must remain secret. He said, "There are special historical circumstances here, and the *Post* signed off on their agreement."[848] Woodward has been an assistant editor of the *Post* for some time now. Bernstein lives in New York and has been writing a book about Senator Hillary Rodham Clinton, whose career began as a young anti-Nixon lawyer in the Senate Watergate Committee. The Watergate scandal started many profitable careers and fortunes.

Bob Woodward published his ninth post-Watergate bestseller, *Plan of Attack,* where he provided plenty of Bush-bashing innuendoes. During the 2004 presidential campaign John Kerry used this type of inference to accuse Bush of arranging a "secret deal" with the Saudi ambassador to lower oil prices before the November 2004 election, as a kind of "October surprise." Anthony Fergusson wrote:

> It all began with Watergate, of course, when Woodward and his partner Carl Bernstein dragged the bloodied body of Richard Nixon from the White House and martyred him on the front page of the *Post*... And who in Washington is more successful than Bob Woodward? Not only is he the best at what he does, he has also become exceedingly rich and famous for doing it...[849]

Bob Woodward has been laughing all the way to the bank since he began profiteering off of Watergate.

John Dean was prominently in the news during the Ford-Carter 1976 election campaign. The *New York Times* headline on October 13, 1976, announced, JOHN DEAN ACCUSED FORD AS NIXON'S GO-BETWEEN IN WATERGATE. On election night David Brinkley, on NBC News, projected Carter's victory and then revealed:

John Dean had finally found two persons in California to vouch for his reliability so that he could obtain a card to a local library...[850]

Brinkley smiled, suggesting a connection between Carter's victory and Dean's "reliability." Indeed, there was a connection.

Perceptions change as time corrects distortions. Eventually the ridiculous break-in will be recognized as not at all a diabolical conspiracy by Nixon, a great statesman who had been twice elected Congressman, twice Senator, twice vice-president, and twice president of the United States, the last time by the greatest landslide in history. With the passage of years the majority of the public will no longer consider Nixon a pariah. Ronald Reagan often sought Nixon's advice on foreign affairs and domestic policies. Nixon wrote several brilliant bestsellers and appeared before large audiences, where he was greeted with standing ovations. The press stopped "kicking Nixon around." Bob Dole and Henry Kissinger cried at Nixon's funeral.

The resignation of Richard Nixon was forced upon him in a public trial by the media without a jury, which shows how democracy and fair play can be subverted by a determined group of ideologues, in this case the left-wing Democrats who long resented the defeats of their fellow leftists Jerry Voorhis and Helen Gahagan Douglas and the exposure of the Soviet spy Alger Hiss, as well as the anti-communist reaction of the 1950s in which Nixon played a prominent role. Irwin Gellman's several volumes of Nixon's biography amply demonstrate how brilliant

Nixon was as a college and university student and how effective he was in directing American foreign policy.[851]

Starting June 1, 2005, swarms of commentators began insisting that W. Mark Felt, a 91-year-old former FBI official, had finally revealed that he was Deep Throat. This "revelation" originally came from a *Vanity Fair* article written by John D. O'Connor, the Felt family lawyer, and from Felt's daughter Joan and his grandson Nick Jones. They propped up Mr. Felt, frail and smiling, in the doorway of his daughter's home in Santa Rosa, California, only to say to a group of reporters:

Hey, look at that. We appreciate you coming out like this.[852]

This was all he said, if he said even that much. All the talking was done by his daughter Joan, his grandson Nick and their lawyer John D. O'Connor. There was a brief controversy around whether Mr. Felt was a hero or a traitor. Almost no attention was paid to the fact that Mr. Felt in 1979, when he was 65 years old, published a book, *The FBI Pyramid From the Inside*, in which he wrote that he had met Bob Woodward only once during the Watergate investigation. Mr. Felt wrote:

> Woodward wanted to check out the information that he and Bernstein had collected and he asked me to tell him which was accurate and which was not. I declined to cooperate with him in this manner and that was that.[853]

The name of Mr. Felt had once in a while been mentioned among dozens of other suspects for the role of Deep Throat, but Mr. Felt always emphatically denied that he ever leaked to Woodward any information about Watergate. In her review of Woodward's book *The Secret Man*, Ms. Kakutani quotes from Mr. Felt's 1979 book *The FBI Pyramid from the Inside*, in which Mr. Felt stated:

> I never leaked information to Woodward and Bernstein or anyone else![854]

Yet numerous newspaper reports and TV commentators declared over and over again that "Mr. Felt revealed that he was Deep Throat." Felt's daughter Joan attempted to persuade Bob Woodward to cooperate with her in writing about Felt's Deep Throat story, but he refused to do that.

In 2003 Joan turned to J. Todd Foster, who at that time worked for *People* magazine, but her offer was rejected, because, as he said, "The Felts wanted payments." In a telephone interview Mr. Foster said:

> This was always about money, and they were very up front with me. [855]

Joan's proposal wound up in the hands of Judith Regan at Regan Books. On June 1, 2005, Ms. Regan said:

> A possible book had collapsed because of the serious concern that Mr. Felt was no longer of sound mind.[856]

Other sources mention Mr. Felt's advance state of dementia or other mental illnesses. Mr. Felt suffered a stroke in 2001. He could not write the "revealing" article in *Vanity Fair* magazine. John D. O'Connor, the Felt family lawyer, wrote the article in which he stated that in the 1970s Mr. Felt was "confronted by the countercultural changes at work and at home when his daughter Joan, one of Mr. Felt's two children, moved to a commune." Mr. Felt reconciled with his daughter decades later. Mr. O'Connor wrote that in 2002 a woman said to Joan that she knew that Joan's father was Deep Throat. Joan smelled money, a lot of it. When she came home she told her father, "I know now that you're Deep Throat." Mr. Felt, by then a frail man no longer of sound mind and totally dependent on his daughter, supposedly replied:

> Since that's the case, well, yes I am. [857]

This was the origin of the frenzy surrounding the revelation of the identity of Deep Throat. Joan said:

> Bob Woodward's gonna get all the glory for this, but we could make at least enough money to pay the bills, like the debt I've run up for the kids' education.[858]

The *New York Post* reported that DVD and video sales of *All the President's Men* and the sale of this book shot through the stratosphere. Bob Woodward rushed into print an article about his forthcoming book, *The Secret Man,* about his relationship with Mr. Felt. The book was published in 2005. Michiko Kakutani, in her *New York Times* review, "An Aura of Mystery Still Hovers Around the Man Who Is Deep Throat," states:

> Deep Throat's identity remained a mystery for more than 30 years... Scattered here and there in *The Secret Man* are some interesting tidbits. Mr. Woodward reveals that the *Washington Post* might have had its own leaker—possibly in the paper's legal department—who was providing "information to the Justice Department and the White House..." Among the tidbits scattered in the book is Woodward's revelation that in 1974, in the wake of the publication of *All the President's Men*, he placed a phone call to Mr. Felt, but Mr. Felt abruptly hung up on him. "For days I was haunted, imagining the worst. The worst ranged from the possibility that he might take his own life to the higher likelihood that he would go public and denounce me as a betrayer and scum who had exploited an accidental friendship."[859]

This was why Woodward did not approach Mr. Felt then. Years later, when

Mr. Felt's daughter, Joan, approached Woodward with an offer to be her co-author in writing a book about her father as Deep Throat, Woodward refused. On July 11, 2005, Woodward was interviewed by James Mann on C-Span 2's Book TV show, about his book *The Secret Man*. Woodward admitted that he did not talk to Mr. Felt for the book, but talked only "briefly" to Joan. For years Woodward promised to reveal the identity of his "deep, deep source" only after this person dies or releases him from his promise to keep his identity secret. Mr. Felt is still alive and he did not release Woodward from anything.

Ms. Kakutani writes:

> The main reason the portrait of Deep Throat in this book is so fuzzy is that Woodward never really tried to dig out an "exacting explanation" until a few years ago, by which time it became evident that Mr. Felt, now 91, was suffering from severe memory loss. Woodward had to put off talking to his old source, this book suggests, because he was fearful about what kind of reception he might receive.[860]

The reason Woodward refused to interview Mr. Felt was because Mr. Felt was not able to recall that he was "the man in the rain coat in the shadows of the garage," whom Woodward described as the Deep Throat in his *All the President's Men*. Ms. Kakutani quotes from Mr. Felt's 1979 book, *The FBI Pyramid from the Inside*, stating:

> I never leaked information to Woodward and Bernstein or anyone else![861]

"Universal Pictures and Public Affairs have agreed to pay close to $1 million to buy the film and book rights to the life story of W. Mark Felt." Tom Hanks's movie company will make the film.[862] Whether Woodward will share his profits with Joan and Nick has not been revealed. Asked whether the Felt family's revealing the identity of Deep Throat had helped Mr. Woodward, Mr. Bradlee said:

> It helps him on the way to the bank, I'm sure.[863]

Yet the whole distasteful affair is not only about the money. The motives of the people involved are mixed. Joan was motivated not only by money, but also by the desire to share in the "glory" that Woodward has enjoyed for the destruction of President Nixon and to relive her youth in the counterculture "hippie commune," where bashing Nixon was the obligatory pastime.[864] As for Woodward, he for one always did follow the money, but having become very rich after publishing twelve books, a few more million would not make much difference to him. As for Carl Bernstein, he still hopes to make millions by publishing the biography of Hillary Clinton, which he has been writing for some time. But both Woodward and Bernstein have been so addicted to wallowing in their Watergate "glory" that they would not mind wallowing in it once again. They did not say explicitly that Mr. Felt was Deep Throat. Instead, they and Bradlee made some confusing noises that Mr. Felt was one of their sources.

Mr. Felt is still alive, but he is senile and incapable of understanding what's happening. So far the media and most people believe he was the real Deep Throat. It appears almost impossible to change this perception. For the time being the case remains open until the real Deep Throat will eventually reveal his true identity. This might be about to happen. John Dean, the widely acclaimed "expert on Watergate," in his article "The Source Runs Dry," dismissed John O'Connor's article "A G-Man's Life: The FBI, Being 'Deep Throat,' and the Struggle for Honor in Washington," as well as Bob Woodward's book, *The Secret Man: The Story of Watergate's Deep Throat,* as total fabrications. Dean described in great detail the wrong information and inconsistencies in both accounts, mentioning Mr. Felt's "current dementia (he's 92)," and adding sarcastically about the "remarkable ability of both authors to enter the mind and memory of a man who is unable to do so himself."[865]

Not being able to enter John Dean's mind it appears that in writing the article he resents Woodward for stealing the secret and running with it all the way to the bank, enriching himself, and advancing his lucrative career as an "investigative reporter" in the process. Dean also made a career out of his Watergate fame as the "expert on Watergate." A footnote to Dean's article states:

John W. Dean is a former Nixon White House counsel. His seventh nonfiction book, *Conservatives Without Conscience,* will be published in July.[866]

Judging by the title, the book will be bashing George W. Bush and his conservative Republican party the same way Dean attacked Richard Nixon and the Republicans with his Watergate "revelations." Perhaps one day he will also reveal that he and Deep Throat were one and the same person.

Chapter 9

Israel's Nightmare:
The Carter Presidency

During the 1976 campaign, Carter told his staff:

I don't want any more statements on the Middle East or Lebanon. Jackson has all the Jews anyway. It doesn't matter how far we go. I don't get over four percent of the Jewish vote anyway, so forget it. We'll get the Christians.[867]

Speaking to a student group on December 9, 1975, Carter said:

The rights of the Palestinian people, whose representative is the PLO, must be recognized. . . . Israel will have to withdraw to the 1967 boundaries.[868]

However, in a speech at a Jewish center in Elizabeth, New Jersey, on June 6, 1976, Carter stated:

Final borders between Israel and her neighbors should be determined via direct negotiations between the parties, and they should not be imposed from outside.[869]

In the 1976 American elections, 87 percent of the Jewish vote went to Carter.

Once elected, Carter made the Middle East the central issue of his foreign policy, and soon began attempting to determine Israeli borders and impose settlements from the outside. In March 1977, he declared:

> The Palestinian people must have a homeland or entity and Israel must withdraw to the 1967 borders with minor adjustments.[870]

Thus began Israel's nightmare during the next four years of Carter's presidency, which proved to be a disaster for the Russian Jews. Carter's hostility to Israel manifested itself immediately after his inauguration. He vetoed the Israeli sale to Ecuador of twenty-four Kfir fighter-bombers outfitted with American engines and ordered the State Department to protest Israeli oil drilling in the Gulf of Suez. The drilling, according to Carter, was "not helpful to efforts to get peace negotiations under way." Carter reneged on President Ford's promise to provide Israel with GBU-72 bombs capable of destroying concrete bunkers and missile sites. Early in February 1977, a top Defense Department official suggested to several American firms "not to deal with Israel." The story was leaked to the press, raising questions in Congress. Referring to Carter's innovations, many Israelis said, "We could tell that he was headed in the wrong direction."

Israeli prime minister Yitzhak Rabin asserted that Israel would not return to the 1967 borders. Carter assailed Rabin a few days later for not having agreed to his demands. Rabin complained that the Israeli Labor Party's defeat in the May 1977 election and Menachem Begin's victory were the result of Carter's unreasonable demands upon Israel. Vitaly Svechinsky, the leader of Soviet Jews since 1968 and a recent immigrant to Israel commented:

> Carter sounds more like an Arab than an American president. There seems to be nobody but Begin to stand up to him. If Begin is elected, let Carter swing his scythe—it will break against Begin's rock.[871]

After Begin's election, Carter declared Israeli settlements on the West Bank "illegal" and "obstacles to peace." Begin authorized scores of new settlements. When the PLO attacked Israeli towns with Katiusha rockets from Lebanon,

Begin retaliated by ordering air strikes upon Palestinian guerrilla bases. Carter's initial reaction was one of strong anger, but "he yielded to advisers who urged him to moderate his public criticism in order to avoid stirring up the American Jewish community." Carter justified the Israeli air strikes as a "regrettable but understandable retaliation." When the UN General Assembly declared the Israeli settlements "illegal," Carter ordered his UN Ambassador Andrew Young to abstain from the vote, thus displaying American "evenhandedness" so as to "avoid stirring up the American Jewish community." But that is exactly what happened.

September 12, 1977, was the beginning of the Jewish New Year. That day Carter invited Israel and "Palestinian representatives" to the Geneva Conference to negotiate a "comprehensive peace." A *New York Times* editorial described Carter's invitation as "sensible," but some Jews felt that the timing of Carter's announcement was not coincidental, and that his "sensitivity" was indicative of a morbidly spiteful nature. It was reported that the turnout of worshipers that year was "unusually high."

In September 1977, Carter and Anatoly Dobrynin, the Soviet ambassador to Washington, discussed Carter's proposal to prepare a Soviet-American statement to be issued during the visit of Soviet foreign minister Andrey Gromyko to Washington on September 22. Carter accepted the Soviet draft of the Soviet-American Joint Declaration, which was published on October 1, 1977. It struck the world, as Hitler used to say, "like a bolt from the blue." The statement dictated the "terms of settlement" of the Arab-Israeli conflict and offered Soviet-Americans "guarantees" to implement those terms. On October 4, 1977, a *New York Times* editorial stated:

> The first and most important question about the new Soviet-American statement on the Middle East is why President Carter must, once again, explain the motives of his diplomacy.[872]

Carter initially described the statement as "an achievement of unprecedented significance," but when confronted with an uproar of protests in the United States and in Israel, he attempted to explain it away as an "innocuous document." On October 5, 1977, Carter, in his exchange with Moshe Dayan, demanded that Israel take part in the Geneva Conference and accept the "principles" of the Soviet-American Joint Declaration "no later than December 1977." This was an ultimatum. The confrontation with Dayan, described as "brutal," lasted late into the night. Carter threatened Dayan that he would "appeal to the friends of Israel in the United States." He accused Israel of "stubbornness," of being "an obstacle to peace," and of "endangering the vital interests of America." Dayan was not impressed, and said:

> We do not depend on the U.S. to save us. Even if you wanted to send us soldiers, you couldn't do it after Vietnam . . . We count only on ourselves.[873]

Carter appeared impressed and perhaps surprised at some of the history that Dayan had recounted. Turning to Secretary of State Cyrus Vance, Carter ordered him to prepare a "working paper" to Dayan's liking. The tension dropped considerably. Then Carter asked Dayan, "Tell me, what makes you dissatisfied with the declaration?" "Everything," replied Dayan. Carter suggested, "Let's study it clause by clause." Dayan replied, "There is no need. The mere fact that you introduced the Russians into the arrangement is enough."

On February 13, 1978, Carter's national security adviser Brzezinski said:

> The statement was good, although we might have dealt with it in a somewhat different way. The Administration might have softened the ground for a greater understanding of the need for a U.S.-Soviet statement on the Middle East.[874]

The "ground" Brzezinski was talking about was public opinion, which needed to be cultivated for Carter's confrontation with Begin, Israel, and the American-Jewish community.

Egyptian president Anwar Sadat realized that Carter's acceptance of a Soviet military presence on the Arab-Israeli border signified a Soviet-American "deal" that was not only a threat to Israel, but also to Egypt. He realized that this declaration was a prescription for war. On November 9, 1977, Sadat, in a long and emotional speech to the Egyptian parliament, announced, "I am ready to go to the Israeli parliament itself to discuss peace." Begin immediately welcomed Sadat's visit, and sent him an official invitation. Sadat insisted that Begin postpone his long-scheduled trip to England so that Sadat could come to Jerusalem within the next few days. His plane touched down at Ben-Gurion Airport minutes after the end of Shabbat, November 19, 1977.

The American media described Sadat's trip to Israel as "largely symbolic." Harry Reasoner pointed to the "sheer drama of the pictures." John D.

O'Connor observed that "as various network commentators rattled on about boggled minds, astonished ears, and startled eyes, the images alone—moving and even thrilling—told all." However, images did not reveal the real drama that had suddenly forced Sadat to fly to Israel and had instilled him with a real sense of urgency. Sadat knew that, had he not gone to Israel, an Arab-Israeli war would have broken out within days, and Egypt would have soon become involved. In his November 9 speech, where he announced his readiness to go to Israel, Sadat mentioned that he had earlier received a telephone call from Hafez al-Assad, the president of Syria, who had told him that "within a week or ten days" Sadat was expected to join the Syrians in the war against Israel. Why would the Syrians start a war at a time when their quick and decisive defeat seemed inevitable? This question was on Sadat's mind, and the answer was obvious: the Soviets were not particularly interested in an Arab victory, and, in fact, they might have preferred another Arab defeat in order to use it as a pretext to intervene and pick up the pieces. They would be most interested in the pieces left of Egypt.

Sadat feared the worst. Various analyses described Israeli military superiority and mentioned Israel's "nuclear option." The Israelis neither confirmed nor denied it. Their superiority in conventional weaponry and their "special relationship" with the U.S. (before Carter's innovations) ruled out the need for a nuclear response. Israelis also took the American determination not to allow a Soviet military presence in the Middle East for granted. Carter's policy left these assumptions in shambles. Israeli leaders bluntly described the situation in which Israel found itself as a "crisis of unprecedented isolation." As Kissinger put it, "Israel, maddened by isolation and the fear of an imposed peace, would withdraw in sullen intransigence." If war would have broken out under such circumstances, it was reasonable to assume that Israel would have struck back with all the power in her possession, including the use of the "nuclear option." Egypt, the strongest Arab military power, would have been the first to come under Israeli attack. One atomic bomb dropped on the Soviet-built Aswan Dam would have released such a gush of water that it could have washed a good part of Egypt off into the sea. Sadat later stated regretfully:

> Before I made that speech in the Parliament, I discussed it only with my Foreign Minister, Ismail Fahmy, who later resigned. He was not with the Knesset initiative at all.[875]

Nothing unites longtime adversaries better than a direct threat from a common enemy. Sadat made his first overtures toward Israel soon after the Soviet-American Declaration of October 1, 1977, was published. DAYAN SHUTTLE A MYSTERY, announced London's *Daily Telegraph*, reporting that Moshe Dayan, the Israeli foreign minister, had conducted a secret meeting with an important Arab official somewhere in Europe. Actually, Dayan, having disguised himself "by taking off his famous black eye patch and donning dark glasses and a diplomat's Homburg hat," flew to Tangier for a secret rendezvous with Morocco's King Hassan, who told him:

> If the Geneva negotiations break down and the alternative is war, Egypt would consider interim talks as a fallback.[876]

Sadat was seeking a separate negotiation with Israel as a "way out" of a war that might bring about Soviet intervention.

Sadat said, "Moscow hasn't liked me or my government for years now. The Russians do not like anybody who rejects their control." The Soviets did not care for Morocco's King Hassan either. They waged a proxy war against in the Western Sahara, where Polisario rebels, supported by "socialist" Algeria, demanded "self-determination" for the vast territory populated by 75,000 desert dwellers. What was actually at stake was a Soviet stronghold along the important Atlantic coastline with its rich phosphate deposits. Sadat noticed that the Soviet-American statement of October 1, 1977, had coincided with the Soviet and Cuban takeover of the Horn of Africa, threatening the sea routes from the oil-rich Persian Gulf into the Indian Ocean, and posing a direct threat to Saudi Arabia, Iran, Oman, and the United Arab Emirates. The Soviets took over Aden Naval facilities and armed their ally, the Marxist regime of South Yemen. For Sadat, the "Palestinian issue" was not at the "core" or the "heart" of the problem in the Middle East, but an emotional smokescreen behind which the Soviets pursued their schemes. It was not a coincidence, said Sadat, that Syria, Libya, Algeria, Iraq, South Yemen, and the PLO had formed the "Rejectionist Front," and that they all "received their arms from Moscow." He broke diplomatic relations with those countries, and expelled the PLO from Egypt. He described the "rejectionist" leaders as being "dwarves," "stooges," "impostors," and "nuts." Sadat found in the pro-Western King Hassan a natural ally and the best possible intermediary in negotiations with Israel.

Carter initially displayed transparent hostility toward the Egyptian-Israeli rapprochement in November 1977 when Sadat's trip to Jerusalem stunned the Carter White House. Then, very slowly, Carter began to exhibit resentful and begrudging approval. The *New York Times* editorial "United States as Sphinx" stated:

> The Carter Administration's enthusiasm for President Sadat's diplomacy could freeze the Nile. It has been grudging, chilling, and altogether unworthy of the United States, which should be cheering and rewarding every act of moderation in the Middle East.[877]

Directly and by innuendo, the White House attempted to create the impression that Sadat's trip to Jerusalem had been prompted by Carter's personal letter to him. This letter has never been published, but Sadat recalled:

> In September, I received a personal letter from Carter, in his handwriting. A special envoy in Cairo delivered it. I read the letter. I wrote the answer in my hand. In my answer—for the first time I am revealing this—I said the whole situation needed some bold action.[878]

Sadat revealed that Carter's letter was wax-sealed in several places, and that it was a highly secret communication. When Sadat was asked whether Carter, in his letter, had advised him to go to Jerusalem, Sadat replied:

> No, the letter did not suggest this, but it made me think of a way out.[879]

People think of a way out when they feel trapped.

This was exactly how Sadat felt when he read Carter's letter. The timing and circumstances under which Carter wrote his letter throw significant light on this letter's true message. On September 12, 1977, the State Department announced that the "Palestinians must be involved in the peacemaking process" and "their representatives will have to be at Geneva for the Palestinian question to be solved." Carter's other ideas had been outlined in the Soviet-American Joint Declaration of October 1, 1977, which sanctioned Soviet military intervention in advance, and formalized both Carter's acceptance of Soviet "guarantees" and his agreement with the Soviets to jointly impose a settlement of the Arab-Israeli conflict on the Soviet and Arab terms. This settlement was to be canonized at the Geneva Conference "no later than December 1977." This was a major provocation.

Sadat remembered the 1973 Yom Kippur War debacles and decided not to play the role of a Soviet stooge. As he explained:

The Soviet Union was starting its own tricks with the Syrians and the Palestinians. Syrian President Hafez al-Assad was not serious at all about going to Geneva. Assad sent a special envoy to me.[880]

The Soviets moved fast to implement their scheme. Assad's special envoy brought a message very similar to the one that he had sent to Sadat in 1973, on the eve of the Yom Kippur War: get ready for combat. It was in effect a Soviet message, or as Sadat put it, a Soviet "trick." It coincided with Carter's "handwritten" letter to Sadat, also delivered by a "special envoy." Sadat told the Egyptian Parliament on November 9, 1977, that he knew that he had only a "week, or ten days, something like that," to extricate himself from the "dilemma" with which the Soviet-American Joint Declaration had presented him. Otherwise, he feared the outbreak, as he put it, of a "terrible, terrible" war.

All intelligence reports, as well as an analysis of Sadat's own military staff, showed that Israel was ready to deliver a quick and decisive defeat to any combination of Arab forces. The Soviets realized this as well, but despite this they moved fast to implement their scheme. Palestinian guerrillas in Lebanon attacked Israeli border towns with volleys of Katiusha rockets on November 8 and 9. PLO leader Yasir Arafat arrived in Cairo on November 9, 1977, and declared that this was the time for "military action." He also said, "Now we welcome war." Israelis responded with massive air strikes against Palestinian bases in southern Lebanon. Israel's defense minister, Ezer Weizman, said, "I regard the cease-fire as no longer existing."

Sadat proved to be a prudent and foresighted statesman, acting in the best interests of his people. The Egyptian masses instinctively understood what was at stake. And so did the Israelis. In an enlightening commentary, Henry Kissinger wrote:

> The absence of alternatives clears the mind marvelously. There is no alternative to the Sadat-Begin negotiations. Geneva as a negotiating forum is dead. This is just as well.[881]

The Geneva Conference, as Carter and the Soviets had proposed it, would have made the Soviets the arbiters of the conflict. For the Israelis Geneva had revived the specter of Munich. Begin pointed out that it was at Munich that Hitler had demanded "self-determination" for the Sudeten Germans and, after his demand had been satisfied, proceeded to dismantle Czechoslovakia. Begin said:

> May I state that never again will that concept [self-determination] be misused, because we'll remember the thirties, the late thirties, and the result of this misuse.[882]

Carter's demands for a "Palestinian homeland or entity," and his statements about the "legitimate rights of Palestinian people for the determination of their own future" were clearly understood in Israel. Neither Sadat nor Begin, and for that matter the press, missed the real meaning of those euphemisms, which disguised Carter's demand for a Palestinian state. The Israeli Cabinet declared:

> A Palestinian state would extinguish any prospect of peace and would create a danger to the very existence of the Jewish state. There has never been, and there will not ever be a government in Israel that would agree to such conditions.[883]

Carter's policy toward Israel nearly plunged the Middle East into a war. Wars that almost happen leave virtually no traces in history textbooks. A review of how and why these wars were avoided might contain some valuable lessons.

Carter's press secretary Jody Powell insisted:

> We do not want a public confrontation with the Jewish community over the Middle East. I suppose we might win it by convincing the majority of Americans that the policy was in the best interests of the country. However, the fallout would be terrible. It would pit a small, identifiable minority against the majority; that is a situation no society wants to get into.[884]

It has happened before in history. A small, identifiable minority had been singled out as a scapegoat on a number of memorable occasions. A new war in the Middle East could have been presented to the public as a "Jewish war" when another energy crisis could have been used to sway public opinion in Carter's favor. Brzezinski threatened to "persuade the President to go to the country to win support for a tough stand against Israel." He said that a confrontation between the Jewish community and Carter "would be a calamity" and "would leave the President no choice but to go to the country and explain that the policy was in our national interest and Israel's as well."

Actually, it was of no importance where Brzezinski stood on this issue. Carter dictated his policies. The tendency "to go to the people and stir up sentiment" was demonstrably Carter's own, and for the Jewish community to make Brzezinski a whipping boy was nothing but a transparent attempt to avoid facing the uncomfortable truth.

Early in February 1978, Carter again "concluded" that "Israel must yield" the West Bank, Gaza, and all of Sinai in order for "peace efforts to succeed," and that "the administration was preparing for the possibility of another period of sharp exchanges with Israel." To convince the public of the Israelis' wickedness, Carter alleged that Begin and Dayan had reneged on a "promise not to build new settlements." Begin and Dayan stated that they had never promised Carter anything like that. Someone was lying. It turned out it was Carter, and it was also he who caught himself lying. The Israeli ambassador in Washington pointed out that in his July 29, 1978, press conference, held after discussions with Begin in Washington, Carter had stated:

> Mr. Begin did not give me any promise about his actions on the settlement question. . . . He did not give me any commitments about what he would do.[885]

Begin was not an "outsider" who had mysteriously appeared from nowhere. He had been around for a long time. What he said then was something he had been saying his whole life, as a Zionist youth leader in Poland; as a prisoner in the Soviet Gulag; as an underground leader in Palestine during the British Mandate; as an opposition leader in the Knesset; and as the prime minister of Israel.

The stand Begin had taken on the settlement issue during the election, and after his victory in May 1976, did not change. In his February 15, 1978, press conference in Jerusalem, he said, "I say what I mean. And I mean what I say." Moreover, when Begin said that the settlements were "legal, legitimate, and essential," and that he would continue to build them, he meant it. The confrontation between "the most powerful man in the world" and "the small, identifiable minority," which from the fullness of its arrogance and impudence refused to submit to his authority, had been in progress since Carter's inauguration. "It is not our desire to in any way further or prolong public debate over the settlements," said Jody Powell on February 13, 1978, after having read Carter's statement on the settlement issue. He also said that the debate "was not a process that we choose to become involved in." Powell was lying again.

When Sadat and Begin took the peace initiative into their hands, White House officials resentfully labeled them "unguided missiles." Unguided by Carter and Moscow they certainly were, but they were guided, most properly, by their national interests and by a mutual desire to avoid war. Sadat was not fooled by Soviet "tricks." Israel broke out of the unprecedented isolation in which Carter's policy had placed it. A separate peace treaty between Egypt and Israel could have been negotiated soon after Sadat's trip to Israel, but it was Carter's objection to such a treaty as being incompatible with his demands for a "comprehensive" peace that prevented any agreement. Sadat wanted to "go to the end" in his negotiations with Israel, but how could he agree to anything less than Carter's demands? Sadat and Begin went out of their way to placate Carter, to praise him, and to save his face. They needed American help against the Soviet threat, not against each other. They went so far as to attribute credit to Carter for Sadat's initiative. Carter, despite all the evidence to the contrary, did not hesitate to accept it.

Carter prolonged and prejudiced the peace negotiations by demanding concessions from Israel and attempting to impose conditions the Israelis could not agree to. Sadat had no alternative but to demand the same concessions from Israel in order not to appear less pro-Arab than Carter did. Begin resisted Carter's demands for a long time, but ultimately found it difficult to withstand the pressure of the mighty President of the United States, which was being widely perceived as Israel's only ally in the hostile world. Begin did not foresee that his retreat from all of Sinai would be used as a historical precedent for future Arab and other countries' demands for Israel to retreat from "all of the occupied territories" that it had captured in the 1967 war. Begin finally agreed to return all of the Sinai peninsula to Egypt, and to dismantle the Israeli coastal city of Yamit. Ariel Sharon, despite his misgivings, was compelled to enforce Begin's order to displace and remove the Israeli settlers from Yamit. Sharon recalled that the "uprooting of settlements in Sinai had broken Begin's heart, even though he saw in it his duty to make painful concessions for the sake of peace."[886]

Begin signed the Camp David Accords with the provision of returning Sinai to Egypt, because he believed that Sinai was not a part of the historical land of Israel, and that the Jews, according to the Bible, had wandered there for only forty years during the Biblical exodus. He thought that Sinai, as a vast desert, could serve as a buffer between Egypt and Israel, no matter who controlled it. He also believed that peace with Egypt would be a major breakthrough from isolation in the midst of the hostile Arab world. Sadat signed the Camp David Accords because, in the shadow of the Soviet threat, peace with Israel was more important to him than Carter's dream of Palestinian "homeland or entity." Sadat and Begin shared the 1978 Nobel Peace Prize. Moshe Arenas, the Israeli Defense Minister and a lifelong Begin supporter, said:

> The retreat from Sinai was Begin's great mistake. Begin lived to see that the peace with Egypt turned out to be a very cold one.[887]

Begin lived to regret his concessions at Camp David, which provoked bitter debate among his supporters. He was reelected prime minister in July 1981, but stepped down in September 1983. He lived in virtual seclusion for the next nine years, and died in 1992.

Although Carter claimed credit for the Camp David Accords, he actually did not intend to honor its letter or its spirit. The U.S. supported the UN Security Council's anti-Israel Resolution of March 1, 1980, which negated the Accords. The uproar in America and in Israel was followed by an unprecedented and bizarre development: Carter disavowed the American vote, and called it a "mistake that resulted from an honest break in communication." Secretary of State Cyrus Vance, who had testified before the House Foreign Affairs Committee, ignored Carter's explanation and stated that the vote was in fact the true expression of the administration's Middle East policy, but it had to be "disavowed in order not to upset the Israeli-Egyptian negotiations." The *New York Times* editorial surmised that Carter had pursued two policies, one official, the other "hidden," and that the hidden policy had reflected Carter's true intentions. On November 6, 1977, the *Times* editorial, "The Jews and Jimmy Carter," stated:

> One of the unsayable things in our political life these days is that most leaders of the American Jewish community are acting as if President Carter is risking Israel's survival. . . . The confrontation now brewing between Carter and the Jews seems to us to transcend any single issue relating to the Middle East negotiations. . . . What is unspoken is the further fear of a revival of anti-Semitism and of the charge of "dual loyalty."[888]

Faced with loud protests in the United States and in Israel, Carter told a group of Jewish members of Congress who had visited him on October 5, 1977:

I'd rather commit suicide, political or otherwise, than hurt Israel![889]

The press reports declared that Carter's statement was "strong," and that it underscored his "unwavering dedication to the security of Israel." The statement was strong indeed, in fact much too strong to be real, especially in view of his ever-escalating hostility towards Israel. If anything, it had all the earmarks of a "reaction formation"—that is, the outwardly strong expression of a no-less-strong, but hidden, opposite impulse. Carter presented himself to the American public as a "born-again Christian" and often spoke of his closeness to God. It is worthwhile to consider Ernest Jones's observation:

> God-complex types vary according to the particular God with whom the person identifies himself, and that in the West, the most common identification is with Christ. With this Christ type there invariably goes an anti-Semitic tendency.[890]

The last year of Carter's presidency was dominated by the Iranian hostage crisis. Some columnists began to refer to him as the "54th hostage." On April 30, 1980, after the failure of the hostage rescue mission, he suddenly announced that the "situation had been alleviated and become more manageable," but failed to explain how this rescue failure had produced such a miraculous improvement. In their article, "Did Carter Send a General to Hasten the Shah's Fall?" Rowland Evans and Robert Novak reported that General Alexander Haig, the NATO Supreme Commander at the time, had "accused the Carter Administration of assigning his NATO deputy to hasten the Shah's fall." The article stated that General Haig disagreed with Carter's order to send Air Force Major-General Robert E. Huyser to Iran because the purpose of the order was ambiguous and it eventually resulted in preventing Iran's military from resisting the takeover of Iran by Ayatollah Khomeini's fanatics. The reporters noted that Haig had "not gone public with his sensational charge." The Pentagon records showed that General David Jones, Chairman of the Joint Chiefs of Staff, had called Haig in December 1978 "to inform him that President Carter wished to send Huyser to Teheran for meetings with Iranian military leaders." Haig asked whether the purpose of Huyser's mission was "to urge the generals to reestablish law and order or to tell the Shah to leave the country." Jones said that the mission was to "keep the Iranian military united and effective." What this phrase meant was not made clear and what else Jones told Haig has not been reported, but Haig's reply was, "I non-concur." He added:

> It was wrong to use a professional military man to execute a political
> mission; if dirty work was in the offing, a political emissary would have
> been more appropriate. An attempt by the United States to force out the
> Shah would lead to disaster in Iran.[891]

Charles Duncan, Deputy Secretary of Defense, discussed Haig's reservations
with the Joint Chiefs (Defense Secretary Harold Brown was in California at the
time), and took the matter to Carter and Brzezinski. Carter told Duncan "to
overrule Haig and to cut the orders for the Huyser mission to Teheran."
Duncan insisted that "the purpose of the Huyser mission was to cause the
military in Iran to have confidence in U.S. support and to avoid disintegration
of the military." He also said that "the military did ultimately decide not to
resist Ayatollah Khomeini." Haig did not take Duncan's explanation
seriously—he regarded it as a "smokescreen." Haig believed that "Huyser was
an instrument of Carter's policy to drop the Shah," pointing to the "leaks out
of Washington that U.S. policymakers have finally concluded that the Shah
must go."[892] These leaks coincided with Huyser's mission and the State
Department's advice to the Shah to leave the country. The Shah's own
memoirs, published in the December 1979 issue of the London magazine *Now!,*
leave no doubt about his interpretation of the Huyser mission. He wrote:

> At the beginning of January 1978, when I was still on the throne of Iran,
> Huyser arrived secretly in Teheran with the clear purpose of neutralizing
> the Iranian army and preventing it from fighting the Khomeini mobs.[893]

He stated that when he received Huyser and Ambassador William H. Sullivan,
"The one thing that was on the minds of both men was to know on what day
and at what time I should be leaving."

The Shah departed Teheran on January 16, 1979. On February 11,
Khomeini took over and began the mass executions that wiped out all of the
generals whom Huyser had "neutralized." General Huyser was appointed chief
of the United States Military Airlift Command at Scott Air Force Base in
Illinois. He refused to comment on either the American reports or the Shah's
memoirs, saying through his spokesman that his statement could be
"counterproductive to our national effort."

Whether Huyser's reticence helped or hurt "our national effort" may be a matter of opinion, but the fall of Iran into the hands of a maniac was definitely not in our interest. Congress has not questioned the participants regarding the events that resulted in Huyser's mysterious mission, although it has been suggested that "Senators Stennis and Tower ought to get to the bottom of this." Secretary of State Ed Muskie, during his May 1980 visit to Brussels, told reporters that Carter had "kept the visibility of the hostage problem alive by tying it to his own campaign plans." Public opinion polls revealed that the hostage issue was actually helping Carter in the presidential primaries.

The tendency to blame America for its support of "corrupt regimes" in South Vietnam, as well as in Iran, was due to the failure to recognize that the choice in Vietnam was between the bestial communist dictatorship of the North and the imperfect democracy of the South. The choice in Iran was between the Shah's imperfect pro-Western government and the brutal regime of the Islamic fanatics led by Ayatollah Khomeini. The war of terror against the United States began with Ayatollah Khomeini's call for "Death to America," and the Iranian Jews were the first victims of his lunacy. The ancient Jewish community that had survived in Persia for two-and-one-half millennia, since the fall of the first Jerusalem Temple, was no more. The ancient synagogue in the city of Shiraz, the traditional place of the tomb of Queen Esther, was left with no Jews to glorify her for saving the Jewish people from their enemy Haman during the holy days of Purim. The few remaining Jews of Shiraz were imprisoned as "Israeli spies."

As the Iranian Jews were being driven out of Iran during the Carter years, Jewish emigration from the Soviet Union suddenly slowed down. It came to a complete halt on December 25, 1979, when Soviet troops invaded Afghanistan. The Soviet leaders intended to occupy Afghanistan in order to encircle China. They had pursued the same goal in Vietnam. Their fear of China was linked to their policy toward Jewish emigration from Russia. They were emboldened by Carter's hostility toward Israel and his acceptance of the Khomeini takeover in Iran.[894] The resumption of the mass emigration of Soviet Jews would have to wait for President Ronald Reagan's demand, "Mr. Gorbachev! Tear down this wall!"

Chapter 10

The Twentieth-Century Hoax

In 1983, a Jewish *refusenik*, Natan Sharansky, then an inmate in a Soviet prison, read a copy of *Pravda,* which fulminated about Reagan's calling the Soviet Union an "Evil Empire." *Pravda* called Reagan's statement a "provocation." Sharansky later recalled:

> Tapping on walls and talking through toilets, the word about Reagan's "provocation" quickly spread throughout the prison. We, the dissidents, were ecstatic. Finally, the leader of the free world had spoken the truth that burned inside the heart of each and every one of us. At the time, I never imagined that three years later, I would be sitting in the White House telling this story to the president.[895]

Ronald Reagan, in his election campaign speech of March 27, 1979, (which he wrote in his own hand), stated:

> When Israel was created as a nation (carrying out a centuries-old Bible prophecy), its borders enclosed less than 20 percent of the area called Palestine. Eighty percent of the former mandate in the area called Palestine was, by the stroke of the pen, turned by the British into the Kingdom of

Trans-Jordan . . . . Yasir Arafat is the leader of terrorist guerrilla bands who have pledged to continue violence and the effort to destroy Israel. The PLO has already assassinated West Bank leaders who might be a threat to Arafat's dream. Nobody elected the PLO or Arafat.[896]

Shortly before the 1980 election, 160 leaders of major U.S. Jewish groups signed an advertisement in the *New York Times* titled "Let's Put an End to Innuendo! Vote to Re-Elect President Jimmy Carter on November 4."[897]

Ronald Reagan and George H. W. Bush were elected. Soon after Reagan was inaugurated, he called the Khomeini fanatics "criminals and kidnappers," and stated that the detention of American hostages would be met by swift and painful retribution. Soon thereafter, Khomeini released fifty-two American hostages. Then Reagan ordered American troops to remove Fidel Castro's puppet clique from the Caribbean island of Grenada. This action signaled the beginning of the uplifting of the American spirit that had been badly damaged by the malaise of the "Vietnam syndrome," the Watergate scandal, and the foreign policy of Jimmy Carter. Reagan increased the military budget threefold, strengthening American armed forces on the assumption that a healthy economy can flourish only when military security is ensured. The eventual collapse of the Soviet regime was caused by the bankruptcy of its economic and social system, which was unable to remain competitive with American military and financial might. When the Berlin Wall tumbled, the Soviet gates were also flung open for the mass exodus of Soviet Jews. Reagan died on June 5, 2004. At the funeral ceremonies mourners praised his achievements, mentioning the ending of the Cold War, the collapse of the "Evil Empire," and the dismantling of the Iron Curtain. However, the miraculous liberation of the Soviet Jews was ignored even by, of all people, Rabbi Schneider, who in his invocation in the Washington Cathedral quoted in Hebrew a Biblical prayer, but failed to mention Reagan's role in freeing the Soviet Jews.

George H. Bush, in his election campaign speech of October 3, 1980, stated:

Jimmy Carter is a small, mean-minded man who undermined Israeli security by condoning pro-PLO and other anti-Israel actions. . . . The Carter administration, by various devices—including the pro-PLO activities undertaken by its former UN Ambassador, Andrew Young—has given Israel less support than any American government since the birth of the Israeli nation in 1948. Jimmy Carter has undermined the security of an

197

ally by encouraging Israel's enemies.[898]

In June 1981, five months after the election of Reagan and Bush, Israeli prime minister Menachem Begin ordered an air strike that destroyed Saddam Hussein's Osirak nuclear reactor near Baghdad. Most of the American and European media protested Israel's "unilateral preemptive strike." The French government declared the strike "unacceptable." A *New York Times* editorial stated:

> Israel's sneak attack on the French-built nuclear reactor near Baghdad was an act of inexcusable and shortsighted aggression.[899]

Years later, an op-ed column in the *Times* stated, "In retrospect, the condemnations were completely wrong."[900]

In 1982, Begin ordered the Israeli army to destroy the Palestinian guerilla bases in Lebanon from where the terrorists had attacked Israeli towns. The Israeli army, led by Ariel Sharon, expelled Arafat and his PLO from Lebanon. For a decade thereafter, they were confined to exile in Tunis. The eight years of Reagan's presidency were a golden era in American-Israeli relations.

Congressman John Kerry, speaking at the 1988 Democratic National Convention, called the eight years of Reagan's presidency a period of "moral darkness." For Soviet Jews, however, this was a time of liberation and great hope. In the 1988 presidential campaign George H. W. Bush defeated Democratic nominee Michael Dukakis. The Soviet Union was on the brink of collapse and the Arab states were losing their mighty ally and supplier of weapons. In August 1990, Saddam Hussein invaded Kuwait, and President Bush assembled a coalition of allies and placed half a million American troops in the Saudi Arabian desert to counter Iraqi aggression. Soviet leader Mikhail Gorbachev sent his emissary, Evgeny Primakov, to Washington to dissuade Bush from taking military action. Primakov, a KGB operative, was well known for his major role in carrying out Soviet anti-Israel policy. He was also the foremost Soviet expert on Arab affairs. Photos of him, hugging and kissing Saddam Hussein in Baghdad, were displayed on the front pages of major American newspapers. Another prominent visitor to Baghdad was Yasir Arafat, who also hugged and kissed Hussein.

While visiting the White House, Primakov promoted the idea of linking the Iraqi occupation of Kuwait to the Arab-Israeli conflict. Bush, in his July 31, 1991, joint press conference with Mikhail Gorbachev, said that the United

States and the Soviet Union would act as "co-sponsors" in the Arab-Israeli talks. This sounded like a reincarnation of the Carter's attempt to solve Arab-Israeli conflict through cooperation with the Soviets. Gorbachev pressed for negotiations with Saddam Hussein, but Bush ordered military action, which began on January 17, 1991. The Iraqis launched thirty-nine SCUD missiles against Israel, hitting Tel-Aviv, while Palestinian Arabs danced on the roofs of their homes, celebrating the attack. In a TV interview some ten years later, Bush's secretary of state, James Baker, recalled these events. He smiled and said that the Bush administration had applied "finesse" to prevent Israel from retaliating against the Iraqi missile strike. "Finesse" was the euphemism he used to describe the heavy pressure to which Israeli prime minister Yitzhak Shamir had succumbed and decided not to retaliate for the Iraqi attack. American troops, half a million strong, and the British expeditionary force drove the Iraqis out of Kuwait in the brief 1991 Gulf War, which lasted some one hundred hours before Bush halted the offensive. Iraqi troops eagerly surrendered to the Americans. One hundred forty-nine American soldiers were killed, and 513 wounded. Estimates of Iraqis killed ranged from 10,000 to 100,000. The ruling Kuwaiti family was returned to power; promptly expelling hundreds of thousands of Palestinian immigrant workers who had sided with Saddam Hussein and helped his troops pillage Kuwait. The Saudis also expelled Palestinian immigrant workers, but the Israelis allowed them to return to their homes in the West Bank and Gaza.

President Bush's policy toward Israel changed drastically after the Gulf War. James Baker declared that the Gulf War victory opened a "window of opportunity" for solving the Arab-Israeli conflict and declared that Israeli "settlements were an obstacle to peace." The *Jerusalem Post* published a cartoon depicting American tanks returning from the Gulf War and lining up in front of Shamir's office, pointing their guns at it. On January 29, 1991, James Baker and Alexander A. Bessmertnykh, the Soviet foreign minister at the time, issued a Soviet-American communiqué in which they linked the Gulf War to "the sources of conflict, including the Arab-Israeli conflict." They agreed to jointly pursue "a meaningful peace process," and "mutual American-Soviet efforts to promote Arab-Israeli peace and regional stability," to achieve a "comprehensive settlement in the Middle East." This communiqué produced an outcry in the United States and in Israel against the linkage of the Gulf War to the Arab-Israeli conflict. The White House attempted to put political distance between Bush and the communiqué. The State Department spokesperson, Margaret D. Tutwiler, said:

We did not, in all candor, view this as any big deal.[901]

But Israeli prime minister Yitzhak Shamir, who remembered well the October 1, 1977, Soviet-American Joint Declaration, was outraged and stated:

> The Baker-Bessmertnykh communiqué is a threat to Israel and a political act that involves us, our fate, and our future, taken without consulting us, without even telling us beforehand.[902]

James Baker went to the Middle East to arrange an Arab-Israeli "peace conference." He portrayed Hafez al-Assad as a man promoting "new thinking." He also said:

> Assad is a partner with whom we share a commitment to seek a comprehensive settlement based upon UN Security Council resolutions 242 and 338.[903]

Assad's interpretation of these resolutions was well known: he insisted that Israel return "all" the territories the Arabs had lost in the 1967 War, including the Golan Heights and East Jerusalem, which would reduce Israel to its 1967 borders and would allow the Arabs to try to overrun Israel's amputated land again.

In his victory speech in Congress, Bush said that the Israelis must achieve a "comprehensive peace" with their Arab neighbors by "trading territory for peace to secure legitimate Palestinian political rights." He added that "anything less would fail the twin test of fairness and security." What is fair is in the eyes of the beholder. The Israelis did not think it was fair to demand that a tiny Jewish state give up land to create one more, twenty-third, Arab state, in addition to the already existing twenty-two hostile, oil-rich Arab countries occupying a colossal territory that stretched from the Indian Ocean to the Atlantic. In effect, Bush was pressing Israel to demonstrate "fairness" by trading its minuscule territory for an illusory "peace" with the hostile Arab world.

In October 1991, Bush and Baker succeeded, despite Yitzhak Shamir's objections, in starting the "Madrid Peace Conference," to which they invited Israeli, Syrian, Lebanese, and Jordanian-Palestinian delegations. Although the West Bank Palestinian Arabs were Jordanian citizens, their inclusion as a "Palestinian entity" was an unprecedented concession made by Shamir's government. At that time, Israeli law considered any diplomatic contact with "Palestinians" and the PLO as a criminal offense. The Madrid conference soon moved to Washington, D.C., and ended without any agreement. Yet the very presence of "Palestinians" at the conference was a new fact-of-life that would have serious consequences. After the Madrid conference, the Israeli political scene underwent a noticeable shift. The left-leaning Labor Party emerged as the most popular force in the upcoming election to the Knesset, which was scheduled to take place in June 1992.

At this point, the issue of ten billion dollars in U.S. loan guarantees came up to enable the cash-strapped Israeli government to borrow money from commercial banks at favorable rates to facilitate the absorption of one million Jewish refugees fleeing to Israel from the former Soviet Union. The loan guarantee emerged as the major issue during both the Israeli and American 1992 election campaigns. Bush decided to use this loan guarantee as a lever to coerce Israel into "freezing the construction of settlements in the occupied territories." Vermont Democratic Senator Patrick J. Leahy, the chairman of the Senate Foreign Operations Subcommittee, stated:

> Unless Israel halts building settlements on the occupied territories, loan guarantees will be dead for 1992. . . . What is more important: receiving full assistance to resettle the immigrants, or continuing to build settlements at the cost of aid?[904]

Israel's foremost priority has always been to prevent itself from becoming a vulnerable, easy-to-overrun deathtrap. The *New York Times* editorial, "Lending for Peace in Israel," praised Bush for stipulating that the freeze on Israeli settlements be a "condition for receiving American loan guarantees." The editorial argued:

> The condition will help nudge this difficult peace process forward by forcing Israel to meet the historic opportunity of absorbing the Soviet Jews.[905]

This argument was a gross distortion of the truth. After the collapse of the "Evil Empire," the Soviet Jews had continued to flee to Israel despite the hardship they knew they would face there. They were caught in the crossfire of ethnic violence that was sweeping the former Soviet Union, where they were the only ethnic group without territory to flee to or the ability to defend themselves in. A million of them, possibly many more (no one really knew how many millions were ready to leave) heard the warning of Russia's president Boris Yeltsin, who on February 6, 1992, said: "I can already feel the breath of the red shirts and brown shirts on our necks." The Jews have felt the breath of these communist and fascist thugs on their necks for a long time. The Soviet leaders, including Gorbachev, have always denied the existence of anti-Semitism in the Soviet Union.[906] The Soviet Jews knew that the only escape route available to them was through the application for exit visas to Israel. Israel continued the absorption of the Soviet Jews without American loan guarantees, as it had done in absorbing previous waves of Jewish refugees from Arab and other countries. It did not accept the "linkage" between the purely humanitarian problems of refugee absorption and the political issues of its borders, which is what the "freeze on settlements" was all about. Similar linkages became familiar "package deals" in future negotiations. They always boiled down to Israeli concessions to placate the Arabs.

The issue of loan guarantees played a crucial role in the June 1992 Israeli election. The influx of one million Soviet Jews, who on their arrival automatically became Israeli citizens, added votes to Yitzhak Rabin's Labor Party because, at that time, the Soviet Jews blamed Shamir for his failure to obtain American loan guarantees. They voted in great numbers for Rabin, because they perceived him as being favored by Bush, which indeed Rabin was. They thought that the loan guarantees would be available and their hardship could be alleviated, if only the stiff-necked Shamir would depart the scene.

After Rabin was elected, the chief of the Mossad, the Israeli intelligence agency, told him that his new deputy foreign minister, Yossi Beilin, was conducting unauthorized, secret talks through emissaries with representatives of Yasir Arafat's PLO. At the time, any contacts with the PLO were illegal. Beilin's men were advising Arafat's lieutenants in Oslo how to maneuver Rabin into negotiating a "peace deal." Rabin did not trust his foreign minister Shimon Peres, and he despised Yossi Beilin, whom he called "Peres's poodle." But "the poodle turned out to be a political pit bull" who took advantage of Rabin's diplomatic weakness. "Leave it to me," Rabin told his Mossad chief. Meanwhile Beilin and Peres maneuvered Rabin into what became known as the "Oslo Accords," and "Beilin became the darling of the Israeli Left, the Arabists in the U.S. State Department, and the European Union."[907]

However, before the Oslo agreement could be signed, President Bush lost the 1992 election to Bill Clinton, who was thereby relegated to overseeing the signing of the "Oslo Accords." The ceremony took place with great pomp on the White House lawn on September 13, 1993. Clinton was jubilant. He prodded a reluctant Rabin to shake Arafat's hand. Rabin later complained to his friends, "I was stuck with the 'bastard' that Oslo had created."[908] But the deal was struck and Clinton claimed credit for it. The Oslo Accords—a "declaration of principles"—had proclaimed "Palestinian self-rule" in the Gaza Strip and the town of Jericho. It also promised the future Israeli withdrawal from some of the West Bank, and a final border agreement within five years. The PLO was recognized as the "representative of the Palestinian people," and Arafat declared that the PLO recognized Israel's "right to exist." The ceremony produced international euphoria. In October 1994, Israel and Jordan signed a peace treaty. Israel recognized Jordan as the custodian of the Muslim holy places in Jerusalem. This provision angered Arafat, who insisted that it was not the Jordanians, but the "Palestinians who were the lawful custodians of the Muslim holy places in Jerusalem." In 1995, Clinton arranged a short-lived agreement between Israel, Lebanon, and Syria, which promised to stop Hezbollah guerillas from attacking Israel. The attacks resumed as soon as the paperwork was signed.

During the entire eight years of his presidency, Clinton kept promoting what he called the "Middle East peace process." He was the first American president to propose the division of Jerusalem into "Israeli and Palestinian sectors," and to promote the idea of granting sovereignty over the Temple Mount to the "Palestinians," while assigning the underground ruins of the two ancient Jewish Temples to Israel. Clinton was the first American president to advocate a "Palestinian state" and to propose the opening of two American embassies in the "Israeli and Palestinian sectors" of Jerusalem. First Lady Hillary Clinton declared her support for a "Palestinian state" even before her husband did, suggesting that the couple might have discussed this idea in private. Clinton held more photo opportunities and conferences with Yasir Arafat than with all other world leaders combined, thus lending a large measure of legitimacy to this gun-toting lifelong terrorist who was continually screaming for Jihad against Israel and the Jews.

On November 4, 1995, an extremist religious student, whose parents had fled to Israel from Yemen in 1950, and who was opposed to ceding any part of the "promised land" to the "Palestinian Authority," shot and killed Yitzhak Rabin during a peace rally in Tel-Aviv. Shimon Peres, who together with Rabin and Arafat had been awarded the Nobel Peace Prize for signing the "Oslo Accords," became prime minister. Benjamin Netanyahu, who had been opposed to the "Oslo Accords," was elected leader of the rightist Likud party.

He was running against Peres in the 1996 Israeli election. During the campaign, Rabin's widow, Leah Rabin, one of the leading Israeli leftists, accused Netanyahu of having played a role in Rabin's assassination.

However, four suicide bombings that had been perpetrated during the campaign and killed fifty-nine Israelis brought about victory for Netanyahu, who became the youngest prime minister in the history of Israel. Clinton invited Netanyahu and Arafat to a conference at the Wye River Plantation in Maryland in October 1998, which lasted for nine days. Clinton succeeded in extracting from Netanyahu an agreement to cede control of Hebron, the first capital of ancient Israel, to the Palestinian Authority. Netanyahu also agreed to cede to the Palestinian Authority additional territory on the West Bank in exchange for Arafat's promise to curtail violence against the Israelis. Netanyahu's concessions, especially his giving Hebron to the Palestinian Authority, produced vehement opposition from his Likud supporters. His days in power were numbered.

The end of 1998 was a tense period for Clinton. In December 1998, the House of Representatives was debating the articles of impeachment in the Monica Lewinsky scandal. The Arab press ran articles suggesting that Monica was a "Zionist agent" planted by the Jews to embarrass Clinton. In December 1998, Clinton went to Gaza to address the "Palestinian National Council." He praised Arafat for revoking the clause in the 1964 PLO Charter that called for the destruction of Israel. This revocation provided Clinton with the opportunity to announce a "great concession" and a "bold step toward peace" by the Palestinians. Arafat proclaimed himself the "Present day Saladin, a liberator of Jerusalem." Hillary Clinton, who had accompanied her husband on this trip, embraced and kissed Arafat's wife Saha Arafat after this "Palestinian First Lady" delivered a vicious, hatemongering speech, accusing Israelis, among other "crimes," of poisoning Arab children. Henry Siegman, a member of the Council on Foreign Relations, who for four decades had been promoting peace between Israelis and Arabs, said of Saha's hatemongering:

> It is an illusion to believe that Palestinians, Egypt, or Saudi Arabia could return their people to sanity.[909]

Bill Clinton survived the impeachment proceedings while Hillary Clinton survived her embrace and kissing of Saha. Fate was favorable to the Clintons when Netanyahu lost the May 1999 election to Ehud Barak, who promised to "revive the stalled peace process." Clinton invited Barak and Arafat to a peace conference at Camp David, after which Dennis Ross, Clinton's peace mediator, recalled:

> Arafat never offered any substantial idea, not once. The only thing he did say was that the Second Temple, destroyed by the Romans almost 2,000 years ago, had never existed in Jerusalem, as the Jews believe.[910]

Ehud Barak, for all his willingness to swallow Arafat's antics and lies, had had enough, and stated:

> When Jesus Christ walked the streets of Jerusalem, he did not see any Muslim mosques or Christian churches there—all that Jesus saw was the ancient Jewish Temple.[911]

It was reported that on his flight to Gaza to address the "Palestinian National Council," Clinton had read Paul Johnson's *History of the Jews*, in which the author noted that the Bible mentions the First and Second Jewish Temples in Jerusalem more than 650 times. Clinton must have read the Bible in his youth, yet he did not tell Arafat that, as far as he knew, the Jewish Temples had indeed existed in Jerusalem. Clinton could have told Arafat to stop alternating between his calls for Jihad against the Jews and his glib declarations of a "peace of the braves," which he had supposedly achieved with his "partner, Yitzhak Rabin."

Arafat constantly threatened to proclaim a "Palestinian State with Jerusalem as its capital." The daily mosque sermonizing continued under his tutelage, calling for the destruction of Israel and for the expulsion of Jews from "Palestine to the countries from which they came." Various Palestinian terrorist organizations were calling for the murder of Jews and for the destruction of the "Zionist entity." Textbooks in Palestinian schools exhibit maps of "Palestine" with no mention of Israel, as if it did not exist. The Palestinian Authority has been running camps where the children are taught to murder Jews and to "liberate Tel-Aviv and Haifa." Hillary Clinton said that the reports about these camps had made her "sick." President Clinton has never complained about such camps.

Clinton's secretary of state, Madeleine K. Albright, devoted much time to having her picture taken with Arafat. She had declared on many occasions that Israel "must withdraw from the occupied territories," and that "illegal settlements are an obstacle to peace." She also said that Israel should "show maximum restraint" in responding to terrorist attacks. When Arafat, his bulging goggle-eyes rolling in one of his tantrums, stormed out of her office at the American embassy in Paris, Ms. Albright ran after him, pleading with him to come back. But Arafat ordered his limousine driver to drive him out of the U.S. embassy grounds. Ms. Albright shouted at the guards to close the embassy gates to prevent Arafat from escaping her pursuit.

There were some even more embarrassing moments during Ms. Albright's tenure in office. Michael Dobbs of the *Washington Post* reported, "Ms. Albright lost three of her Jewish grandparents, among other close relatives, to the Holocaust." She described these revelations as "obviously a major surprise."[912] This denial of her Jewish roots turned the story into a "big *megillah*" (big deal). Numerous other articles, containing photos of her murdered relatives and letters to the editor condemning or justifying her denial of her Jewish origin, appeared in the press.[913] There was nothing in Ms. Albright's pronouncements to indicate any sympathy to Israel because of her real or alleged Jewish ancestry.

A *New York Times* editorial of February 6, 1997, stated:

Secretary of State Madeleine K. Albright has been hit by a thunderbolt from the past.[914]

One of the readers, Leonard S. Berkowitz, responded the next day:

And just what is this thunderbolt? Ms. Albright has just learned that her parents were born Jewish. That anyone would describe this as a "thunderbolt" is a slap in the face to all Jewish people.[915]

Joseph L. Birman, in another letter to the editor, wrote:

The tragedy of the Korbel family (Secretary Albright's grandparents) is that they were killed twice—once by Nazis and the second time by their own children (the Secretary's parents), who suppressed the facts of their lives and deaths.[916]

Ms. Albright's spokesman, James Rubin, a Jew, said on February 6, 1997:

Questions that Ms. Albright might have Jewish origins have come up for some time. When I have asked her about them, she has always replied that she was raised as a Catholic and became Episcopalian when she married. At the end of last year [1996], Ms. Albright advised me to be less categorical in denying her Jewish origins because letters and other accounts were becoming more persuasive.[917]

In July 2000, Clinton persuaded Israeli prime minister Ehud Barak to agree to withdraw 1,500 Israeli soldiers from the security zone in Lebanon. Barak declared that Israel would not walk away from this zone "with its tail between its legs." Major General Amos Malka, chief of Israeli intelligence, stated, "Syria will continue to use Hezbollah to operate against the Israeli army." Malka confirmed that Hezbollah has surface-to-surface missiles that can hit targets deep inside Israel. Barak stated that his predecessors had agreed to withdraw from the Golan Heights. Shamir, Peres, Netanyahu, and Leah Rabin, however, emphatically refuted such allegations. Forty thousand Syrian troops and Syrian secret police agents remained in Lebanon. With its historical ties to the West and the diversity of its many ethnic and religious groups, Lebanon could have been a natural ally of Israel. But the Lebanese government has been a puppet of Damascus for a long time. At the Arab League meeting, the foreign ministers of the twenty-two Arab countries justified the Hezbollah attacks on Israel and demanded a "price that Israel should pay for the right to withdraw its troops in peace." The "price" included the "Israeli withdrawal from the Golan Heights" and the "repatriation to Israel of 360,000 Palestinian refugees" from Lebanese camps. The foreign minister of Lebanon stated that these "refugees, if not guaranteed repatriation to Israel, would remain a time-bomb threatening peace in Lebanon and the entire peace process." Lebanese president Emile Lahoud also threatened, "A unilateral Israeli withdrawal will not work, and will lead to another war."[918]

These demands greatly surprised Yossi Beilin and Shimon Peres, the architects of the "Oslo Accords." Beilin called these demands "surreal," while Peres asked in amazement, "Have you ever heard anything like that in history?" Some amazing historical events have transpired before Peres's very eyes: 300,000 Arab refugees from the 1948 Arab-Israeli War have been kept for more than a half-century in Lebanese "refugee camps" where they have been denied citizenship and the right to work among their "Arab brothers," who speak the same Arabic and practice the same Islam. This abuse of Palestinian refugees has been financed by billions of dollars of United Nations funds. By contrast, Israel has absorbed millions of Jewish refugees from the Arab countries, from the war-ravaged Europe, from Ethiopia, and from the former

Soviet Union. These Jewish refugees did not have twenty-two oil-rich Jewish countries to shelter them. They did not turn their refugee status into a profession. All they had was the 4,000-year-old title to the land of their ancestors.

Israel walked away from Lebanon with 10,000 members of the SLA (South Lebanese Army), Israeli allies, and members of their families, who had escaped from their Hezbollah "liberators" and were resettled in Israel. In January 2003, they petitioned the Israeli High Court, "demanding Israeli citizenship and financial benefits equivalent to the benefits of Israeli soldiers, as well as compensation for their lost property in Lebanon."[919] Barak's retreat from Lebanon emboldened Hezbollah and other terrorist groups, who interpreted the Israeli retreat as a sign of weakness. Hamas supporters in Gaza proclaimed: "The Jews are tired! Let's finish them off!" Attacks by Hezbollah, Hamas, and other terrorist groups intensified. Barak naively believed that his concession would reduce Israeli casualties and bring Israel closer to peace. But, as the saying goes, "The road to hell is paved with good intentions." History is littered with disasters caused by wishful thinking. British prime minister Neville Chamberlain had believed that by agreeing to Hitler's demanded for the "self-determination" of the Sudeten Germans, he would be preserving "peace for our time." Upon his return from Munich, crowds had greeted Chamberlain as a hero. It did not take long before it was realized that the Munich agreement was a major provocation that had encouraged Hitler to unleash the Second World War.

Other provocations, born out of good intentions, could have also ended in disaster. John F. Kennedy had argued during the 1960 election campaign that Matsu and Quemoy, two small islands off the coast of Communist China, had no strategic importance and were not worth defending. The Chinese communists could have interpreted this statement as an invitation to conquer these islands. But they were too weak at the time. In 1961, during the Vienna summit with Khrushchev, Kennedy jumped off his rocking chair and ran across the hall to shake Khrushchev's hand, not realizing that he was shaking a "pig's hoof." During this summit, Kennedy signed the "Neutralization of Laos" agreement with Khrushchev. The North Vietnamese communists immediately started to use Laos as a route to infiltrate their troops in South Vietnam. When Kennedy failed to provide the military support that he had promised to the group of Cuban exiles in their Bay of Pigs landing, and watched helplessly as they were captured by Castro's troops, this was a provocation: Khrushchev could not understand how an American president, with so much power in his hands could fail to ensure the success of an operation just ninety miles off American shores. Khrushchev convinced himself that Kennedy was an pushover and decided to blackmail America by placing Soviet nuclear rockets in Cuba, assuming that he would get away with it. Luckily, he was mistaken and he blinked.

When Ariel Sharon visited the Temple Mount in Jerusalem, the *New York Times* depicted this visit as a "provocation" that had triggered the "second *intifada.*" The media repeated *ad nauseam* the myth about Mohammed, on flying horses, ascending to Heaven from the Al-Aqsa Mosque on the Temple Mount, which for the Muslims became the "third holiest place." Mohammed died in 632 AD, never having set foot in Jerusalem. In 691 AD, fifty-nine years after Mohammed's death, a Jewish convert to Islam built the Al-Aqsa Mosque on the site of the two ancient Jewish Temples. Jerusalem is not mentioned in the Koran even once, while the two Jewish Temples are mentioned in the Bible more than 650 times. For two millennia, countless generations of Jews have prayed to their God, begging Him to take them "Next Year to Jerusalem" so that they could pray at the Western Wall, which is all that remains of the two Jewish Temples. The Western Wall is not the second or third holiest place for the Jews, but their first and only holy place. These are the historical facts, not myths fabricated for propaganda purposes.

At the Camp David conference and at Taba conferences, Clinton was able to wring major concessions from Barak. Sari Nusseibeh, a Palestinian Arab official, and Barak's emissary Ami Ayalon signed an agreement, which stated:

> The Palestinian people and the Jewish people each recognize the other's historical right with respect to the same land, which will have two states for two people with Jerusalem to serve as the capital of both states. Palestinian refugees are to be compensated by an international fund and will return.[920]

Israelis took a look at what kind of "peace" with the Palestinian Authority lay in wait for them. What they saw was a very frightening picture.

On October 12, 2000, three Israeli soldiers took a wrong turn into the West Bank. Palestinian policemen led them to the Ramallah police station. Then they let a Palestinian mob torture and murder the soldiers. Their bodies were tossed through the window to the bloodthirsty mob, which proceeded to mutilate them. Then the mob dragged the corpses through the streets in a trail of blood, triumphantly chanting, "Sharon, have a look! Barak, have a look! We are clearly killing your soldiers." A photo of the bestial orgy showed Aziz Salha, a young Arab, outstretching his blood-covered hands at a window to the cheering mob, who were triumphantly chanting, "Here is where we gouged his eyes! Here is where we ripped off his legs! Here is where we smashed his face!" The Palestinian Authority stated that the soldiers were Israeli "undercover infiltrators on a secret mission to assassinate Arabs," ignoring the fact that the soldiers wore military uniforms and drove an Israeli-licensed Mazda. A Palestinian police officer urged a photographer to "film the blood that dribbled out the station door and through the courtyard," saying, "We want their mothers to see what our mothers had to endure."[921]

Reservist Vadim Novesche, a thirty-three-year-old recent immigrant from the former Soviet Union, was survived only by his pregnant wife, his nine-year-old daughter, and a brother, Mikhail Novesche. Choking back sobs, Mikhail spoke in a soft Russian-accented Hebrew at the funeral:

> I insisted upon seeing him, and I opened the coffin at Tel Hashomer cemetery, and I saw what they did to him. Only animals could do such a thing. You cannot make peace with the devil. But Jews, I ask you on behalf of my family and my brother: Don't stoop to their level; let the army deal with them.[922]

On Barak's orders, the Israeli army at first responded with a slap on the wrist. But later it captured Aziz Salha who on June 27, 2001, appeared in a published photo, reenacting his jubilation. His outstretched arms were this time in handcuffs.[923] The Palestinian police officer who had supervised the murder of the soldiers was also arrested and received a life sentence in prison.

Anti-Jewish violence has been prevalent throughout history. Willard Gaylin, author of the book *Hatred*, cites an example as to the kind of pathological hatred Polish Jews have had to endure: in July 1941, during the German occupation, Poles in the town of Jedwabne murdered 1,600 of their Jewish neighbors.

> They gouged out their eyes with kitchen knives, dismembered them with crude farm instruments, and drowned the women in shallow waters. Infants were pitchforked in front of their mothers and thrown onto burning coals. All activities were accompanied by the shrieks of delight, indeed the laughter, of their neighbors.[924]

Gaylin states, "The Palestinians have become a community of hatred and the Israelis have not," adding, "Hatred is a pathological state." In his 1966 study *Warrant for Genocide*, historian Norman Cohn wrote about the causes of twentieth-century anti-Semitism and of its significance to the destiny of nations:

> A grossly delusional view of the world, based on infantile fears and hatreds, was able to find expression in murder and torture beyond all imagining. It is a case history in collective psychopathology, and its deepest implications reach far beyond anti-Semitism and the fate of the Jews.[925]

While Jimmy Carter in 1977 extracted from Begin the Sinai Peninsula, which was not a part of ancient Israel and amounted to 90 percent of the territory seized by Israel in the 1967 Six-Day War, Clinton managed to extract from Barak an agreement to cede to the Arab Palestinians 97 percent of the remaining part of the "occupied territory" in the West Bank and Gaza, which were parts of ancient Israel and were natural springboards for Arab aggression. Lieutenant-General Thomas W. Kelly, former Director of Operations of the U.S. Joint Chiefs of Staff, pointed out:

> The West Bank Mountains, especially their approaches, are the critical terrain. If an enemy secures those passes, Jerusalem and all of Israel will be uncovered. Without the West Bank, Israel is only eight miles wide at its narrowest point, making it indefensible.[926]

On January 18, 2001, Clinton recounted his achievements, some of them real and some the products of a masterful spin. But he did not say a word about his extraordinary eight-year involvement in what he used to call the "peace process," but later renamed the "political process." Having pushed Israel to the brink of disaster by extracting major concessions from Barak, Clinton forced the Israelis to take a hard look down the abyss that faced them. They kicked Barak out of office and elected Ariel Sharon in the greatest election landslide in Israeli history. But some Jews still continue to think of Clinton as Israel's protector. In a speech given at a fundraising dinner in Toronto to 350 Jews, who paid $1,000 per person to break bread with him, Clinton glibly declared:

> If Iraq came across the Jordan River I'd grab a rifle and fight and die for Israel.[927]

211

This declaration was met with wild applause. A newspaper headline read, G. I. BILL-BUBBA: I'D FIGHT AND DIE FOR ISRAEL.[928] Some readers recalled Jimmy Carter's similarly glib declaration on October 5, 1977, when he said that he'd "rather commit suicide, political or otherwise, than hurt Israel."[929] Another headline announced: CLINTON LOBBIED FOR NOBEL PEACE PRIZE, revealing that Clinton had promoted his candidacy for the 2000 Nobel Peace Prize and that his emissaries had approached two Norwegian public-relations firms and a member of the Norwegian parliament with a "six-figure" offer, which the paper regarded as "unscrupulous, unethical behavior."[930]

Gunnar Berge, chairman of the Nobel Peace Prize committee, presented the 2002 Nobel Prize to Jimmy Carter, saying that Carter's "exclusion from the 1978 prize had been a mistake that the committee was proud to correct." Berge linked U.S. policy toward Iraq to the Arab-Israeli conflict, pointing to "decades of Carter's untiring effort to find peaceful solutions to international conflicts," and praising "Jimmy Carter's Camp David triumph." But when asked whether the award was meant to be a "kick in the leg" to the White House of George W. Bush, Berge replied:

> The answer to your question is an unequivocal yes. The prize must be interpreted as a criticism of the present U.S. administration.[931]

Kaare Kristiansen, who had resigned from the Nobel Peace Prize committee in 1994 rather than endorse the awarding of the prize to Yasir Arafat, called Berge's remark "inexcusable." On December 10, 2002, Carter accepted the Nobel Peace Prize "with a broad smile and an air of satisfaction" and then repeated his scathing assault on President Bush's Iraq policy, which he had also criticized in an earlier article.[932] He then demanded that Israel accept United Nations Resolution 242, which "calls for Israel to withdraw from the occupied territories."[933] In reply to a question during the CNN interview, Carter said that it had bothered him that he did not receive the Peace Prize in 1978 for his Camp David peacemaking efforts with Anwar el-Sadat and Menachem Begin, adding, "It was hard for me to understand it. I have to admit: I really wanted to earn the Nobel Peace Prize."[934] The myth of Jimmy Carter's "Camp David Triumph" was at the root of the "land for peace" formula that provided the foundation for the 1993 Oslo Accords, for which Arafat, Rabin, and Peres had shared the Nobel Peace Prize.[935]

Carter and Clinton found allies among the Israeli and American leftists who advocated Israeli concessions to placate the Arabs. At the time of Israel's birth, the Communist party in Israel had advocated the creation of an Arab-Jewish state allied with the Soviet Union. The Socialist party *Mapam* advocated the creation of a secular socialist Jewish state that would be allied with the Soviet Union. On December 15, 1972, the Israeli security service Shin Bet arrested forty-six members of a spy-and-terrorist organization, who were preparing acts of sabotage in places frequented by Christian visitors. Four of the arrested were Jews, members of the extremist anti-Zionist group Mazpen, which advocated the return of all territories captured in the 1967 War to the Arabs. Most of the saboteurs were Arab members of the Israeli Communist party. They also advocated a "socialist revolution" in the Near East and a "classless society" to replace all the states in the area. Ehud Adiv, one of the four arrested Jews, had gone to Athens and then flown to Syria, where he had undergone training in espionage. The Jewish members of Mazpen formed the "Revolutionary Communist Union" and published the newspaper *Red Front*, which advocated an alliance with the Palestine Liberation Organization and called for the liquidation of the "Zionist entity." Daniel Cohn-Bendit, a German-French Jew known also as "Danny the Red," had visited Israel in 1968 and called for a "socialist revolution."

Such excesses are a thing of the past in present-day Israel. Today's Israeli leftists are ideological descendants of the wild-eyed extremists of yesterday. The traces of this lineage have survived in the ideology and sloganeering of the modern-day Israeli doves. One of these doves was the late Abba Eban, the fabulously eloquent Israeli diplomat who believed that Israel should exchange the territories captured in the 1967 War for a negotiated peace with the Arabs. He declared:

> Israel was tearing its own birth certificate, which is intrinsically and intimately linked to Israel's conception and with the idea of sharing territory and sovereignty.[936]

Eban was deeply involved in the diplomatic maneuvering that resulted in the very narrow November 1947 UN majority vote that authorized the partition of Palestine into Jewish and Arab states and he accepted the UN resolution as Israel's "birth certificate." He viewed himself as a kind of midwife at Israel's birth. Eban and the Israeli delegation accepted the idea of "sharing territory and sovereignty" with the Arabs as a legal foundation of the legitimacy of Israel. However, the Arabs never accepted the right of Israel to exist and launched four wars against the Jewish State in 1948, 1956, 1967, and 1973. For half a century they have subjected Israel to terror. The truth of the matter is that the State of Israel was born in the crucible of her victory in the first War of Independence in 1948, and of all of her victories in the three subsequent wars with Arab states. Israel's birth certificate is "intrinsically and intimately" linked to its victories in these wars, not to any UN resolutions.

But Abba Eban had not always sanctified the UN resolutions. He strongly objected to the resolution in 1975 that equated Zionism with racism, stating:

> The United Nations began its life as an anti-Nazi alliance. Thirty years later it is on the way to becoming the world center of anti-Semitism. The horrifying truth is that Hitler himself would often have felt at home in the forum, which gave applause to the gun-toting Yasir Arafat. . . . It is as natural for Arabs to be citizens and members of Parliament in Israel today as it is inconceivable for non-Muslims to be citizens, much less officeholders, in Saudi Arabia or Yemen.[937]

Eban condemned many subsequent anti-Israeli UN resolutions. He spoke with equally brilliant eloquence from both the right and left side of his mouth, and, reportedly, could do this fluently in ten languages. What are we to make out of his exquisite oratory? Perhaps Levi Eshkol was right when in 1967 he drew a bottom line:

> Eban doesn't live in reality. He never gives the right solution, only the right speech.[938]

Privately Eshkol referred to Eban in Yiddish as *der gelernter naar* (that overeducated fool).[939] Many Israelis doves have openly contradicted themselves with less eloquence than Abba Eban. Shimon Peres and Yossi Beilin are the most prominent among them.

Numerous prominent Jews scattered throughout the Diaspora have also advocated the idea of "trading land for peace." Rabbi Jonathan Sacks, the head of Britain's Jewish community (which numbers some 280,000 members) said in his interview with the British newspaper *The Guardian*:

> I have long been convinced that Israel had to give back all the land on the West Bank and Gaza Strip that had been captured in the 1967 Six-Day War.[940]

Rabbi Sacks' book, *The Dignity of Difference: How to Avoid the Clash of Civilizations*, was serialized in the *Guardian*. Rabbi Sacks wanted to meet with Sheikh Abu Hamza, the militant cleric in London who believed that "it is okay to kill non-Muslims"—and who, proclaiming his support for Osama bin Laden, equated the Jews with "Satan." Sacks disclosed that at a UN conference of religious leaders in New York in 2000, he had met with one of Iran's most notorious anti-Semites, the high-ranking cleric Ayatollah Abdullah Javadi-Amoli. Rabbi Sacks stated, "We established a common language within minutes."[941] He wants very much to appease the Muslims who often make anti-Semitic and anti-Israel statements. Petronella Wyatt, in her column in the *Spectator*, noted that "since September 11, open expressions of anti-Semitism have become respectable at London dinner tables." She reported that the French ambassador to London "politely told a gathering in my home that current troubles in the world were all because of that shitty country Israel. Why should the world be in danger of a World War Three because of these people?" After a suicide-bomber killed twenty-six and injured 200 Israelis, columnist Charles Glass, "an old anti-Israeli hand at the *Evening Standard*," wrote that: "Palestinians kill Israelis, Israelis kill Palestinians. Who killed first? No one remembers, and it does not matter."[942] London Mayor Ken Livingstone called Ariel Sharon "a war criminal who should be in prison" and charged that "Sharon continues to organize terror" and that "Israel is engaged in a campaign of ethnic cleansing against the Palestinians similar to that of the Serbs in Bosnia." and that the Israeli government is trying to frame Muslims for European anti-Semitism."[943]

The picture is gloomier in France. A *New York Times* editorial, "Defending France's Jews," stated:

> Last year the number of Jews moving from France to Israel doubled . . . It remains sadly common for French intellectuals to suggest that if only Israel would do right by the Palestinians, the problem of France's Jews would disappear. This is a cynical argument.[944]

Sharon expressed his concern over "the wave of dangerous anti-Semitism that is sweeping France," but Shimon Peres, after meeting French president Jacques Chirac, asserted, "I am convinced the French leadership is staging a serious and determined effort to battle anti-Semitism in France." Dr. Shimon Samuels commented, "Peres's appeasement encouraged the denial of Jew-hatred in France."[945]

Hillary Clinton, having discovered some rattling bones of a Jewish step-grandfather in her family closet, courted Jewish voters during her election campaign for a New York Senate seat in 2000. HILLARY SEEKING LIEBERMAN'S HELP, declared a *New York Times* headline.[946] The article discussed Mrs. Clinton's courting Senator Joseph I. Lieberman, who was running as the vice-presidential candidate on the Democratic ticket with Al Gore. Lieberman had stated that it was a good idea to establish an understanding with Louis Farrakhan, the well-known anti-Semite who had called the Jews "bloodsuckers." The British government did not allow Farrakhan to enter Britain because of his virulent anti-Semitism. In 1998, Palestinian gunmen murdered an Israeli rabbi, Hillel Lieberman, who had gone to pray at the Joseph Tomb near Nablus. His family claimed that Senator Lieberman was their relative, but the senator denied it. All Liebermans are certainly not related. Avigdor Lieberman, a recent immigrant from the former Soviet Union (and the leader of the right-wing Israeli party "Israel *Beitenu*" [Israel Is Our Home]), said, "A Palestinian state would be a disaster for Israel."[947] He never claimed to be the senator's relative. There was another Lieberman who definitely was not related to Senator Lieberman, because he was a Palestinian Arab. In 1938 he fled from British-ruled Palestine to Paris and asked the French communists to help him to travel to Moscow. They provided him with a forged passport with a fictitious name, "Ali Lieberman"; he chose this name because he had a Jewish communist friend in Palestine by the name of Lieberman. "Ali Lieberman" taught Arabic at the Moscow Oriental Institute (where I was his student), and worked at an Arabic-language radio station broadcasting Soviet propaganda to the Arab countries. We, his students, called him *Rafik* Ali (Comrade Ali).

Some American Jews feel an irresistible urge to portray themselves as "impartial, evenhanded, and progressive" arbiters in the Arab-Israeli conflict. One of them, Dr. Alan Sokal, a professor of physics at New York University, placed an ad in the *New York Times:* "An Open Letter from American Jews to Our Government." This "Open Letter" advocated the Israeli retreat to "borders along the pre-1967 line"; "the evacuation of "all settlements"; "equal sovereignty for Palestinian and Jewish states"; the "right" of Arab refugees to return to Israel with "financial compensation"; and "Palestinian self-determination."[948] It turns out that Dr. Sokal was involved not only in anti-Israel advertisements, but also in scientific "nonsense." In his article in the Science section of the *New York Times*, Denis Overbye referred to Dr. Sokal as "the physicist who had published a nonsense article about quantum gravity in the cultural journal *Social Text* in 1994."[949] Dr. Sokal and his ilk represent a dwindling group of left-leaning Jewish appeasers who break their spines bending over backwards to parade their "fairness and impartiality" while proudly calling themselves "progressives." These Jewish "lemmings" are not interested in Israel. Dictionaries describe lemmings as "rodents . . . notable for recurrent mass migrations often terminated by jumping into the ocean and drowning in it." They are like the character in Lion Feuchtwanger's novel *Jew Süss*: a Jew who lived a life of privilege at the court of a German king but was hanged for being Jewish.

American policy toward Israel drastically changed with the election of George W. Bush. For a brief period he toyed with the notion that, in order to build a broad coalition against Saddam Hussein, he would have to placate the Arab states by speedily resolving the Israeli-Palestinian conflict. But on October 4, 2001, Ariel Sharon stunned the White House when he said:

> The United States should not repeat the terrible mistakes of 1938, when the enlightened European democracies decided to sacrifice Czechoslovakia so as to reach a convenient temporary solution. Do not appease the Arabs at our expense; we cannot accept it. Israel is not Czechoslovakia.[950]

The reference to the appeasement policy of British prime minister Neville Chamberlain was obvious. This was not the first time Israeli leaders had warned foreigners not to appease the Arabs at Israeli expense. In January 1969, Moshe Dayan and Yigal Allon warned the Soviets that "Israel is not Czechoslovakia."[951] In 1979 Menachem Begin also issued the same warning.

Secretary of State Colin Powell called Sharon the same night to convey Mr. Bush's displeasure. The next day, White House spokesman Ari Fleischer said:

> The prime minister's comments are unacceptable. Israel can have no better or stronger friend than the United States, and no better friend than President Bush. Bush is an especially close ally of Israel.[952]

This was true enough. President Bush has been a great friend of Israel. But George F. Will in his column pointed out:

> On an emotional, visceral level, Bush is Israel's very good friend—its best presidential friend since Ronald Reagan, or perhaps even Harry Truman. But Bush's policy, bent by persons determined to nuance into inanity his

war against terrorism, may teach this lesson: although it is dangerous to be America's enemy, it can be fatal to be America's friend.[953]

It was reported that Colin Powell was going to deliver a "very important speech" at the United Nations on October 11, 2001, to declare a new U.S. policy of support for a "Palestinian state." But on the morning of September 11, 2001, Al-Qaeda terrorists struck the Pentagon and New York's Twin Towers. On that day, Palestinian crowds surged into the streets, dancing and shouting praise for bin Laden while Arafat's police tried to confiscate filming equipment and deter TV crews from preserving the ugly scene. It was asserted on numerous occasions that "9/11 has changed everything." Powell later joked, "This was the most important speech that was never delivered."

In retaliation for suicide bombings that had killed scores of civilians, the Israeli army entered Ramallah in February 2001. It surrounded Arafat's headquarters, but Colin Powell stated, "Arafat is central to the peace process" and demanded "immediate Israeli withdrawal from the occupied territory." Netanyahu retorted, "Arafat is our bin Laden. The only difference is that you do not know where bin Laden is, while we know where Arafat is." He proposed to place Arafat on a ship and let it drift on the high seas, precisely because of his central role in the reign of terror. President Bush extracted from Sharon a promise not to harm Arafat, and Sharon kept his word. Arafat bragged that he was the only Arab general to have defeated Sharon. He shouted, "I defeated Sharon in Beirut—I defeated him!"[954] He had in mind the Israeli invasion of Lebanon in 1982, during which Sharon had ordered an Israeli sharpshooter, who had Arafat in his crosshairs, not to kill him.

In February 2001, President Bush was insisting on major reform within the Palestinian leadership in order to deter those involved in terrorism. In response to the renewed wave of violence, Israeli forces again seized and largely destroyed Arafat's Ramallah compound in September 2002. President Bush criticized this move as "unhelpful." A senior Bush administration official said:

> Bush would like Sharon to refrain from any action in the Palestinian West Bank and Gaza that would enflame the Arab region while the potential of a U.S. invasion of Iraq remains high. They have a common problem: each wanted to support the other's war against terror.[955]

At the opening of the UN General Assembly on September 12, 2002, Secretary-General Kofi Annan warned that the Israeli-Palestinian conflict was the "prime threat to world peace," and advanced the view that the "Israeli-Palestinian conflict should be solved before the world moves against Iraq."[956] Some Americans also cited the need to resolve the Arab-Israeli conflict before invading Iraq. The old Primakov formula of "linking" the Arab-Israeli conflict to the American policy toward Iraq emerged again. Brent Scowcroft, who had advised President George H. W. Bush during the Persian Gulf War, warned:

If the United States were seen to turn our backs on the Israeli-Palestinian dispute in order to go after Iraq, there would be an explosion of outrage against us.[957]

Richard N. Pearle, a former adviser to President Reagan, said:

Mr. Scowcroft's arguments were misguided and naïve. . . . To believe that we can produce results in the fifty-year-old dispute between the Israelis and the Arabs is naïve, and this is, therefore, an excuse for not taking action.[958]

Senator Chuck Hagel of Nebraska introduced another argument against attacking Iraq, stating:

A war with Iraq could create the political cover for Israel to expel Palestinians from the West Bank and Gaza.[959]

Senator Edward Kennedy argued that if the United States attacked Iraq, Saddam Hussein might launch rockets at Israel, and Israel in turn would respond with an atomic bomb; the United States should therefore refrain from attacking Iraq.

The British press also joined in "linking" the Israeli-Arab conflict with the policy toward Iraq. A *Financial Times* editorial, "The Right Road to Baghdad," suggested a "winning package," declaring:

Iraq would be easier to deal with if the Arabs felt the international community was dealing evenhandedly with the Israeli-Palestinian conflict. . . . A cohesive coalition would in turn make it easier for the U.S. to restrain Mr. Sharon.[960]

Tony Blair followed up on this suggestion by demanding creation of a

"Palestinian state within the 1967 borders," but he failed to "restrain" Sharon, who responded by recalling the bitter lesson of 1938–39, when the British cabinet headed by Prime Minister Neville Chamberlain issued the "White Paper," following Chamberlain's 1938 Munich Agreement with Hitler, allowing only 75,000 Jews to enter Palestine between 1939 and 1944 and further restricted Jewish immigration to Palestine in the following years, preventing thousands, perhaps millions, of Jews, from escaping from Nazi-occupied Europe. The purpose of the "White Paper" was to appease the Arabs and gain their support in the looming war with the Nazis. However, after Winston Churchill replaced Chamberlain as prime minister, he and his War Cabinet allowed the formation of a Jewish brigade in Palestine to fight the Nazis. Some British ministers objected, citing their fears of antagonizing the Arabs, but Churchill replied, "To hell with the Arabs! They haven't helped us to win the war anyway!"[961]

Israel did not expel the Palestinians from the West Bank and Gaza as Chuck Hagel predicted; and Israel did not use an atomic bomb as Edward Kennedy feared. In June 2002, President Bush revealed his "vision of a Palestinian state," hoping in this way to help Tony Blair, his staunch British ally, to overcome the public's opposition to the Iraq war. Britain has a large Arab and Muslim population, which supports the Palestinian cause and is opposed to the war with Iraq. Bush also hoped to include some Arab states to join in the anti-Saddam "coalition of the willing." These hopes were the origin of Bush's support for the "road map to peace," which was proposed on September 17, 2002, by the so-called "Quartet" of the United Nations, European Union, Russia, and the United States. The "Quartet" agreed to pursue a three-stage plan that would enable Israel and the Palestinians to reach an agreement on the best way to create a "Palestinian state with provisional borders." Israeli leaders found it difficult to ignore the "Quartet," despite their realization that all the members of the "Quartet," except for the United States, have a long history of hostility toward Israel. The future will tell whether Bush's "vision of a Palestinian state" and his support for the "road map," were the products of wishful thinking, or delusion.

Kofi Annan said, "We should hopefully give the Palestinians the incentive to work with us and focus their energy on institution-building and preparing for the state on the horizon."[962] But Sharon, in his January 19, 2003, press conference, dismissed the UN, the European Union, and Russia as credible members of the "so-called diplomatic quartet." In response to a question by a *Washington Post* correspondent he said, "Oh, the quartet is nothing. Don't take it seriously." Addressing the Europeans, he said, "Your attitude toward Israel and the Arabs should be balanced." When asked to explain his widely predicted defeat in the January 28, 2003, election Sharon smiled and said, "Maybe they tried to bury me too early, and maybe not deep enough."[963]

Israel should not underestimate the world's propensity for Jew-phobia. In 2002, Kofi Annan presided over the "UN Conference on Racism" at Durban, South Africa, which was dominated by Arab leaders who, in an orgy of hatemongering oratory, spewed virulent anti-Jewish and anti-Israeli propaganda. Izzat Ibrahim, Saddam Hussein's second-in-command, shouted: "We demand that the Islamic and Arab nations rise quickly to expel the sons of monkeys and pigs, strangers in the land." Abdel-Razzaq al-Saadi, another participant, urged Arab countries to "open their borders to volunteers who want to fight Israel." The top *imam* in Saudi Arabia, Sheikh Abdul-Rahman al-Sudais, delivered a sermon in the Grand Mosque in Mecca that was carried live by Arab TV and radio networks, calling upon Muslims "to say farewell to a peace initiative with these people, the Jews." He prayed "to terminate the Jews: the scum of humanity, the rats of the world, prophet-killers, pigs, and monkeys." Ghazi Algosaibi, Saudi Arabia's ambassador to Britain, published a poem praising the Palestinian homicide-bombers who had "died to honor my God's world."[964]

Russian foreign minister Igor Ivanov went to the Middle East to "revitalize the peace process." Russian president Vladimir Putin glibly proclaimed that his support for the "road map" was motivated by his concern for the safety of the "former Russian citizens who had immigrated to Israel." He said nothing about the safety of other Israeli Jews. The Russians again assumed the role of champions of the "self-determination of Palestinian people" and voted for all the UN anti-Israeli resolutions. The abysmal Soviet record of monumental abuse of the rights of peoples of various ethnic, religious, and historical identities, especially in Chechnya, flies in the face of such pretensions. A leopard does not change its spots overnight, and the dozen or so years since the collapse of the "Evil Empire" are much too short a time. It was reported on March 15, 2004, that Putin had been reelected by seventy percent of the vote. "In one recent poll, 45 percent of Russians remained loyal to Stalin and said that Stalin had played a positive role in the country's history," reported Interfax News Agency.[965] It also reported that "another survey has found that only 26 percent of respondents would describe Stalin as a 'bloody dictator.'"[966] Putin received more than ninety-two percent of the vote in Chechnya, according to the official results.[967] Stalin used to receive ninety-nine percent of the vote during his rule. American writer Anne Nivat, who visited Chechnya in December 2003, was shocked when two days before the election a young Russian told her, "I will vote for *Volodia* [Vladimir Putin], of course, because he stopped the war. Putin has told us many times on television about what he did in Chechnya. It's over, we won this war, and I am proud of it." Nivat concluded her op-ed article: "Don't be surprised if the Russians continue to live their illusions for a long time to come."[968]

Many Russians applauded Putin's assault on the Jewish "oligarchs," whom he accused of corruption and tax fraud. Mikhail Khodorkovsky, the chief executive of the enormously successful oil company Yukos, is now in prison on charges of financial irregularities. His shares are worth some eight billion dollars. He transferred control of his shares to Leonid Nevslin, who flew to Israel and offered to give their shares, worth fourteen billion dollars, to the Russian government in exchange for the release of Khodorkovsky from prison. Khodorkovsky says that he has no intention of leaving Russia. He considers himself a Russian, but the Russians consider him a *polukrovka* (half-breed) because his father is Jewish. Putin held a press conference with Italian prime minister Silvio Berlusconi, during which Putin said that Khodorkovsky was "in prison because he was caught committing a fraud, and was grabbed by his—," and he pointed to his crotch.

Boris A. Beresovsky, an "oligarch" and a supporter of the anti-Putin Liberal party, now lives in London. Media magnate Vladimir Gusinsky and few other Jewish "oligarchs" escaped to Israel. They supported liberal parties and opposed the war in Chechnya.[969] Putin asked the Israeli government to extradite all the Jewish tycoons who had settled in Israel, but the Israeli government refused. "Oligarchs" have been perceived by many Russians as "Jews who stole Russia blind." Putin thrives on the envy of the poverty-stricken Russian people, who resent the few Jews who enriched themselves during the wild privatization campaign after the collapse of the Soviet Union. Putin must have been very skilful at playing the role of a "freedom-loving man" when in November 2001 he visited President Bush at his Crawford, Texas, ranch. Bush said, "I looked Putin in the eyes, liked what I saw, and trusted him."[970] President Bush is likely one day to regret this statement.

Putin was present at the regional economic conference in Bangkok when Malaysia's prime minister Dr. Mahathir Mohamad said:

The Europeans killed six million out of twelve million Jews, but today the Jews rule the world by proxy. They got others to fight and die for them.[971]

This statement was met with wild ovation. The next speaker was Putin, who received a similar welcome. Putin did not object to Dr. Mahathir Mohamad's blatantly anti-Semitic rhetoric. Putin's speech was reported in Russia to the dismay of many people there.[972] No one at the conference mentioned Russia's brutal war against the Muslim Chechens.

The infamous forgery, *Protocols of the Elders of Zion*, has been gaining popularity in the Arab world. The Arab propaganda television station Al Jazeera declared, "Zionism exists and it has controlled the world since the dawn of history."[973] This forgery was used in Russia and in Nazi Germany for the persecution of Jews.[974] Sami Al-Arian, the Palestinian fundraiser in Florida who was arrested and charged with financing terrorist organizations, for once dared to tell the truth about the source of the Arab hatred for Israel:

Israel's prosperity and strength is a continuous reminder of the weakness of Arabs as a people, of their society and political system; as well as an indication of their impotence and the corruption of their regimes.[975]

Arafat used to constantly proclaim "days of rage" for his "Palestinian people" who live in perpetual rage because they envy Israeli prosperity. They see the Jewish settlements' manicured gardens and beautiful villas with red-tiled roofs and they compare their squalid slums with Israel's prosperous cities, towns, and settlements. They dream of driving the Jews out, not only from the settlements in the "occupied territory," but also from Israel proper. Nothing short of allowing them to slit Jewish throats will appease their envy and satisfy their bestial thirst for revenge. "The pitiful Gaza Strip residents, used by Arab states as political hostages for decades, have a per capita GNP of only $1,000 per year, compared with $19,000 for Israelis. The West Bank Arabs are little better off at $2,300 per year. Arafat and his henchmen have done nothing to improve the lives of Palestinian Arabs, despite the huge infusion of Western aid and Arab oil money."[976]

Salman Rushdie, for whom Iran's ayatollahs had issued a death sentence for his book *The Satanic Verses*, wrote:

Even if an Arab-Israeli settlement were reached tomorrow, anti-Americanism would probably not abate. . . . What America is accused of— is what its accusers would see if they looked into a mirror.[977]

In a November 29, 2002, interview with Kuwait's *Al Siyasa* newspaper, the interior minister of Saudi Arabia, Prince Nayef bin Abdel Aziz, stated:

> It is impossible that nineteen youths, including fifteen Saudis, carried out the operations of September 11. Who committed the events of September 11? I think the Zionists are behind these events.[978]

A member of Hamas, usually an advocate of the murder of Jews, proposed:

> There are many open areas in the United States that could absorb the Israeli Jews.[979]

This was an intriguing idea. The twenty-two oil-rich Arab countries have "lots of open areas" that stretch from the Indian to the Atlantic Oceans and are populated by only one hundred million Arabs. They can absorb not only the "Palestinian refugees," but also, for good measure, all the Palestinians from the West Bank and Gaza and all of the "Israeli Arabs" who have often acted as a "fifth column" in Israel, despite the fact that they enjoy living standards and human rights that are unimaginable in any Arab country.

UN Secretary General Kofi Annan declared the "Israeli occupation of the Palestinian areas illegal." Actually, the wars in 1948, 1956, and 1967, and the Yom Kippur War of 1973, had all been illegal aggressions by Arab states. It is illegal for the UN to provide a forum to the Arab states to wage the venomous, hatemongering campaign against the Jews and Israel. It is criminal for the UN to provide funds for half a century to the "Palestinian refugees" in the UN refugee camps and to use the refugees as a cannon fodder in attacking Israel and murdering the Jews. These camps are the breeding ground for aggression against Israel. The "Palestinian refugees" have been used for the virulent anti-Jewish propaganda under the pretense of "fairness and objectivity."

Columnist Anthony Lewis, employing his tortured "evenhanded reasoning," wrote:

> Serbs in the grip of religion and mystical nationalist history killed thousands and expelled millions in their ethnic cleansing in Bosnia. Fundamentalist Judaism and extreme Israeli nationalism have fed the movement to plant settlements in Palestinian territory, fueling Islamic militancy among the Palestinians.[980]

Lewis equated the "killing of thousands and expulsion of millions of Muslims in Bosnia" (he forgot to mention Kosovo) to the Israeli "settlements." Such logic should remind the Jews that the threat to them is not "Islamic militancy among Palestinians," which Israel will handle, but the Jew-phobia masquerading as phony "evenhanded fairness." After visiting Riyadh in February 2002, Thomas Friedman began promoting the Saudi Crown Prince Abdullah's "peace initiative," which called for Israel to "repatriate" all the Palestinian refugees to Israel and to retreat to the 1949 Armistice Line in exchange for which the Arab world would normalize its relations with Israel.[981] Reporting from Cairo about this "peace initiative," Friedman wrote:

> I am not talking about what is right or what is fair, or even what is rational. If we ignore it, if we dismiss it all as a fraud, we will never harvest the positive change that could come from a regime change in Iraq.[982]

As President Reagan used to say, "Here we go again." Friedman had applied the old Primakov formula and "linked" the Iraq war with American support for Israel. He likes to predict Israel's demise:

> The Israelis will control the whole area by apartheid, or they will control it by expelling Palestinians, or they will grant Palestinians the right to vote and it will no longer be a Jewish state. Whichever way it goes, it will mean the end of Israel as a Jewish democracy.[983]

In his report "One Wall, One Man, One Vote," Friedman again prognosticated Israel's disintegration. He wrote that Israel "is still wrestling with all the unintended consequences of its victory in 1967." He did not mention the *intended* consequences of the Arabs' victory in that war. He wrote:

> Today Israel is building fences and walls around the West Bank to deter suicide-bombers. But, having looked at this wall extensively from both sides, I am ready to make a prediction: it will be the mother of all unintended consequences.[984]

Friedman predicts that the fences will force the Palestinians to demand Israeli citizenship, and that a "One Man, One Vote" would result in the end of Israel, which would gradually dissolve into the Arab majority. He glibly reassures his readers that he has "enormous sympathy for Israelis trying to deter suicide-bombers."[985]

Thomas Friedman might be in for a major disappointment. The fence, as "the mother of all unintended consequences," might very well ensure Israel's survival by preventing the Palestinians from unleashing their fury toward the Jews. Their hatred needs an outlet. And if the Palestinians are unable to find such an outlet in the murder of the Jews, they might very well direct their hatred inward. When the fence is complete, it will channel this hatred against the terrorist gangs and against the Palestinian Authority, which would have to fight for control over the people in Palestinian areas and confront Hamas, the Palestine Islamic Jihad, and other terrorist organizations. The Palestinian Authority would have to defend itself in order to survive. This clash might lead to a civil war among the Palestinian factions, which the Palestinian Authority has so far avoided by refusing to suppress terrorist gangs.

Another prediction of the "end of Israel" came from Andrea Koppel, the State Department correspondent at CNN, who declared that Israeli soldiers had committed "slaughter in the Janin refugee camp." When Israelis complained that this was not true, Andrea Koppel answered: "Palestinians told us about the slaughter," adding, "Yes, you will lose your country. Yes, I believe we are now seeing the beginning of the end of Israel."[986] Another "evenhanded" Jew, Jeffrey Goldberg, demonized the settlers in the West Bank and Gaza in his article "Among the Settlers: Will They Destroy Israel?," calling them a "vanguard of Israel's demise as a Jewish democracy."[987] The Israeli press accused Goldberg of being a "self-hating Jew" and even compared him to the *"kapos"* (Jews who had cooperated with the Nazis in murdering their fellow Jews in gas chambers). Another strange case of an anti-Israel Jew is Adam Shapiro, a Brooklyn native dubbed the "Taliban Jew," who came to prominence as a pro-Palestinian activist. He huddled with Yasir Arafat in his Ramallah bunker and married a Palestinian woman. Pictures of this happy couple have been prominently displayed by the media.[988]

Yasir Arafat used to urge Arab and Muslim countries to put Israel on trial at The Hague's International Court, which proclaimed the Israeli building of the barrier illegal. Arafat accused Israel of building what he called a "Berlin Wall." He turned the truth upside-down. The Soviets built the Berlin Wall to prevent East Germans from escaping from the Soviet-occupied "German Democratic Republic" and seeking freedom in West Germany. Israelis built the fence to prevent Palestinian terrorists from entering Israel and murdering innocent people in the free and democratic Israel. The Israeli government responded by predicting that this decision would find its place in the ash heap of history among many other anti-Israeli UN declarations.

Dr. Gustav Hendrikssen, a member of the Swedish Nobel Prize committee, advised Israel not to rely on the support of Europeans. He wrote:

> For a Christian who has managed to divest himself of the hatred of Jews, Israel is a divine message. . . . It gives a "goy" like me a reason to believe that humanity is not just a band of primitive savages that tear each other's throats every few years. . . . For the first time in 2,000 years, the Jew is seen as an equal among equals. . . . Arafat is the heir of Hitler . . . This miserable butcher crawled out of the human sewer, and his entire purpose in life has been to destroy the people of Israel on their own land.[989]

Dennis Ross, who advised President Clinton on the Israeli-Palestinian "peace process," held a different opinion of Arafat:

> Yasir Arafat is the symbol of the Palestinian movement. Anyone who thinks he is going to disappear doesn't understand the importance of what Yasir Arafat means to the Palestinian people. From a Palestinian standpoint, he put them on the map.[990]

It is true that Arafat "put Palestinians on the map" and that he is "the symbol of the Palestinian movement." More than that, he invented the "Palestinian people" and he invented himself as the "Palestinian leader." Amr Musa, the Secretary-General of the League of Arab Nations, stated, "Arafat is the elected representative of the Palestinians." George F. Will commented, "Yes, and Stalin had been elected by the Politburo."[991] The oft-repeated mantra "Yasir Arafat is an elected leader of the Palestinian people" is a myth perpetrated by Arafat, whose opponent in the sham 1996 "election" was an elderly woman whose name was barely known then and is not remembered today. The striking fact is that Arafat is not even a "Palestinian." He was born in Egypt to Egyptian parents. His mother died when he was four years old. His father sent him to live with an uncle who had migrated from Egypt to Jerusalem in search of employment in the prosperous Jewish communities of British Palestine, as did many Egyptians at that time. This uncle sent his unwelcome nephew back to Egypt, where Arafat's sister supported him through school and at Cairo University. Arafat served in the Egyptian army before moving to Syria, where in 1969 he created his *Fatah* terrorist group and used it to take over the PLO.

When his father died in 1964, Arafat did not go to his funeral, thus discarding both his paternity and his Egyptian origin. He postulated a "Palestinian" identity for himself by always carrying a gun and wearing Palestinian *skuffiyah*, his customary headdress.

Arafat, who is dead now, was not the first "outsider" to leech onto a people to usurp their identity and establish a "Palestinian" identity for himself. Hitler had discarded his Austrian origins and took over a collapsed German empire, while Stalin, a Georgian, had convinced himself that he was a "Russian" in order to outsmart his rivals and usurp power in post-revolutionary Russia. Hitler and Stalin insinuated their pathological personas into the emotional vacuum created by the loss of legitimacy by the two great empires. Both Stalin and Hitler were mass murderers and psychopaths, as well as Jew-haters. Arafat lied smugly and shamelessly; and he also was a Jew-hater. He believed in everything he pontificated, no matter how ridiculous his fabrications were; he lived in a world of endless denial. Looking straight into President Clinton's eyes, Arafat denied that Jewish Temples in Jerusalem had ever existed.[992] He also stated that Jesus Christ was "Palestinian" because he had been born in Bethlehem. On March 20, 2004, a delegation of Muslim and Christian clergy from various countries brought Mel Gibson's movie, *The Passion of the Christ*, to the besieged Arafat compound in Ramallah. To his adviser Abu Rudeneh, who watched the film with him, Arafat said that the picture was "historic and impressive," adding: "The Palestinians are still exposed daily to the kind of pain Jesus was exposed to during his crucifixion."[993] Hanan Ashrawi, Arafat's "spokeswoman," stated, "the Palestinians were the first Christians." Arafat made many ridiculous assertions, among them:

> I am Yasir Arafat and this land is my land and the land of my grand-grand-grand-grand-grandfathers. I am one of the sons of Abraham from the beginning.[994]

Arafat used to organize parades of his followers dressed in strange attire, who proclaimed that they were "descendants" of Canaanites, the ancient people who were, as the ancient Philistines, briefly mentioned in the Bible. Yet it is true that the majority of "Palestinians" identify with Arafat because they sense in him the same emotional need to postulate an identity for themselves as he had done for himself. They also share his hatred for the Jews and his dream for the destruction of the Jewish State. It was not the sham 1996 "election" that made Arafat the true "Palestinian leader," an assertion that Arafat's Western supporters repeated *ad nauseam* when he was alive, with their shared loathing of the Jews. Palestinians eagerly identify with the Biblical "Philistines" and "Canaanites," and dream of robbing the Jewish people of their history and of the land of their ancestors. They also hope to take over the Jewish homes and property in Israel.

Ariel Sharon called Arafat a "murderer and a pathological liar." Benjamin Netanyahu called Arafat "our Osama bin Laden." Anthony Lewis, who often used his columns to promote the pro-Palestinian cause, wrote:

> Predictably, this intifada has hardened Israeli attitudes. The peace movement has dwindled; politics has moved to the right. In a poll of Israelis just published by the newspaper *Maariv*, fifty percent said they favored the "transfer" of all Palestinians from the West Bank and Gaza—sending them to Arab countries.[995]

The increasing majority of Israelis indeed reject the "Oslo Accords" with its "trading territory for peace" provision, recognizing in it a stepping-stone to the creation of a hostile Arab state on Israel's borders. Menachem Begin's son Benny Begin observed:

> There is no group of Arabs west of the Jordan River that is distinct from other Arabs and that is eligible for the self-determination. The Palestinians as a different nation is the greatest hoax of the twentieth century after the Nazi hoax.[996]

Yoram Hazony, in his *New York Times* op-ed piece, cites Israeli opinion poll numbers: Ariel Sharon had more than 80% support among Israeli Jews, while the architects of Oslo, Shimon Peres, was down to 28%, and Yossi Beilin down to 7%. Another revealed that over 50% of Israeli Jews support the "transfer" of Palestinians to twenty-two Arab countries, home to more than 100 million Arabs. A leftist Israeli wrote a letter to the editor of the *New York Times*, stating:

> Ariel Sharon's victory means the final death of Oslo with no viable alternative except transfer. Many of us on the left are disappointed, and I, for one, hope that we are wrong.[997]

Although the idea of "transfer" continues to gain support in Israel, this word does not exist in either Yiddish or Hebrew and had to be borrowed from English. This language "deficiency" reflects the historical fact the Jews have not done to other people what other people have done to them. The Jews had been exiled from ancient Israel, from Spain, from many other European countries; and, more recently, from Arab and Muslim nations. The Palestinian Arabs could have been absorbed into Arab countries with a fraction of the oil billions that had been wasted on acquiring weapons for wars with Israel. The Israelis do not have another Jewish country to which to flee or be exiled.

On May 2, 2002, the former Texas Republican House Minority leader Dick Armey, in an interview with Chris Matthews on MSNBC, said, "the Palestinians should leave," which caused much furor. He had to "politically correct" himself by saying, "Individuals who support terror may properly be expelled." Tom DeLay, the majority leader, said:

> I can't imagine the president supporting a sovereign state of terrorists. You'd have to change almost an entire generation's culture. . . . When they talk about a road map, I question whether this is a road map based upon the President's speech, or a road map based upon some State Department concept of another peace process.[998]

DeLay said that politics had nothing to do with his pro-Israel stance, predicting that "Jews would never leave the Democratic party in large numbers." He said that his attitude toward Israel is driven by his support for its democratic values and by his faith:

> I recognize that my faith came from this part of the world. And in my faith, fighting for right and wrong, and understanding good and evil, is pretty apparent and straightforward.[999]

Israelis are very much heartened by the support of the estimated sixty million evangelical Christians in the United States.

Benny Elon, a member of the Knesset, met with Jewish organizations and U.S. Senators and Congressmen. He presented them with the "Elon Peace Initiative," a seven-part plan which called for the nullification of the "Oslo Accords"; the resettlement of Palestinian refugees in the countries of their present residence, with the help of international funds; and the establishment of a Jordanian-Palestinian state with Amman as its capital. Under this plan,

Palestinians in the West Bank and the Gaza Strip would have Jordanian-Palestinian citizenship and could opt to remain in their homes in Israel, but those who violated the terms of the plan would "be expelled to their state on the other side of the Jordan River." Elon said that he had received quiet support from several U.S. legislators, adding, "I can say one thing: Dick Armey and Tom DeLay are not alone."[1000]

According to Palestinian opinion polls, more than eighty percent of Palestinians support terror. President Bush's "vision of two states living in peace with each other" might encounter a problem. PLO representatives Sari Nusseibeh, Diana Buttu, and Michael Terazi stated that the PLO might abandon the two-state solution and declare that "Israel would eventually have to consider giving citizenship to Palestinians living in the West Bank and Gaza." A spokesman for the State Department dismissed this idea, saying that it threatens Israel's Jewish character. But the PLO wants the destruction of Israel as a Jewish state by whatever means, if not by terror and military conquest, then by "peaceful" demographic aggression.

Israel did not use the Iraq war to expel Palestinians, as Senator Chuck Hagel had predicted. Israel did not drop atomic bombs on Iraq as Senator Ted Kennedy had feared it would. These two Senators linked the Israeli-Palestinian conflict to the Iraqi war as the justification for their opposition to President Bush's decision to remove Saddam Hussein from power. It is doubtful that the Palestinian Arabs, had they been expelled from the "occupied territories," would have remembered for one hundred, let alone two thousand, years this land as the Jews have remembered the land of their ancestors.

Senator Edward Kennedy has expressed his support for the Palestinian cause on several occasions. An article "Kennedy Praises Bush Road Map," revealed that he and Congressman James Moran, a Democrat from Virginia, were "among the personalities who had appeared at a gala dinner for the Arab-American Institute that was sponsored in part by the Kingdom of Saudi Arabia." Kennedy, the keynote speaker, "praised President Bush for his road map for peace between Israel and Palestinian Arabs." He was greeted by loud applause. When Kennedy praises Bush for supporting the "road map," Israelis should beware and take note. Congressman Moran, who had earlier declared that "without the support of the Jews, America would not have gone to war in Iraq," was also greeted "with enthusiastic applause and a standing ovation." Also present was the family of Rachel Corrie, an anti-Israel member of the "National Student Conference of the Palestine Solidarity Movement," which supports Palestinian homicide-bombers. Rachel Corrie had earlier gone to

Gaza to "defend Palestinian homes" and had been run over by an Israeli army bulldozer, which was destroying a home used for smuggling weapons from Egypt. Her supporters proclaimed her a "hero and a martyr," but the Israeli army called her death a tragic accident.[1001] Charlotte Kates, 23, a Rutgers University law student and a leader of the National Student Conference of the Palestine Solidarity Movement, declared:

> Palestinian resistance has been a very powerful tool of justice in all its forms, from armed struggle to mass protest. Israel is an apartheid colonial-settler state. I do not believe that apartheid colonial-settler states have a right to exist.[1002]

John Kerry spoke at the same Arab-American Institute in October 2004, and declared:

> I know how disheartened Palestinians are by the Israeli government's decision to build a barrier off the green line, cutting deeply into Palestinian areas. We do not need another barrier to peace. Provocative and counterproductive measures . . . increase the hardship of the Palestinian people.[1003]

Kerry believes that the construction of the Israeli fence against suicide bombers is "another barrier to peace." He is worried that this barrier would "increase the hardship of the Palestinian people" while ignoring the fact that the Israeli people are "disheartened" by being blown up to pieces by Palestinian terrorists.

Kerry said that he intended, if elected, to send former Secretary of State James Baker to mediate Israeli-Palestinian negotiations. In a speech to the Council on Foreign Relations in December 2003, Kerry said that he would also dispatch former presidents Jimmy Carter or Bill Clinton to the Middle East "as special envoys to deal with the Israeli-Palestinian crisis."[1004] He dropped Baker from that list of envoys either because Carter and Clinton were perceived by him as a less of an anathema to Israel than Baker, or because Kerry perceived Baker as being too friendly with the Bush family. Kerry often criticized President Bush for "mismanaging" American foreign policy, stating that he wanted to improve relations with Arabs and Muslims. He never explained how he would perform such a miraculous feat without turning his back on Israel. He wanted Bush to undergo a "global test" which meant to get approval from the United Nations and many foreign countries before making decisions to defend the United States. Dr. Mahathir Mohamad, the former prime minister of Malaysia, who had made anti-Semitic statements, said, "John Kerry would keep the world safer than President Bush."[1005]

To attract the Jewish vote, Kerry made statements about his commitment to Israeli security. He said repeatedly that he would ask for the support of the United Nations before taking any military action. It is difficult to imagine how he would deliver on any commitment to Israeli security without having to endlessly plead for the support of the anti-Israel UN majority in the event of a new Arab-Israeli war. Kerry did not mention the "road map" in his speeches, and did not say what kind of Arab-Israeli peace he would pursue.

A December 2003 newspaper headline announced, BUSH THREATENS TO SUSPEND ROAD MAP.[1006] The major point of this article was that in his State of the Union speech of January 20, 2004, Bush did not mention the "road map" among his foreign-policy priorities. Ahmed Qurei, the prime minister of the Palestinian Authority, objected to that omission. Democratic Senator from California Dianne Feinstein said that she wished to hear from President Bush "something about the United States pushing the peace process." She described the Israeli-Palestinian conflict as the "number-one issue precipitating a real clash of civilizations between the Western world and the Muslim world."[1007] President Bush proposed economic, political, and cultural reforms in the Middle East. Arab and several European leaders criticized the United States for its failure to insist upon a "peaceful end to the Israeli-Palestinian conflict as a precondition for such reforms."[1008] In the op-ed article, "The Wrong Way to Sell Democracy to the Arab World," Zbigniew Brzezinski, a national security adviser to the Carter administration, joined this chorus of anti-Bush criticism and accused Bush administration officials of delaying "serious American effort to push the Israelis and Palestinians to reach a genuine peace settlement."[1009] More then two decades earlier, Brzezinski characterized as a "good document" the Soviet-American Joint Declaration of October 1, 1977, an ultimatum to Israel to surrender to a Soviet-American dictate "by December 1977."

The *Jerusalem Post* used to be a dovish Israeli newspaper, but recently one of its directors, Barbara Amiel, in her article "Getting Beyond Arafat," stated:

> We are at a point where neither Arafat's exile nor death would resolve the Arab-Israeli conflict. . . . Muslims are increasingly being pulled into a malicious myth in which the antagonist is named Israel, and, by extension, America and its allies. . . . If you are a nation of six million surrounded by

seventy million enemies who don't accept your existence, the only option is to fight to the death.[1010]

Before Arafat's death, the Israeli press had aired several suggestions as to how best to deal with him: to put him on a ship and let it drift helplessly in Mediterranean sea; or exile him to France to be reunited with his "wife Saha and her eight-year-old daughter living on an entire floor of a posh hotel in Paris," where the family could enjoy the "secretly amassed $1.3 billion in assets hidden around the world."[1011] Another suggestion was to place Arafat in the glass cage that had not been used since the trial of Nazi mass-murderer Adolf Eichmann (who had been executed by hanging in 1962, the only case thus far in Israeli history of capital punishment). Also mentioned was killing Arafat if he tried to resist capture.

Arafat is now dead, but his legacy has survived. Arab and Muslim countries, and some European countries, remain hostile to Israel. On May 16, 2004, a French representative at the European Union Parliament, Paul-Marie Couteaux, denounced Israel as a "theocratic religious state" and said:

> I have no hesitation in saying that we must consider giving the Arab side a large enough force, including a large enough nuclear force, to persuade Israel that it cannot simply do whatever it wants. This is the policy my country pursued in the 1970s when it gave Iraq a nuclear force.[1012]

Couteaux ignored the fact that Israel is the only free and democratic state in the entire Middle East region, where it is surrounded by twenty-two hostile, theocratic religious states that are ruled by autocrats and dictators. He also neglected to mention what Israel had done to the Iraqi nuclear force. Israel, like the marshal in *High Noon*, is pretty much on its own in its lonely struggle for survival.

President Bush declared that the United States would not allow Israel to be crushed. The Israelis, of course, appreciate his assurance. But they had won their own battles for survival. There will be a lot of howling and passing the blame onto the Jews if a new Arab-Israeli War breaks out. What else is new? For centuries the Jews have survived massacres, the Inquisition, pogroms, and the Holocaust. And now there is something new: for the first time in two thousand years the Jews have a country of their own and an army to defend it. An elderly woman, Merka Shevach, who survived a Nazi concentration camp and now lives in Israel, said it best during a gathering of survivors for the sixtieth anniversary of the liberation of Auschwitz-Burkenau concentration camp where the few former inmates placed candles at the death camp memorial. In her impromptu statement Merka Shevach said:

> I was here naked as a young girl, I was 16. They brought my family here and burned them. They stole my name and gave me a number.[1013]

She pulled back her sleeve to show the tattoo: 15755. She continued:

> Now I have a country, I have my army. I have a president. I have a flag and this will never happen again.[1014]

The only reason the Arab states do not attack Israel today is because they know what a crushing defeat awaits them. The only thing Israel needs is for the United States not to appease the Arabs by pressuring Israel for dangerous and unacceptable concessions.

Vitaly Svechinsky, my childhood friend and codefendant, called me after hearing reports of the exit polls suggesting John Kerry's victory in the 2004 election. He, like many Israelis, was worried. I was worried, too. I told him that Israel had survived eight years of Bill Clinton and even survived four years of Jimmy Carter, and it would survive Kerry as well. Mikhail Margulis, my other childhood friend and codefendant, called me after President Bush's victory. He was in high spirits and shouted: "Bush won! Arafat is dropping dead!" He exclaimed in Hebrew, "*Am Israel hai!*" (People of Israel live!). Knowing that I was writing a book, *Israel at High Noon*, Svechinsky sent me an article by Amnon Lord, the editor at the Israeli newspaper *Makor Rishon* (*The Source*). Lord compared President Bush and Israel to Gary Cooper in the movie *High Noon*. The article included a large still from the film with Gary Cooper standing alone on an empty street to confront the four killers, who are about to turn the corner.[1015]

Chapter 11

Putin's Deadly Schemes and the Shadow of Primakov

Vladimir Putin arrived in Israel on April 28, 2005. Israeli newspapers announced that Evgeny Primakov was part of Putin's entourage and that Putin had an ambitious agenda which included his proposal to convene an international conference in Moscow on May 8–9, 2005, "to discuss efforts to push forward the long-stalled peace process."[1016] Putin announced that he intended to provide the Palestinian Authority with two helicopters, training for its security forces and rebuilding the infrastructure in the Gaza Strip. He did not mention the fifty armored vehicles that he had promised to deliver earlier to the Palestinian Authority. Ariel Sharon said that he would not allow the armored personnel carriers into the West Bank and Gaza Strip. He also said that he was against the sale of Russian anti-aircraft missiles to Syria because these missiles could fall into the hands of terrorists and that he was against Russia's assistance in developing nuclear power stations in Iran.[1017]

The beginning of the talks was marked by a confusion about the fate of Mikhail Khodorkovsky, a Russian oligarch who, as many Israelis believed, has been imprisoned because of his criticism of Putin's policies and because Khodorkovsky, whose father is Jewish, was being persecuted as a wealthy Jew, who had "stolen Russia blind." Israeli newspapers reported that that a Russian court in Moscow would sentence Mikhail Khodorkovsky on April 29. But on the day of Putin's arrival in Israel it was announced that the Russian court decided to delay the sentencing to the middle of May. The sentencing was again postponed and on May 30 Khodorkovsky and his partner Platon Lebedev were sentenced to nine years in prison. Representative Tom Lantos of California, the ranking Democratic member of the House International Relations Committee, spoke outside the Moscow court, stating:

> This political trial, tried before a kangaroo court, has come to a shameful conclusion. The conclusion of this trial was predetermined politically.[1018]

Kodorkovsky's Russian mother, Marina, who is Russian, said:

> We lost our son the day Putin came to power. We know who these people are, these KGB people. How could our country elect such a person from this organization?[1019]

Andrew Meiler, in his "A Modern K.G.B. Colonel," a review of *Kremlin Rising—Vladimir Putin's Russia and the End of Revolution,* summed up the book's major point:

> For all of Putin's talk, Russian officialdom remains what it was in Pushkin's [and Lermontov's] time—a mess.[1020]

Vladimir Bukovsky, a prominent Russian dissident now living in Britain, observed:

> Russia has undergone a bloodless revolution but it did not affect the soul of its people and social conscience was not changed by the fact of the great epochal change—the demise of the Evil Empire.[1021]

Yuri N. Afanasiev, a historian and honorary president of the Russian State University of Humanities, lamented what he called a "restoration of official, incomplete and dishonest Russian history," stating:

> An attempt is being made to vindicate the official history of Russia. This is the same history of Stalin's time—falsified, biased, and ideological.[1022]

Putin visited the President of the Palestinian Authority, Mahmoud Abbas, in his Mukata presidential compound. Abbas expressed satisfaction over the "historic" visit of the Russian president and stated his hope that Moscow would serve as a balance to Washington's bias toward Israel. Abbas welcomed "our precious friend and comrade" and said:

> Your visit is a historic event reflecting the deep historical connection, strong friendship between the peoples of Russia and Palestine.[1023]

Putin responded:

> If we expect Chairman Abbas to fight terrorism effectively, he can't do it with slingshots and stones. We must understand this.[1024]

In Soviet times Abbas studied at Moscow State University, where he wrote his dissertation in which he denied that the Holocaust ever took place.

Talal Okal, a Palestinian political analyst, said:

> Russia does not have enough power to reactivate its role in the Middle East. Its economy is too weak and it has too many internal problems, such as Chechnya. All we Palestinians can do is receive Putin warmly as an ally. But to achieve peace, we need the intervention of a strong superpower.[1025]

While in Jerusalem, Putin visited the Yad Vashem Holocaust memorial museum and, according to tradition, covered his head with a yarmulke to honor the Holocaust victims. Evgeny Primakov did not go to Yad Vashem. Wearing a yarmulke was apparently too much of a burden for this son of a Jewish mother. While in Ramallah, Putin laid a wreath on Yasir Arafat's grave and quickly moved away. Primakov also laid a wreath on Arafat's grave and stood there for some time honoring his old friend. Primakov made no TV appearances on this visit to Israel. But during his previous visit as a Soviet official he castigated Israel for not retreating from to the "occupied territories." In his interview on Israeli TV Primakov was asked why the Soviet Union had occupied Konigsberg and other German territories and was still occupying them. Primakov replied, "Because we are a Great Power."

On Friday, May 13, 2005, a few days after Putin returned to Moscow, Muslim preacher Ibrahim Mdaires delivered his sermon at a Gaza Strip mosque, declaring:

> We have ruled the world before, and by Allah, the day will come when we will rule the entire world again. The day will come when we will rule America. The day will come when we will rule Britain and the entire world—except for the Jews. The Jews will not enjoy a life of tranquility under our rule, because they are treacherous by nature, as they have been throughout history. The day will come when everything will be relieved of the Jews—even he stones and trees which were harmed by them. Listen to the Prophet Muhammad, who tells you about the evil end that awaits Jews. The stones and trees will want the Muslims to finish off every Jew.[1026]

Mdaires also blames the Jews for the World War II and questions the Holocaust:

> Yes, perhaps some of them were killed and some burned, but they are inflating this in order to win over the media and gain world sympathy.[1027]

Palestinian Authority Information Minister Nabil Shaath called for the suspension of sermons by Mdaires but the Palestinian Waqf (religious authority) stated:

> We won't suspend him just because Israel and the US want it.[1028]

Officials in Ramallah expressed fear that publication of the sermon would reflect negatively on Mahmoud Abbas's upcoming talks with President George W. Bush, stating:

> This is the last thing we need now. This preacher has done grave damage to our cause.[1029]

Adil Sadek, a prominent political analyst in Gaza, said:

> We must polish our messages very carefully, especially those that are broadcast on the air.[1030]

Almost 170 years ago, Marquis Astolphe de Custine, a French aristocrat, visited Russia. In his book *Nicholas' Russia: La Russie en 1839*, he wondered why the

Russian people, some ninety percent of them enslaved serfs, felt so resentful and aggressive towards the Western countries. He explained why:

> The kneeling slave dreams of world domination.[1031]

Palestinians as well as other Arab people have been ruled by kings and dictators for centuries and most of them still are enslaved. To compensate the misery of their lives the Islamist fanatics dream of defeating the Western democracies. Marquis de Custine was also shocked by the contradictions between pretense and reality in Russia, stating:

> I do not blame the Russians for being what they are. I blame them for pretending to be what we are.[1032]

The Palestinian Authority should be blamed not for what the Palestinians are but for pretending that the Palestinians behave and think the way people in the democratic countries do.

The great Russian poet Mikhail Lermontov, who was exiled for his criticism of the Tsarist regime at the time of Marquis de Custine's visit to Russia, wrote:

> Goodbye unwashed Russia, the land of slaves and masters; and goodbye to you, blue uniforms; and to you, obedient people who obey them.

In Lermontov's and Pushkin's time, the "blue uniforms" were the officers of the Russian secret police. Grigory Yavlinsky, the leader of the Yabloko Party in the *Duma*, described the alliance of Putin's supporters and the large Communist faction in the Duma as an "aggressive and obedient majority."

Prime Minister Tony Blair, in his interview with the BBC, spoke of "very deep roots" of the mentality that produced the terrorist attack on the London transit system. Blair's reference to "underlying issues and deep roots" produced joy among leaders of the Palestinian Authority. The Associated Press also reported that Palestinian leaders said Blair had "touched the reality and spoke strategically of the need to deal with the problems of this region" and that a number of Arab leaders expressed the view that such terrorism was the "inevitable consequence of the Arab-Palestinian conflict." Actually Blair did not mention Israel or the Palestinians. In response to the terrorist suicide bombing, he said:

Evil ideology must be faced directly, head-on, without compromise or delusion. Their cause is not founded on injustice. It is founded on a belief, one whose fanaticism is such that it can't be moderated. It can't be remedied. It has to be stood up to.[1033]

The Associated Press retracted its original story, stating:

The BBC erroneously reported that Blair spoke of easing the conflict between Israel and Palestinians in his interview with the British Broadcasting Corp.[1034]

Andrea Levin, executive director of the Committee for Accuracy in Middle East Reporting, commented:

There is something disturbing about the rush to link Israel to each terror attack around the world. The leap to implicate Israel is automatic and so is seeing Israel as the core of the conflict.[1035]

When President Bush was asked whether the photo of Saddam Hussein wearing underwear would inflame the insurgents or trigger anti-Americanism in the Middle East, he replied:

You know, I don't think a photo inspires murderers. I think they're inspired by an ideology that is so barbaric and backwards that it's hard for many in the Western world to comprehend how they think.[1036]

President Bush found in the British prime minister a kindred soul and a strong ally in their joint response to the global terrorist threat.

In his op-ed article, "The Speech the President Should Give," John Kerry gave President Bush this advice:

It's time to change course on Iraq and take up the offer that the Saudis have made but have yet to fulfill and acknowledge their concern about our fitful mediation between Israel and the Palestinians in return their help in rebuilding Iraq, protecting its borders, and bringing its Sunnis into the political process.[1037]

Kerry's advice boils down to the "Primakov formula" of linking the Iraqi war to the Israeli-Palestinian conflict. "The Primakov Formula" has been firmly implanted in the minds of Senators Kerry and Kennedy, who go to the pro-Palestinian dinner parties sponsored by Arab-American organizations and Saudi money.

There have been many anti-Israeli resolutions at the United Nations, but the most notorious of them all was the infamous "Zionism-is-Racism" resolution in 1975. John Bolton was an Assistant Secretary of State at the time that he and Daniel Patrick Moynihan led the fight to reverse this resolution. In May 1991 they succeeded despite the resistance of many UN delegations and the cadre of "Arabists" in the Near East section of the US State Department. In 2005 the Democratic minority in the Senate blocked the Bolton nomination to represent the United States in the UN. No one mentioned Bolton's role in reversing the "Zionism-is-Racism" resolution.[1038] Senators Schumer and Lieberman, who are Jewish, as well the junior Senator Hillary Clinton, who has been courting Jewish voters in New York, opposed Bolton's nomination.[1039] President Bush appointed Bolton US representative at the United Nations, using his constitutional right for a recess appointment to avoid a filibuster in the Senate.

On March 11, 2005, at the Madrid international conference on terrorism, Kofi Annan selected a panel, which included Brent Scowcroft and Evgeny Primakov, to work out a definition of terrorism. President Bush stripped General Scowcroft of chairmanship of the Foreign Intelligence Advisory Board after Scowcroft sided with Senator Kerry's presidential campaign in criticizing Bush's Iraq policy and after telling the *Financial Times* that Prime Minister Sharon had "mesmerized Mr. Bush and had him wrapped around his finger." Mr. Scowcroft appeared with President Carter's national security adviser Zbigniew Brzezinski and told reporters that "the election in Iraq would lead to a civil war."[1040] Nasser el-Kidwa, Yasir Arafat's nephew, who was the Palestinian Authority UN ambassador and is now the foreign minister of the Palestinian Authority, has for years led the Arab fight against a definition of terrorism.[1041]

Scowcroft's remark that Sharon "mesmerized Mr. Bush and wrapped him around his finger" has a point. He was referring to the letter Bush wrote to Sharon on April 14, 2004, stating that "any future status resolution must reflect the new realities on the ground, especially the existing major population centers in the West Bank" and that "it is unrealistic to expect that the outcome of negotiations will be a full and complete return to the 1967 lines."[1042] Sharon assumed that this statement meant American agreement not to side with the Palestinians in demanding Israeli withdrawal from major settlements on the West Bank. Only the future will tell whether Sharon's assumption was correct. But it is true that Sharon and Bush drew closer because of their shared view on the war against global terrorism and their mutual trust and loyalty. It all began when Bush asked Sharon not to harm Yasir Arafat when Israeli troops surrounded Arafat in his Ramallah headquarters. Sharon kept his promise. Tony Blair needed Bush to help him withstand the strong opposition of the British public to his alliance with Bush in the war to topple Saddam Hussein. The strong pro-Palestinian bias in England had to be mollified by some kind of prospect of solving the Israeli-Palestinian conflict on terms favorable to the Palestinians. Bush and Blair decided on the "road map to peace" initiative by the "Quartet" (the United States, Britain, Russia, and the UN) formed to promote the establishment of an "independent, democratic state of Palestine, living in peace with the independent, democratic state of Israel." This noble solution to the long and bloody conflict was in essence Bush's agreement to offer a Jewish bone to the British pro-Palestinian public.

Except for the United States, the people of Israel do not have a true friend in the world. Former Spanish prime minister Jose Maria Aznar, whose Popular Party lost the elections in the spring of 2004 following the deadly Madrid train station bombing, said:

> In Europe, Israel is not very popular... Most Europeans support the Palestinian cause. Europeans sincerely wish for a peace agreement and support the peace process, but the reality is that the peace process is closed... The only possible way to make something work is to work closely with the US...[1043]

More than eight million Muslims live in France, most of whom are immigrants from Arab countries. There are millions of Muslims in England, among them many Arabs and Pakistanis. Many of them are citizens who vote in the elections and are able to influence the political parties. The most outspoken British official, who is a strong supporter of pro-Palestinian opinion in Britain, is the Mayor of London, Ken Livingstone, also known as "Red Ken," who in his angry anti-Israeli outbursts stated:

> The Israeli government threatens all of us by inspiring groups such as al-Qaeda to attack the West... Only a just and lasting peace in the Middle

East, including peace between Israel and Palestinians, will bring long-term security.[1044]

Livingstone also called a Jewish reporter "a concentration camp guard." He accused Sharon of being "a war criminal who should be in prison for engaging in a campaign of "ethnic cleansing" against the Palestinians similar to that of the Serbs in Bosnia."[1045] Britain's Chief Rabbi Jonathan Sacks, who has been promoting the pro-Palestinian causes in his sermons and writings, was knighted on June 11, 2005, as part of the celebration of Queen Elizabeth's 79th birthday. His knighthood was justified by his role in "improving interfaith relations."[1046]

The reality of pro-Palestinian sentiment in Britain that Blair faced was a major factor in Sharon's agreement to go along with the proclaimed "road map." He also agreed to withdraw Jewish settlers from Gaza Strip and from four settlements in Samaria in the northern West Bank as a token of his contribution to solving the problem Bush and Blair faced with the British public's opposition to their alliance in the Iraq war.

Sharon also faced a very strong and emotionally charged opposition to his "disengagement plan." In a speech at the Caesarea Economic Conference he declared, "We must leave Gaza—to build Israel." He warned against "the nightmare of nonimplementation of the disengagement plan on our political position and how we are treated in the global markets." He attacked "the extremist gangs who are trying to terrorize Israeli society and tear it to pieces."[1047] He strongly believed that carrying out this plan would help him "build Israel." This belief was based on his assumption that he got the best possible deal when President Bush wrote his April 14, 2004, letter to him, stating:

Any future status resolution must reflect the new realities on the ground, especially the existing major population centers and it is unrealistic to expect that the outcome of negotiations will be a full and complete return to the 1967 lines.[1048]

On August 12, 2005, on the eve of the Gaza withdrawal, Sharon, in an interview with the daily newspaper *Yediot Aharonot*, recalled that while, as a senior member of Menachem Begin's government, he was haggling with the Egyptians in Cairo over the terms of 1979 peace treaty, he called his eighty-year-old mother, who was still managing their farm. He said that as a child he remembered her sleeping with an ax under her bed. After telling him what was happening on the farm, she would end with a maternal admonition, "Never trust the Arabs." Sharon gave a succinct justification for the Gaza withdrawal:

> I've reached a deal with the Americans. I prefer a deal with the Americans to a deal with the Arabs.[1049]

Menachem Begin believed that by signing the 1979 peace treaty with Egypt, the most powerful Arab country, Israel was breaking out of isolation in the midst of the hostile Arab world. It turned out that this peace treaty amounted to a very cold peace. Begin lived to regret the withdrawal from Sinai, but at least he signed some kind of a peace agreement with an Arab country. Sharon's unilateral withdrawal from Gaza without any type of treaty with the Palestinian Authority doesn't even offer an illusory promise of peace. The second problem is that Sharon did not "reach a deal with Americans"—he made a deal with George W. Bush, who will not be in the White House forever. Bush could be replaced, as it had happened before, by a president unfriendly to Israel, at least as far as Israel's security is concerned, a weak president like Jimmy Carter or Bill Clinton, despite their glib assurances to the contrary. In this case Sharon would have certainly regretted his decision to withdraw from Gaza the same way Begin regretted his decision to withdraw from Sinai.

So far all indications point to the Palestinian assumption that the Israeli withdrawal from the Gaza Strip and four northern West Bank settlements was a victory for the al-Aksa intifada, which erupted in September 2000. If this assumption becomes the guiding spirit of Palestinian society it will make the withdrawal not a step toward peace, but an inducement for more violence and a major provocation for bloodshed. The *Jerusalem Post* reports:

> There appears to be a growing number of Palestinians who are truly convinced that the pullout is nothing but a retreat by Israel achieved through the blood of thousands of shahids, or martyrs. Still, many Palestinians consider it a conspiracy designed to tighten Israel's grip on the West Bank and Jerusalem. Hamas and Islamic Jihad leaders were the first to refer to the disengagement as a "fruit of the resistance attacks" against Israel and to use the word "indihar" (banishment and defeat). In recent days even senior Palestinian officials have begun labeling the pullout an Israeli defeat [1050]

The President of the Palestinian Authority, Mahmoud Abbas, has been engaged in fierce competition with Hamas and Islamic Jihad over who will be credited with the Gaza pullout. In a speech to a Palestinian crowd on August 19, 2005, Abbas praised the "martyrs and their patience" for Israeli withdrawal. He also promised a great improvement in the lives of the Gaza population. Mahmoud Zahar, overall Hamas leader in the Gaza strip, in an interview published September 17, 2005, in the London-based pan-Arab daily *Asharq Al-Awsat*, said:

> Now, after the victory in the Gaza Strip, we will transfer the struggle first to the West Bank and later to Jerusalem. We will continue the struggle until we liberate all our lands. This is an important day for the Palestinians and proof that the armed struggle has born fruit. Neither the liberation of the Gaza strip, nor the liberation of the West Bank, or even Jerusalem will suffice us. Hamas will pursue the armed struggle until the liberation of all our lands. We don't recognize the state of Israel or its right to hold onto one inch of Palestine. Palestine is an Islamic land belonging to all the Muslims. The disengagement would boost morale in the Arab and Muslim world and positively influence the anti-US campaign in Afghanistan and Iraq. We are part of a large global movement called the international Islamic Movement.[1051]

Muhammed Abdel-Al, who is better known by his nickname Abu Abeer, one of the leaders of the Popular resistance Committees, an alliance of various Palestinian militias operating in the Gaza strip, declared:

> We will make every effort to transfer all forms of resistance to the West Bank. We have already begun transferring the technology of rockets and military experts to the West bank. We will transfer two-thirds of our budget to the West Bank. Our rockets have a range of 18 kilometers. This means that if we fire them from Kalkiliya, they will hit the occupied city of Tal al-Rabi [Tel-Aviv].[1052]

Muhammad Deif, the commander of Hamas's armed wing, the Izzedine al-Qassam Brigade, issued a video with a harsh warning to Mahmoud Abbas and the Palestinian Authority not to try to disarm Hamas:

> We warn all those who try to touch the weapons of those who liberated Gaza. These arms must be used to free our occupied motherland. The war

must continue to free the West Bank, Jerusalem, and, under the Hamas charter, all of the British mandate Palestine, including Israel. We tell the Zionists who have tarnished our soil, we tell you that all of Palestine will become hell.[1053]

These and similar declarations confirm Netanyahu's prediction that the Gaza withdrawal would turn Gaza into the major terrorist base. Netanyahu challenged Sharon for the leadership of the Likud party, aiming to replace him as prime minister. The Gaza withdrawal will no doubt be one of the most important issues and whether it signals the beginning or the end of any further Israeli concessions. The *New York Times* editorial "Only the Beginning" provides a glimpse at what kind of a pro-Palestinian president the editors of the *Times* hope to see in the White House after the end of Bush's term. This editorial insists that the withdrawal from Gaza is "Only the First Step" and adds:

> Mr. Sharon, the architect of Israel's settlement policy, might have imagined a different legacy, but he will go down in history as the man who rammed the plan to dismantle the Gaza settlements through Parliament, taking on, and defeating, extreme right-wing members of his own Likud party. Mr. Sharon should be cheered for taking this step. But he must also be forewarned: if there is to be any chance for peace, there are many more steps that must be taken.[1054]

The editors of the *Times* might be gloating prematurely in announcing Mr. Sharon's legacy. The Jewish people in Israel and in the Diaspora will remember his heroic service in the battle for Israel's survival. They will remember him leading his troops across the Suez Canal, bringing about the surrender of the Egyptian army, the heroic deed which ended the Yom Kippur War. They called him "Arik, Melekh Israel" (Arik, King of Israel). As for his decision to withdraw from Gaza, even if it turns out to be a major provocation of Arab violence, the Jewish people will not hold it against him and will see it as his only mistake. They will figure that he acted on his best judgment at the time and will probably forgive him, saying, "It's only one short step from the glorious to the ridiculous," or might recall the old Russian proverb, "Horses have four legs, but even horses stumble some time." The lionizing of Sharon for his decision on the Gaza withdrawal will eventually turn to vilification for refusing to make other concessions to the Arabs. On February 20, 2005, the

Israeli cabinet approved a fence that included in Israel the settlements of Ma'aleh Adumim and Kedar, Nofel Prat, Kfar Adumim.[1055] In July 2005 Sharon visited Ariel, one of the largest Israeli settlements in the West Bank, telling the settlers there that their settlement and other settlements in the West Bank would always be a part of Israel.

Thomas Friedman prophesized dreadful consequences of Sharon's policy for Jews, Israel, and America:

> Sharon's vision of getting out of Gaza in order to take over the West Bank will probably win by default. If that happens, "Jews, Israel, and America" will be bound more tightly than ever as enemies of Arabs and Muslims.[1056]

For all the gloom and doom emanating from such a prediction, Israel continues to grow in population and prosperity. Stuart Hershkiwitz, head of the international department at the Bank of Jerusalem, states:

> Purchases by foreign residents have taken off beyond anybody's wildest dreams. This is a real revolution. I dealt with million-dollar purchases every couple of months. Now, it is almost on a weekly basis… up at least 30 to 40% from a couple of years ago. They wanted to have a place here. Period. You can't imagine how many people have told me, "I have a dream to own a place in Israel"[1057]

In the debates that followed Sharon's decision to withdraw from the Gaza Strip, the proponents of the withdrawal insisted that the settlers' homes not be destroyed. Defense Minister Shaul Mafaz argued that razing the 1,600 or so dwellings and bringing the rubbish back to Israel would cost $46 million and take eight months, declaring:

> I'm not prepared, as defense minister of the state of Israel, to endanger Israeli soldiers in order to destroy the houses of the settlers…[1058]

On April 6, 2005, Secretary of State Condoleezza Rice praised Sharon's plan to pull all 9,000 settlers out of the Gaza Strip as a "huge historical opportunity," adding:

> We want it to succeed and we want Israel not to engage in wanton destruction of the homes to be abandoned by settlers.[1059]

Isaac Herzog, Housing and Construction Minister in Sharon's government, wrote about his school teacher who had protested the removal of settlers from Gaza. Herzog's father, a former President of Israel, was a British soldier during World War II and took part in the liberation of a German concentration camp in which this teacher was an inmate. Herzog told his former teacher that the disengagement from Gaza was necessary and the destruction of settlers' houses was the right thing to do in order to save the lives of Israeli soldiers. He expressed his concern about the possibility of Hamas terrorists dancing on the roofs of settlers' homes, raising Hamas flags in front of CNN and Al Jazzira TV cameras, and proclaiming victory over Israel. This possibility frightened Sharon and the Bush administration. Their fear was that such a TV show might produce a public upheaval in Israel akin to the prehistoric volcanic eruption that sent the ancient Philistines fleeing from the exploding Greek Islands to the Eastern Mediterranean shores where the present day Gaza and Israeli coast is today. Secretary of State Condoleezza Rice was urgently dispatched to negotiate with Israeli and Palestinian leaders a way to avoid such a catastrophe that might threaten the "road map." She announced an agreement with Israeli leaders to destroy the settlers' houses and for the Palestinians to clear up the rubble and to be paid $40 million raised by the international community.

Uri Dan, the veteran political commentator, in an article "Arik's mission impossible," wrote:

> The destruction of flourishing Jewish settlements in the Gaza Strip and northern Samaria will be a political and social earthquake, compared to which what happened in Yamit [the Israeli town in Sinai from which Begin agreed to withdraw as the result of Carter's pressure at Camp David] was just a minor tremor. At the same time it is necessary to minimize the risk of a civil war, something that only Sharon, with his authority and experience, is capable of doing. The threats to his life that accompany him during his public trips and even when he visits his wife's grave have reached unprecedented levels of gravity.[1060]

The Bush administration was worried about a poll in Israel, conducted by Maagar Mihot, which found that only 48% of the public supported Sharon's Gaza Strip withdrawal plan, 38% were opposed, and 19% were undecided. Support for disengagement has fallen significantly from its peak of 65% in February 2005. In response to the poll Sharon, pretending not to be concerned, said:

I didn't get excited when the polls were in my favor, and I don't get depressed when the polls are different.[1061]

Sharon was a man of strong convictions and abounding faith in the destiny of Israel. He liked to repeat what the late Pope John Paul II told him:

I would like you to remember that the land of Israel is holy to Muslims, Christians, and Jews—but it was only to the Jews that it was promised. That is the difference between terra sancta and terra promissa.[1062]

Sharon believed that his agreement with President Bush, which to Sharon meant that most Israeli settlements in the West Bank, will remain a part of Israel. He believed that Bush supported this vision. He remembered the nightmare Israel lived through during Jimmy Carter's presidency when Carter demanded an Israeli retreat to the "1967 borders with minor adjustments." Carter monitored the 1996 election of Yasir Arafat, saying that the election was "free and fair." He also led a team of observers who monitored the January 9, 2005, election in the Palestinian Authorities and also declared it to be "free and fair." While meeting with Israeli president Moshe Katsav, he said:

Prime Minister Ariel Sharon's commitment to withdraw from Gaza and some settlements in the West Bank is a major step in the right direction.[1063]

The "right direction" for Carter always has been Israeli retreat to the "1967 borders with minor adjustments."

On June 9, 2005, shortly after the release of a report in *Newsweek* about American soldiers flushing a Koran down the toilet at the Guantanamo Bay prison, Abdulmalik Dehamshe, a member of the Knesset from the United Arab Party, accused the Megiddo prison administration in Israel of the desecration of Korans. He demanded to see the alleged defiled holy books and broke prison regulations by trying to sneak his assistant into the prison with a photo camera. The same day the Islamic Jihad released pictures of torn Koran pages, stating that it had "received them from inmates who took the pictures with cellular phone cameras." The same day Taleb A-Sanaa, another Arab member of the Knesset, led dozens of protesters outside Megiddo prison. He met with Prisons Service Chief Yaakov Ganot and "demanded the establishment of an inquiry commission to investigate the accusations." Sheikh Kamel Hatib, deputy head of Islamic Movement's northern branch in Israel, said:

The Muslim world would react harshly to the desecration of its holy book. Someone will need to pay for this. They have harmed all Muslim women, children, and men by desecrating the word of god.[1064]

Several undisputable facts emanate from these bizarre statements: Israeli Arabs elect representatives from several Arab parties to the Knesset. The members of these parties and Muslim clergy are involved in spreading vicious anti-Israeli propaganda and are getting away with it with impunity. Palestinian terrorists have cell phones with photo cameras in Israeli prisons and are able to smuggle photos from their prison cells. Israeli prisons, like the Guantanamo Bay prison, do not resemble the Gulag.

"Rafik Maraabi is a precise, mild-mannered father of five and mid-level official in the Palestinian Authority, not a wild-eyed ideologue," states the June 25, 2005, article in the *Economist*. It quoted Rafik Maraabi, who declared:

Israel wants to take over Jordan, Egypt, Syria Lebanon, and Saudi Arabia.[1065]

If Rafik Maraabi believes this nonsense, he could believe the nonsense about the Jewish conspiracy to take over the world which has been propagated by the *Protocols of the Elders of Zion*, the infamous forgery that is part of the textbooks in Palestinian schools. He could also believe Saha Arafat's statement that Israelis poison Palestinian children. He could also believe the sermons of the Muslim preacher Ibrahim Mdaires who declared:

We have ruled the world before and, by Allah, the day will come when we will rule the entire world again. The day will come when we will rule America. The day will come when we will rule Britain and the entire world—except for the Jews.[1066]

If Rafik Maraabi, "a precise, mild-mannered father of five and mid-level official in the Palestinian Authority, not a wild-eyed ideologue," could believe this nonsense, it is hard to imagine what kind of thoughts ordinary Palestinians entertain.

At this writing it is impossible to say whether the "road map" will lead to peace or end up in a ditch. It was impossible to say whether the withdrawal of settlers from Gaza, after several delays, scheduled to start on August 16, 2005, would actually take place. Asher Mivtzari, a settler in Kfar Darom, said:

Everything here is miracles. I am certain that Mr. Sharon's Gaza plan would be derailed somehow. Visit me here a year from now. I don't believe Israeli defense minister Shaul Mofaz's statement that giving up Gaza would mean that Israel would be able to keep its largest settlements in the West Bank and a united Jerusalem. Giving up Gaza would just whet the appetites of Palestinians for Jerusalem and the West Bank. This is just an example of what all Israel will face if we leave Gaza.[1067]

After a Palestinian mortar hit her house on May 20, 2005, Mrs. Tamar Shwartz, another settler in Kfar Darom, holding her frightened four-year-old daughter, said:

This war didn't start today, it started many years ago. To fight it you need not just arms, but faith, and we are here because of our faith.[1068]

As most settlers in Gaza, Mrs. Schwartz vowed not to leave willingly. She believed that a way would be found to stop Sharon's plan to withdraw Israeli civilians.

Thomas Friedman, in his column "Tyranny of the Minorities," equated Moktada al-Sadr's terror gangs with the Jewish settlers in the West Bank and Gaza.[1069] Michael Rosenbluh wrote in a Letter to the Editor of the *New York Times*:

I am one of the settlers… This does not make me a messianic extremist who disdains man-made laws. I believe, as Jewish people did for thousands of years and the Zionist movement more recently, that the Jewish homeland includes Gush Katif, Hebron and all of land from the Mediterranean to the Jordan River. Non-Jews who live in this small strip of land are welcome to live with us as long as they are peaceful and law-abiding.[1070]

Shalom Freedman, a Jerusalemite, in another Letter to the Editor, stated:

Thomas Friedman compares Shiite militia at war with the United States to people whose sympathy and identification with American democracy is extremely strong.[1071]

Uzi Landau, a member of Sharon's Likud party, who opposed Sharon's plan to withdraw from Gaza, said:

> The closer disengagement gets, the more people see the price. Now the plan is under 50%, and when you take out the Arabs, it's even less. In the couple of months, after support for the plan continues to fall, it will be clear to the Members of the Knesset that they are doing something with no public legitimacy of support.[1072]

Supporters of Finance Minister Benjamin Netanyahu said that public opinion was changing because of Kassam rockets fired from Gaza Strip on Sderot and Gush Katif and because recent criticism of disengagement plan from former Army Chief of General Staff Moshe Ya'alon and former Shin Bet chief Avi Dichter.[1073] Moshe Ya'alon stated:

> If Israel does not agree to more pull outs after the upcoming disengagement, then an increase of terror attacks on Israeli targets can be expected. The establishment of a Palestinian state will lead to war at some time. The idea that such a state will bring stability is divorced from reality. I do not rule out the possibility that the army will return to the Gaza Strip at some time.[1074]

Moshe Ya'alon's prediction found confirmation in Mohammed Dahlan, the Palestinian cabinet minister, who warned that if Israel does not agree to further withdrawals, "the third intifada is on the way."[1075]

Seymour D. Reich, president of the Israel Policy Forum, in his Letter to the Editor, quotes Ehud Olmert, Israel's deputy prime minister, who in his speech in New York in June 2005 stated:

> We are tired of fighting, we are tired of being courageous, we are tired if winning, and we are tired of defeating our enemies.[1076]

Ehud Olmert, a former mayor of Jerusalem and a leading member of the Likud party, a hawk-turned-dove, was appointed deputy prime minister in the Sharon government. Because public support for the withdrawal from Gaza was declining with every passing day, Olmert joined Shimon Peres, the perennial dove, in proposing to move the day of withdrawal from August 16 to end of July, but the Knesset members voted against this proposal. Peres, the main architect of the Oslo Accords, has been a leading proponent of appeasement.

But Ehud Olmert's conversion from hawk to dove was a surprise, often explained by the fact that his wife is one of Israel's outspoken leftists. Mr. Reich concluded:

> It is time for Secretary of State Condoleezza Rice to revive shuttle diplomacy to help the first step: a successful Israeli withdrawal from Gaza.[1077]

At the end of July 2005 Ms. Rice visited Sharon in his Negev ranch. They discussed the problem of Israeli withdrawal from Gaza. Ms. Rice also suggested an international conference, sponsored by the United States and Russia, to promote, after Israeli withdrawal from Gaza, close cooperation between Israel and the Arab countries. An American official in the region said:

> Ms. Rice was planning by August 16, 2005, to go to Israel to monitor the Gaza pullout, has since decided against the idea. She'll get credit if it works, and she doesn't want to be here if it doesn't.[1078]

Who could blame Ms. Rice for hedging her bets? The situation in Israel has been unpredictable since the beginning of disengagement.

Haim Yavin, Israel's "Mr. TV," who has been regarded as an objective political commentator, released a documentary in which he criticized the settlers and deplored "occupation of Palestinian territory." He recalled the impact of CBS anchor Walter Cronkite on American foreign policy during the Vietnam war, about whom President Lyndon Johnson said, "If I lost Cronkite, I've lost Middle America." Five weeks later, Johnson decided not to seek reelection. The message of Yavin's documentary is contradictory and confusing. He concluded by stating:

> Don't compare me to Cronkite! This will not have such strong repercussions. The Israeli-Palestinian conflict is entirely different. I am not sure any power on earth can move people to give any land to your enemy, one that really wants to harm you.[1079]

Yuli Edelstein, once a Soviet prisoner of conscience, now a member of the Israeli Knesset, decided to move to live in his new home in a Gaza settlement of Gadoid to show his opposition to withdrawal. In a phone interview he said:

Some people are sure it's all over, and we've lost. But others have religious feelings that it will never happen or have a strong sense of personal optimism that they won't have to leave.[1080]

Benjamin Netanyahu resigned his post as finance minister in Sharon's government in protest against the Gaza pullout. He appealed to Israeli legislators to stop the pullout, saying the Gaza strip could become a base for terrorism that would put Israel in "mortal danger." In his first speech after his resignation he said:

> We are allowing the creation of an independent terrorist base in Gaza to which arms will flow from Syria, Afghanistan, and Iraq. Don't give them guns, don't give them missiles.[1081]

In her August 11, 2005, report, "Gaza settlers Make Room for Opponents of the Pullout," Dina Kraft states that thousands of opponents of the pullout infiltrated Gaza. She wrote:

> Some newcomers are living in the attics of settler homes. Others are living in tent camps by the sea and in shacks cobbled together from tarpaulin and poles.... Udi Amar, 28, has moved in from a small West Bank settlement. He said: "We came here to prevent the evacuation. The mood here is good because new families are arriving all the time."[1082]

Cal Thomas presents a pessimistic view in his article "The End of Israel?" of what retreat from Gaza bodes for the future of the Jewish state. He cites the H. G. Wells novel and subsequent film *The Invisible Man,* in which the main character takes a dangerous drug and slowly disappears, as a metaphor for "Israel slowly disappearing, and the twin drug of appeasement and self-delusion are responsible."[1083]

For all the contradictions and confusion surrounding the Arab-Israeli conflict there is a glimmer of light at the end of the long dark tunnel. The major reason for hope is the growing understanding of the extremism of modern Islamic Jihadists. David Brooks in his op-ed article writes:

> Humiliated and oppressed, they lash out against America, the symbol of threatening modernity. Off they go to seek martyrdom, dreaming of virgins who await them in the afterlife. Now we know that the story line

doesn't fit the facts. We have learned a lot about the jihadists, from Osama bin Laden down to the Europeans who attacked the London subways... We know, thanks to the database gathered by Mark Sageman formerly of the C.I.A., that about 75 percent of anti-Western terrorists come from middle-class or upper-middle-class homes. An amazing 65 percent have gone to college...[1084]

Brooks also cites the book *Globalized Islam* by the French scholar Oliver Roy, who states:

Today's jihadists have a lot in common with the left-wing extremists of the 1930s and 1960s. Ideologically, Islamic neofundamentalism occupies the same militant space that was once occupied by Marxism. [1085]

Anne Applebaum argues essentially the same point in her article, "The Discreet Charm of Terrorism."[1086]

There are other hopeful indications that the Islamofascism will eventually wind up in the dust bin of history as did the left-wing extremists of the 1930s and 1960s, as well as wild-eyed Marxists and Bolsheviks of the earlier times. The *New York Times* editorial stopped mentioning "resistance fighters" and "insurgents" and finally called them by their proper name—"terrorists." The editorial quoted a Joseph Conrad character who said that a terrorist "must be purely destructive" and added:

It must be that and only that because madness alone is truly terrifying, in as much as you cannot placate it either by threats, persuasion, or bribes.[1087]

The editorial continued:

There is nothing remotely articulate in bombings like the one that took place in London on Tuesday... In Conrad's day, it may have persuaded ordinary people of the implacable madness of terrorists. We still use that language—madness—because it still applies to the murder of innocent people... But it's always surprising how quickly something like normal life resumes after a terrorist incident. By next morning many London trains were running again... We do not teeter on the brink of madness or catastrophic irrationality. We may find ourselves flung into our fears for a time. But as London itself has shown us in the past, to be flung into our fears is the way of discovering who our adversaries really are—and that they are not ourselves.[1088]

Such an editorial may have been published hundreds of times after each of the many suicide bombings in Israel, but it never was.

Another glimmer of light came from, of all places, the article "A Poverty of Dignity and a Wealth of Rage" by, of all people, Thomas Friedman, who apparently was tired of bashing Israel and the settlers and asked:

> Why are young Sunni Muslim males, from London to Riyadh and Bali to Baghdad, so willing to blow up themselves and others in the name of their religion?[1089]

Friedman did not mention the Jerusalem or Nataniya suicide bombers, but carefully wrote with a glib qualifier:

> I can understand, but never accept, suicide bombings in Iraq or Israel as part of nationalist struggle. But when a British Muslim citizen, nurtured by that society, just indiscriminately blows up his neighbors and leaves behind a baby and pregnant wife, to me he has to be in the grip of a dangerous cult or preacher—dangerous to his faith, community, and to the world.

Freedman can understand, but never accept, the young suicide bomber who murdered shoppers in a Nataniya mall in August 2005. Possibly he can even understand his mother who said that she was proud of her son the "martyr" and wanted her other teenage son "to grow up to be a martyr." Friedman quotes a Muslim scholar who said:

> When the inner conflict becomes too great, some are turned by recruiters to seek the sick prestige of "martyrdom" by fighting the alleged unjust occupation of Muslim lands and the "decadence" of our own. This is about the poverty of dignity and the rage it can produce.

Another flicker of hope came from the Palestinian Authority, which promised to remove any reference to the *Protocols of the Elders of Zion* from textbooks in Palestinian schools. Publication of these textbooks has been financed by the governments of Italy, Finland, Netherlands, and Belgium. These governments decided to stop such funding.[1090]

A look back into history offers hope that a future Arab leader will strive for a peace with Israel as Anwar Sadat did in 1979, although at that time he was influenced by the Soviets nearly having provoked a "terrible, terrible war" that he managed to avoid by going to Jerusalem and concluding peace with Israel at Camp David. For Sadat, the "Palestinian issue" was not at the "core" or the "heart" of the problem in the Middle East, but an emotional smokescreen behind which the Soviets pursued their schemes. It was not a coincidence, said Sadat, that Syria, Libya, Algeria, Iraq, South Yemen, and the PLO had formed the "Rejectionist Front," and that they all "received their arms from Moscow." He broke diplomatic relations with those countries, and expelled the PLO from Egypt. He described the "rejectionist" leaders as being "dwarves," "stooges," "impostors," and "nuts."

The withdrawal from Gaza is unlikely to signal the end of Israel's conflict with Palestinians. As Greg Myre reported from there:

> The Palestinian Authority is planning rallies as if it were the homestretch of an election campaign. Small sewing factories are cranking out thousands of Palestinian flags and street banners, T-shirts, and backpacks that proclaim, "Today Gaza, tomorrow the West Bank and Jerusalem." That is the message intended to give Palestinians hope that Gaza first will not be Gaza last...[1091]

Such sloganeering points to a strong possibility that Israel's withdrawal from Gaza might very well turn out to be a major provocation for another intifada and also for a civil war between the Palestinian Authority and terrorist organizations like Hamas and Islamic Jihad. It was revealed that the UN Agency in Gaza was financing the production of such propaganda material. Iran is not the only state to pose a threat to Israel. The possibility of a resurgence of the Muslim Brotherhood in Egypt is quite real. Israel's Defense Minister Shaul Mofaz said that members of the Palestinian military intelligence agency helped terrorists to smuggle several *Strela*—Russian-made shoulder-fired missiles, from Egypt to Gaza. "This crosses a red line for us," said Mofaz.[1092]

On December 18, 2005, John Bolton, America's ambassador to the United Nations, gave a keynote speech at the Zionist Organization of America in which he said that Mahmoud Ahmadinejad's calling for Israel to be wiped off the map, "drew almost no attention at the UN" and that the Iranian nuclear program threatens not only Israel, but all the nations of the region and may eventually threaten the US itself." He pointed out that on November 29, 2005, the anniversary of the UN vote approving the 1947 creation of Israel, the UN Headquarters sponsored an official "Day of Solidarity with the Palestinian People." UN Secretary General Kofi Annan, as well as the presidents of the General Assembly and the Security Council, presided at this event at which, behind them, was displayed a map of the Middle East with Israel displaced by a country called "Palestine." Israel was literally "wiped off" this official UN map. No one, except for John Bolton, protested:

> This is not simply a mistake that the three men made not speaking about the map.... They did not see anything unusual. And in fact there isn't anything unusual... We need to take this instance and to slam the people involved for not criticizing the map, for not walking out. We need to say this is a pivotal point.[1093]

Thirty years ago the UN General Assembly passed Resolution 3379, which denigrated Zionism as "racism." Chaim Herzog, Israel's ambassador to the UN at the time, warned: "We, the Jewish people, will not forget this resolution." In 1991 this UN resolution was repealed. On January 10, 2005, Bolton, who was instrumental in repealing this resolution, stated:

> It's incredible that this resolution was passed to begin with. It's incredible that it took 16 years to repeal it.[1094]

Israel needs John Bolton more than ever. His appointment as head of the US delegation to the UN is encouraging, especially in view of the nuclear threat Iran poses to Israel.

Iran's recently elected president, Mahmoud Ahmadinejad, speaking at anti-Israeli rallies, called for the destruction of Israel, stating, "As the imam said, Israel must be wiped off the map." "Death to Israel!!" has been a rallying slogan in Iran ever since the imam Ayatollah Ruhollah Khomeini led the 1979 Islamic coup in Iran. Ahmadinejad was identified by former hostages as one of the most fanatical "students" who brutalized them in the American embassy in Teheran during the Khomeini coup. On a number of occasions he also declared that the Holocaust was a myth invented by "infidels." He stated:

> This is our proposal: If they committed this crime, then give a part of your land in Europe, the United States, Canada or Alaska to the Jews so they can establish their country. [1095]

At public rallies and on the official Islamic Republic News Agency, he proclaimed that the Western countries intended to complete the genocide by establishing of a "Jewish death camps" in the Muslim countries as the best means of ridding themselves of Jews. In October 2005 he again called for Israel to be "wiped off the map."[1096] As far back as December 2001, Ali Akbar Hashemi Rafsanjani, the Iranian president, explained his rationale for nuclear war with Israel:

If a day comes when the world of Islam is duly equipped with the arms Israel has in its possession... application of an atomic bomb would not leave anything in Israel but the same thing would just produce minor damage in the Muslim world.[1097]

Mahmoud Ahmadinejad predicted:

After just a short period ... the process of the elimination of the Zionist regime will be smooth and simple.[1098]

The Israeli Foreign Ministry issued a statement:

The combination of fanatical ideology, a warped sense of reality and nuclear weapons is a combination that no one in the international community can accept.[1099]

Mohammed ElBaradei, chairman of the International Atomic Energy Agency, has failed to curtail Iran's fanatical rulers who have been feverishly working at acquiring atomic weapons and proclaiming their intention to destroy Israel. Instead of exposing the danger to Israel of Iran acquiring atomic weapons, ElBaradei declared:

Disarming Israel of its nuclear weapons is the key to achieving peace in the Middle East. It is a very emotional issue in the Middle East.[1100]

ElBaradei failed to mention that the existence of Israel has been an emotional issue in the Arab countries. He suggests that "stripping" Israel of its very existence might be the key to achieving peace. On December 10, 2005, he was awarded the 2005 Nobel Prize, thus joining Yasir Arafat on the top of the list of Nobel Prize gaffes. At the Nobel Prize ceremony, he stated that "no smoking gun had emerged to prove Iran's intent was horrible." The Norwegian newspaper, *Aftenposten,* referring to the increasingly open discussion about the possibility of Israel attacking Iranian nuclear installations, reported ElBaradei's warning to Israel:

> You cannot use force to prevent a country from obtaining nuclear weapons. By bombing them half to death, you only delay the plans. But they will come back and they will demand revenge.[1101]

Where ElBaradei does not see a smoking gun, Israelis see a mushroom cloud.

On December 11, 2005, the British Sunday *Times* reported that Ariel Sharon ordered the Israeli air force to prepare to attack Iran's nuclear facilities at the end of March 2006. On December 13, 2005, Lt.-Gen. Dan Halutz, Chief of Staff of the Israeli Defense Forces, reported that "Iran could begin enriching uranium by March 2006 and approach the point of no return and would have the technological capacity to manufacture a nuclear weapon."[1102] On December 27, 2005, Meir Dagan, the head of the Mossad, told the Defense and Foreign Affairs Committee that in a few months Iran would be able to develop a nuclear bomb. On December 14, 2005, the German newspaper *Der Spiegel* reported that the Mossad had "marked six Iranian nuclear facilities that the Israeli air force would hit in a pre-emptive strike." Also on December 14, 2005, the *Los Angeles Times* reported that Israel had modified American-made *Harpoon* cruise missiles in order to launch them from *Dolphin* submarines recently purchased from Germany "as a means to further dissuade Iran from becoming a nuclear power." On December 27, 2005, *Ma'ariv* reported that Prime Minister Sharon was coordinating intelligence on Iran with the United States."[1103] The German newspaper *Der Tagesspiegel* reported that CIA Chief Porter Goss visited Turkey on December 12, 2005, and requested access to military bases for American forces to launch an assault on Iran. The German news agency DDP reported that Saudi Arabia, Jordan, Oman, and Pakistan were also informed.[1104]

Wednesday night, January 4, 2006, Ariel Sharon had a stroke and massive brain hemorrhage. Israel and the world were confronted with the possibility of his demise. But Ra'anan Gissin, the prime minister's long-time spokesman, stated:

> Let's stop the festival of eulogies. I believe that he has the capability, stamina, and life force to pull through. He had pulled himself out of worse

situations, where anybody could not survive. He is a real warrior. Don't jump to conclusions about irreversible, terrible brain damage. How do you know?[1105]

Gissin was referring to the Battle of Latrun during the 1948 War of Independence in which Sharon was shot in the stomach and thigh and barely survived. Just a few years ago he became a national and international pariah in the wake of the 1982 Lebanon invasion and the massacre in the Palestinian refugee camps of Sabra and Shatilla, but he survived the investigation and eventually became prime minister, again to survive the political earthquake during the painful Gaza pullout, that only he could see through. President Bush, in a speech, offered warm wishes to Sharon:

> Our nation sends our deepest sympathies to Ariel Sharon... We pray for his recovery. He is a good man, a strong man who cares deeply about the security of the Israeli people and a man who had a vision for peace. May God bless him.[1106]

President Bush did not mention the "road map to peace" and the "two states, Israel and Palestine, living in peace side by side," which for some time has been his vision for the Middle East. He did not say what kind of "vision for peace" Sharon had. In fact, Sharon never told what kind of "painful concessions" he was prepared to make to the Palestinians except for vaguely stating that he would adhere to the "road map." Edward Walker, former Assistant Secretary of State for Middle East and now president of the Middle East Institute said:

> The US-backed road map peace plan was fundamentally dead some time ago and Mr. Sharon's illness left the Bush administration's policy hanging by a thread. The Bush administration is in the position of hanging on to a figment of imagination of the road map. They will probably sustain it.[1107]

To sustain the road map, let alone revive it, President Bush would need Sharon at the head of his new Kadima Party, but also Mahmoud Abbas at the head of the Palestinian Authority. One thing is clear: the virtually dysfunctional Palestinian Authority, in Gaza and in the West Bank, is in the grip of an orgy of looting, arson, and kidnapping of hostages. Shimon Peres, the architect of the Oslo Accords and a perennial dove, declared: "The road map is in question if Hamas takes over."[1108] Another perennial dove, Amnon Rubinstein, wrote in desperation:

> Experience shows that sanity is not a highly prized commodity in the Arab Street. The West Bank situation should be seen in the context of the danger of a mad, nuclear-armed Iran, with its missiles aimed at the tiny, vulnerable Israeli island. The one possibly effective response to this danger is Israel's entry into NATO—or alternatively a defense pact with the US—which may deter Teheran. What is left? The only practical possibility is that the Western powers undertake responsibility for the West Bank or, at least, that Israel makes such an offer. Or, if this idea is not acceptable, that the UN mandatory regime be entrusted to the two Arab states which made peace with Israel—Egypt and Jordan. If the Palestinians cannot rule themselves, then Israelis should not rule over them, let other Arabs rule the Palestinians under UN mandate.[1109]

In his 2005 State of the Union speech President George W. Bush said:

> The beginnings of reform and democracy in the Palestinian territories are now showing the power of freedom to break old patterns of violence and failure.

On the eve of Bush's 2006 State of the Union address Hamas won a landslide victory. Secretary of State Condoleezza Rice stated

> I have asked why nobody saw it coming. It does say something about us not having a good enough pulse.[1110]

Delusional good intentions take time to fade away. The spin began immediately: It was asserted that the corruption and mismanagement by the Palestinian Authority, its failure to collect garbage and improve the life of Palestinians led to the Hamas victory. One of the elected Hamas legislators from Gaza was Mariam Farhat, a mother of three suicide bombers whom she proudly proclaims "martyrs" and said she "felt sorry for not having 100 sons as martyrs."[1111] At least 75% of Palestinian Arabs voted for Hamas not because they believed Hamas would collect their garbage better, but because Hamas clearly stands for the destruction of Israel. They hate the Jews and the Jewish state and this very hate makes the fuzzy vision of "two states living peacefully side by side" a ridiculous wishful thinking.

The Bush administration exerted strong pressure on the acting Prime Minister Ehud Olmert to allow Jerusalem Arabs to vote in the January 25th Palestinian elections because Abbas demanded it and threatened to postpone the vote. Despite Sharon's earlier statement that Jerusalem Arabs should not be allowed to participate in the Palestinian elections, Olmert succumbed to American pressure. Jerusalem Arabs, waving green Hamas flags, drove *en masse* to voting places in Jerusalem and elected four Hamas representatives. Jerusalem Arabs have been enjoying social welfare, financial benefits as well as free medical services. Their garbage has always been collected by the Jerusalem municipality. They pray on their knees in the mosques built on the ground of ancient Jewish Temples. This reminds one of Marquis de Custine's memorable words: "The kneeling slave dreams of world domination." They dream of destroying Israel, the country which insures their freedoms to worship and to travel and provides a standard of living unimaginable in any Arab country. Not one of the Arab countries, except for the recently liberated Iraq, has free elections. They are ruled by potentates and dictators.

In electing Hamas, Jerusalem and Palestinian Arabs voted for the destruction of Israel. This plain truth should not be obscured by the "politically correct" spin. But the world is getting wobbly. A *New York Times* editorial explained away Hamas's electoral victory by suggesting that it was motivated by Palestinian anger at the corruption and mismanagement by the regime of Mahmoud Abbas, although the editorial also mentioned in passing that Hamas "revels in terrorism and is sworn to destroy Israel." It blamed "Ariel Sharon and other Israeli "hardliners" for their failure to give Mahmoud Abbas any concessions" and ridiculed "Sharon's doctrine of unilateral separation from the Palestinians." Not long ago the *New York Times* lionized Sharon for removing settlers from Gaza and Northern Samaria and for promising other "painful concessions." The editorial also expressed the hope that "Hamas will renounce its call for the destruction of a sovereign state, disarm its private army and try to negotiate the creation of a real Palestinian state."[1112]

Another *New York Times* editorial, "Hamas at the Helm," stated that "the acting Israeli Prime Minister, Ehud Olmert, may be trying to win an election by appearing tough, but pouring gas over an inflamed situation is not the way to go." The editorial suggested that the way to go was for the United States to "continue to press Israel to hand over the $50 million a month in tax receipts it collects from the Palestinian Authority…"[1113] Olmert succumbed to American pressure and delivered more than $50 million to the Palestinians.

The day after the Hamas victory the former US President Jimmy Carter, speaking at a Jerusalem Press Conference, proclaimed:

> The Palestinian elections were completely honest, completely fair, and completely safe and without violence… The Palestinian Government is destitute and in desperate financial straits. I hope that support for the new government will be forthcoming via non-government channels such as UN agencies.[1114]

George F. Will wrote:

> Jimmy Carter, an even worse ex-president than he was a president, responded to the Hamas victory by quickly suggesting a way to evade the U.S. law against providing funds to terrorists. He suggested that the executive branch of the U.S. government could launder money destined for Hamas by passing it through the UN.[1115]

It is worth recalling that Jimmy Carter during his one term presidency devoted an excessive amount of time to bashing Israel. Immediately after his election in 1977 Carter demanded a "homeland or entity for the Palestinian people," a euphemism for the "two states solution" which was not a politically correct idea at the time. He also insisted that "settlements on occupied territory were illegal." He demanded Israel's "retreat to the 1967 borders with minor adjustments" and he signed the "Soviet-American Joint Declaration of October 1, 1977," demanding Israel's compliance with his and Soviet demands to be accepted by Israel "no later than December 1977." This was an ultimatum which Israel rejected.[1116]

After the Hamas victory Russian President Vladimir Putin declared that "Russia never regarded Hamas as a terrorist organization and did not rule out financial aid for the Hamas-led government." On January 9, 2006, at a joint press conference with Spain's Prime Minister Jose Luis Zapatero, Putin stated:

> Hamas has arrived at the doors of power through legitimate elections. We must respect the Palestinian people… Contacts with Hamas must continue. Preserving our contacts with Hamas, we are willing, in the near future, to invite the authorities of Hamas to Moscow to carry out talks.[1117]

It must be recalled that Adolf Hitler also "arrived at the doors of power through legitimate elections," which suggests that elections are not always a panacea for calamities. Putin, too, had "arrived at the doors of power through legitimate elections." In an article to the *New York Times* op-ed page, Andrey Illarionov, a former economic adviser to Putin, wrote:

> Russia today is not the same country it was only six years ago, when Vladimir Putin became president.... Today Russia is richer—and not free.[1118]

Russia is richer today because the price of oil has risen to $70 a barrel. But despite this wealth, most people in Russia still venerate Stalin more than half a century since the dictator's death. They had no qualms electing a former KGB colonel to the highest office in their country.

US State Department spokesman Sean McCormack said that the US was on the record condemning the violent views of the Hamas. He said that the US ambassador to Russia, William J. Burns, has requested clarification of the massage Putin intends to give the Hamas officials.[1119] No clarification is needed. It is already clear that Putin's Russia has reverted to its old ways of rivalry with the United States and the Free World and will use the Arab-Israeli conflict to advance its goals, as it did during the Cold War. Putin will press Hamas leaders to adopt the language and tactics of Yasir Arafat and Mahmoud Abbas in hoodwinking the world into believing their peaceful protestations. But now the charade is over. The Palestinian Arabs, at least 75% of them, by voting for Hamas, revealed their hatred for the Jewish state. The fuzzy vision of "two states living peacefully side by side" can no longer cloud the eyes of Israeli "doves." The question is: will the rest of the world also refuse to be hoodwinked?

On February 10, 2006, Defense Minister Sergei Ivanov of Russia reiterated Putin's invitation to Hamas, saying: "Hamas won the democratic elections and other countries would follow Russia's lead." Indeed, this prediction proved to be true. A spokesman for the French Foreign Ministry said: "Although the invitation was offered by Russia without consulting the other members of the Quartet, the talks between Russia and Hamas may serve to advance the Quartet's goals of two nations [Israel and Palestine] living side by side in peace and security."[1120] Israel's radio announced: "Israeli-Russian relations stood at the precipice of the most serious crises in years."[1121] The fuzzy vision of "two states living peacefully side by side" refused to yield to the reality of the abyss between the goals of Hamas and the aspirations of the Jewish people.

Flynt Leverett, in his *New York Times* op-ed article "The Gulf between Us," quotes Saudi Foreign Minister Prince Saud al-Faisal: "If the Iranian nuclear weapons were deployed against Israel, they would kill Palestinians, and if they missed Israel, they would hit Arab countries." Prince Saud worries about the Arabs and he does not give a damn about the Jews. Mr. Leverett agrees with Prince Saud's suggestion to establish "a region-wide nuclear–weapons-free zone" as a way out of the quandary, which boils down to "the long standing Arab insistence that the regional arms control cannot begin without Israel's denuclearization." Mr. Leverett states: "The United States and its partners should build on this idea and support the creation of the Gulf Security Council…" He described Ahmadinejad as a "populist nationalist" who is "engaged in execrable rhetoric about Israel and the Holocaust."[1122] Ahmadinejad is actually a raving lunatic who threatens to "wipe Israel off the map" and calls the Holocaust a "myth."

Mahmoud Abbas called the Holocaust a "myth" long before Ahmadinejad did. In his dissertation, which he wrote at Moscow University while studying there during Soviet times, Abbas described the Holocaust as an invention of the Jews to justify their oppression of the Palestinian people. Today the appeasers of Arabs insist on retaining Abbas as the "elected president of the Palestinian people." This is all about money. They want to keep Abbas in his figurehead office as a fig leaf to justify the "funding of the Palestinian Authority" in order to pretend that the election of Hamas did not change anything. The problem is, and always was, that Arafat and Abbas for years have been hoodwinking the world into believing their peaceful protestations in order to keep money flowing into their coffers.

On the twenty-seventh anniversary of the Islamic Revolution Ahmadinejad, a fanatical follower of the Ayatollah Khomeini, told tens of thousands of Iranians that the United States and Europe will pay a "heavy price for the publication of caricatures of the Prophet Muhammad," saying, "the West had become the tool of Zionism. Now, in the West insulting the Prophet is allowed, but questioning the Holocaust is considered a crime."[1123] Our trouble in Iran began a long time ago. It must be recalled that late in 1979 Jimmy Carter sent Air Force Major-General Robert E. Huyser to Iran with an order to prevent Iran's military from resisting the takeover by Khomeini's fanatics. General Alexander Haig stated at that time: "Huyser was an instrument of Carter's policy to drop the Shah."[1124]

Day after day crowds of angry Muslims went on violent rampages all around the world and especially in Europe. David Brooks, in his *New York Times* op-ed article "Drafting Hitler—A Clash of Cartoons and Civilizations," described a demonstration in London where the protesters held signs reading: "Freedom Go to Hell," "Exterminate Those Who Mock Islam," "Be Prepared for the Real Holocaust," and "Europe, You Will Pay, Your 9/11 is on the Way." An Imam in Copenhagen declared, "In the West freedom of speech is sacred; to us, the Prophet is sacred."[1125] People in Europe began to feel the rage engulfing the Muslim mob when cars were set on fire in Paris and other cities. This rage is similar to the rage of the Palestinian mobs against the Jews and Israel.

Actually cartoons have nothing to do with the Prophet Muhammad, or with what Islam represented throughout the ages. The cartoons revealed the artists' view of today's Islamic extremists who blow up busses, cafes, and the World Trade Center towers, who take hostages and behead them for the world to see these grizzly murders on television screens. In the artist's mind the bomb fuse was burning not on the Prophet Muhammad's turban, but in the heads of those who profess to be his followers. The phrase "Clash of Civilizations" is actually a misnomer—the clash is not between civilizations but between the Western civilization and the uncivilized barbarians of Hamas and Al-Quaeda. The civilized world is to blame for letting this poison penetrate its life. This rage feeds on bottomless envy and a burning desire to avenge the misery of life in Arab and Muslims countries. These mobs are out to intimidate the Free World into submission to their whims.

Israel must isolate itself from this poisonous hatred. Ariel Sharon's legacy is his idea to unilaterally disengage from the hate-ridden Palestinian society and to build the barrier separating Israel from the Arab-populated areas. The desire to complete the barrier and for unilateral disengagement unites Israeli doves and hawks alike. Some hawks even go so far as to agree to cede to Palestinians the Arab-populated part of Jerusalem. Avigdor Liberman, leader of the "Israel Beiteinu" (Israel is Our Home) party, said that he would like to give up the Arab-populated neighborhoods of Jerusalem, such as Sur Baher and Jabal Mukaber, along with heavily Arab populated areas in the Galilee in return for expanded settlement blocks in Judea and Samaria. He explained:

There are Arabs in Jerusalem whose only connection to the state is that they go once a week to Salah a-Din Street to get their National Insurance

Institute payments. I don't think Israeli taxpayers should be paying for them anymore.[1126]

Liberman's suggestion makes sense, especially after Arabs in Jerusalem voted to elect four Hamas member to the Palestinian parliament. Israeli Arabs are Israeli citizens and they amount to some twenty percent of the population. They elect ten members of the Israeli parliament who openly identify with their "Palestinian brothers" and demonstratively refuse to stand up in Knesset to pay respect to the Israeli national hymn. Asmi Bshara, an Israeli citizen and member of the Knesset, in an interview with Palestinian television declared:

> The Palestinian people sooner or later will defeat its mortal, heartless, and bloodthirsty enemy—Israel.[1127]

Ahmoud Tibi, another Israeli citizen and member of the Knesset, declared:

> The Palestinian resistance is a great heroic movement, which is a matter of pride for the entire Arab nation.[1128]

Another Arab in the Israeli Knesset, Taleb A-Sanaa, shouted:

> Let's proclaim our devotion to shahids (martyrs, the suicide bombers), our real heroes.[1129]

Except for Israel, no country in the world would allow its citizens, let alone members of its parliament, to engage in such treasonous rhetoric.

Israel faces the threat of being wiped off the map by an Iranian nuclear attack as well as by the Hamas murderers. When President Bush was asked whether America would defend Israel against the Iranian threat, he answered, "You bet, we will defend Israel." Most probably, Bush would not wait for Israel to strike first at Iranian targets. He will be going through the motions in the UN Security Council as long as it takes before taking any military action. Defense Secretary Donald Rumsfeld said that contingency plans to bomb Iranian nuclear installations were ready. According to the Israeli press, Israel has its own contingency plans. If Iran does not comply with the Security Council's demands, Bush and America's allies would have the choice of bombing Iranian nuclear sites with bunker-busting bombs and using a naval blockade of the Strait of Harmus to strangle Iran economically and induce an internal uprising.

The Israeli military can take care of the Hamas threat. The major problem for Israel is its internal enemy—the Israeli-Arab population. A growing number of Israelis are coming to believe that Israeli Arabs are its "fifth column." This problem could only be solved partly by ceding parts of Arab-populated East Jerusalem and part of the Arab-populated Galilee to the Palestinian Authority. Israel's democracy is incapable of forcefully expelling people even if they constitute a threat to the Jewish state. The "peace at any price" crowd around the world would turn against Israel even if Palestinian Arabs would support Iranian aggression. The wobbly Republican Senator Chuck Hagel of Nebraska was against the American invasion of Iraq, using this argument:

> A war with Iraq could create the political cover for Israel to expel Palestinians from the West Bank and Gaza.[1130]

The Jews did not expel the Palestinians, as Hagel predicted. Throughout history the Jews never exiled any people, but other people exiled the Jews many times and from many lands. Yet the Jews survived to return to the land of their ancestors. In the Gaza Strip and Northern Samaria, Jews expelled Jews from their homes.

During the Senate debate over pullout from the Iraq War the Democrats were divided over a deadline for the withdrawal of American troops, offering various arguments in support of their opinions.[1131] But Dianne Feinstein, a California democrat, came up with a strikingly novel argument for withdrawal, stating that American troops might be needed to quell the looming crisis in the Israeli-Palestinian conflict.[1132] Presumably, she assumed that they would be needed to protect Israel. If so, Senator Feinstein should be reminded that Israel defended its people in four wars against armies of several Arab states and two Palestinian intifadahs.

Israel is faced with the danger of these Islamic lunatics but also by the anti-Israeli bias of members of American academia and some prominent members of the media. Jessica T. Mathews, president of the Carnegie Endowment for International Peace, in her *New York Times* op-ed article, "Speaking to Teheran, With One Voice," pointed to the "error that led us into Iraq" and argued that Democrats should stop "currying favor with pro-Israel voters by vying to see who can be the most anti-Iranian."[1133] One of the media's most prominent Bush bashers, Helen Thomas, sitting in the front row at the president's press conference, insisted in asking whether Bush decided to topple Saddam Hussein "because of oil or Israel." She kept interrupting Bush's response, determined to hear a confirmation from Bush of her suggestions. She pointed fingers and made facial grimaces which betrayed her disappointment in his answer. But the eighty-one-page report, published by two scholars, John J. Mearsheimer and Stephen M. Walt, for the Kennedy School of Government at Harvard University, was the most hostile attack on the "pro-Israeli lobby."

They stated:

> The United States has a terrorism problem in good part because it is so closely allied with Israel, not the other way around. The United States would not be worried about Iran, Iraq, and Syria, if not for its ties with Israel.[1134]

These authors argue that the pro-Israeli lobby has been manipulating American policy to support Israel, which is contrary to America's own interests. They accused Jewish officials in the Bush administration, namely Paul Wolfowitz, Douglas Feith, and David Wurmser, of being behind the push for war with Iraq. The bottom line of their argument is that the Jews are guilty of dragging America into war against Saddam Hussein. The authors also assert that Israel is "not a true democracy." This report may become as popular with Islamic Jew-haters of the world as the *Protocols of the Elders of Zion* was with the Nazis.

John J. Mearsheimer and Stephen M. Walt did not indicate how much their views had been influenced by Senator Kennedy's pro-Palestinian views. Kennedy and Congressman James Moran, a Democrat from Virginia, were "among the personalities who had appeared at a gala dinner for the Arab-American Institute that was sponsored in part by the Kingdom of Saudi Arabia." Kennedy was the keynote speaker and was greeted by loud applause. Congressman Moran was invited because he earlier declared that "without the support of the Jews, America would not have gone to war in Iraq." He was also greeted "with enthusiastic applause and a standing ovation." Also present was the family of Rachel Corrie, an anti-Israel member of the "National Student Conference of the Palestine Solidarity Movement," which supports Palestinian homicide-bombers. Corrie went to Gaza in 2003 to "defend Palestinian homes" and was run over by an Israeli Army bulldozer, which was destroying a home used for smuggling weapons from Egypt. Her supporters proclaimed her a "hero and a martyr," but the Israeli army called her death a tragic accident.[1135]

Twenty-one British Jews wrote a Letter to the Editor to the *New York Times*, stating:

We are Jewish writers who support the Royal Court Theater's production of *My Name Is Rachel Corrie*. We are dismayed by the decision of the New York Theater Workshop to cancel or postpone the play's production. In London it played to sell-out houses. Critics praised it. Audiences found it intensely moving. We believe that it is an important play… and the crucial issues it raises about Israeli military activity in the occupied territories… Rachel Corrie gave her life standing up against injustice.[1136]

British anti-Semites gleefully pat these twenty-one groveling Jewish lemmings on the back.

Israel should not pay attention to Jewish sycophants or wait for the United States, United Nations, or the Quartet to give it a green light, or to advise it as to when or how to deal with its enemies. It should start immediately to wean the Palestinian people off suckling at Israel's breast. Let the Palestinians learn the consequences of their hate. Sealed by the separation barrier and not finding an outlet for their hatred in murdering the Jews, the Palestinian people in the "occupied territories," including the Hamas-infested Arab neighborhoods of East Jerusalem, will start killing each other for a share of the few handouts they receive from Arab countries. Most probably hunger riots will be the final outcome of Hamas' victory at the polls. This will be the end of the pipe-dream of the "Palestinian state" and it will ensure Israel's survival.

On April 29, 2006, acting Prime Minister Ehud Olmert said in an interview with the German newspaper *Bild*:

Ahmadinejad speaks today like Hitler before taking power. He speaks of the complete destruction and annihilation of the Jewish people. We are dealing with a psychopath of the worst kind, an anti-Semite."[1137]

Describing how Ahmadinejad eclipses Iranian clerics and consolidates power, a political science professor in Tehran said:

Ahmadinejad is reshaping the identity of the elite. Being against Jews and Zionists is an essential part of this new identity."[1138]

In May 2006 Olmert traveled to Washington to confer with President Bush about his unilateral disengagement plan to pull some 70,000 Israeli settlers from the West Bank. The *New York Times* article, "West Bank Pullout Gets a Nod From Bush," described Bush's response as "A gingerly 'yes,' while insisting that Olmert find a way to negotiate with the Palestinians"[1139]

Prime Minister Blair was even less accommodating. At the joint press conference with Ehud Olmert, he declared:

> I don't want to go down any path other than a negotiated settlement. The only answer is a negotiated settlement. There really isn't another way to move forward… We the international community have got a choice. We either put our best effort into making sure that a negotiated settlement becomes a reality or we are going to face a different reality.[1140]

Blair did not specify what kind of "different reality" he had in mind. What is clear is that he was trying to appease the substantial part of the British electorate which is afflicted by a pro-Palestinian bias, especially true in the case of British academics, thousands of whom call for the boycott of Israel, denouncing "Israeli apartheid policies, including construction of the exclusion wall and discriminatory educational practices."[1141] It was Blair's "Quartet" idea of the "road map to peace" which Bush supported to help him, Bush's staunchest ally in the Iraqi war, as he was facing strong opposition to this war at home. Now, three years later, the idea of the "road map to peace" went full circle. The difference is that then Yasir Arafat's double "peace talk" was a cover for at least some faint hope, which is how, with Hamas in charge of the Palestinian Authority, the "road map to peace" wound up in the deep hole.

During the Kadima party election campaign Ehud Olmert presented himself as an heir of Ariel Sharon. Polls predicted Kadima winning forty-four seats in the Knesset, but final results were only twenty-nine. Olmert insisted that he would continue Sharon's policy of unilateral disengagement by removing some 70,000 settlers from the West Bank by the end of his term in 2010. But then he changed his mind and said that he would complete unilateral disengagement by the beginning of 2008, which would coincide with the end of President Bush's last term in office. This suggests that Olmert wraps himself not only in Sharon's mantle, but that he is also the heir of the Sharon-Bush agreement to leave the large blocks of Israeli settlements in Israel's hands. This delusion reminds one of a memorable phrase: in the Russian playwright Griboedov's drama *Trouble Out of Wisdom,* the hero says, "One cannot travel too far in a stagecoach of the past." These words are especially true when the stagecoach belongs to someone else.

Iran's President Mahmoud Ahmadinejad reemerged as the reincarnation of such pathological Jew-haters as Hitler and Stalin. History threatens to repeat itself, with Ahmadinejad looking like a mix of a miniature smiling Mickey Mouse and Lucifer who inflames large enthralled crowds of adoring Iranians to a frenzy.[1142] This frenzy finds an echo in a *New York Times* op-ed article, "The Persian Complex" by Abbas Amanat, a Yale University professor of history and author of the forthcoming book *In Search of Modern Iran*. Amanat starts his article by heaping scorn on those who find it "easy to label Iran's quest for nuclear energy a dangerous adventure" and on those who also find it comforting to heap scorn on President Mahmoud Ahmadinejad for his "denial of the Holocaust and his odious call for the obliteration of the state of Israel." Having mentioned in passing the "rambling intransigence" of Ahmadinejad's "recent letter to President Bush, Amanat indulges himself in an invective against foreigners—Mongols, Arabs, Russians, Europeans, Americans—who for centuries, as he suggests, have abused and exploited the Persians. The bottom line of Amanat's article is that the mistreatment of Iranians explains the "The Persian Complex" of blaming "outside powers for their misfortune." He concludes his article by warning the Bush administration: "If the United States resorts to sanctions, or worse, to some military response, the outcome would be not only disastrous, but, in the long run, transient." And he ends his article with a chilling prophecy: "Iran will most likely succeed, for ill or for good, in finding its own nuclear holy grail."[1143]

On June 25, 2006, three Palestinian terrorist factions, including the "Hamas Military wing," dug a tunnel from Gaza to Israel, killing two Israeli soldiers and abducting Cpl. Gilad Shalit, 19, who was wounded in the process. The terrorists demanded the release of some 15,000 Palestinian prisoners as a ransom for the Israeli soldier. Abu al-Muthana, a spokesman for the Army of Islam, one of the factions involved, declared:

> Whether he [Gilad Shalit] will be killed or not killed, we will not disclose any information. We do not kill captives. Our Islam requires that we treat captives well and fairly.[1144]

Yet, another young Israeli, Eliahu Asheri, 18, who was abducted at the same time as Cpl. Gilad Shalit, was executed with a single bullet in the head. His body was found in a shallow grave.[1145]

Prime Minister Olmert took a seemingly uncompromising and tough stance in trying to save Cpl. Shalit. He ordered his military "to do whatever was necessary to free the soldier. He told his cabinet that he "intended to make the lives of Gazans ever more miserable" until Shalit was released. His interior minister, Roni Bar-On, warned Hamas that if the soldier was harmed or killed, "the sky will fall on them."[1146] But Israel also yielded somewhat to outside pressure on Sunday, July 3, 2006, by allowing a limited supply of fuel and food into Gaza." On Saturday, Defense Minister Amir Peretz, one of Israel's perennial doves, approved opening two border crossings for four days to allow basic supplies in:

> By early Sunday evening, 50 trucks of wheat, corn, meat, cooking oil passed through the Karni crossing … about 265 gallons of diesel fuel, 21,000 gallons of gasoline and 200,000 tons of natural gas were shipped through the fuel terminal at Nahal Oz.[1147]

Olmert and his ministers talked tough but at the same time sent mixed signals by providing essential goods to the hostile Palestinian population. These signals were confusing to the outside world. They encourage wishful thinking in Palestinian terrorists who, as delusional as they are, might interpret it as a sign of vacillation by Israeli government. In this case these signals will serve as a provocation and encouragement of terrorism. A resolution proposed by the 57-member Organization of the Islamic Conference was approved with a few meaningless amendments on July 6, 2006, by a vote of 29-11, with five abstentions in the UN Human Rights Council, which decided to send "an urgent fact-finding mission to the West Bank and Gaza Strip after the Council deplored Israeli Defense Forces operations in the region as breaching international humanitarian and human rights law in the occupied Palestinian territory." Cuba, Russia, and China, the most notorious human rights violators, voted for this resolution. Canada and the European countries voted against it. The United States and Israel are not members of this Council.[1148]

On July 10, 2006, Hassan Nasrallah, the leader of the Lebanese terrorist group Hezbollah, ordered an attack on an Israeli military patrol. Several soldiers were killed and two soldiers were taken as hostages. Nasrallah demanded the release of Arab prisoners in Israeli jails in exchange for the two captured soldiers. Israel responded by bombing Hezbollah-controlled areas to deplete its arsenal, supplied by Iran and Syria. Mujtaba Bigdeli, Hezbollah's spokesman in Teheran, boasted that his group has trained 2,000 volunteers, ready to attack America and Israel. He declared:

> We are ready to dispatch them to every corner of the world to jeopardize Israel and America's interests. If America wants to ignite World War III … we welcome it.[1149]

Iran has supplied Hezbollah with much of its firepower, including long-range (120 miles) Zelzal missiles transported through Syria.[1150]

But Iranian and Syrian leaders were having second thoughts about the adventure of their proxy Hezbollah. On July 15, 2006, Ahmadinejad, who had on numerous occasions called for the destruction of Israel, suddenly called on the "international community" to end the conflict by "restraining Israel."[1151] On July 19, 2006, President Bashar al-Assad of Syria called Prime Minister Recep Tayyip Erdogan of Turkey and asked him to promote a "cease-fire which is necessary in order to stop the Israeli attack on Lebanon."[1152] This was not the first time anti-Israeli organizations began their war cries and shed crocodile tears on behalf of the "innocent Palestinian people," promising to come to their aid. Such pleadings are simply another form of provocation, promising a reward for terrorism. Just talking about "painful concessions," let alone making them, is a deadly form of appeasement.

On August 14, 2006, the UN Security Council, after protracted negotiations, adopted a resolution calling for a cease-fire. The Hezbollah leader, Sheik Hassan Nasrallah, President Ahmadinejad, and President Bashar Assad all proclaimed a victory over the "Zionist entity" and its American and British supporters. As of this writing the cease-fire still holds. There were no victory speeches in Israel, but a reckoning began. Prime Minister Olmert and his defense minister, Amir Peretz, were gravely wounded by the perception of having poorly conducted the war. They both were no match for Ariel Sharon, whose mantel they intended to inherit. Benjamin Netanyahu, the leader of the opposition Likud Party, stated:

> The government failed to destroy an Iranian army division, fighting in a war conceived, organized, trained, and equipped by Iran, with Iran's goal of destroying Israel and its fantasy ideology of building a once-glorious Muslim empire in which we are merely the first pit stop.[1153]

The major reassessment of the war claimed two significant political casualties: Olmert's campaign promise of the unilateral withdrawal of some 70,000 settlers from a large part of the West Bank and the completion in building the separation fence. Itamar Rabinovich, a former Israeli ambassador to Washington, said bluntly:

> Two notions have died. First, unilateralism, and second, separation by the fence. Missiles dwarf the fence. Part of the reckoning will be our reputation as a strategic partner of the Americans. ... Part of our self-image is of military miracle workers, and we didn't do that this time. Still, Lebanon reinforces Israel's view that the real danger in the region is Iran,

Hezbollah's patron, and that the threat of a nuclear-armed Iran is aimed at Egypt, Saudi Arabia, and Jordan too.[1154]

Itzhak Levanon, Israeli ambassador to the UN, commented on the UN resolution which was vetoed by the United States: "Obviously, this resolution isn't evenhanded. It's not equitable and it's not balanced."[1155] The point is that the result of the vote was not only obvious, but given the history of UN anti-Israel votes, it was ridiculous even to expect a different vote. Russia and China do not condemn the daily barrage of rockets fired by Hamas or Hezbollah terrorists against Israeli citizens and they do not condemn the North Korean regime for denying human rights to the starving millions kept in prison camps. If they, instead of Israel, were attacked by Hamas or Hezbollah terrorists, they would respond by starving the people who supported the terrorists and sending them fleeing from a sinking ship to the neighboring Arab countries.

Israel should not wait for the United Nations or the Quartet for a green light, or advise them as to when or how it should deal with its enemies, or pay attention to Jewish lemmings and their opinions. It should act immediately to cut off the Palestinian people from Israel. After all, why continue to feed those who bite your hand? Talking about "painful concessions," let alone making them, is a deadly form of appeasement, similar to running away from a vicious dog which only invites continued aggression. Let the Palestinians experience the consequences of their hate. Sealed by the separation barrier and without an outlet for their hatred by murdering the Jews, the Palestinians in the West Bank, Gaza, and in the Hamas-infested Arab neighborhoods of East Jerusalem will start killing each other for a share of the handouts from the oil-rich Arab countries. Most probably hunger riots will be the final outcome of Hamas' rule, ending the pipe-dream of a "Palestinian state," thus insuring Israel's survival, which ultimately depends on the strength and determination of its citizens to fight and win.

Notes

1. *Jerusalem Post,* February 20, 2006.
2. Ibid.
3. Picture of Ahmadinejad in *New York Times,* May 28, 2006, p.14.
4. *Jerusalem Post,* January 22, 2004, "Bush Skips Road Map in the State of the Union Address," by Janine Zachariah.
5. I. I. Etinger, "Eto nevozmozhno zabyt," Moscow, *Ves Mir,* p. 226.
6. Ibid., p. 236.
7. V. Kirpichenko, *Razvedka: Litza I lichnosti,* Moscow, 1998, p. 282.
8. Roman Brackman, *The Secret File of Joseph Stalin: A Hidden Life,* Frank Cass, London Portland, 2001, Chapter 24, pp. 249–50.
9. Ibid., Chapter 27.
10. Copyright 1992, Soviet Data Day Line, *Soviet Press Digest,* January 22, 1992.
11. Interview with Russian journalist German Broido, October 2004.
12. Russian-language newspaper, *v Novom Svete,* November 5–11, 2004, p. 14.
13. *New York Times,* November 8, 2002, p. A31.
14. Fox News, *Special Report with Brit Hume,* April 4, 2003.
15. Reprint from *Times* (London) in *New York Post,* March 18, 2004, p. 4.
16. Erica Goode, "Stalin to Saddam," *New York Times,* May 4, 2003, WK, p. 5.
17. See "Blavatnik Archive," Published by Len Blavatnik, President of Access Industries, NYC and London.
18. *Evreiskaya Entsiklopedia,* vol. III, p. 651.
19. V. Kaminsky and I. Vereshchagin, *'Detstvo i yunost': documenty zapiski, rasskazy (Childhood and Adolescence of the Leader,* Stalin's childhood biography), p. 24f.
20. Kaminsky and Vereshchagin, pp. 20–25.
21. Personal interview with Nugzar Sharia in Sag Harbor, New York, in 1971.
22. See *Evreiskaya entsiklopediya* ["Jewish Encyclopedia" in Russian], vol. VI, p. 808f, for the analysis of the Georgian language by the academician Niko Marr, and his claim that the Georgian language is of Semitic origin. Other linguists have argued that the Georgian language is related to a group of Caucasian languages.
23. Edvard Radzinsky, *Stalin,* p. 19 (quoting from the Gori archive).
24. Kaminsky and Vereshchagin, *Detstvo i yunost,* p. 26.
25. Knickerbocker. See also Isaac Deutscher, *Stalin: A Political Biography,* p. 2.
26. Edvard Radzinsky, *Stalin,* p. 12.
27. Okhrana Report no. 5500, dated May 1, 1904, published in Roy Medvedev's *New Pages from the Political Biography of Stalin,* in Robert C. Tucker, ed., *Stalinism,* p. 200f.
28. The historian Andrey Amalrik related this popular belief in an interview with the author in Chappaqua, New York, 1976.
29. J. Iremaschwili, *Stalin und die Tragödie Georgiens,* pp. 8–11.
30. Personal interview with Nugzar Sharia in Sag Harbor, New York, in 1971.
31. *Evreiskaya Entsiklopedia,* vol. IX, pp. 938–40.
32. Personal interview with Nugzar Sharia in Sag Harbor, New York, in 1971.
33. Iremashvili, p.11f.
34. Personal interview with Nugzar Sharia in Sag Harbor, New York, in 1971.
35. Lev Trotsky, *Stalin,* p. 8.
36. Boris Souvarine, *Stalin: A Critical Survey of Bolshevism,* p. 3.
37. Roy Medvedev, *Let History Judge,* p. 337.
38. Robert Conquest, *Stalin: Breaker of Nations,* pp. 4, 9, 12. Also *Kazakhstanskaya pravda,* November 10, 1988. See also L. Kafanova, "O velikom druge i vozhde," *Novoe Russkoe slovo,* March 23 and 24, 1977.
39. Kaminsky and Vereshchagin, p. 38.

40. Related to Nugzar Sharia by Stalin's bodyguard Gogi Zautashvili. Personal interview with Nugzar Sharia.

41. Felix Svetlov, a former Soviet lawyer and son of a high-ranking Soviet Secret Police official, told me about Stalin's "rabbit" during an interview in New York in 1989.

42. Personal interview with Nugzar Sharia.

43. Iremaschwili, p. 11f.

44. Kaminsky and Vereshchagin, p. 28.

45. Anatoly Rybakov, "Deti arbata," *Druzhba norodov*, no. 4–5. See also L. Kafanova, "O velikom druge i vozhde," *Novoe russkoe slovo*, March 23, 1977. Kafanova quotes the prominent Soviet composer Vano Muradeli, a native of Gori.

46. Ibid., p. 43f.

47. Personal interview with Nugzar Sharia in Sag Harbor, New York, in 1971.

48. Svetlana Allilueva, *Only One Year*, p. 360.

49. Joseph Darvichewy, *Ah! Ce qu'on Rigolait Bien avec Mon Copain Staline*, p. 34. Quoted in Daniel Rancour-Lafferiere, *The Mind of Stalin*, and p. 36f.

50. Ibid., p. 45.

51. F. D. Volkov, *Vzlet i padenie Stalina*, p. 24. Volkov quotes from oral testimony by Anna Allilueva, Nadezhda Allilueva's sister-in-law.

52. Andrey Amalrik related the story of Vissarion's imprisonment in an interview with the author in Chappaqua, New York, in 1976.

53. Iremaschwili, p. 5f.

54. A. Kazbegi, "Otseubiitsy," *Izbrannye Sochineniya*, vol. I.

55. For a discussion of Hitler's similar rejection of his father, see Walter C. Langer, *The Mind of Adolf Hitler*, pp. 146–60.

56. L. Kafanova, "O velikom druge i vozhde," March 23, 1977. She quotes a prominent Soviet composer and native of Gori, Vano Muradeli, who recalled, "Koba seemed to have learned the truth about how this kind and loving priest was related to him." It is unlikely that in all his years at Gori Koba never once encountered the rumor that Egnatashvili was his real father.

57. Iremaschwili, p. 16.

58. Anatoly Rybakov, "Deti arbata," *Druzhba norodov*, no. 4–5, 1987.

59. Iremaschwili, pp. 16–18.

60. Kaminsky and Vereshchagin, p. 71.

61. Iremaschwili, pp. 19–22.

62. Andrey Amalrik interview. Also S. Vereshchak, "Stalin v tur'me," *DNI*, January 22 and 24, 1928.

63. R. Arsenate, "Is vospominanii o Staline," *Novy zhurnal*, no. 72, June 1963. Vereshchak, "Stalin v tur'me," Andrey Amarlik interview.

64. Ibid., p. 86.

65. Iremaschwili, p. 24.

66. Ibid.

67. Brackman, *The Secret File*, Chapter 1, "The Roots of Evil."

68. A. T. Vasiliev, *The Okhrana*, p. 57f.

69. Ibid., p. 63f.

70. Ibid., p. 95f.

71. A. T. Vasiliev, *The Okhrana*, p. 63f.

72. J. Iremaschwili, *Stalin und die Tragödie Georgiens*, p. 27f.

73. I. V. Stalin, *Sochineniya*, vol. I, pp. 314f.

74. N. Vakar, *Stalin . . .*, p. 2.

75. Ibid.

76. Lev Trotsky, *Stalin*, pp. 34f.

77. For a brief account of Colonel S. P. Shabelsky's career, see Smith, p. 103. Also see Roy Medvedev, *Let History Judge*, pp. 319–23. Medvedev states that in the early thirties, the historian Professor

Sepp, author of *The October Revolution in Documents*, happened upon the file of a police agent, Iosif Dzhugashvili, and that the file contained Dzhugashvili's request to be released from prison. A note on the request stated: "Free him, if he agrees to give the Gendarmerie Department information about the activity of the Social Democratic Party."

78. "Batumskaya demonstratsiya 102—go goda," pp. 120–22. See also Vereshchak for similar incidents of Koba accusing other prisoners of being Okhrana agents.

79. Okhrana Report no. 5500, dated May 1, 1904, on file at the Hoover Institution and published in Robert C. Tucker (ed.), *Stalinism*, pp. 200f.

80. B. Souvarine, *Stalin*, p. 44.

81. Okhrana report no. 53-c, dated March 14, 1911, and other Okhrana documents, including the circular letter attached to Okhrana report no. 97984, dated April 19, 1913, which states that I. V. Dzhugashvili was exiled by the "Highest Authority decree of June 9, 1903, for a state crime."

82. R. Bagratuni's letter to I. D. Levine, dated May 8, 1967. In I. D. Levine's archive. Copy in the author's archive.

83. S. Alliluev, *Proidennyi put*, p. 63f.

84. Personal interview with Nugzar Sharia in Sag Harbor, New York, in 1971. Nugzar Sharia related recollections of his uncle, Peter Sharia, Stalin's assistant. Starting in 1937, Stalin ordered publication of numerous articles and books glorifying Ketskhoveli. One of the many authors was Lavrenty Beria—see, for instance, his *Lado Ketskhoveli*.

85. Dr. Norman Syrkin, in a letter addressed to the author dated January 4, 1975. Also Syrkin's interview with the author and Vitaly Svechinsky in Haifa, Israel, in January 1972. Syrkin's father, Zalman Syrkin, who worked for many years in the USSR Academy of Science, learned in 1964 that this telegram had been found in the Irkutsk Okhrana archive, but was not published because Khrushchev was deposed that year and his de-Stalinization campaign ended with Leonid Brezhnev's assumption of power.

86. E. Yaroslavsky, *Vazhneishie vekhi zhizni i deyatelnosti tovarishcha Stalina*, p. 31.

87. "Batumskaya demonstratsiya 102—go goda," p. 140. See also M. A. Bulgakov, *Sobranie sochinenii* in five volumes, Volume 3, Moscow, Khudozhestvennaya Litratura, 1990, p. 697.

88. I. Dubinsky-Mukhadze, *Kamo*, p. 32f.

89. Lev Trotsky, *Stalin*, p. 46, fn. 9.

90. Okhrana Report no. 101145, dated March 31, 1911, signed by the vice-director of the Department of Police, Vissarionov, and the chief of the Special Section, Colonel Eremin. On file at the Hoover Institution. Copy in the author's archive.

91. I. V. Alekseev, *Provokator Anna Serebriakova*.

92. Okhrana Report no. 5500, dated May 1, 1904.

93. Budu Svanidze, "My Uncle Joe," p. 6 and p. 16. "Budu Svanidze" was a pen name of the Soviet diplomat Bessedovsky, who knew Stalin personally and who, having defected in 1930, wrote several books under various pen names. Bertram Wolfe points out that Bessedovsky did not invent anything but invariably wrote of what he actually knew.

94. Brackman, *The Secret File*, Chapter 3, "Meeting the 'Mountain Eagle.'"

95. Ibid., Chapter 5, "The Betrayal of Avlabar Press."

96. This name is mentioned in a police record in the Stockholm City Police Archive. Copy in Edward Ellis Smith's archive; see *The Young Stalin: The Early Years of an Elusive Revolutionary*, pp. 176, 396; ref. no. 363.

97.. Stockholm City Police Archive. A copy of the archive record is in Smith's archive; see E. E. Smith, *The Young Stalin*, p. 176 and fn. 363 on p. 396. See also H. M. Hyde, *Stalin*, p. 76.

98. *Padenie tsarskogo rezhima*, vol. VII, p. 322; also vol. I, p. 327, and vol. III, pp. 75 and 494.

99. G. I. Uratadze, *Moi vospominaniya*, p. 140, on file at the Hoover Institution, cited in Smith, p. 396, fn. 363a.

100. Brackman, *The Secret File*, Chapter 6, "Hotel Bristol."

101. *Padenie tsarskogo rezhima*, Burtsev's testimony, vol. I, p. 311f.

102. V. D. Bonch-Bruevich, quoted in Dubinsky-Mukhadze, *Kamo*, p. 62.

103. Garting's report no. 152, dated April 24, 1907 (Old Style), on file at the Hoover Institution; see also Smith, p. 183 and p. 397, fn. 375b.

104. Lev Trotsky, *Stalin*, p. 90.

105. Garting's "top-secret" report no. 225, dated May 26, 1907 (Old Style), to the director of the Department of Police. On file at the Hoover Institution; see also Smith, p. 186f and p. 397, fn. 387.

106. Lev Trotsky, *Stalin*, p. 108.

107. For a detailed account of Koba's second encounter with Garting, see Brackman, *The Secret File*, Chapter 6, "The Hotel Bristol."

108. I. M. Dubinsky-Mukhadze, *Kamo*, pp. 71–85.

109. The events are described in Rafael Bagratuni's handwritten testimony, dated May 8, 1967, on file in Isaac Don Levine's archive. Copy in the author's archive. In his testimony, Bagratuni relates information he received from his relative, Alexander Bagratuni, a gendarmerie officer who served in the Tiflis Okhrana until the end of summer 1907.

110. Ibid.

111. V. I. Lenin, *Polnoe sobranie sochinenii*, vol. XV, p. 571, and vol. XVI, p. 680–86.

112. For a detailed account of Koba's second encounter with Garting, see Brackman, *The Secret File*, Chapter 7, "The Great Tiflis Bank Robbery."

113. For a detailed account of the Tiflis bank robbery, see Brackman, *The Secret File,* Chapter 7, "The Great Tiflis Bank Robbery."

114. Rafael Bagratuni's testimony, dated May 8, 1967, on file in I. D. Levine's archive. Copy in the author's archive.

115. "Krasny arkhiv," no. 2, 1934, p. 3.

116. See Martynov's letters to Eremin in Lavrenty Beria, *K Vosprosy ob istorii bolshevitskikh organizatsii v Zakavkazie*, p. 90, and M. D. Bagirov, *Iz istorii bolshevitskoi organizatatsii Baku i Azerbadzhana*, p. 101f.

117. I. Dubinsky-Mukhadze, "Kamo," pp. 64f. See the photocopy of Colonel Eremin's wire, dated April 22, 1908.

118. S. Vereshchak, "Stalin v turme," *DNI*, January 22 and 24, 1928.

119. Ibid.

120. R. Arsenidze, "Iz vospominanii o Staline," *Novyi zhurnal*, no. 72, June 1963, pp. 218–21.

121. I. V. Stalin, *Sochineniya*, vol. II, p. 46f.

122. L. Beria, "K voprosu ob . . .," p. 90.

123. Ibid. See also Okhrana report no. 101145, dated March 31, 1911, and Smith, p. 230.

124. I. Dubinsky-Mukhadze, *Kamo*, p. 124f.

125. M. D. Bagirov, *Iz isetorii . . .*, p. 101f.

126. Roy Medvedev, *Let History Judge*, p. 319 and fn. 61.

127. Ibid.

128. J. Iremaschwili, *Stalin und die Tragödie Georgiens*, p. 40.

129. Ibid. See also N. Vakar, "Stalin po vospominaniyam N. N. Zhordania," *Poslednie novosti*, December 16, 1936.

130. E. E. Smith, *The Young Stalin*, pp. 208–10.

131. L. Zhgenti, *Prichiny revolutsii na Kavkaze i rukovodstvo*, pp. 58–62.

132. *Padenie tsarskogo rezhima*, vol. VII, p. 339.

133. See *Spisok obschego sostava chinov otdelnogo korpusa zhandarmov*, 1911, p. 613; quoted in Smith, p. 401, fn. 482.

134. For a detailed account, see Brackman, *The Secret File*, Chapter 9. Colonel Pastrulin, Eremin's successor in Tiflis, discovered in 1911 that Koba's file in the Tiflis Okhrana archive was almost empty.

135. For a detailed account, see Brackman, *The Secret File*, Chapter 8, "Colonel Eremin."

136. V. Rudich's taped testimony citing Olga Shatunovskaya's statement that a commission of Old

Bolsheviks during the Khrushchev era investigated the rape case against Stalin at the time of his exile in Solvychegodsk. See also S. Vereshchak's articles, recounting Stalin's conversation with S. Surin, one of the exiles there and an Okhrana agent, about his stormy relations with Kuzakova.

137.   Alexander Kolesnik, *Mify i pravda o Staline*, p. 10.

138.   Yevgeny Zhirnov, "K. Kuzakov-syn I. V. Stalina," *Argumenty i fakty*, #39, 1995.

139.   This was a widely held opinion at the time.

140.   I. Dubinsky-Mukhadze, *Kamo*, pp. 142–54. See also his book *Ordzhonikidze*, pp. 70–72.

141.   *Krasny arkhiv*, vol. 2 (105), 1941, p. 23.

142.   On Malinovsky's career, see *Delo provokatora Malinovskogo*, Respublika, Moscow, 1992. Also Paul Sacardy, "Lenin's Deputy: The Story of a Double Agent," unpublished manuscript on file at the Radio Liberty Committee; also B. K. Erenfeld, "Delo Malinovskogo," *Voprosy istorii*, no. 7, 1965; *Padenie tsarskogo rezhima*, vol. VII, p. 374 and listed references; "Ot ministerstva yustitsii," *Vestnik vremennogo pravitelstva*, June 16, 1917; "Bolsheviki," p. x.

Evno Azef, an engineer by profession, was the head of the terrorist arm of the Social Revolutionary Party and at the same time a top-secret Okhrana agent. He masterminded many terrorist acts, among them several assassinations of high government officials. Driven by dark predatory impulses, Azef managed for many years to remain beyond the suspicion of both the Okhrana and the revolutionaries. General A. A. Lopukhin (to whom Koba and Kamo in 1905 had attributed their forged "Lopukhin Report") was outraged by Azef's duplicity and confided to Vladimir Burtsev, a Social-Revolutionary journalist and self-appointed exposer of Okhrana spies, that Azef was an Okhrana agent. Lopukhin was exiled for his exposure of Azef, who managed to escape and died in anonymity in Berlin. His handler, the Chief of the St. Petersburg Okhrana, General Gerasimov, was forced to resign. The Azef scandal resulted in a long and thorough investigation of Okhrana practices and in the firing of many of its agents and informers. (It was in the course of this investigation that Okhrana Colonel Zasypkin submitted the report about the exposure and liquidation of the Avlabar Press.) The Okhrana purge created a vacancy for Eremin's transfer to St. Petersburg and Beletsky's appointment to the post of Acting Vice-Director of the Department of Police. On Azef's career, see B. I. Gul, *Azef*; see also *Padenie tsarskogo rezhima*, vol. VII, p. 300, and listed references. On Lopukhin and Gerasimov, see *Padenie tsarskogo rezhima*, vol. VII, pp. 323, 369, and listed references.

143.   Ibid.

144.   Medvedev, *Let History . . .*, p. 337 and fn. 88. Medvedev's "famous Bolshevik in Moscow" in 1912 can refer only to Malinovsky.

145.   Brackman, *The Secret File*, Chapters 9 and 10.

146.   *Padenie tsarskogo rezhima*, vol. III, p. 281, and vol. V, pp. 212–13. See also "Ot ministerstva yustitsii," *Vestnik vremennogo pravitelstva*, June 16, 1917; "Bolsheviki i departament politsii," *Russkoe slovo*, May 19, 1917, p. 1.

147.   *Padenie tsarskogo rezhima*, vol. III, pp. 108 and 280.

148.   See Vasiliev's signature "for the Chief of the Special Section" on the copy of Colonel Pastrulin's Report No. 53-c, dated March 14, 1911. On file at the Hoover Institution. Copy in the author's archive.

149.   See E. Evseev, "Istoriya sionizma v tsarskoi rossii," *Voprosy istorii*, #5, May 1973, p. 72.

150.   *Padenie tsarskogo rezhima*, vol. III, p. 176, and vol. VII, p. 314.

151.   See N. Karganov, "Iz proshlogo Stalina," *Vozrozhdenie*, Paris, January 13, 1929.

152.   S. Vereshchak, "Stalin v tur'me: vospominaniya politicheskogo," *DNI*, January 24, 1928.

153.   See Brackman, *The Secret File*, Chapter 29, for I. A. Zelensky's "confession" at the Bukharin Show Trial. Zelensky "confessed" that he had sent from his place of exile in Narym two letters to an officer of the gendarmerie he knew only by the man's name "Vasily Konstantinovich." From Zelensky's forced "confession"—one of many instances in which Stalin forced his victims to confess slightly altered versions of events in his own life—Stalin's relations with Vasiliev can be inferred.

Notes

154. Boris Souvarine, *Stalin: A Critical Survey of Bolshevism*, p. 128; Karganov; Vereshchak; Edward Ellis Smith, *The Young Stalin: The Early Years of an Elusive Revolutionary*, p. 260.
155. See Alexander Orlov, "The Sensational Secret Behind the Damnation of Stalin," *Life*, April 23, 1956.
156. *Padenie tsarskogo rezhima*, vol. V, p. 62.
157. Evidence of Koba's employment by the St. Petersburg Okhrana is found in a report written by Eremin summarizing Koba's activities in the Okhrana. See the end of this chapter.
158. Bolsheviki, Introduction, *Padenie tsarskogo rezhima*, vol. III, p. 280; vol. V, p. 212.
159. I. V. Stalin, *Sochineniya*, vol. II, p. 437.
160. L. Trotsky, *Stalin*, p. 244.
161. Ronald Hingley, *Joseph Stalin: Man and Legend*, p. 72; also E. E. Smith, *The Young Stalin*, p. 294.
162. Alexander Orlov, *Life*.
163. Ibid.
164. Bolsheviki, p. 227. Also F. N. Samoilov, *Vospominaniya*, vol. III, p. 27f.
165. Ibid., pp. 164–68.
166. S. Shumsky, "Troyanovsky," *Poslednie novosti*, Paris, January 1, 1934, p. 3. Also see Shumsky's unpublished manuscript in the Nikolaevsky Collection at the Hoover Institution.
167. S. Shumsky, "Troyanovsky," p. 3.
168. E. E. Smith, The Young Stalin, p. 297; K. Sharikov, "Vazhneishie mesta prebyvaniya i revolutsionnoi deyatelnosti I. V. Stalina v Peterburge-Petrograde-Leningrade, 1909–1934," *Propaganda i agitatsiya*, 1939, no. 32, p. 60.
169. David Shub, *Politicheskie . . .*, p. 122.
170. See Brackman, *The Secret File*, Chapter 28, for the reconstruction of the original text of Eremin's report. For the reproduction of Stalin's forgery of Eremin's report, see I. D. Levine, "A Document on Stalin as Tsarist Spy," *Life*, vol. 40, no. 7, April 23, 1956. See also I. D. Levine, *Stalin's Great Secret*.
171. For a detailed account of this period, see Brackman, *The Secret File*, Chapter 10, "The Great State Scandal."
172. *Padenie tsarskogo rezhima*, vol. I, p. 317; V. Maksakov, "Arkhiv revolutsii i vneshnei politiki XIX–XX vekov," *Arkhivnoe delo*, no. XIII, 1927.
173. For a detailed account of this period see Brackman, *The Secret File*, Chapter 11, "Iosif Dzhu . . . ? We Have Forgotten. It Is Very Important."
174. *Padenie tsarskogo rezhima*, vol. 1, p. 313f. Bertram D. Wolfe, *Three Who Made a Revolution*, Cooper Square Press reprint, 2003, vol. II, p. 537.
175. Bertram D. Wolfe, *Three Who Made a Revolution*, vol. II, p. 537.
176. *Padenie tsarskogo rezhima*, vol. VII, p. 307.
177. Ibid., vol. VII, p. 317.
178. *Padenie tsarskogo rezhima*, Burtsev's testimony, vol. I, p. 315. Also I. M. Dubinsky-Mukhadze, *Ordzhonikidze*, p. 78.
179. *Padenie tsarskogo rezhima*, vol. V, p. 85.
180. Rodzianko, *Byloe*, no. 12, 1923, p. 249.
181. Ibid., vol. XXV, p. 341.
182. The newspapers *Russkoe slovo*, September 16, 1914, and *Golos*, October 13, 1914, reprinted this report as front-page news. See Elwood, p. 58 and p. 94, fn. 110.
183. *Sotzial-Demokrat*, no. 33, November 1, 1914 (October 19 Old Style), p. 2. See also Lenin's letter to V. A. Karpinsky in *Lenin*, vol. XLIX, p. 18, and Elwood, p. 58 and p. 94, fns. 111 and 112.
184. V. I. Lenin, *Polnoe Sobranie Sochinenii*, letters to Zinoviev and Inessa Armand, vol. XLIX, pp. 261, 282–83. Lenin's correspondence with Malinovsky was submitted to the Investigatory Commission of the Provisional Government in May 1917 (see P. B. Pisma, *Akselroda i Yu O. Martova*, p. 292) but never published. See Ralph Carter Elwood, *Roman Malinovsky*, p. 94, fn. 116.
185. David Shub, "Politicheskie deyateli rossii," *Novy zhurnal*. See also Z. A. B. Zeman and W. B.

Notes

Scharlau, *The Merchant of Revolution: The Life of Alexander Israel Helfand (Parvus), 1867–1924.*
186. David Shub, *Politicheskie deyateli rossii*, p. 205f.
187. Gerard Walter, *Lenin*, p. 251; quoted in Ralph Carter Elwood, *Roman Malinovsky* . . ., p. 59 and p. 94, fn. 119.
188. Ralph Carter Elwood, *Roman Malinovsky*, p. 94, fn. 119.
189. Colonel Eremin's letter no. 125483, dated May 13, 1910, to the chief of the Okhrana Foreign Agency A. A. Krasilnikov. On file at the Hoover Institution. Copy in the author's archive.
190. Okhrana Report no. 933 from Paris, dated August 11, 1915 (July 29 Old Style). On file at the Hoover Institution. Copy in the author's archive.
191. *Leninski sbornik*, ed. 2, vol. XI, p. 193.
192. Nadezhda Ulanovskaya, Personal interview, Israel, 1979. Her husband was an anarchist exile in Krasnoyarsk and knew Stalin personally.
193. Anton Antonov-Ovseenko, *Portret tirana*, p. 178.
194. For a detailed account, see Brackman, *The Secret File*, Chapter 11, "Iosif Dzhu . . . ? We Have Forgotten. It Is Very Important."
195. Ibid., p. 35.
196. *Russkoe slovo*, April 14, 1917, p. 3.
197. Letters from the Tolstoy Foundation, dated October 9, 1974, and December 9, 1974, report on the results of the search for Eremin's family in Chile. In the author's archive. In 1957, Eremin's two daughters came to New York with the intention of selling Eremin's papers; they found no buyer. After their return to Chile, they disappeared, most probably lured to Russia by a Soviet agent. I obtained this information when interviewing Isaac Don Levine.
198. P. E. Shchegolev, *Okhranniki i avanturisty*, pp. 138–49.
199. Ibid., p. 140.
200. *Leninsky sbornik*, vol. XIII, p. 271.
201. Maksakov, *Archiv revolutsii* . . . , p. 39.
202. V. I. Lenin, *Polnoe sobranie sochinenii*, vol. XXXI, pp. 79–82 and 521f. See also Elwood, p. 96, fn. 8.
203. Lenin's letter, dated March 17, 1917 (Old Style), in V. I. Lenin, *Polnoe sobranie sochinenii*, 5th ed., vol. XLIX, p. 423.
204. *Pravda*, no. 73, June 17, 1917, p. 3.
205. B. V. Nikitine, *The Fatal Years: Fresh Revelations on a Chapter of Underground History*, p. 24.
206. Lev Trotsky, *Stalin*, p. 211. See also I. Dubinsky-Mukhadze, *Ordzhonikidze*, p. 150.
207. Roy Medvedev, *Let History Judge*, p. 200f.
208. V. Maksakov, "Arkhiv revolutsii i vneshnei politiki XIX–XX vekov," p. 33.
209. All materials and Okhrana files of the Extraordinary Commission were delivered to Moscow at the end of 1919. In Stalin's file, see Chapter 17.
210. Bolsheviki, Introduction, p. ix.
211. Ibid.
212. Bolsheviki, Introduction, p. xxix.
213. Trotsky, *Stalin*, p. 222f.
214. For a detailed account, see Brackman, *The Secret File*, Chapter 12, "Vasily . . . So Far Unidentified."
215. Lev Trotsky, *Stalin*, p. 239.
216. N. N. Sukhanov, *The Russian Revolution*, p. 229f. Also Lev Trotsky, *Stalin*, p. 194.
217. Lev Trotsky, *Stalin*, p. 243f.
218. For a detailed account, see Brackman, *The Secret File*, Chapter 13, "The Grey Blur."
219. Ibid., Chapter 14, "The Red Terror."
220. *Proletarskaya revolutsiya*, no. 9, 1922, and David Shub, *Politicheskie deyateli rossii*, p. 218.
221. David Shub, *Politicheskie deyateli rossii*, p. 186, quoting *Rabochy soldat*, July 26, 1917.
222. Lev Trotsky, *Stalin*, p. 372.
223. Ibid., p. 375.
224. V. I. Lenin, *Polnoe sobranie sochinenii*, vol. XLV, p. 346.

225. Ibid., p. 107. Also Moshe Lewin, *Lenin's Last Struggle*, p. 96f.

226. Lev Trotsky, *Stalin*, p. 374.

227. Ibid., 376f.

228. See Elizabeth Lermolo, *Face of a Victim*, p. 136f.

229. For a detailed account, see Brackman, *The Secret File*, Chapter 15, "The Old Man Wants Poison."

230. Lev Trotsky, *Stalin*, p. 382.

231. Ibid., 419.

232. Ibid.

233. A. Avtorkhanov, *Zagadka smerty Stalina*, p. 50.

234. Personal interview with Pavel Litvinov (grandson of Maxim Litvinov) in Chappaqua, New York, 1975.

235. Yulian Semenov, in a conversation with the author in the presence of publisher I. Levkov, April 3, 1988.

236. Roy Medvedev, *Let History Judge*, p. 44.

237. See L. Horwitz, "Lenin and the Search for Jewish Roots," *New York Times*, August 5, 1992, p. A22. The author reports that archival documents about Lenin's grandfather were on display in Lenin's Museum in Moscow in June 1992. (The museum was closed in October 1993.) Soviet archivist V. V. Tsapen reported in the Spring 1992 edition of the journal *Arkhivy rodiny* (Native Land Archives) that he had found documents about Lenin's Jewish ancestry in Russian and Ukrainian archives. Lenin's grandfather, Israel Blank, was born in 1804 to Moshke and Miriam Blank and in 1820 applied for conversion to the Russian Orthodox Church to gain admission to the Medical-Surgical Academy, having changed his name to Alexander Dmitrievich Blank. He graduated in 1824. This information, suppressed by Stalin (who had found out about it earlier), was nevertheless known to Lenin's biographer Margarita Shaginian (Radio Liberty Committee, N.Y. Program no. 103/72) and is referred to by Louis Fisher in *The Life of Lenin*, p. 34.

238. I. V. Stalin, *Sochineniya*, vol. V, p. 308.

239. Dr. I. Frankel, editor, *Jerusalem University Collection of Documents on Soviet Jews*. See there M. I. Kalinin, *Yevrei-zemledeltsy v soyuze narodov SSSR*, p. 35f, and A. Bragin and M. Koltsov, *Sudba evreiskikh mass v sovetskom soyuze*, pp. 21–26.

240. Lev Trotsky, *Stalin*, p. 417.

241. V. I. Lenin, *Polnoe sobranie sochinenii*, vol. XLV, pp. 356–60.

242. Ibid., p. 345f.

243. Lev Trotsky, *Stalin*, p. 375f.

244. Isaac Deutscher, *The Prophet Unarmed*, p. 137.

245. Ibid., p. 258.

246. Isaac Deutscher, *Stalin: A Political Biography*, p. 307.

247. On Voroshilov's ties to the Okhrana, see Lev Trotsky, *Stalin*, p. 388f.

248. Ibid., p. 388.

249. For a detailed account, see Brackman, *The Secret File*, Chapter 16, "Jewish Origin."

250. Ibid., p. 41.

251. David Shub's notification of the discovery of Stalin's Okhrana file and his reaction to it are described in a letter by Isaac Don Levine to the author dated August 7, 1976. In the author's archive.

252. Personal interview with Isaac Don Levine. Levine's letter is in the author's archive.

253. Ibid., p. 374f.

254. Ibid.

255. Isaac Deutscher, *The Prophet Unarmed*, p. 279.

256. Ibid. See also Anton Antonov-Ovseenko, *Portret tirana*, p. 334.

257. Abram Belenky's sister, Emilia Solomonovna Belenkaya-Ravich, an architect, was the author's neighbor in a Moscow apartment building on Lobkovsky Street. She mentioned her brother and spoke of Dzerzhinsky's death.

258. A. Tishkov, *Dzerzhinsky*, p. 377f.

259. Ibid., p. 376f.

260. For a detailed account of the discovery of Stalin's Okhrana file, see Brackman, *The Secret File*, Chapter 17, "Stalin's Okhrana File Found in 1926."

261. Ibid., p. 390.

262. Oleg Moroz, "Poslednii diagnoz," *Literaturnaya gazeta*, September 28, 1988.

263. Taped personal interview with Vasily Rudich, 1976.

264. Sigmund Freud, "Psychoanalytic Notes Upon an Autobiographical Account of a Case of Paranoia (Dementia Paranoides)," *Collected Papers*, vol. 1, ch. 3.

265. Ibid. Oleg Moroz quotes from the journal *Vestnik znaniya*, no. 24, 1927.

266. Pravda # 90, April 18, 1928; See also H. Montgomery Hyde, *Stalin: The History of a Dictator,* New York, 1971, p. 279

267. H. Montgomery Hyde, *Stalin,* p. 279.

268. Lev Trotsky, *Stalin*, p. 392.

269. I. Frankel, editor, *Jerusalem University Collection of Documents on Soviet Jews*, pp. 98–136, citing *Tribuna*, no. 6, 1928, p. 1.

270. Ibid., quoting M. I. Kalinin, *Evrei v SSSR*, pp. 12–15.

271. Y. Larin, *Evrei i antisemitism v SSSR*, p. 183f; quoted in *Collection of Documents on Soviet Jews*, p. 102f.

272. Roy Medvedev, *Let History Judge*, p. 224f.

273. Lev Trotsky, *Stalin*, p. 399f.

274. For a detailed account of this period, see Brackman, *The Secret File*, Chapter 18, "Castrated Forces."

275. Roy Medvedev, *Let History Judge*, p. 140, quoting a Latvian Old Bolshevik, I. I. Sandler, who had been imprisoned in Varkuta.

276. Dmitry Volkogonov, "Demon revolutsii," *Pravda*, September 9, 1988.

277. Alexander Orlov, *The Secret History of Stalin's Crimes*, p. 192f.

278. Personal interview with I. P. Itskov, who knew Rabinovich, the assistant chief of the GPU Secret Political Department in the late 1920s. Also see Brackman, *The Secret File*, Chapter 26, describing how I. L. Stein, the assistant chief of the NKVD Secret Political Department, discovered Stalin's Okhrana file in Menzhinsky's office in 1936. Also see *Bulleten Oppositsii*, #10, April 1930, p. 1 on Rabinovich and Silov.

279. Alexander Orlov, *Tainaia istoriya stalinskikh prestuplenii*, pp. 191–93.

280. For a detailed account, see Brackman, *The Secret File*, Chapter 19, "Blumkin's Failed Mission."

281. Alexander Orlov, "The Sensational Secret Behind the Damnation of Stalin," *Life*, April 23, 1956. Orlov relates the 1936 discovery of Stalin's Okhrana file in Menzhinsky's office by the assistant chief of the Secret Political Department, I. L. Stein.

282. *Biulleten oppositsii*, vol. I, no. 10, 1930, p. 1.

283. H. Montgomery Hyde, *Stalin: The History of a Dictator*, p. 282.

284. Ibid., p. 114.

285. H. Montgomery Hyde, *Stalin*, pp. 281–83.

286. Roy Medvedev, *Let History Judge*, p. 119, quoting *Proletarskii prigovor nad vrediteliami-interventami* (record of court proceedings), Moscow, 1930, p. 32.

287. E. Lyons, *Stalin: The Tsar of All the Russias*, p. 370. Also quoted in H. Montgomery Hyde, *Stalin*, p. 280.

288. H. Montgomery Hyde, *Stalin*, p. 283.

289. Roy Medvedev, *Let History Judge*, pp. 132–37.

290. Ibid., p. 132f.

291. Ibid., p. 132.

292. Even the grammatical mistakes provide evidence of Stalin's authorship: the book contains the same type of mistakes found in Stalin's other writings, which are common to people who are not native speakers. There are improper usages of the word *starchestvo* instead of the correct *starost* to describe Sebriakova's advanced age and non-Russian-sounding phrases: *"proshedshee s nastoyashchim"*

instead of the correct "*proshloe s nastoyashchim*"; "*ludi odnogo poriadka*" instead of "*ludi odogno poshiba*"; and "*krepkie sviasi*" instead of "*prochnye sviasi.*"

293. I. V. Alekseev, *Provokator Anna Serebriakova*, p. 3f.

294. Ibid., p. 4.

295. Ibid., pp. 160–80.

296. Ibid., p. 175f.

297. See Sigmund Freud, "Psychoanalytic Notes upon an Autobiographical Account of a Case of Paranoia (Dementia Paranoides)," *Collected Papers*, vol. 1, ch. 3. See also Walter C. Langer, *The Mind of Adolf Hitler*, pp. 183–85.

298. I. V. Alekseev, *Provokator Anna Serebriakova*, p. 180.

299. P. E. Shchegolev, *Okhranniki i avanturisty*, pp. 138–49.

300. Roy Medvedev, *Let History Judge*, p. 319.

301. *Novoe Russkoe Slovo*, August 20, 2001, p. 17.

302. N. S. Khrushchev, *Khrushchev Remembers*, p. 40f. Khrushchev does not reveal if he ever found out that the letter had been written by Stalin.

303. Ibid., pp. 37–42.

304. Robert Conquest, *Stalin: Breaker of Nations*, p. 11.

305. *Poslednie novosti*, Paris, August 8, 1934.

306. Svetlana Allilueva, *Dvadtzat pisem k drugu*, p. 107f.

307. Aleksandr Orlov, *The Secret History of Stalin's Crimes*, p. 301f.

308. *Izvestia*, November 12, 1932.

309. Aleksandr Orlov, *Tainaya istoriia stalinskikh prestuplenii*, p. 306f.

310. For a detailed account of this period, see Brackman, *The Secret File*, Chapter 20, "I Know What Kind of Revolutionary You Are!"

311. Isaac Don Levine, "Stalin Suspected of Forcing Trials to Cover His Past," *American Journal*, March 3, 1938, front page.

312. Walter G. Krivitsky, *I Was Stalin's Agent*, p. 182.

313. Robert Conquest, *The Great Terror*, p. 52, quoting Boris Nikolaevsky, *Power and the Soviet Elite*, p. 29. Also Lev Razgon, "Nakonez."

314. Walter G. Krivitsky, *I Was Stalin's Agent*, p. 182.

315. *Komsomolskaya Pravda*, November 13, 1964.

316. *Izvestia*, August 31, 1964.

317. Arkady Vaksberg, *Kak zhivoi s zhivymi*.

318. Isaac Don Levine, *Stalin*, p. 337. Roy Medvedev, *Let History Judge*, p. 295. Medvedev quotes from papers in the archive of the Petrovsky family.

319. Roy Medvedev, *Let History Judge*, p. 295. Medvedev quotes from papers in the archive of the Petrovsky family.

320. Arkady Vaksberg, *Kak zhivoi s zhivymi*.

321. Lev Razgon, *Nakonez*.

322. Aleksandr Orlov, *The Secret History of Stalin's Crimes*, p. 259f.

323. For a detailed account, see Brackman, *The Secret File*, Chapter 22, "Why Did You Kill Such a Nice Man?"

324. Robert Conquest, *The Great Terror*, pp. 86–88.

325. Ibid., pp. 89–92.

326. Vitaly Rapoport and Yury Alekseev, *Izmena rodine*, p. 277. Also Robert Conquest, *The Great Terror*, p. 133, and Anton Ciliga, *The Russian Enigma*, p. 283.

327. For a detailed account, see Brackman, *The Secret File*, Chapter 22, "Why Did You Kill Such a Nice Man?"

328. Bulanov described this type of poisoning in his "confession" at the Bukharin show trial. See *Bukharin Trial*, pp. 480–85.

329. See Brackman, *The Secret File*, Chapter 26, for a detailed account of the discovery of Stalin's

Okhrana file.

330. For a detailed account, see Brackman, *The Secret File*, Chapter 22, "Why Did You Kill Such a Nice Man?"

331. Robert Conquest, *The Great Terror*, pp. 86–88.

332. Ibid., pp. 89–92.

333. Vitaly Rapoport and Yury Alekseev, *Izmena rodine*, p. 277. Also Robert Conquest, *The Great Terror*, p. 133, and Anton Ciliga, *The Russian Enigma*, p. 283.

334. *Krasny Arkhiv*, no. 68, 1935, p. 12.

335. Roy Medvedev, *Let History Judge*, p. 319.

336. Written testimony of Raphael Bagratuni in Isaac Don Levine's and in the author's archives. Bagratuni stated: "Svanidze gathered over many years materials in Soviet archives to compose a biography of Stalin. But this was a ruse. Svanidze, heading a group of loyal Georgians, destroyed documents in the Soviet archives that were compromising to Stalin under the pretext that they had been fabricated by Trotskyites. While he was shredding documents, Svanidze, backtracking in time (using the old orthography), reissued certain historical documents."

337. For a detailed account, see Brackman, *The Secret File*, Chapter 23, "The Stalin Institute."

338. Lev Trotsky, *Stalin*, p. xiv.

339. J. Perus, *Correspondance Romain Rolland et Maxime Gorki*, p. 320, quoting Romain Rolland's diary. See Michele Nike, *K voprosu o smerti M. Gorkogo*, p. 343f, fn. 90 and 93. Also P. Moroz, "Gorky v SSSR: Vstrechi s Gorkim," *Sotsialisticheskii vestnik*, 1954, no. 1, pp. 15–18.

340. The author has known Yevgeny Primakov well since they were classmates in the Moscow Oriental Institute (Arabic Division) in 1948–50.

341. N. Berberova, *Zheleznaya zhenshchina*, p. 269.

342. *Izvestia*, June 18, 1936, p. 2. See also Michele Nike, *K voprosu . . .*, pp. 344–46.

343. *Pravda*, June 19, 1936.

344. For a detailed account, see Brackman, *The Secret File*, Chapter 23, "Old Bear with a Ring in His Nose."

345. Aleksandr Orlov, "The Sensational Secret Behind the Damnation of Stalin," *Life*, April 23, 1956.

346. Robert Conquest, *The Great Terror*, p. 666. Also B. I. Nikolaevsky, "Letter of an Old Bolshevik," p. 64; Walter G. Krivitsky, *In Stalin's Secret Service*, p. 207.

347. *Zinoviev Trial*, Holtzman's testimony, pp. 155–78.

348. Brackman, *The Secret File*, Chapter 6.

349. Dewey Commission Report, *Not Guilty*, p. 85.

350. Aleksandr Orlov, *Tainaya istoriia stalinskikh prestuplenii*, pp. 66–69.

351. Ibid., p.165–169.

352. For a detailed account, see Brackman, *The Secret File*, Chapter 10.

353. Ibid., Chapter 26, "The Fatal Find in Menzhinsky's Office."

354. Vitaly Rapoport and Yury Alekseev, *Izmena rodine*, p. 359.

355. Aleksandr Orlov, "The Sensational Secret Behind the Damnation of Stalin," p. 35f.

356. Aleksandr Orlov, *Tainaya istoriia stalinskikh prestuplenii* p. 88.

357. Ibid., p. 88.

358. Robert Conquest, *The Great Terror*, p. 167f.

359. Ibid., p. 170.

360. Ibid., p. 335.

361. For a detailed account of the fabrication of the "Tukhachevsky Dossier," see Brackman, *The Secret File*, Chapter 27, "The Tukhachevsky Dossier."

362. Roy Medvedev, *Let History Judge*, p. 174.

363. Dewey Commission Report, *Not Guilty*, New York, 1937.

364. Aleksandr Orlov, *Tainaya istoriia stalinskikh prestuplenii*, p. 204.

365. Robert Conquest, *The Great Terror*, p. 259f.

366. Ibid., p. 260. Also personal interview with I. P. Itskov.

367. Ibid., p. 260f.
368. Robert Conquest, *The Great Terror*, p. 261, quoting the *Great Soviet Encyclopedia*, 2nd ed., under "Ordzhonikidze."
369. Gustav Hilger and Alfred G. Meyer, *The Incompatible Allies*, p. 271.
370. Aleksandr Orlov, "The Sensational Secret Behind the Damnation of Stalin."
371. Aleksandr Orlov, *Tainaya istoriia stalinskikh prestupleniy*, p. 253.
372. Walter Krivitsky, *I Was Stalin's Agent*, p. 237. Also *Dla vas*, no. 48, November 27, 1938, p. 12.
373. *Panorama*, no. 56, July 3, 1988, quoting from Paul Karell, *Hitler's War on Russia*.
374. Lev Nikulin, *Marshal Tukhachevsky*, pp. 189–94.
375. Robert Conquest, *The Great Terror*, p. 302.
376. *Panorama*, no. 56, July 3, 1988, quoting from Paul Karell.
377. Yury Kogan, the son of one of the executed top officers from General Uborevich's staff. Yury Kogan learned of this from one of his father's friends, who had survived the purge. Personal interview with Michael Meerson-Aksenov, a Russian Orthodox priest, in 1979 in Jerusalem. Personal interview with Viktor Shwartzburg in 1981 in Beersheva, Israel.
378. Walter G. Krivitsky, *In Stalin's Secret Service*, pp. 229–31.
379. *Bukharin Trial*, p. 582.
380. Brackman, *The Secret File*, Chapter 19.
381. Walter G. Krivitsky, *In Stalin's Secret Service*, pp. 229–31.
382. Boris Viktorov, "Zagovor krasnoi armii," *Pravda*, April 29, 1988.
383. I. Rachkov, *Iz vospominaniy o Y. B. Gamarnike*, p. 69.
384. P. Yakir has heard of Tukhachevsky having being interrogated by Stalin in the camps. The author heard of it in the Norilsk camp from an inmate, the former NKVD officer A. Y. Tsynman.
385. Lev Nikulin, *Marshal Tukhachevsky*, pp. 189–94.
386. Unpublished memoirs of Olga Shatunovskaya, an Old Bolshevik and a member of a Party committee that investigated Stalin's crimes during the Khrushchev era. Shatunovskaya's recollections were related by Vasily Rudich in a taped interview with the author. In the author's archive. Also, Rachkov, *Iz vospominaniy o Y.B. Gamarnike*, pp. 69–72, and Vitaly Rapoport and Yury Alekseev, *Izmena rodine*, p. 300.
387. I. Rachkov, *Iz vospominaniy o Y. B. Gamarnike*, p. 69f.
388. *Pravda*, June 1, 1937, p. 4.
389. Walter Krivitsky, *In Stalin's Secret Service*, p. 232.
390. L. Gaglov and I. Selishchev, *Komissary*.
391. I. Viktorov, "Zagovor krasnoi armii."
392. Ibid.
393. Ibid.
394. The award citation, dated June 11, 1937, and signed by Zinovy Katsnelson, is among the papers of the author's father Yakov I. Brakhtman, a former prisoner in the Dmitrov camp, who received the award on this day.
395. Genady Zhavoronkov, "I edinozhdy ne solgavshiy," *Moskovskie novosti*, April 10, 1988. Also Iosif Kosinsky, "Za chto borolis," *Novoe Russkoe slovo*, April 22, 1988.
396. See Brackman, *The Secret File*, Chapter 10, for Colonel Eremin's cover letter, dated June 11, 1912, with attached *Spravka bez no. 5/18*, p. 7.
397. Aleksandr Orlov, *Tainaya istoria . . .*, p. 262.
398. Yulia Piatnitskaya, *Dnevnik zheny bolshevika*, p. 172. Also Zhavoronkov, "I edinozhdy ne solgavshiy," and Kosinsky, "Za chto borolis."
399. Roy Medvedev, *Let History Judge*, p. 244f.
400. Alvin D. Coox, "L'Affaire Lyushkov," *Soviet Studies*, January 1968, p. 62.
401. Personal interview with R. S. Osinina, widow of Lyushkov's assistant Osinin.
402. Alvin D. Coox, "L'Affaire Lyushkov," p. 408.
403. Personal interview with General T. V. Gerbov, a Russian émigré in Kharbin who knew

Golovachev personally, in Nyack, New York, in 1975. In the author's archive.

404. Russianov's son, who had emigrated to Australia, sent this package of Okhrana material to Isaac Don Levine. It was examined by the author in Levine's archive at his Virginia farm.
405. N. M. Ulanovskaya spoke in a taped interview about her husband, Soviet intelligence officer A. Ulanovsky, who met Stalin during his exile in Yeniseysk. She recalled that Stalin was known among the exiles for visiting the Okhrana office there.
406. Aleksandr Orlov, *Tainaya istoriia stalinskikh prestuplenyi*, p. 223.
407. Isaac Don Levine received information about the file from Wolf and Klement. Their subsequent murders convinced him that their claims were authentic. Personal interview with Isaac Don Levine in Chappaqua, New York, in 1976.
408. J. Dziak, *Chekisty* . . . , p. 99f. Also Stephen Schwartz, *Intellectuals and Assassins: Annals of Stalin's Killerati.*
409. Aleksandr Orlov, *Tainaya istoria* . . ., p. 224.
410. S. Rozhdestvensky, "Pokhishchenie generala Millera," *Novoe russkoe slovo*, May 19, 1979.
411. Stephen Schwartz, *Intellectuals and Assassins: Annals of Stalin's Killerati*, pp. 3 and 29–31. The first reports about Max Eitingon's ties to Skoblin and Plevitskaya appeared in the Russian-language émigré newspaper *Vozrozhdenie*, Paris, December 9, 1938, and in an earlier unsigned Russian-language manuscript, dated December 1937. See J. Dziak, *Chekisty* . . ., p. 99, fn. 79.
412. Robert Conquest, *The Great Terror*, p. 444. Also Pavel Antokolsky, *Novy mir*, no. 4, 1966. Also Marina Tsvetaeva, *Izbrannye sochineniya*, introduction. Efron is listed among prisoners executed in October 1941.
413. *Bukharin Trial.*
414. For a detailed account, see Brackman, *The Secret File*, Chapter 28, "The Forgery That Tells the Truth."
415. Aleksandr Orlov, *Tainaya* . . ., p. 228–32.
416. Isaac Don Levine, *American Journal*, March 3, 1938. The article's subtitle reads: "Levine Probed Reports of Secret File Proving Red Leader Tsarist Spy."
417. Isaac Don Levine in a conversation with the author in 1976 in Chappaqua, New York.
418. Aleksandr Orlov, *Tainaya* . . ., pp. 144–49.
419. *Bukharin Trial*, p. 478–99.
420. See Robert Conquest, *The Great Terror*, pp. 561–62, quoting from *Bukharin Trial*, pp. 622–23.
421. Ibid., p. 666. Stalin's deep distrust of Dostoyevsky's insight into a certain type of mind is indicated by his banning Dostoyevsky's works.
422. For a detailed account, see Brackman, *The Secret File*, Chapter 29, "The Staged 'Trifle.'"
423. Walter Duranty, *The Kremlin and the People*, p. 37.
424. Ibid., p. 55.
425. Joseph E. Davies, *Mission to Moscow*, vol. 1, p. 39.
426. Robert Conquest, *The Great Terror*, p. 673.
427. *Krasny arkhiv*, vol. 2 (105). Ogiz, Chief Archive Administration of the NKVD of the USSR, 1941, p. 30f.
428. Roy Medvedev, *Let History Judge*, p. 200f.
429. The author has heard these rumors from various people.
430. Robert Conquest, *The Great Terror*, p. 617f.
431. Alvin D. Coox, "L'Affaire Lyushkov," *Soviet Studies*, January 1968, p. 411.
432. Ibid.
433. V. Mikhailov and V. Bondarenko, *Kurier*, no. 58, June 3–9, 1993, pp. 1 and 24.
434. Alvin D. Coox, "L'Affaire Lyushkov," p. 400, citing *Pravda* report on Lyushkov dated December 20, 1937.
435. Ibid., p. 413, fn. 21.
436. R. S. Osinina, who was earlier divorced from Gregory Osinin-Vinnitsky, provided this information in a personal interview with the author in Haifa, Israel, in 1979. She was an aunt of Vitaly

Svechinsky. In the author's archive.

437. Roy Medved, *Let History Judge*, p. 323.
438. Brackman, *The Secret File*, Chapter 28.
439. The author examined this package at Isaac Don Levine's farm in Waldorf, Virginia. It is in Levine's archive.
440. Brackman, *The Secret File*, Chapter 34.
441. Aleksandr Orlov, *Tainaya storiia stalinskikh prestuplenii*, p. 13.
442. Ibid., pp. 309–11.
443. Personal interview with I. P. Itskov, a lawyer who represented Evgenia Alliluev in her "rehabilitation case." See also Svetlana Allilueva, *Twenty Letters to a Friend*, p. 182f.
444. Aleksandr Orlov, *Tainaya storiia stalinskikh prestuplenii*, p. 13.
445. Aleksandr Orlov, *The Secret History of Stalin's Crimes*, p. 240.
446. Aleksandr Orlov, "The Sensational Secret Behind the Damnation of Stalin," *Life*, April 23, 1956, pp. 34–44.
447. H. Montgomery Hyde, *Stalin: The History of a Dictator*, p. 377.
448. Robert Conquest, *The Great Terror*, pp. 348–50.
449. Roy Medvedev, *Let History Judge*, p. 140, fn. 23. See also Volkogonov's article on Trotsky, "The Demon of the Revolution," published in *Pravda*, September 9, 1988, p. 4.
450. See Brackman, *The Secret File*, Chapter 36, for a detailed account of the murder of Mikhoels in 1948. For the murder of Vissarion, see Chapter 4 of the same title.
451. Ibid., p. 480f.
452. *Pravda*, August 24, 1940.
453. For a detailed account, see Brackman, *The Secret File*, Chapter 32, "The Murder of Trotsky."
454. Robert Conquest, *The Great Terror*, p. 603.
455. Boris Shragin, personal interview in Chappaqua, New York, in 1976.
456. Personal interview with Felix Svetlov in New York, August 4, 1991. Also personal interview with Vladimir Gutkin in New York in 1993. Gutkin worked with Louis Mercader in Moscow. In the author's archive.
457. Lev Trotsky, *Stalin*, p. 421.
458. *Biulletin oppositsii*, vol. 65, 1938. Quoted in Volkogonov, *Demon revolutsii*.
459. J. Pilsudski, *Rok 1920 z povody pracy M. Tuchaczewskiego, 'Pochod za Wisle.'* Tukhachevsky's Polish "origin" was the reason he was appointed commander of the Soviet forces as they advanced on Warsaw during the 1920 Soviet-Polish war. Also, V. Primakov, in his "last word" (which was almost certainly penned by Stalin), referred to the non-Russian ethnic origin of his fellow defendants at the June 11, 1937, trial. (Brackman, *The Secret File*, Chapter 28.)
460. Robert Conquest, *The Great Terror*, p. 582.
461. R. Coulondre, *De Staline à Hitler*, p. 165.
462. *Documents on German Foreign Policy, 1919–1945*, series D, vol. VII, pp. 225–29.
463. Adam B. Ulam, *Stalin*, p. 508, quoting R. J. Sontag and J. S. Beddie, eds., *Nazi-Soviet Relations, 1939–1941: Documents from the Archives of the German Foreign Office*, p. 2.
464. *Documents on International Affairs, 1928–1963*, vol. II, 1939–1946, p. 446.
465. *International Military Tribunal*, vol. XXXVII, p. 550.
466. Ibid., p. 510.
467. The secret protocol, including the map and Stalin's signature, was published by the Yeltsin government. See the *New York Times*, August 19, 1989, pp. A1–5.
468. *Documents on German Foreign Policy, 1919–1945*, series D, vol. VII, pp. 225–29.
469. Alan Bullock, *A Study in Tyranny*, p. 531.
470. Hitler's Table Talk—Hitlers Tischgespreche in Führerhauptquartier, 1941-2, edited by Dr. Henry Picker, Bonn 1951
471. Adam Ulam, *Stalin*, p. 512.
472. Albert Speer, "Nazi Invasion of Poland: September 1, 1939," *New York Times*, August 31, 1979, p.

A23.

473. N. S. Khrushchev, *Khrushchev Remembers*, p. 128.

474. Galina Vishenevskaya, Bolshoi Theater singer and the wife of cellist Mstislav Rostropovich, states in her recollections that in Stalin's box "there was always a big bowl of hard-boiled eggs on a table." See the excerpt from her autobiography, *My Russia, My Love*, in the *New York Post*, September 26, 1984, p. 31.

475. Oleg Moroz, "Poslednii diagnoz," *Literatura gazeta*, September 28, 1988.

476. *New York Times*, October 15, 1992, pp. 1 and 8.

477. For a detailed account of the murder of Polish prisoners-of-war, see Brackman, *The Secret File*, Chapter 33.

478. *Documents on German Foreign Policy, 1918–1945*, series D, vol. VIII, p. 160.

479. For a detailed account, see Brackman, *The Secret File*, Chapter 34, "The War and the October 1941 Massacre."

480. Solomon F. Bloom, *Commentary*, May 1957, p. 417.

481. Robert G. L. Waite, *The Psychopathic God: Adolf Hitler*, p. 76.

482. Solomon F. Bloom, *Commentary*, May 1957, p. 417.

483. *Nazi-Soviet Relations, 1939–1941*, pp. 234–37.

484. Ibid., p. 221f.

485. Ibid., pp. 247–54.

486. Ibid.

487. Ibid., p. 258f.

488. Ibid., p. 258f.

489. G. Hilger and A. Meyer, *The Incompatible Allies*, p. 323.

490. Alan Bullock, *A Study in Tyranny*, p. 622.

491. George E. Kirk, *A Short History of the Middle East*, pp. 194–99.

492. Ibid.

493. *Documents on German Foreign Policy, 1918–1945*, series D, vol. XI, p. 899.

494. Ibid., vol. XII, p. 126.

495. H. Montgomery Hyde, *Stalin: The History of a Dictator*, p. 426.

496. For a detailed account, see Brackman, *The Secret File*, Chapter 34.

497. *Documents on German Foreign Policy, 1918–1945*, series D, vol. XII, p. 870.

498. G. Hilger and A. Meyer, *The Incompatible Allies*, p. 336.

499. H. Montgomery Hyde, *Stalin*, p. 435, quoting Khrushchev's "Special Report to the Twentieth Party Congress" (his secret speech).

500. Khrushchev's secret speech.

501. H. Montgomery Hyde, *Stalin*, p. 438f.

502. Albert Speer, *Inside the Third Reich*, p. 306.

503. Roy Medvedev, *Let History Judge*, p. 310.

504. I. P. Itskov in a taped interview with the author.

505. Sir Ernest Llewellyn Woodward, *British Foreign Policy in the Second World War*, p. 152f.

506. Robert E. Sherwood, *The White House Papers of Harry L. Hopkins*, vol. I, pp. 343–45.

507. A. N. Kolesnik, "Voennoplennyi starshii leitenant Yakov Dzhugashvili," *Voenno-istoricheskii zhurnal*, Moscow, December 1988.

508. Albert Speer, *Inside the Third Reich*, p. 306.

509. A. N. Kolesnik, "Voennoplennyi starshii leitenant Yakov Dzhugashvili."

510. *New York Times*, February 19, 1968, p. 7.

511. Svetlana Allilueva, *Dvadtsat pisem k drugu*, p. 151f. See also Ya. L. Sukhotin, "Iosif Vissarionovich bolshoe gnezdo . . . ," *Novoe Russkoe Slovo*, April 8–9, 1996.

512. A recollection of Nadine Brackman, the author's wife, who was a classmate of Gulia's in the second through sixth grades. She remembers that Yulia and her daughter Gulia lived in the secret police building on Bolshoi Komsomolsky Lane, not far from the Lubyanka. Gulia attended School

no. 644 on nearby Armiansky Lane. In the morning, a maid would accompany her to school, carrying her books and notes. After classes, the maid escorted her home. The girl was a loner. She hardly talked to her classmates and usually stood alone near a corridor window during breaks between classes. In 1950, after finishing the sixth grade, Gulia left the school and, according to gossip, enrolled in a special art school.

513. Beatrice Farnsworth, *William C. Bullitt and the Soviet Union*, pp. 3 and 173.
514. Ibid.
515. Winston Churchill, *The Second World War*, vol. III, pp. 405 and 411.
516. Robert Sherwood, *The White House Papers of Harry L. Hopkins*, vol. I, p. 392.
517. V. A. Chalikova, "Arkhivnyi yunosha," *Neva*, October 1988, p. 153.
518. Roy Medvedev, *Let History Judge*, p. 311. Also Khrushchev's secret speech.
519. The "J" letter is on file in Isaac Don Levine's archive, and a copy of it is also in the author's archive. This confidential letter, dated July 17, 1956, was from a high State Department official, who signed the letter "J," to Isaac Don Levine. The letter referred to two secret cables, dated November 26, 1941, and January 5, 1942, from the German mission in Shanghai to the German foreign office in Berlin. The cables were discovered in File AA/18 of the Alexandria repository of captured German World War II documents.
520. Ibid.
521. H. Montgomery Hyde, *Stalin*, p. 459f.
522. N. S. Khrushchev, *Khrushchev Remembers*, pp. 203–05.
523. Ibid.
524. A. Antonov-Ovseenko, "Katyn," *Novoe russkoe slovo*, May 27, 1988, p. 20.
525. Stanislaw Kot, *Conversations with the Kremlin and Dispatches from Russia*, p. 106.
526. Ibid., p. 140.
527. V. A. Chalikova, "Arkhivnyi yunosha," *Neva*, October 1988, p. 153.
528. A. Antonov-Ovseenko, "Katyn."
529. Lord Moran, *Winston Churchill: The Struggle for Survival 1940–1965*, p. 141f.
530. Ibid.
531. Frances Perkins, *The Roosevelt I Knew*, p. 70f.
532. Lord Moran, *Winston Churchill: The Struggle for Survival 1940–1965*, pp. 133–35.
533. Albert Speer, *Inside the Third Reich*, p. 390.
534. Ibid., 390f.
535. Ibid., 128.
536. Arthur D. Morse, *While Six Million Died*, p. 290.
537. *New York Times*, December 28, 1991, p. 6.
538. Ibid.
539. Ibid.
540. I. P. Itskov, taped interview with the author in New York in 1989. Itskov investigated the murder of his former wife, Bronislava, and searched the Lubyanka archives, as well as the records of the Moscow crematorium. He was also interested in the fate of Raoul Wallenberg, and in doing his research kept Wallenberg in mind. He came to the conclusion that Wallenberg was poisoned in 1947 and had been cremated. The author remembers Dr. A. L. Smoltsov, a man of medium height, about forty years old, with a very low forehead and cold, small black eyes, who made regular visits to Lubyanka prison cells.
541. "Churchill, Stalin Made Polish Deal," *New York Times*, August 5, 1974.
542. The Earl of Avon, *The Reckoning*, p. 513.
543. I. V. Stalin, *Stalin's Correspondence with Churchill, Attlee, Roosevelt, and Truman 1941–1945*, vol. II, p. 214.
544. H. Montgomery Hyde, *Stalin*, p. 331.
545. G. K. Zhukov, *Vospominaniya i razmyshleniya*, p. 631f.
546. Erich Kuby, *The Russians and Berlin, 1945*, p. 175.

547. Winston Churchill, *The Second World War*, vol. II, p. 903.
548. G. K Zhukov, "Bitva za Berlin," *Voenno-istoricheskii zhurnal*, June 1965.
549. James MacGregor Burns, *Roosevelt: The Soldier of Freedom, 1940–1945*, p. 68.
550. Winston Churchill, *The Second World War*, vol. VI, p. 552.
551. James F. Byrnes, *Speaking Frankly*, p. 263.
552. Ibid., 76.
553. V. Mikhailiv and V. Bondarenko, "Zhizn i smert komissara Lyushkova," *Kurier*, June 3, 1993. See also Alvin D. Coox, "L'Affaire Lyushkov," *Soviet Studies*, January 1968, p. 418; also A. Antonov-Ovseenko, *Portret tirana*, p. 208f.
554. *Times* (London), March 6, 1946.
555. *Pravda*, March 13, 1946.
556. *Daily Herald*, London, August 16, 1946.
557. H. Montgomery Hyde, *Stalin*, p. 555, citing Field Marshal Montgomery, *Memoirs*, p. 445.
558. Harry S. Truman, *Years of Trial and Hope, 1946–1953*, p. 111.
559. Milovan Djilas, *Conversations with Stalin*, pp. 157–61.
560. *Forward*, May 10, 2002, #337.
561. G. B. Kostyrenko, *Tainaya Politika Stalina*, p. 240.
562. Y. A. Gilboa, *The Black Years of Soviet Jewry*, pp. 42–56.
563. *Pravda*, August 25, 1941.
564. Ibid.
565. S. Redlich, *Propaganda and Nationalism in Wartime Russia: The Jewish Anti-Fascist Committee in the USSR, 1941–1948*.
566. G. B. Kostyrenko, *Tainaya Politika Stalina*, p. 236.
567. Personal interview with Boris Guriel, director of Chaim Weizman's archive, in Tel-Aviv in 1969. In the author's archive.
568. George E. Kirk, *A Short History of the Middle East*, pp. 202–06.
569. Personal interview with Mordechai Oren in Israel in 1969. In the author's archive.
570. Y. A. Gilboa, *The Black Years of Soviet Jewry*, pp. 42–56.
571. Samuel Volkovich, interview with the author, Tel-Aviv, 1969. In the author's archive. See also Y. A. Gilboa, *The Black Years of Soviet Jewry*, pp. 64–65.
572. Personal interview with Samuel Tornopoler, Tel-Aviv, February 1969. In the author's archive.
573. Ibid.
574. Personal interview with David Ben-Gurion, Sde-Boker and Tel-Aviv, 1969. In the author's archive. See also Ben-Gurion's letter to Y. A. Gilboa, dated January 31, 1967, in Y. A. Gilboa, *The Black Years of Soviet Jewry*, p. 352, fn. 20.
575. George E. Kirk, *A Short History of the Middle East*, pp. 202–06.
576. Edward R. Stettinius, Jr., *Roosevelt and the Russians*, p. 278.
577. "V komissii Politburo TK KPSS," *Izvestia TK KPSS*, January 1989, Protocol no. 7, December 29, 1988, p. 37.
578. Yakov Aizenshtat, *O podgotovke Stalinym genotsida evreev*, p. 38.
579. "V komissii Politburo TK KPSS," *Izvestia TK KPSS*, January 1989, Protocol no. 7, December 29, 1988.
580. Personal interview with Vasily Rudich. In the author's archive. See also N. S. Khrushchev, *Khrushchev Remembers*, p. 261f. Vasily Rudich related the testimony of Olga Shatunovskaya, a member of the Special Commission of the Presidium of the Central Committee. She, together with the Special Commission's chairman N. M. Shvernik; the general prosecutor of the USSR, R. A. Rudenko; the chairman of the KGB, A. N. Shelepin; and the director of the Central Committee Section on Administrative Organs, N. R. Mironov, interrogated Politburo member G. M. Malenkov, who described Stalin's order to murder Mikhoels.
581. A. Borshchagovsky, *Obviniaetsia krov*, pp. 5–8, and Yakov Aizenshtat, *O podgotovke. . . ,* pp. 39–41, quoting a report by Beria, dated April 2, 1953, to the Presidium of the Party Central Committee.

582. Ibid. Also Robert Conquest, *Stalin: Breaker of Nations*, p. 306.

583. Svetlana Allilueva, *Only One Year*, p. 154.

584. The author and his classmate Mikhail Margulis were present at the funeral and heard the rumor. Two years later, Soviet movie director Mikhail Kalik was arrested and accused of stating that Mikhoels had been murdered by MGB agents.

585. Svetlana Allilueva, *Only One Year*, p. 154.

586. Personal interview with Lidia Shatunovskaya and Lev Tumerman, Rehavot, Israel, 1975. In the author's archive.

587. Personal interview with Natalia and Alexander Rodovsky in Haifa, Israel, 1979. In the author's archive.

588. Personal interview with Lidia Shatunovskaya and Lev Tumerman, Rechavot, Israel, 1973.

589. Henry Kamm, "Inquiry on Jan Masaryk's Death in 1948 is Demanded in Prague," *New York Times*, April 3, 1968. Also C. L. Sulzberger, "Foreign Affairs: Murder Will Out," *New York Times*, April 17, 1968.

590. Personal interview with David Ben-Gurion, Sde-Boker and Tel-Aviv, Israel, 1969.

591. G. V. Kostyrchenko, *Tainaya politika Stalina*, p. 418.

592. Personal interview with author Saul Avigur, Tel-Aviv, Israel, 1969. Personal interview with Matetiahu Shmulevich, Jaffa, 1969. Both interviews in the author's archive.

593. Boris Guriel, quoting Weizman's diary. Personal interview, Tel-Aviv, 1969. In the author's archive.

594. Personal interview with Samuel Mikunis, Jerusalem, Israel, 1969. In the author's archive.

595. Personal interview with David Lifshitz in Tel-Aviv, Israel, 1969. In the author's archive. Personal interview with Matetiahu Shmulevich in Jaffa, Israel, 1969. In the author's archive; G. S. Nikitina, *Gosudarstvo Izrail*, p. 58f., fn. 74.

596. Personal interview with David Lifshitz, interview with the author, Tel-Aviv, Israel, 1969. In the author's archive.

597. G. S. Nikitina, *Gosudarstvo Israel*, pp. 58–59, note 74.

598. Personal interview with Matetiahu Shmulevich, Jaffa, Israel, 1969. In the author's archive.

599. Personal interview with David Lifshitz, Israel, 1969. In the author's archive.

600. The author was a cellmate of Goldman's in Lubyanka prison in the summer of 1950.

601. Ekaterina Solomonova, "Rely Only on Yourself," *Vesti*, September 18, 1997, p. 6.

602. Personal letter to the author, dated January 25, 2005.

603. A. Vaisberg, "Evreisky antifashistsky komitet u M. A. Suslov," *Zveniya-istorikeskii almanakh*, Moscow, 1991, pp. 535–54.

604. Ibid., p. 546.

605. "V komissii Politburo TK KPSS," *Isvestia TK KPSS*, January 1989. Protocol no. 7, dated December 29, 1988. See also Arkady Vaksberg, *Stalin Against the Jews*, pp. 198–202.

606. Ibid.

607. Personal interview with Anna and Boris Glick, inhabitants of Davydkovo and victims of the exile order from Davydkovo. New York, 1967. In the author's archive.

608. Interview with Mikhail Meerson-Aksenov, the son of Georgy Meerson. New York, 1989. In the author's archive.

609. Anton Antonov-Ovseenko, *Portret Tirana*, p. 325.

610. S. Allilueva, *Dvadtzat pisem k drugu*, p. 150.

611. Nikita S. Khrushchev, *Khrushchev Remembers*, p. 264 and pp. 258–69. Also Nikita S. Khrushchev, *Khrushchev Remembers: The Last Testament*, pp. 78 and 150.

612. S. Tsirulnik, "'Ispoved' na pepeleshche," *Vremia i my*, no. 42, June 1979, pp. 186–87. Complete text of the article, pp. 170–208.

613. Aleksandr Orlov, *The Secret History of Stalin's Crimes*, p. 313.

614. S. Tsirulnik, "'Ispoved' na pepeleshche," *Vremia i my*, no. 42, June 1979, pp. 186–87. Complete text of the article, pp. 170–208.

615. Personal interview with Aaron Cohen, Haifa, Israel, 1969. In the author's archive.

616. *Evreiskaya Entsiklopediya* ("Jewish Encyclopedia" in Russian), St. Petersburg, 1912–1913, Vol. VI, pp. 808–09.
617. M. Gorbanevsky, "Tovarishch Stalin vy bolshoi ucheny," *Nedelia*, no. 45, November 5–11, 1990, p. 4.
618. Ibid.
619. Roy Medvedev, *Let History Judge*, pp. 332–33.
620. Nikita Khrushchev's secret speech. Also, *Khrushchev Remembers*, pp. 282–86.
621. Boris Nikolaievsky, "The Strange Death of Mikhail Ryumin," *New Leader*, October 4, 1954, pp. 15–18. See also John J. Dziak, *Chekisty*, p. 127.
622. Svetlana Allilueva, *Only One Year*, p. 386.
623. Nikita S. Khrushchev, *Khrushchev Remembers*, p. 312.
624. Personal interview with Nugzar Sharia, Chappaqua, New York, 1972.
625. Personal interview with I. P. Itskov, New York, 1988. In the author's archive.
626. Boris Nikolaievsky, "The Strange Death of Mikhail Ryumin," *New Leader*, October 4, 1954, pp. 15–18. See also John J. Dziak, *Chekisty*, p. 127.
627. Iakov Iakovlevich Etinger, *Eto Nevozmozhno Zabyt*. Ves Mir: 2001, p. 91.
628. Ibid. 95–96
629. Ibid. 95.
630. G. V. Kostyrchenko, *Tainaya politika Stalina*, Moscow, "Mezhdunarodnye otnosheniya," 2001, p. 660.
631. Ibid., 663.
632. Krishna P. S. Menon, *The Flying Troika*, p. 29. Also H. Montgomery Hyde, *Stalin*, p. 591.
633. Hans Frank, memoirs, quoted in Robert G. L. Waite, *Afterward*; and in Walter C. Langer, *The Mind of Adolf Hitler*, p. 234. Also Andor Klay, quoting novelist Hans Habe, *Newsweek*, October 3, 1977, p. 14.
634. Quoted in Robert G. L. Waite, *The Psychopathic God: Adolf Hitler*, p. 222.
635. Ibid., 223.
636. Sigmund Freud, *The Wolf-Man*, pp. 181–83. On fear of castration, see Sigmund Freud, *Moses and Monotheism*, p. 99.
637. Sigmund Freud, *Moses and Monotheism*, p. 99.
638. Walter C. Langer, *The Mind of Adolf Hitler*, p. 151.
639. Adolf Hitler, *Mein Kampf*, p. 38; also Robert G. L. Waite, *The Psychopathic God: Adolf Hitler*, pp. 162–68; also Walter C. Langer, *The Mind of Adolf Hitler*, pp. 142–45.
640. Robert G. L. Waite, *The Psychopathic God: Adolf Hitler*, p. 227.
641. Ibid.
642. Brackman, *The Secret File*, Chapter 1.
643. Hervey Cleckley, M. D. *The Mask of Sanity*, p. 259. Dr. Cleckley cites two sources in support of this opinion: George W. Henry, *Essentials of Psychiatry*, Williams and Wilkins Co. Baltimore, 1938 and William Sadler, *Theory and Practice of Psychiatry*, The C. V. Mosby Co., St. Louis, 1936, pp. 880–85.
644. Vladimir Maximov, dissident Soviet writer, told this story to Rita Lipson at New York University.
645. Boris Ilizarov, *Novoe Russkoe Slovo*, August 20, 2001.
646. Iakov Iakovlevich Etinger, *Eto Nevozmozhno Zabyt*, Ves Mir, 2001, p. 101.
647. Sigmund Freud, *Moses and Monotheism*, pp. 115.
648. Ibid., 115–16.
649. Ibid., 116.
650. Ernest Jones, *Psycho-Myth, Psycho-History*, Vol. II, Chapter XII, "The God Complex," pp. 263–64.
651. I. V. Stalin, *Sochineniya*, vol. XIII, p. 28. Also *Pravda*, November 30, 1936.
652. Isaac Deutscher, *Stalin: A Political Biography*, p. 91.
653. "V komissii Politburo TK KPSS," *Izvestia TK KPSS*, January 1989. Protocol no. 7, dated December 29, 1988.
654. Nikita Khrushchev's secret speech.

655. Personal interview with Israeli diplomat Yakov Yanai in Tel Aviv, Israel, 1971. In the author's archive. Yanai met a Soviet general in a prison camp who told him about Stalin's interest in the building of a long-range bomber that would enable the attack of the U.S. with nuclear weapons.

656. Personal interview with Mordekhai Oren, Israel, 1969.

657. Svetlana Alliluyeva, *Only One Year*, p. 392.

658. Iakov Iakovlevich Etinger, *Eto nevozmozno zabyt*, Ves Mir, Moscow, 2001, p. 136.

659. Personal interview with Nugzar Sharia, Sag Harbor, New York, 1971.

660. *Evreiskaya Entsiklopedia*, vol. IX, pp. 938–40.

661. *Pravda*, January 18, 1953.

662. Yuri Druzhnikov, "Saga o Pavlike Morozove," *Strana i mir*, no. (2) 44, March–April 1988, p. 119.

663. Zenon Pozniak and Evgeny Shygalev, "Kuropaty—doroga smerti," *Novoe russkoe slovo*, June 24, 1988, p. 6. Also Yury Turin, "S odnoi storony, s drugoi storony," *Ogonek*, no. 39, Moscow, 1988.

664. Personal interview with Yakov and Diana Vinkovetsky (Pavel Litvinov's friends) in Chappaqua, New York, 1975. They took part in this censoring operation.

665. Roy Medvedev, *Let History Judge*, p. 508.

666. Yakov Aizenshtat, *O podgotovke Stalinym. . . .*, p. 79. Also, Z. Sheinis, *Grozila deportatsiya*.

667. A. Antonov-Ovseenko, *Portret Tirana*, p. 325f. Also Medvedev, *Let History Judge*, p. 496, and interview with Boris Zubok, who saw the Novaya Zemlia barracks. Zubok's interview with the author in Chappaqua, New York, 1975.

668. Z. Sheinis, *Provokatsiya veka*, Moscow, 1994, quoting the record of the testimony of the Secretary of the Deportation Commission, N. N. Poliakov.

669. Yakov Aizenshtat, *O podgotovke Stalinym . . .*, pp. 70–74.

670. Ibid.

671. *Pravda*, January 13, 1953.

672. Ibid.

673. Robert Conquest, *Stalin: Breaker of Nations*, p. 306.

674. Personal interview with Nugzar Sharia, Sag Harbor, New York, 1972. Sharia told the author about the recollections of his uncle Peter Sharia, one of the arrested "Mingrelian bandits" to whom Beria had shown the files.

675. Ibid. Nugzar Sharia recalled the account of the Hero of the Soviet Union Meliton Kantaria, a Mingrelian. Also *New York Times*, December 31, 1993, p. A24.

676. G. V. Kostyrchenko, *Tainaya politika Stalina*, Moscow, "Mezhdunarodnye otnosheniya," 2001, p. 656.

677. The author witnessed incidents of Jewish prisoners being attacked in the Norilsk prison camp by criminal inmates.

678. Roy Medvedev, *Let History Judge*, p. 495f.

679. Ibid.

680. Ibid.

681. Arkady Vaksberg, *Stalin Against the Jews*, p. 272. See also Nikita S. Khrushchev, *Khrushchev Remembers*, p. 308.

682. Personal interview with Lidia Shatunovskaya, Rechavot, Israel, 1973. She was one of the prisoners in Vladimir Central.

683. Milovan Djilas, *Conversations with Stalin*, p. 160f.

684. A. Antonov-Ovseenko, *Portret Tirana*, p. 327.

685. A. N. Kolesnik, "Glavny telokhronitel vozhdia," *Voenno-istoricheski zhurnal*, no. 12, 1989, pp. 85–92.

686. Personal interview with I. P. Itskov, New York, 1988.

687. Iakov Iakovlevich Etinger, *Eeto Nevozmozhno Zabyt*, Ves Mir, 2001, p. 122–23.

688. Ibid.

689. Ibid.

690. Ibid.

691. G. V. Kostyrchenko, *Tainaya politika Stalina*, Moscow, "Mezhdunarodnye otnosheniya," 2001, p.

681.
692. Ibid., 678.
693. A. Antonov-Ovseenko, *Portret Tirana*, p. 325. Also Roy Medvedev, *Let History Judge*, pp. 495–97.
694. Nikita Khrushchev, *Khrushchev Remembers*, p. 243.
695. *Pravda*, February 14, 1953, p. 1.
696. Svetlana Allilueva, *Only One Year*, p. 155.
697. A. Antonov-Ovseenko, *Portret Tirana*, p. 326.
698. Personal interview with Alexander Radovsky, Haifa, Israel, 1990.
699. N. A. Bulganin's statement to Professor Iakov Etinger in "Khronika dela vrachey," pp. 4–7. Quoted in Yakov Aizenshtat, *Podgotovka Stalinym genotsida evreev*, p. 70 and pp. 74–75.
700. The historian and academic E. V. Tarle, quoted in Yakov Aizenshtat, *Podgotovka Stalinym genotsida evreev*, p. 83.
701. Svetlana Allilueva, *Only One Year*, p. 155.
702. Personal interview with Nugzar Sharia in 1972 in Sag Harbor, New York. Gogi Zautashvili had described these events to Sharia. In the author's archive. Also A. Rybin, "Riadom s I. V. Stalinym," *Sotsiologicheskie issledovaniya*, no. 3, 1988.
703. Personal interview with Nugzar Sharia, Sag Harbor, New York, 1972. Sharia recounted the recollections of his uncle Peter Sharia and other Mingrelian generals. Peter, one of the top Mingrelian officials in the Kremlin, was the only one to survive.
704. Recollection by Peter Sharia, one of the arrested Mingrelians.
705. Andrey Sukhomlinov, Kto Wy Lavrenty Beria, Detektiv Press, Moscow, 2004, p. 228 and 239
706. Ibid. p. 316.
707. V. A. Chalikova, "Arkhivnyi yunosha," *Neva*, October 1988, p. 152.
708. Pavel Sudoplatov, *Operazii Lubyanka I Kreml [Operations Lubyanka and Kremlin], 1930–1950*, p. 156. Olma Press: Moscow, 2003.
709. A. Rybin, "Riadom s I. V. Stalinym."
710. V. Likholitov, "Interview c meditsinskimi rabotnikami prisutstvovavshimi pri smerti," *Meditsinskaya gazeta*, November 11, 1988, p. 8.
711. Svetlana Alliluyeva, *Dvadtzat, pisem k drugu*, pp. 5–10.
712. Ibid.
713. Interview with Felix Svetlov.
714. Vladimir Karpov, *Novy Meridian*, May 12, 2004, Brooklyn, New York.
715. Svetlana Alliluyeva, *Dvadtzat, pisem k drugu*, pp. 5–10.
716. V. Likholitov, "Kak balzamirovali Stalina," *Meditsinskaya gazeta*, August 10, 1988.
717. Personal interview with Nathan Feingold, New York, June 13, 1974. Also recollections of Nadine Brackman, author's wife.
718. Personal interview with Nugzar Sharia, who provided recollections of Georgians recalling how Beria had bragged about his humanitarian exploits.
719. Vladimir Naumov and Jonathan Brent, *Stalin's Last Crime*.
720. Michael Wines, *New York Times International*, March 5, 2003.
721. H. G. Wells, *Ostrov Doktora Moro*.
722. H. Montgomery Hyde, *Stalin*, p. 316.
723. Personal interview with Vitaly Svechinsky. In the author's archive.
724. The author heard Romanyuk's jubilant words.
725. *Pravda*, April 4, 1953.
726. *New York Times*, September 15, 1979, p. 12.
727. *Pravda*, March 28, 1953.
728. Ibid., April 6, 1953.
729. Amy Knight, "Beria, the Reformer," *New York Times*, November 3, 1993.
730. S. Bystrov, "Dozvoleno k pechati," *Krasnaya Zvezda*, March 18–20, 1988.
731. Chabuk Amiragibi told the author about this message during his incarceration at the "101-

Kilometer Camp" in August–September 1953.

732. Bystrov, "Dozvoleno k pechati."

733. Andrey Sukhomlinov, *Kto vy Lavrenty Beria?*, p. 239

734. Personal interview with Nugzar Sharia.

735. Pavel Sudoplatov, *Operazii Lubyanka I Kreml* [*Operations Lubyanka and Kremlin*], *1930–1950*, p. 157. Olma Press: Moscow, 2003.

736. Personal interview with Felix Svetlov, February 8, 2003.

737. Felix Svetlov interview in May 2005 who received this information from a former nurse at the Policlinic #112

738. S. Bystrov, "Dozvoleno k pechati." Also A. Antonov-Ovseenko, "Beria," *Yunost*, December 1988.

739. Nikita S. Khrushchev, *Khrushchev Remembers*, p. 344, fn. 14; also p. 345, fn. 15.

740. Ibid. p. 44; also fn. 12 at the bottom of the page.

741. Ibid. pp. 347–51.

742. The author was present at the reading of Khrushchev's secret speech at the Rossmetaloproekt firm in Moscow in March 1956.

743. A member of the Polish Communist Party, Seweryn Bialer defected to the West with a copy of Khrushchev's speech.

744. Russian historian Z. I. Peregudova, in a BBC interview with the author in June 2001, denied that Stalin had ever been an Okhrana agent.

745. G. V. Kostyrchenko, *Tainaya politika Stalina*, p. 671–85.

746. Ibid., 678, note at the bottom of the page.

747. Ibid., 679.

748. Ibid., 698.

749. Aleksandr Orlov, "The Sensational Secret Behind the Damnation of Stalin," *Life*, April 23, 1956, p. 44.

750. F. D. Volkov, *Vzlet i padenie Stalina*, p. 23.

751. Roy Medvedev, *Let History Judge*, pp. 315–23. Also Roy Medvedev, "Dvadtsatyi vek," *Obshestvenno-politicheskii i literaturnyi almanakh*, #2, London, 1977, p. 10f.

752. O. G. Shatunovskaya and C. B. Shaboldaev, *Moskovskaya Pravda*, July 2, 1989. Letters, p. 4. Also Aleksandr Orlov, "The Sensational Secret Behind the Damnation of Stalin," p. 37.

753. F. D. Volkov, *Vzlet i padenie Stalina*, p. 23.

754. *Moskovskaya Pravda*, March 30, 1989. Also F. D. Volkov, *Vzlet ipadenie Stalina*, p. 16.

755. Personal interview with Nugzar Sharia in Sag Harbor, New York, in 1972.

756. B. Ravich, a chemistry professor and secretary of the Communist Party organization at the Moscow Institute of Nonferrous Metals (and my neighbor in Moscow), related Khrushchev's behavior to me. It was well known at that time among Party officials. Also Svetlana Alliluyeva, *Dvadtzat, pisem k drugu*, p. 6. Svetlana recounts Khrushchev crying at the time of Stalin's death. Also Nikita S. Khrushchev, on p. 318 of *Khrushchev Remembers*, confuses his own outbursts with Beria's, stating: "Beria threw himself on his knees, seized Stalin's hand, and started kissing it."

757. T. T. Rigby, *The Stalin Dictatorship: Khrushchev's Secret Speech and Other Documents*, p. 95.

758. Personal interview with Vasily Rudich in Chappaqua, New York, in 1975. Rudich related the testimony of O. G. Shatunovskaya, a member of the Party Control Committee, who recalled that A. N. Shelepin, the KGB chief at the time, had kept Khrushchev from delivering the planned part of the speech relating to Kirov's murder. Shelepin, nicknamed "Iron Shurik" at the time, "re-Stalinized" the Soviet secret police. In November 1961, he was promoted to the Central Committee secretariat. See John J. Dziak, *Chekisty: A History of the KGB*, p. 152.

759. F. Konev, "Kak perezakhoranivali Stalina," *Voenno-istoricheskii zhurnal*, Moscow, 1989.

760. *New York Times*, April 28, 1963, and July 29, 1963. See also Robert Payne, "A Man Like No Other," *New York Times*, September 8, 1963.

761. S. M. Dubrovsky, "Protiv idealizatsii deyatelnosti Ivana IV," *Voprosy istorii*, no. 8, August 1956, pp. 121–28.

762.   *Pravda*, March 10, 1963.
763.   Personal interview with Yury Krotkov, the author of the book *The Red Monarch* and a KGB agent who had defected to the West, in New York in 1972. Krotkov related the inside story of Khrushchev's intention to make public the Stalin-Malinovsky rivalry in the Okhrana. The article he mentioned was published in censored form after Khrushchev had been removed, although the part detailing the Stalin-Malinovsky Okhrana rivalry was suppressed. See B. K. Erenfeld, "Delo Malinovskogo," *Voprosy istorii*, no. 7, 1965, pp. 106–16.
764.   *Pravda*, July 20, 1964.
765.   Radio Moscow I, July 19, 1964, monitoring tape recording. Radio Liberty Archive.
766.   Robert Conquest, *The Great Terror*, p. 172.
767.   B. K. Erenfeld, "Delo Malinovskogo."
768.   Nikita S. Khrushchev, *Doklad na zakrytom zasedanii XX s'ezda KPSS*.
769.   Michael B. Oren, *Six Days of War*, pp. 8–10.
770.   The author was in the crowd lining the motorcade route.
771.   The author knew Yuri Ivanov as a student in the philosophy department of Moscow University.
772.   Michael B. Oren, *Six Days of War*, p. 28.
773.   G. V. Kostyrchenko, *Tainaya politica Stalina*, p. 404.
774.   The author interviewed the Eshkol family in Israel in 1968.
775.   Michael B. Oren, *Six Days of War*, p. 59.
776.   *Pravda*, May 22, 1967
777.   Michael B. Oren, *Six Days of War*, p. 117.
778.   Ibid., 118.
779.   Ibid.
780.   Ibid., 117–31.
781.   Rabin, *Memoirs*, p. 83; also Carmit Guy, *Bar-Lev*, Am Oved: Tel-Aviv, 1998, p. 103.
782.   Michael B. Oren, *Six Days of War*, pp. 156–158
783.   Ibid.
784.   Ibid., 99.
785.   *Le Monde*, December 3, 1967, and *New York Times*, December 4, 1967.
786.   Michael B. Oren, *Six Days of War*, p. 151–152.
787.   Ibid., p. 146.
788.   Ibid., pp. 100–63.
789.   The author was present in the election-campaign crowd in Kiryat Ata, Israel.
790.   Moshe Yasser, a soldier in the IDF during the 1956 and 1967 wars.
791.   For a detailed, day-by-day account of the conflict, see Michael B. Oren, *Six Days of War*, p. 170–304.
792.   Michael B. Oren, *Six Days of War*, p. 299.
793.   Ibid., 117.
794.   Ibid., 299
795.   Ibid., 304.
796.   Ibid.
797.   Ibid. 317.
798.   Ibid., 317.
799.   Ibid.
800.   Interview with Efim Spevakovsky.
801.   B. Morozov, *The Jewish Emigration in Light of New Documents*, Tel-Aviv, 1998, p. 62.
802.   Ibid., p. 63.
803.   Vitaly Svechinsky's letter, dated August 19, 2002. Svechinsky maintains a close personal relationship with Nechemia Levanon, who retired and died in August 2003.
804.   The author and Leonid Rigerman, one of the Soviet dissidents, took part in arranging this merger and in the press conference announcing it.
805.   Leonid Averbukh, *Rasechennye sudby*, Optimum: Odessa, 2001, pp. 154–58.

806. Russian magazine *Rodina* [Motherland], 1996, issues 7 and 8.
807. Roman Brackman, "Atkofa She Lo Haya" [The Confrontation That Did Not Happen], *Ma'ariv*, February 7, 1969, p. 27.
808. Ibid.
809. Roman Brackman, "Dramatic Nixon Change: President Seeking to Move Soviets out of Middle East," *Jerusalem Post*, March 23, 1969, p. 9; Roman Brackman, "Nixon's Middle East Message: The U.S.A. Will Not Tolerate Any Soviet Takeover," *Jerusalem Post*, January 16, 1969, p. 3; Roman Brackman, "Israel Need Not Fear Nixon Foreign Policy," *Jerusalem Post*, August 1, 1969, p. 3; Roman Brackman, "Jordan, the Laos of the Middle East: How the Soviet Union is Manipulating Hussein," *Jerusalem Post*, December 9, 1968, p. 3.
810. The author participated in James Buckley's campaign.
811. Vitaly Svechinsky was present at the scene and told this story to the author.
812. G. V. Kostyrchenko, *Tainaya politika Stalina*, p. 698.
813. Roman Brackman, "Dramatic Nixon Change—President seeking to move Soviets out of Middle East," *Jerusalem Post*, March 23, 1969, p. 9; also Roman Brackman, "Nixon's Middle-East Message—The U.S.A. will not tolerate any Soviet take-over," *Jerusalem Post*, January 16, 1969, p. 3; also Roman Brackman, "Israel Need Not Fear Nixon Foreign Policy," *Jerusalem Post*, August 1, 1969, p. 3; also Roman Brackman," Jordan, the Laos of the Middle East—How the Soviet Union is manipulating Hussein," *The Jerusalem Post*, December 9, 1968 p. 3.
814. Roman Brackman, "The Middle Eastern Vietnam," *National Review*, June 4, 1968.
815. *New York Post*, "The Lying Begins" February 14, 2004, p. 17.
816. Donald H. Wolfe, *The Last Days of Marilyn Monroe*, New York: William Morrow, 1998, p. 383n.
817. Leonard Garment, *In Search of Deep Throat—The Greatest Political Mystery of Our Time,* Basic Books, 2000.
818. *New York Times,* July 24, 2000.
819. Ibid., p. 222.
820. www.romanbrackman.com
821. See the Watergate Tapes; also see Leon Jaworski, *The Right and the Power*, p. 255
822. *Will—The Autobiography of G. Gordon Liddy*, p. 21.
823. Ibid., 40.
824. www.romanbrackman.com
825. Ibid.
826. *New York Times*, January 30, 2001.
827. Ibid., p. A19.
828. Ibid., June 27, 2005, p. 11.
829. Ibid.
830. Ibid., November 19, 2000, p. WK 15.
831. Leon Jaworski, *The Right and the Power*, pp. 286–287.
832. Also *New York Times*, June 2, 2005, The Tipster, p. A16.
833. Ibid.
834. Roman Brackman's Letter to the Editor, *"If the President Withdrew...",* The New York Times, April 12, 1974.
835. Watergate, Deep Throat and the Yom Kippur War," at www.romanbrackman. com.
836. Ibid.
837. Ibid.
838. Carl Bernstein and Bob Woodward, *All the President's Men,* p. 349.
839. *RN—The Memoirs of Richard Nixon*, Grosset & Dunlap, New York 1978, pp. 884–885.
840. See Stewart Steven, *Spymasters of Israel*. See also "Why Intelligence Fails," TV Discovery Times, channel 113.
841. Len Colodny and Robert Gettlin, *Silent Coup*, pp. 421–425.
842. Ibid.
843. Jaworski, *The Right and the Power*, pp. 151–152.

844. *Jerusalem Post,* June 28, 2005, p. B1.
845. Ibid.
846. At the risk of personalizing too much, I may say that I am as Jewish as they come and a member of the "Zionist Prisoners" organization in Israel, but even I often rant against the "progressive, liberal Jews," using either Russian or English expletives.
847. John W. Dean, *Unmasking Deep Throat—History's Most Elusive New Source,* a Salon.com Book, 2002, p. 140.
848. *New York Times,* April 8, 2003, p. A14.
849. Andrew Fergusson, "Bob Woodward's Washington," *The Weekly Standard,* May 3, 2004, pp. 23–26.
850. NBC News, November 4, 1968.
851. Conversation with Irwin Gellman, author of *The Contender.*
852. *New York Times,* June 2, 2005, June 1, 2005, "Deep Throat" Unmasks Himself…, p. A16
853. Ibid., June 2, 2005, "The Tipster," p. A16.
854. Ibid., July 6, 2005, *Books of the Times,* pp. E1-E6.
855. Ibid., June 2, 2005, "In Saga's Final Chapter," pp. A1-16.
856. Ibid.
857. Ibid., June 1, 2005, "The Source," p. A17.
858. *New York Post,* June 1, 2005, p. 9.
859. *New York Times,* July 6, 2005, *Books of the Times,* pp. E1-E6.
860. Ibid.
861. Ibid.
862. Ibid., June 16, 2005, p. A 22.
863. Ibid., June 2, 2005, "In Saga's Final Chapter," p. A16.
864. *New York Post,* June 6, 2005, p. 29.
865. *New York Times Book Review,* June 7, 2006, p.18.
866. Ibid.
867. Roman Brackman, *Jimmy Carter, Provocateur-in-Chief,* Deerfield Publishers, 1980, p. 71.
868. *New York Times,* December 10, 1975.
869. Ibid., June 7, 1975.
870. Ibid., March 15, 1975.
871. Vitaly Svechinsky's letter to the author.
872. *New York Times,* October 4, 1977.
873. Ibid., October 6, 1977.
874. Ibid., February 14, 1977.
875. Brackman, *Jimmy Carter,* p. 76.
876. Ibid.
877. *New York Times,* November 18, 1977.
878. Brackman, *Jimmy Carter,* p. 76.
879. Ibid.
880. Ibid., p. 78.
881. Ibid., p. 84.
882. Ibid., p. 95.
883. Ibid.
884. Brackman, *Jimmy Carter,* p. 87.
885. *New York Times,* July 30, 1978.
886. *Jerusalem Post,* June 16, 2004.
887. Ibid.
888. *New York Times,* November 6, 1977.
889. Ibid., October 6, 1977.
890. Ernest Jones, M. D., *Psycho Myth, Psycho-History,* Volume Two, pp. 263–64.
891. Brackman, *Jimmy Carter,* p. 99.
892. In 1980 the author submitted his book *Jimmy Carter: Provocateur-in-Chief* (including Chapter VII,

"The 54th Hostage," dealing with General Huyser's mission to Iran) to General Al Haig, asking the general to confirm or deny the correctness of the report prepared by Rowland Evans and Robert Novak. At the time Haig was the Chief Executive Officer of the United Technology Corporation. He responded through his assistant, verifying this report.

893. Brackman, *Jimmy Carter*, p. 99.
894. *New York Times*, October 25, 1980.
895. Natan Sharansky, "The Prisoner's Conscience," Opinion, *Jerusalem Post*, June 6, 2004.
896. *Reagan in His Own Hand*, foreword by George P. Schultz. The Free Press: New York, 2001, pp. 215–18.
897. *New York Times*, October 25, 1980.
898. B. Drummond Ayres, Jr., article, *New York Times*, October 3, 1980.
899. *New York Times*, "The Osirak Option," November 15, 2002, p. A31.
900. Ibid.
901. *New York Times*, January 28, 1991.
902. Ibid., January 30, 1991.
903. Ibid., Editorial, February 3, 1992.
904. Ibid., February 5, 1992.
905. Ibid., Editorial, February 6, 1992.
906. G. V. Kostyrchenko, *Tainaya politika Stalina*, p. 698.
907. *New York Post*, December 15, 2002, p. 22.
908. A. M. Rosenthal, "Barak Risks It All for Political Gain," *New York Daily News*, December 22, 2000, p. 53.
909. *New York Times*, April 15, 2002, p. A11.
910. *Jerusalem Post*, May 15, 2002.
911. Ibid.
912. Frank Rich, "The Albright Question," *New York Times*, February 19, 1997, Op-Ed, p. A21.
913. *New York Times*, February 12, 1997, p. A4; *New York Times*, February 7, 1997, p. A8; Louis Begley, *New York Times*, February 12, 1997, Op-Ed, p. A25.
914. *New York Times*, February 6, 1997.
915. Ibid., "When 'Elegance' Meant Denying a Jewish Past," February 19, 1997, Letters.
916. Ibid.
917. *New York Times*, February 7, 1997, p. A8.
918. Ibid., March 13, 2000.
919. *Jerusalem Post*, January 9, 2003, front page.
920. Ibid., November 27, 2002, front page.
921. *New York Times*, October 13, 2000, pp. A1 and A8.
922. Ibid., June 27, 2001.
923. *New York Daily News*, June 27, 2001, p. 2.
924. Willard Gaylin, *Hatred*, quoted in the review by Melvin Konner, *New York Times Book Review*, Sunday, August 3, 2003, p. 12.
925. *Jewish Press*, April 2, 2004, front and back pages.
926. Ibid., October 21, 2000.
927. *New York Post*, August 2, 2002, pp. 1–6.
928. Ibid.
929. See preceding chapter.
930. Fox News report, October 15, 2000. See also the *Jewish Press*, October 21, 2000, p. 1.
931. *New York Times*, December 11, 2002, pp. A1–14.
932. *International Herald Tribune*, October 15, 2002, pp. 1–7.
933. *New York Times*, December 11, 2002, pp. A1–14.
934. Ibid.
935. Brackman, *Jimmy Carter*, and website www.romanbrackman.com article "I'd Rather Commit

Suicide, Political or Otherwise, Than Hurt Israel!"
936. *New York Post*, November 18, 2002, p. 16.
937. *New York Times*, November 3, 1975, Op-Ed, p. 35.
938. Michael B. Oren, *Six Days of War*, p. 100.
939. Ibid.
940. *Jerusalem Post*, August 28, 2002, front page.
941. Ibid.
942. Barbara Armiel, "Islamists Overplay Their Hand but London Salons Don't See It," *Jerusalem Post*, December 21, 2001.
943. *Guardian*, March 4, 2005; also in *Jerusalem Post*, March 8, 2005.
944. *New York Post*, January 15, 2003, Editorial.
945. Ellis Shuman, Israelinsider.com article, March 1, 2002.
946. *New York Times*, August 9, 2000, p. B1.
947. *Jerusalem Post*, Internet edition, "Today, Mine is the Only Right-Wing Party," December 27, 2002.
948. *New York Times*, July 17, 2002, p. A13.
949. Ibid., November 8, 2002, p. B1.
950. Ibid., October 6, 2001, p. B3.
951. Roman Brackman, "The Confrontation That Did Not Happen," *Maariv*, February 7, 1969, p. 21.
952. *New York Times*, October 6, 2001, p. B3.
953. *New York Post*, April 10, 2002, p. 27.
954. *New York Times International*, "Waiting Out the Siege, Arafat Remains Defiant," February 4, 2001.
955. *International Herald Tribune*, October 16, 2002, p. 4.
956. *Jerusalem Post*, September 13, 2002, front page.
957. *Wall Street Journal*, August 15, 2002.
958. Ibid.
959. *New York Times*, August 16, 2001, pp. A1–A11.
960. *Financial Times*. October 9, 2002, p. 12.
961. Michael Beschloss, *The Conquerors*, Simon and Schuster: New York, 2002.
962. *Jerusalem Post*, September 18, 2002, front page.
963. *New York Times*, January 20, 2003, p. A6.
964. Ibid., April 20, 2002, p. A9.
965. Ibid., March 6, 2004, p. A3.
966. Ibid.
967. *New York Times*, March 16, 2004, p. A9.
968. Ibid., March 13, 2004, p. A17.
969. Michael McFaul, "Vladimir Putin's Grand Strategy," *Weekly Standard*, November 17, 2003, pp. 18–19.
970. *New York Times*, October 27, 2002, p. A1.
971. Ibid., October 11, 2003, p. A8.
972. Irina Mintz, who heard Putin's speech in Moscow.
973. *New York Times*, October 26, 2002, p. A1.
974. Brackman, *The Secret File*, Chapter 10.
975. Nicholas D. Kristof, "Behind the Rage," *New York Times*, April 16, 2002, Op-Ed, p. A27.
976. "Deadline Diplomacy," *Wall Street Journal*, Review & Outlook, December 27, 2000.
977. *New York Times*, February 4, 2002, p. A23.
978. *New York Post*, December 4, 2002, pp. 1–2.
979. Ibid., April 10, 2002, p. 27.
980. *New York Times*, December 15, 2001, Op-Ed.
981. Caroline Glick, "Fighting Tom Friedman," *Jerusalem Post*, January 17, 2003.
982. *New York Times*, January 15, 2003, Op-Ed, p. A21.
983. Ibid.

984. *New York Times*, September 14, 2003, Op-Ed, p. A30.
985. Ibid.
986. *New York Post*, January 15, 2003, Editorial.
987. *New Yorker*, May 31, 2004.
988. *New York Post*, May 28, 2002, p. 7.
989. Gustav Hendrikssen (Professor Emeritus of Bible Study at Uppsala University, Sweden), *Nativ* magazine, September 1995.
990. *Jerusalem Post*, May 15, 2002, front page.
991. *New York Post*, April 10, 2002, p. 27.
992. *Jerusalem Post*, May 15, 2002.
993. Ibid., March 20, 2004.
994. *New York Times*, November 14, 2002, p. A12.
995. Ibid., October 27, 2001, Op-Ed.
996. *Jerusalem Post,* January 5, 2003.
997. *New York Times*, January 30, 2003, p. A22.
998. Ibid., May 3, 2002.
999. Ibid., July 25, 2003, p. A8.
1000. *Jerusalem Post*, June 27, 2002, front page.
1001. *New York Sun*, April 24, 2003, p. 2.
1002. *New York Post*, July 9, 2003, p. 2.
1003. *Jewish Week*, February 13, 2004, p. 28.
1004. Ibid.
1005. Arnold Ahlert, "Kerry's Overseas Fans," *New York Post*, March 20, 2004, p. 17.
1006. *New York Sun*, October 24, 2003, p. 7.
1007. Janine Zacharia, "Bush Skips Road Map in the State of the Union Address," *Jerusalem Post*, January 22, 2004.
1008. *New York Times*, March 12, 2004, p. A11.
1009. Ibid., March 8, 2004, p. A19.
1010. *New York Sun*, September 16, 2003, p. 8. Reprinted from the *Daily Telegraph*.
1011. *New York Post*, February 11, 2004, p. 8.
1012. Caroline Glick, "Column One: What Europe Wants," *Jerusalem Post*, May 28, 2004.
1013. *New York Times,* January 28, 2005, p. A6.
1014. Ibid.
1015. Amnon Lord, "The Open Window in the Cell of Everyone," Israeli newspaper *Makor Rishon*, November 5, 2004.
1016. *Jerusalem Post*, May 1, 2005, p. 3.
1017. Ibid., February 16, 2005.
1018. *New York Times Book Review*, Sunday, July 17, 2005, p. 26.
1019. Ibid.
1020. *New York Times Book Review*, Sunday, July 17, p. 26.
1021. Vladimir Bukovsky in conversation with Vitaly Svechinsky in Israel at the end of 1999.
1022. *New York Times,* May 4, 2005.
1023. *Jerusalem Post*, "Palestinians roll out red carpet for 'ally' Putin," May 1, 2005, p. 3.
1024. Ibid.
1025. Ibid. Victor Shvrzburg saw Primakov's interview on Israeli TV.
1026. Ibid., May 19, 2005.
1027. Ibid.
1028. Ibid.
1029. Ibid.
1030. Ibid.
1031. Marquis de Custine, *Journey for Our Time: The Russian Journals of Marquis de Custine*, Henry Regnery

Co. Chicago, 1951.
1032. Ibid., p. 363.
1033. *New York Times,* July 17, 2005, p. A8.
1034. Ibid., July 17, 2005, p. A8.
1035. *Jewish Week,* July 15, 2005, p. 3.
1036. *New York Times,* May 21, 2005, p. A3, David E. Sanger and Alan Cowell, "Hussein Photos in Tabloids Prompt U.S. Call to Investigate."
1037. Ibid., June 28, 2005, p. A23.
1038. Paul Greenberg, "A Test For the Senate," *AM New York,* June 10–12, 2005.
1039. *New York Times,* June 21, 2005, p. A10.
1040. *New York Sun,* January 1, 2004, Editorial "Sidelining Scowcroft."
1041. Ibid., Benny Avni, "Annan to Push for Definition of Terror."
1042. *Jerusalem Post,* "Kurtzer: I did not cast doubts on Bush-Sharon accord," March 24, 2005.
1043. *Jerusalem Post,* January 6, 2005.
1044. Ibid., July 11, 2005.
1045. Ibid., March 8, 2005.
1046. Ibid., July 11, 2005.
1047. Ibid., July 1, 2005.
1048. *Jerusalem Post,* "Kurtzer…," March 24, 2005.
1049. *New York Times,* Zef Chafets, Mother Knows Best," August 16, 2005, p. A15.
1050. *Jerusalem Post,* "Palestinian Authority: "Banishment and Defeat," August 11, 2005.
1051. Ibid., August 20, 2005.
1052. Ibid.
1053. *New York Times,* August 28, 2005, p. A11.
1054. Ibid., August 16, 2005, p. A16.
1055. *Jerusalem Post,* March 1, 2005.
1056. *New York Times,* October 24, 2004, p. Wk 11.
1057. *Jerusalem Post,* August 20, 2005.
1058. *New York Times,* May 12, 2005.
1059. *New York Post,* "Rice: Don't Raze Gaza," by Uri Dan, April 7, 2005, p. 30.
1060. *Jerusalem Post,* April 7, 2005.
1061. *New York Sun,* "Breakfast with Sharon," by Seth Lipsky, May 24, 2005, p. 9.
1062. Ibid.
1063. *Jerusalem Post,* January 7, 2005.
1064. Ibid., June 10, 2005.
1065. *Economist,* "They Don't Believe Israel Will Leave," June 25, 2005, p. 44.
1066. Ibid.
1067. *New York Times,* May 21, 2005, p. A5, Steven Erlander, "Palestinian Attack Hardens Israeli Settlers' Resistance."
1068. Ibid.
1069. *New York Times,* May 16, 2004, Op-Ed page.
1070. Ibid.
1071. Ibid.
1072. *Jerusalem Post,* June 1, 2005.
1073. Ibid., June 9, 2005.
1074. Ibid., June 1, 2005.
1075. Ibid., June 11, 2005.
1076. *New York Times,* Letters to the Editor, July 11, 2005, p. A16.
1077. Ibid.
1078. Ibid., August 7, 2005, p. A3.
1079. *New York Times,* May 31, 2005, p. A3.

1080. *New York Post*, August 8, 2005, p. 25.
1081. Ibid.
1082. *New York Times,* August 11, 2005, p. A8.
1083. *New York Sun,* August 4, 2005 p. 13.
1084. *New York Times,* August 7, 2005, p. A-19.
1085. Ibid., August 7, 2005, p. A19.
1086. *New York Sun,* August 4, 2005 p. 13.
1087. *New York Times,* July 9, 2005, p. A12.
1088. Ibid., July 9, 2005, p. A12.
1089. *New York Times,* November 9, 2003, p. wk p.11.
1090. *Jerusalem Post,* July 14, 2005, p. 25.
1091. *New York Times,* July 12, 2005, p. A1.
1092. *Jerusalem Post,* March 24, 2005, p. A3.
1093. Ibid., December 21, 2005.
1094. Ibid., November 11, 2005.
1095. *New York Times,* December 15, 2005.
1096. Ibid., October 27, 2005; *New York Times,* January 2, 2006.
1097. *Jerusalem Post,* November 2, 2005, Daniel Pipes "Genocidal Design."
1098. *New York Sun,* Daniel Pipes, "Iran's Final Solution," November 1, 2005 p. 6.
1099. *New York Times,* December 15, 2005.
1100. *Jerusalem Post,* November 9, 2004.
1101. *New York Times,* December 10, 2005; *Jerusalem Post,* December 11, 2005.
1102. *Jerusalem Post,* December 13, 2005.
1103. Ibid., December 28, 2005.
1104. Ibid., January 1, 2006.
1105. Ibid., January 8, 2006.
1106. Ibid.
1107. *Financial Times,* January 6, 2006, p. 2.
1108. *Jerusalem Post,* December 31, 2005.
1109. Ibid., December 28, 2005.
1110. *New York Times,* January 30, 2006, p. A-1.
1111. Ibid., February 2, 2006, p. A-10.
1112. Ibid., January 27, 2006, Editorial.
1113. Ibid., February 2, 2006, p. A22, Editorial.
1114. *Jerusalem Post,* January 26, 2006, Edgar Lefkovits, "Carter Calls for Funding Palestinians."
1115. *New York Post,* January 31, 2006, p. 23.
1116. See Chapter 9, "Israel's Nightmare During Jimmy Carter's Presidency"; also Brackman, *Jimmy Carter,* Chapter VII, "The 54th Hostage," pp. 98–99.
1117. *Jerusalem Post,* February 9, 2006; also *New York Times,* February 10, 2006, p A12.
1118. *New York Times,* February 4, 2006, p. A13.
1119. *Jerusalem Post,* February 9, 2006.
1120. *New York Times,* February 11, 2006, p. A7.
1121. *Jerusalem Post,* February 12, 2006.
1122. *New York Times,* January 24, 2006, Op-Ed page.
1123. *Jerusalem Post,* February 11, 2006.
1124. See Chapter 9, "Israel's Nightmare during Jimmy Carter's Presidency"; also Brackman, *Jimmy Carter,* Chapter VII, "The 54th Hostage," pp. 98–99.
1125. *New York Times,* February 9, 2006, p. A27.
1126. *Jerusalem Post,* December 27, 2005.
1127. Avigdor Liberman, *Nothing but the Truth,* Ivrus Ltd., Israel, p. 78.
1128. Ibid.

1129. Ibid.
1130. *New York Times,* August 16, 2001, p. A11.
1131. Ibid., June 16, 2006, pp. A1-8.
1132. Fox News, June 16, 2006.
1133. *New York Times,* Op-Ed, March 21, p. A17.
1134. *Jerusalem Post,* March 19, 2006.
1135. *New York Sun,* April 24, 2003, p. 2.
1136. *New York Times,* March 22, p. A24.
1137. *New York Times International,* April 30, 2006, p. 14.
1138. Ibid., May 28, 2006, p. 14.
1139. Ibid., May 24, 2006, p. A6.
1140. *Jerusalem Post,* June 13, 2006.
1141. *New York Times International,* May 30, 2006, p. A11.
1142. Picture of Ahmadinejad in *New York Times International,* May 28, 2006, p. 14.
1143. *New York Times,* May 25, 2006, p. A27.
1144. *New York Times International,* July 5, 2006, p. A6.
1145. Ibid.
1146. Ibid.
1147. *New York Times,* July 3, 2006, p. A1.
1148. *Jerusalem Post,* July 7, 2006.
1149. *New York Post,* July 19, 2006, p. 7, "We welcome World War 3" : terror fiends, by Ury Dan
1150. Ibid.
1151. Ibid.
1152. *Jerusalem Post,* July 20, 2006, article, "Assad: Cease-fire is needed to stop Israel."
1153. *New York Times,* August 13, 2006, p. 12.
1154. Ibid.
1155. Ibid.

Index

Index